PENGUIN BOOKS
THE CHINA HANDS

E. J. Kahn, Jr., became a staff writer for *The New Yorker* after his graduation from Harvard in 1937. He has reported for that magazine and for others from Africa, Mexico, New Guinea, Japan, Israel, Micronesia, Germany, Korea, the Soviet Union, and China. Books to his credit include *The First Decade, Fraud,* and *The American People,* which is also published by Penguin Books. Mr. Kahn is married to the writer Eleanor C. Munro. The Kahns divide their time among New York City; Truro, Massachusetts; and West Cornwall, Connecticut.

By E. J. Kahn, Jr.

* Available in paperback.

The China Hands

America's Foreign Service
Officers and What Befell Them

E. J. Kahn, Jr.

Penguin Books

Penguin Books Ltd, Harmondsworth, Middlesex, England
Penguin Books, 625 Madison Avenue, New York, New York 10022, U.S.A.
Penguin Books Australia Ltd, Ringwood, Victoria, Australia
Penguin Books Canada Ltd, 41 Steelcase Road West, Markham, Ontario, Canada
Penguin Books (N.Z.) Ltd, 182–190 Wairau Road, Auckland 10, New Zealand

First published by The Viking Press 1975
Published in Penguin Books 1976

LIBRARY OF CONGRESS CATALOGING IN PUBLICATION DATA

Kahn, Ely Jacques, 1916—
　The China hands.
　Bibliography: p.
　Includes index.
　1. United States—Foreign relations—China. 2. China
—Foreign relations—United States. 3. United States—
Diplomatic and consular service—China. I. Title
[JX1428.C6K34 1976]　　327.73′051　　76–18692
ISBN 0 14 00.4301 2 (pbk.)

Printed in the United States of America by
Offset Paperback Mfrs., Inc., Dallas, Pennsylvania
Set in Video Avanta

A small portion of this book appeared, as a profile of John S. Service, in different form in *The New Yorker*.

For Ellie, of course

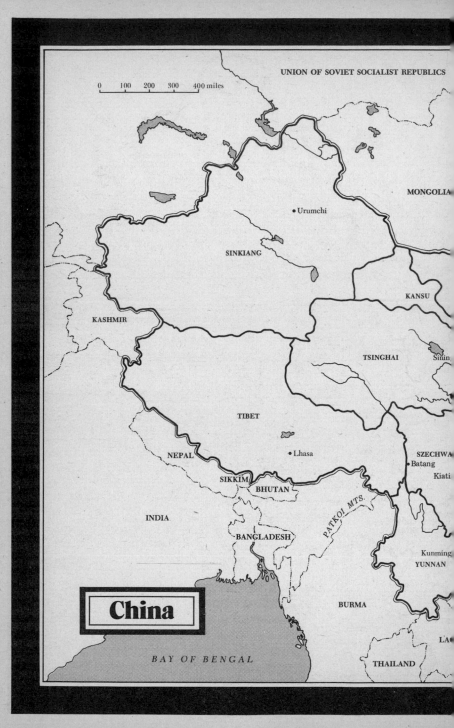

Contents

Author's Note

Henry Kissinger's reintroduction of the United States and some of its diplomats to China may be remembered as the greatest—perhaps the only —accomplishment of the Nixon presidency. This book is a reintroduction of sorts itself—to those American diplomats who, had they been listened to during earlier administrations, might have significantly influenced, or at the very least maintained, mid-twentieth-century relations between their country and the largest one on earth.

For journalist and scholar alike, to resurrect the past becomes in major part a sifting of past printed records. Much of what appears in the pages that follow, however, is the result of personal interviews with onetime Foreign Service officers whose knowledgeable reports from China during the Second World War went mainly unheeded, and who themselves suffered, in varying degrees, for having sent home messages unpalatable to their superiors in Washington.

I am indebted for assistance to many men and women who have shared with me their information and insights, among them Doak Barnett, David Biltchik, Sheila V. Cox, John K. Fairbank, Wilma C. Fairbank, Adrian Fisher, Stuart Gates, Max Granich, Marshall Green, Dr. Ma Hai-teh, John H. Holdridge, Chalmers Johnson, Joyce Kallgren, George Kennan, Herbert Levin, Philip Lilienthal, Gary May, Virginia S. McCormick, John F. Melby, Shirley R. Newhall, Dr. Julius Pearson, Joseph L. Rauh, Jr., John C. Reid, Gerard D. Reilly, Mrs. C. Edward Rhetts, Harold Roser, Alexandra D. Schnurman, Philip Service, Robert Service, Walter S. Surrey, James C. Thomson, Jr., Lyman Van Slyke, Mrs. Burton E. Vaughan, Mrs. John Carter Vincent, John Carter Vincent, Jr., Theodore H. White, Allen S. Whiting, Clifford F. Young, and—a clear-cut case of the first coming last—Donald J. Munro, without whose urging and introductions I might never have met any Old China Hands at all.

This book could not have been written, though, without the generous cooperation of the men whom it is about; and my special deep thanks, accordingly, go to those who deserve special mention for their patiently shared memories of good and bad times: Robert W. Barnett, Colonel David D. Barrett, Oliver Edmund Clubb, Donald Davies, John Paton

Davies, Jr., Everett F. Drumright, John K. Emmerson, F. McCracken Fisher, Fulton Freeman, Raymond P. Ludden, James K. Penfield, Edward E. Rice, Arthur R. Ringwalt, Laurence E. Salisbury, John S. Service, Richard M. Service, and Philip D. Sprouse. They made the book possible, in more ways than one.

New York, New York
7 March 1975

E.J.K.

The China Hands

1

"How do you say that in Chinese?"

When John F. Kennedy and Richard M. Nixon held their four celebrated television debates toward the end of the 1960 presidential campaign, the substantive issue that seemed most to preoccupy both of them was the fate of Quemoy and Matsu, the two small island clusters lying between the People's Republic of China, on the Asian mainland, and the Republic of China, on Taiwan. The candidates had some differences of opinion as to just what the United States could or should do about Quemoy and Matsu, but they agreed—for it would have been all but politically suicidal at that moment in history to take any other public stance—that the unbending support of Chiang Kai-shek, presiding over *his* Republic in Taipei, was vital to American interests.

In the fall of 1960, when so much of what was happening in the United States was influenced by attitudes toward China, Everett F. Drumright was the American ambassador at Taipei, and Edward E. Rice, who a year after Kennedy won would become deputy assistant secretary of state for Far Eastern affairs, was a member of that department's Policy Planning Staff. Drumright and Rice were largely unknown, except to people whose thoughts were almost exclusively focused on China, but that they were where they were was significant. For they were the only two China-language experts in the Foreign Service with pre-Second-World-War experience in their field who still had anything to do with China. At the outbreak of the war, there had been more than a score of specialists like them in the service. But in the fifteen years that had elapsed since V-J Day—and the eleven years since Mao Tse-tung had displaced Chiang in China—the rest of the "Old China Hands" of the Foreign Service had been eased out, or thrown out, of any consequential participation in Chinese affairs, on the ground that they had had a hand in "losing" China.

1

They had not lost it. They had not had it in their power to lose it or keep it. China had been lost by Chiang Kai-shek—and won by Mao—through a convulsive, probably unstoppable revolution. If any outside influences deserved credit for abetting Mao's victory, the aggressiveness of the Japanese in the 1930s certainly eclipsed the acts of omission or commission of any American Foreign Service officer anywhere at any time. Whatever American responsibility there may have been for Chiang's downfall should be ascribed, probably, not to any professional diplomats but to a swashbuckling amateur, Major General Patrick J. Hurley, who on November 17, 1944, was named by President Franklin Roosevelt to be his ambassador to Chiang's capital at Chungking. From that day on, both major political parties in the United States found themselves inextricably hooked on the China question—the Democrats because they were to be principally accused of having helped to lose China, the Republicans because they principally made the accusations. A characteristic comment was that of Senator Robert A. Taft, sometimes thought to be the conscience of the Republican party and undeniably one of its senior spokesmen, who spoke of a "pro-Communist group in the State Department who . . . promoted at every opportunity the Communist cause in China." In the similar view of Senator Arthur H. Vandenberg, the principal Republican on the Foreign Relations Committee, Chiang Kai-shek had been "sold down the river."

It was ironic that no Americans—unless one included John Reed, who was not a Foreign Service officer—were ever accused of losing Russia. George F. Kennan was barred from having anything to do with United States-Soviet relations from 1938 to 1944, not because he was thought to be too tolerant of communism but because he was considered too *anti*-Communist.

The loss of China became so enshrined in American diplomatic mythology that it was often alluded to in connection with later Communist successes. Thus, in the autumn of 1960 a press release handed out by the Internal Security Subcommittee of the United States Senate—an investigative group led and staffed by men who no doubt hoped that Nixon would defeat Kennedy—would declare that "Cuba was handed to Castro and the Communists by a combination of Americans in the same way that China was handed to the Communists." A few months afterward, Senator Thomas J. Dodd, a Democrat from Connecticut, would declare with respect to widely circulated charges that the State Department had given Castro's revolution a leg up, "I am not interested in punishing anybody.

I will go so far as to say that I am confident these were errors of judgment only. I don't suggest anything more. But I do say we must stop this sort of thing, we must get our people in the State Department who will not make continually this kind of errors. This is not anything new. This is what happened in China. This is why we lost China. . . ."

One of the China-language specialists who by 1960 had long since been punished, John Carter Vincent, had in the early spring of 1953 given the fledgling Eisenhower administration some unsolicited advice. "As a so-called Old China Hand," Vincent said, "I would suggest to the new administration that it study with great sincerity of purpose the idea that we 'lost' China. It has been a phony idea all along peddled by the China Lobby. Let's drop it. Then and only then can the administration, with the aid of career officers free from a fear that loyalty to Chiang Kai-shek is a test of loyalty to the U.S.A., begin to evolve and pursue an objective and, we hope, effective policy regarding China."

It might have been safe then to follow Vincent's suggestion. (A Gallup Poll taken a few months later would reveal that only 7 per cent of all Americans thought that Foreign Service officers had lost China, whereas considerably more of them thought that the weakness of Chiang's Nationalist government was the root cause.) Instead of dropping the old idea, however, the new Republican administration summarily dropped Vincent.

Another of the Old China Hands was John Service, who had always stood high on the list of the China-losers, even though the concept of *not* losing China had been much on his mind. On March 20, 1944, for instance, eight months before General Hurley's appointment as ambassador, Service had written to his superiors, "China is in a mess. . . . for the sorry situation as a whole Chiang, and only Chiang, is responsible. . . . Chiang will cooperate if the U.S., upon which he is dependent, makes up its mind exactly what it wants from him and then gets hard-boiled about it. . . . This may mean taking an active part in Chinese affairs. But unless we do it, China will not be of much use as an ally. And, in doing it, *we may save China.*" (Italics added.)

Service, too, was banished from the government, although thanks to the Supreme Court he was restored to State Department duty, after a fashion, following a six-year involuntary absence from it. Perhaps the most notorious of all the Old China Hands, Service had by 1960, when he was fifty years old and in excellent health, periodically mused about how his eventual obituaries would probably begin. They would say, he could be fairly certain, that he was one of the men accused of losing China, and that he had been most specifically accused of espionage in the celebrated *Amerasia* case of 1945, when he was thirty-five. The obits would almost surely also contain a middle name, Stewart, which he himself scarcely ever used, but which his disparagers appeared to agree had a marvelously sinister ring.

The repeated use of "John Stewart Service" served, moreover, to weave its bearer into a nomenclatural conspiratorial web with two of his principal colleagues, John Carter Vincent and John Paton Davies, Jr. By 1960, indeed, there were probably quite a few casual followers of diplomatic history who could not tell the three apart, let alone distinguish them from, among others, the diplomat John Kenneth Emmerson, the doyen of Sinologists John King Fairbank, or John Leighton Stuart, the last American ambassador to China before the Bamboo Curtain was drawn. Another Foreign Service officer whose career roughly paralleled those of Service, Vincent, and Davies was less frequently linked with them than he might logically have been because his name happened to be Oliver Edmund Clubb. On the other hand, one right-wing writer, Geraldine Fitch, the second wife of a missionary who officiated at the marriage of Chiang Kai-shek to Meiling Soong, once linked Service, Vincent, and Davies with a Foreign Service officer who was *not* a China specialist, apparently just because his name was John.

By 1971 Service could make wry jokes about all the confusion. Appearing before the Senate Foreign Relations Committee with Davies and Fairbank after the United States rapprochement with the People's Republic, Service would draw a laugh by recalling how the fall of Chiang's China had once been attributed to four Johns—himself, John Davies, John K. Fairbank, and "John" Kai-shek.[1]

General Hurley, for his part, on the occasion of being awarded the Legion of Merit in 1946 by Secretary of War Robert P. Patterson (it was a decoration routinely conferred on senior officers who had performed their duties without egregious misfeasance), had wisecracked that what he really deserved was a "John Service Cross." As many of the GIs in China rudely elected to treat the familiar syllables of the Generalissimo's name and to refer to him as "Chancre Jack," so would General Hurley refer to

[1]The confusion was rampant. An editorial in the Sacramento *Bee* commenting on the committee hearing was headed "Davies, Stewart win final vindication for their recommendations on China."

Mao Tse-tung as "Moose Dung" (or, as some heard it, "Mouse Tongue").
Among the printable sobriquets that Hurley himself acquired in China
were "Paper Tiger" and "Small Whiskers."

The mix-up of names was, however, by no means always amusing, as
was exemplified by some of the statements made about Service by one of
his dogged pursuers, Paul Yu-pin, the Roman Catholic vicar apostolic of
Nanking and administrator apostolic of Kiating. Bishop Yu-pin, who
spent much of the stressful war period not with his flock in China but in
the United States as a propagandist for Chiang, alleged that Service had
once gone to Moscow and while there had helped the cause of the
Chinese Communists. It would not have been exceptional for a Foreign
Service officer like John Service to serve a tour in Russia, but as it happened he had never set foot on Soviet soil. John *Davies* had been posted
to Moscow for a while, though, helping the cause of the United States;
Yu-pin may well have taken the one for the other.[2]

Service, whose friends called him not "John" but "Jack" or "Jake,"
shrugged off much of the tomfoolery about names. He had long been
inured to that kind of thing. Because of his *surname*, when he was an
eleven-year-old schoolboy in Shanghai his classmates had taken to calling
him "Slave." His parents did their best to make him feel better by
pointing out that the motto of the then Prince of Wales was *"Ich Dien,"*
but that was small comfort. Outside the home he ultimately retired to in
the hills of Berkeley, California, he put up a sign salvaged from an earlier
residence in Peking. It had "Service" on it and also the character for the
Chinese name he had inherited from his missionary father—Hsieh. The
components of the character mean "tongue-self-inch" and add up to
"Speak of yourself in a modest way," or "Be of service." (While in Peking,
Service *fils* had acquired a further Chinese name of his own, Wei-ssu,
which more or less means "great thoughts.") Because the English surname could perplex visitors, just beyond the "Service" sign he put up
another: "The front door is straight ahead."

John Service liked to say after he was long grown up that he had had
three lives. For most of the first one, between his birth in 1909 and the
harrowing year of 1945, he was in China, engaged in studies on his own
behalf and on his country's. In 1971, for one heady, six-and-a-half-week

[2]So little did the Russians know about Service, or at any rate about how his name was
customarily rendered by people inimical to him, that in an unfriendly review of a book
of his in the Moscow journal *Problemy Dal'nego Vostoka* the critic called him "J. Service."

stretch of the third life, which began in 1962 and was also dedicated to China studies, he was back in China. During the greater part of the seventeen years of the middle life, he lived in limbo. Both before and after that period, he had talked extensively with the highest Communist Chinese leaders, and during the war he was one of a very few American diplomats whom Mao Tse-tung and Chou En-lai knew well. The fact that this Foreign Service officer, whom the future rulers of Peking grew to like and, it seemed, to trust, was quiet, dignified, candid, and compassionate, and that he represented the very best in America, could have been most helpful to his country.

Indeed, history might have taken a different turn if anybody in power in Washington, instead of deriding Service as just another China-loser, had heeded his accounts of his 1944 and 1945 conversations with the Communist chiefs and some of the reports that he and his Foreign Service contemporaries were submitting around that time. Most of them were saying then that, no matter what hopes they or anybody else entertained about China's future, and no matter how much they or anybody else might wish to see Chiang Kai-shek retain control of a unified China, in the struggle between the Generalissimo and the Communists, Chiang was sure to lose. That the Old China Hands were correct their later detractors considered irrelevant; the detractors could not perceive the difference between predicting an eventuality and preferring it. Among some of the crueler jabs at Service, in his years of limbo, was the charge that he was somehow personally responsible for the deaths of American young men in the Korean War. The fact was that if he had been listened to, and if the United States had taken a realistic view of China and its Communists, there might not have *been* any Korean War.

Service, moreover, though he did not dwell unduly on his uncomfortable past, suggested in 1971 that if anyone in a position of authority roughly a quarter of a century earlier had reflected on what he and the other knowledgeable China hands were then reporting, there might not have been any Taiwan problem either. "Mao's China, having come to power in a different way and not thrust into isolation by a hostile West, might be quite a different place," he wrote. "It might be one, for instance, where Chinese-American ping-pong matches were normal occurrences instead of being a world-shaking event." At about the same time, a Japanese television commentator asked Service to summarize his feelings about the whole tangled postwar course of relations between the United States and China. Service replied, "I think we missed a great opportunity," and when in 1974 a book of his wartime dispatches was published, it was entitled *Lost Chance in China.*

The people who tried to destroy Service and the other China-losers—operating sometimes with the merciless savagery of rabbit-clubbers, sometimes with the subtlety of the Chinese water torture—were professional killers: Senator Joe McCarthy, Senator Pat McCarran, and the grubby men and women who served as their informers, investigators, and counselors. Like other armies, they too had their chaplains; they went about their homicidal work bolstered by the pious prayers or averted heads of men like Dwight Eisenhower, Richard Nixon, and John Foster Dulles. "If there is any organization that should have the highest morale based firmly in its own convictions as to the importance of its work, the necessity for successful accomplishment regardless of what critic or opponent may say, a morale based in that high belief in a cause," President Eisenhower said at the State Department on October 19, 1954, at a time when Service, Vincent, and Clubb were out of the department and the skids for Davies were being greased, "then that should be the Foreign Service and the State Department." The sentiments were so awkwardly phrased that they had the ring of authentic Eisenhower authorship. The president did not mention that applications to take the Foreign Service examination, which had totalled 2701 the year he was elected, were down to 1261.

The fact was that State Department morale was terrible, and Foreign Service morale even worse. Any mention at State of China in words that did not emanate from the lips of the Generalissimo himself was regarded with suspicion. The department had one woman in its ranks, for instance, who handled "Chirep," the then still moot question of which republic would represent China at the United Nations. She construed her responsibility, reasonably enough given the state of State, to be that of doing everything she could to keep the Nationalists in and the Communists out. One Foreign Service officer with many years of experience in China behind him heard her say one day that all the Chinese on the mainland were murderers. On his uttering the mild rejoinder, "Wouldn't it be more accurate to say that only *some* Communist Chinese are murderers?" she gave him so scathing a look that he feared for several days he'd be exiled to Liberia.

There were senior Sinologists in other fields, too, whose advice was neither much sought nor, because of earlier intimidation, much proffered. "I can testify from personal knowledge that in the early 1950s . . . the widespread subpoena of China scholars had the public effect of inhibiting realistic thinking about China," Professor Fairbank has stated, "and I believe the result carried over into unrealistic thinking about Chinese relations with Vietnam and helped to produce our difficulties there."

The State Department found itself in a peculiar spot when the Vietnamese situation escalated—an escalation that might not necessarily have occurred as it did had a trained corps of senior men with Far Eastern experience been available for advice. In the late 1950s and early 1960s, there were few Foreign Service officers who could speak Vietnamese, so some of the postwar crop of China-language specialists, who hadn't been old enough to lose China, were sent to Saigon, where it was hoped they could pick up some useful information from the Chinese-speaking indigenes. But for the most part they had unrewarding tours of duty. It did not sit well with their superiors when, from their knowledge of Asian history, they perceived and reported that there appeared to be certain basic similarities between what was going on in Vietnam and what had gone on in China in the 1940s. When it came to corruption, Ngo Dinh Diem was just another Chiang.

As for much of the intelligence they gathered, they might as well not have bothered. One of them spent a good deal of time, to establish his credentials, in Cholon, the Chinese quarter of Saigon. After he had hung out there, attending operas, frequenting restaurants, and letting himself be beaten at mah-jongg, he began asking questions and got what seemed to him some illuminating answers. But some of these made the Viet Cong appear to be much more redoubtable than the American government chose to believe, and the embassy refused to pass his findings along to Washington. As for the Foreign Service officer, he was taken off political reporting and put in charge of the embassy motor pool.

The purge of the Old China Hands, and of those who emulated them in trying to tell what was truly happening in their bailiwick, was not without historical precedent. Had not the ancient Persians killed off their messengers who delivered unacceptable messages? "Those Foreign Service Officers in China served their country well," Senator J. William Fulbright would say to his Foreign Relations Committee in 1971, "but their country did not always serve them well. Because they reported that the Nationalist cause was moribund and because they reported what they saw and heard in Yenan and other Communist-controlled areas, they were treated as were messengers of bad news in less civilized times. Bearers of bad tidings, they were seen as advocates and even as the authors of the catastrophe which soon befell the Nationalist regime."

In the summer of 1944, for example, John Service happened to be available as an interpreter when an American general called on Chiang Kai-shek to convey a couple of tart messages from President Roosevelt. The Generalissimo spoke no English, and the general no Chinese; he took Service along simply to translate. But inasmuch as Roosevelt's unwelcome words reached Chiang's ears by way of Service's mouth, the messenger was thereafter held inseparable from the message.

In 1950, during one of innumerable loyalty-and-security hearings to which Service would subsequently be subjected, John Fairbank sent a letter to Secretary of State Dean Acheson. "There is no more loyal act than a statement to one's superiors of truths which are unpleasant for them to hear," Fairbank said. "But since no policy founded on wishful thinking can be a safe one, Mr. Service deserves the thanks of all patriotic American citizens for his courage in stating the truth of the situation in China as he saw it, even though it was not at the time and has not since been palatable to some Americans. In stating the truth as he saw it, he performed his duty with courage; and the soundness of his appraisal of the Chinese scene has been in my judgment amply borne out by the record of history." The following year Acheson made one of his less elegant contributions to the historical record. He fired Service.

In 1960, at the time of the Kennedy-Nixon television confrontations, Old China Hands had been blown like dead leaves all over the earth. (In *Journey to the Beginning,* published in 1958, Edgar Snow, after noting that "not a Chinese-speaking officer from the senior career service was left in the chambers where vital United States policies and decisions on Asia were made," had concluded, "Only a nation of very great power and wealth can afford such 'conspicuous waste' and even the United States could not afford it much longer.") Many individuals by then had felt the crunch of being identified with China, among them old academic hands like Owen Lattimore; but the men who were censured most severely were the Foreign Service officers who had been reporting the truth as they saw it to their government. For having had the temerity to bear bad tidings, they had nearly all, Drumright and Rice excepted, been relegated to spots where they could not effectively exercise their expertise.

John Service, in the fall of 1960, was United States consul at Liverpool, England.

Raymond P. Ludden, a man of rare courage who like Service was assigned to Lieutenant General Joseph W. Stilwell during much of the war, and who once spent four wintry wartime months on a reconnaissance, much of it on foot, behind Japanese lines in Northwest China, was, after nearly thirty years of diplomatic service, United States consul at Düsseldorf. In the earlier postwar years Ludden had been shuttled from Dublin to Brussels to Paris to Stockholm. "From 1949 on," he reflected long after his retirement, "I was just putting in my time. I couldn't get a job as dogcatcher."

A blunt-speaking man, Ludden, like many of his Foreign Service colleagues, didn't like to be called an Old China Hand. That term was to be reserved, the diplomats would say, for foreign bankers and businessmen who spent most of their time consorting with other foreigners in treaty ports like Shanghai or Tientsin and were by and large as unacquainted with the Chinese people as they were with the Chinese language. "The only Chinese that most Old China Hands ever knew," Ludden said, "was the translation for 'whiskey-and-soda.' "

While Ludden was sequestered in Düsseldorf handling routine consular chores, David Bruce, who would of course end up a long diplomatic career in Peking himself, was in Bonn as the American ambassador to West Germany. Bruce would drop in on Ludden every now and then and would sit down in his office and look around uncertainly, as if he sensed something was missing but couldn't quite figure out what it was. Ludden knew what it was all right: It was the portrait of President Eisenhower that official American functionaries were supposed to have on view on their premises. In anticipation of one Bruce visit, Ludden, who felt not without justification that he was in Düsseldorf because the Eisenhower administration considered him to be too controversial to be any place where an Old China Hand could be of real use to his government, hung up a reproduction of a Gilbert Stuart painting of George Washington. When Bruce arrived and began craning his neck searchingly, Ludden pointed to the presidential portrait and said, "Mr. Ambassador, I have that one up because it's noncontroversial."

John Paton Davies, another Stilwell staff man, who was often considered the most intellectual of the China specialists, was in Lima, Peru, in the fall of 1960, having been cashiered from the Foreign Service six years previously by John Foster Dulles, whose name was never confused with anyone else's. Davies, who had spurned an opportunity to resign and,

Stilwell's third John—who was technically a
officer but spent much of the war years in China—had
reported in to Salisbury, Rhodesia, as American consul
. He got there by way of Karachi, Beirut, Paris, and Lagos, Nigeria.
Emmerson had earlier been accused of losing China by, among others,
Lieutenant General Albert C. Wedemeyer, Stilwell's successor.
Wedemeyer testified before a Senate committee that if while he was in
command in China he had paid any attention to what Emmerson had
reported to him there, China would have fallen even faster than it did.
Emmerson thereupon wrote to Wedemeyer reminding him that *his* reports to the general had dealt exclusively with Japanese, not Chinese,
matters, and Wedemeyer had written back saying yes, of course, Emmerson was correct and he was sorry. When Wedemeyer published his memoirs, however, there was the same accusation all over again.

One of the minor crosses Emmerson had to bear was that *his* name
usually appeared in print with only one *m*. That was how Wedemeyer
spelled it in his book. But the explanation in this instance may have been
that the general's reminiscences were in large part compiled by Freda
Utley, who in an earlier work of her own had also used "Emerson"
throughout. A journalist born in London, Mrs. Utley had led an ideological life as dizzying in its swoops as a roller coaster. She had been an ardent
left-winger until her Russian first husband, with whom she lived in the
Soviet Union between 1930 and 1936, was spirited off by the secret police.
On arriving in China in 1938, though aggrieved at the Russians, she was
still sympathetic to the Communists; but she soon soured toward them,
and by the time she became a United States citizen in 1960, she was a
solid right-wing warrior.

John Carter Vincent in 1960 was living in retirement in Cambridge,
Massachusetts, tending a vegetable garden. He had once been in charge
of all Far Eastern affairs for the State Department, but his last post, just
before he was scuttled by Secretary Dulles, had been a crushingly insignifi-
cant one at Tangier. Dulles offered Vincent the choice of dismissal or
retirement because he had failed "to meet the standard which is demanded of a Foreign Service officer." Vincent, who abhorred contentious-
ness, elected to quit and afterward refrained, for the most part, from any

derogatory opinion of him was cited, [...]
dryly that he had served under eight secretari[...]
that, as secretaries went, "Mr. Dulles does not mea[...]
dards."

Oliver Edmund Clubb, another man of gentle disposition, who had
been bullied into retirement in 1952, was teaching part-time at New York
University, Brooklyn College, and Columbia in 1960; later he would
become a research associate of Columbia's East Asian Institute. Upon
being forced to leave the Foreign Service after serving nearly twenty-four
years, Clubb had graciously declared, "Should my knowledge and experience in future circumstances be deemed potentially useful to the Department of State, I should of course be glad to be of service in any way
feasible." Nobody from the department ever took him up on the offer,
though it was logical to surmise that somebody there had at least glanced
at one or two of his books about China, which had been highly praised
for their insights and evaluations.

Richard M. Service, John Service's younger brother, was counselor at
The Hague. A few years previous, while stationed in Brussels as political
officer, he had attended a dinner that the American ambassador to Belgium gave for a junketing United States senator from the Southwest.
Service was describing the American election system to the woman next
to him, a daughter of the Belgian prime minister, and he happened to
remark that, having been born in China and stationed abroad much of
his life, he had never voted. The senator, well gone in drink, overheard
him and exploded. "I know all about you, Service," he bellowed to a now
hushed table, "and it's inexcusably shocking that you're over here purporting to represent your country when you have never even voted!"
Service tried to calm the senator, but he raged on, casting further
aspersions. To spare the host any more embarrassment, Service excused
himself, went to his residence, and wrote the ambassador a memorandum
saying he had no idea what had triggered the outburst, but that he
suspected the senator thought he was his brother John, whose name had
long been anathema to many members of Congress. The next morning
the ambassador, hoping to get everything smoothed over before word
reached home that a legislator had been affronted by a diplomat, made

delicate inquiries and learned that the senator had no recollection of anything that had occurred the evening before, except that the wine had been unexceptionable.

Horace Smith, whom the State Department had assigned to that senator as an escort on the Brussels trip (conceivably because he had a black belt in judo), had by 1960 actually achieved the conventional goal of most career Foreign Service officers—an embassy of his own. He had been ambassador to Laos, at a time when Laos was of little account, but he resigned and went to work for an oil company.

Philip D. Sprouse was an inspector for the Foreign Service. For most of the 1950s he had been stationed in Paris and Brussels. When he became an inspector, the inspector general advised him that State had imposed one restriction on his new assignment: Sprouse was not to inspect any missions in Asia. Sprouse, too, finally became an ambassador—in Cambodia, where he presided briefly at the start of the Kennedy administration, before being invalided home. But he only received his embassy after he handed in his resignation from the Foreign Service, having decided to quit, in despair, because thirty men junior to him had already become ambassadors. Dean Rusk, receiving the resignation, asked him what the trouble was. "I'm not thin-skinned," Sprouse told the secretary, "but I'm also not stupid. I've been behind the China eight ball far too long."

Arthur R. Ringwalt had just retired as United States consul general at Kingston, Jamaica. It was an undemanding assignment, but a good deal more agreeable than some jobs he had had when he was concerned with Chinese matters. In Chungking fifteen years earlier, for instance, he had been political officer under Ambassador Hurley. One day the volatile Hurley, displeased with a report Ringwalt submitted to him, had pulled a gun on him.

James K. Penfield, who had served in Prague, London, Vienna, and Athens after being separated from Chinese affairs, was in Washington as deputy assistant secretary for African affairs. When he finally received an embassy in 1961, it was the one at Reykjavik, Iceland. There was at least some logic to his being there. In 1940 he had been the first Foreign Service officer assigned to Greenland, where he had come to be through a combination of circumstances. First, he was considered hardy enough for the rugged environment, having established his credentials not long before by walking from China to Burma. Second, the last man picked for the slot had been considered potentially too effete, having asked to have four cases of champagne shipped along with him so he could celebrate the Fourth of July with proper protocol.

Robert W. Barnett was a counselor at Brussels, responsible for Common Market problems. He had spent most of his postwar years working on European affairs. Once, in the early fifties, he decided to put his knowledge of China to some use and to look into the Asian connections of European nations. He got to be a great favorite of the Portuguese, because he was the only European-affairs man they had ever encountered who seemed to know or care about Macao. There was to be a conference in Lisbon about whether or not NATO would have to get involved if anything happened to Macao. Barnett, to the delight of his Portuguese friends, was slated to head the American delegation. At the last moment, however, someone above him in Secretary Dulles's chain of command remembered that Barnett was an Old China Hand, and his orders were canceled.

John Fremont Melby had left the Foreign Service.[3] Late in 1948, while Chiang Kai-shek was offering his last frail resistance to the Communists, Melby had stood at the Peking airport and watched planes coming in and unloading two kinds of cargo that some of the Generalissimo's subordinate generals evidently considered high priority—their gold bars and their concubines. (Richard Service similarly reported having once watched with amusement as a Kuomintang official tried in vain to climb the boarding steps of an American transport plane. He couldn't make it because he was overburdened with gold.) Three years later in Washington, Melby had been present, as an adviser to the accused, during a State Department

[3]This John related in his *The Mandate of Heaven* how in the summer of 1947 General Wedemeyer, at a Chungking cocktail party, had addressed Raymond Ludden as "Jack." On being corrected, Wedemeyer said, "Since three of the four State Department officers . . . at Yenan during the war were named John, I thought I was entitled to have the fourth one wild to make it four of a kind." Melby recalled that the ensuing laughter was forced. (Wedemeyer was not alone in his confusion. In another book, published in 1975 and entitled *The World and China, 1922–1972*, the author, whose name also happened to be John, said at one point, "Jack Ludden, one of the four Foreign Service officers in Yenan . . .")

Loyalty Security Board investigation of Edmund Clubb, in which Clubb's inquisitors gave a high priority to the charge that he had "viewed some aspects of Communism favorably in the period 1932–1934." In 1960 Melby was director of foreign students for the University of Pennsylvania and also executive vice-president of something called the National Council of Asian Affairs, a nongovernmental outfit.

Fulton Freeman was another counselor at Brussels. Like Sprouse, he had earlier been a Foreign Service inspector. He had traveled widely in that capacity, through, among other places, Africa and South America; but he had never been permitted to do any inspecting in Asia. Indeed, after leaving China in 1948, he never again set foot in East Asia.

Born in California in 1915, Fulton Freeman early on acquired the nickname "Tony"; General Hurley, who tended to get confused about even relatively uncomplicated facts, would now and then allude to him as "Anthony Fulton." Freeman had family reasons for becoming interested in the Orient. His mother's sister was Ruth Fulton Benedict, the anthropologist whose *The Chrysanthemum and the Sword* has long been staple reading for Americans studying Japan. When Freeman was a sophomore at Pomona College in 1934, he spotted an announcement of a student-exchange program between Pomona and Lingnan University in Canton; the president of Pomona, Charles K. Edmunds, had previously been president of Lingnan. Bored with his courses, Freeman applied for an exchange scholarship and got it—tuition, room, board, and full credit at Pomona for a year's study abroad.

By 1940 Freeman was back in China as a student, this time enrolled in a two-year language program that had been regularly conducted there for young Foreign Service officers since shortly after the turn of the century. In December 1941 he was interned by the Japanese in Peking for seven months. The experience was not overly taxing; a number of his fellow American members of a social group called the Thousand Aces Club (each had his own pewter beer mug with his name on it in Chinese characters and all the other members' names in English) were herded together with him at the residential quarters they had occupied all along, San Kuan Miao, which means "the Temple of Three Officials."[4] They

---

[4]A few of the residences in the compound were designed by an American architect who had come to China initially to design post offices. "He had a one-track mind," an Old China Hand who dwelt there recalled. "My living room looked exactly like a post office except for the window where they sold stamps." The architect was held blameless for what

diverted themselves with poker and volleyball, and Freeman spent most of his other waking hours studying Chinese. He wasn't allowed to leave San Kuan Miao, and his Chinese-language teachers couldn't visit him; but like the other internees he'd been permitted to keep his servants, and he worked out a very satisfactory modus vivendi with his Number One Boy. That factotum knew how to read and write, but he didn't understand much of what was going on in the world. So in return for language lessons, Freeman would explain to the boy what the editorials in the local newspapers meant.

After a while, when the pattern of Japanese surveillance of San Kuan Miao was fairly well established and Freeman's grasp of Chinese fairly secure, he would sometimes sneak out of the compound at night, disguised in a long Chinese gown. He was strolling along a dark street once when a genuine Chinese accosted him and asked if he knew where a certain alley was. Freeman offered to lead him to it. They walked along chatting in Chinese until they reached a street light, whereupon the Chinese looked at his guide, exclaimed in Chinese, "My God, a foreign devil!" and scurried away. Freeman was quite pleased at having been taken, however briefly, for a native. "It was my finest moment as far as linguistic achievement was concerned," he reflected years afterward.

Freeman eventually came to be regarded as one of the finest Chinese linguists the Foreign Service had ever turned out. Early in 1943, after being repatriated during a swap of internees, he was shipped back to China. He was a lowly $3500-a-year third secretary, but because of his fluency in Chinese was given an imposing assignment. A few months before, as a very belated gesture to Chinese nationalism, the United States had decided to waive the extraterritorial rights it had had for a century. Under extraterritoriality, Americans had enjoyed quite a few perquisites that impinged on Chinese sovereignty. Those who got into legal difficulties, for instance, had the privilege of being tried in American consular courts rather than in Chinese courts; if one American shot somebody during a poker game, he could hope that an American consul deciding his fate would react more sympathetically to such a crime of passion than, say, a Chinese magistrate raised on fan-tan. Now, in 1943, such foreign devils were to be treated juridically just like everybody else.

The abandonment of extraterritoriality was very well and good, but the

---

befell one young diplomat, who complained that his fireplace didn't draw properly; what had happened was that his servants didn't like him and had bricked up his chimney.

trouble was that few Americans had any idea of what Chinese law was all about. The codes that governed Chinese courts had never been translated into English. Freeman was instructed to do this, so that non-Chinese-speaking Americans could know what constituted a felony and what a misdemeanor, and how one went about getting a divorce or claiming an inheritance, or whatever. He recruited two English-speaking Chinese lawyers and a couple of bilingual secretaries and drew up a list of the one hundred Chinese laws that struck them as most consequential. Then the Chinese lawyers made a rough translation of these statutes. The results were incomprehensible. Freeman thereupon sat down with twenty-eight dictionaries—Chinese-English, Chinese-French, Chinese-Italian, Chinese-Anything-he-could-follow-at-all—and endeavored to produce English versions of the hundred laws that would be both intelligible and more or less faithful to the Chinese originals. He devoted a little over a year to the task, averaging a law about every three days.

Freeman worked in Washington, in the Chinese Affairs division of the State Department, from 1948 to 1950—two years so harrowing for anyone in that field at that time in that place, that at the end of the stint he had to have three-fifths of his stomach removed. By 1951, much to his relief, he was detached from Chinese affairs entirely and sent to Rome. He served there under two veteran ambassadors, James C. Dunn and Ellsworth Bunker. Then Eisenhower took office, and the usual diplomatic shuffle took place. One of the new president's first appointments was that of Clare Boothe Luce as ambassador to Italy. Mrs. Luce almost didn't get there. Eisenhower had revealed her selection at a press conference without first clearing it with the Italian government; according to the protocol that governs such matters, Rome could have reacted to the inadvertent snub by demanding that Washington name someone else. So great was Eisenhower's prestige, however, that Italy overlooked his gaffe.

Freeman would probably have preferred to have had the niceties of protocol rigidly observed. From where he sat in Rome early in 1953 the roof seemed to have fallen in on him—as dreadfully as a bedroom ceiling in the embassy there would later shed flaked arsenic on the new ambassador. Clare Boothe Luce, of all people! For more than a decade her husband Henry had been an unflagging supporter of Chiang Kai-shek, and in the Luce publications the Old China Hands—of whom Freeman was unarguably one—had received short shrift. Only a few weeks had passed since *Time*'s acerb coverage of the forced retirement of John Carter

Vincent[5]—the same *Time* that had so slanted or scrapped the wartime stories of its own hand in China, Theodore H. White, that he had put a sign on his office door: "Any similarity between this correspondent's dispatches and what appears in *Time* is purely coincidental." And had not Mrs. Luce herself, when she was a member of Congress in 1945, performed like a China Lobby lobbyist on the floor of the House, and later assumed the presidency of the resolutely pro-Chiang American China Policy Association? Clare Boothe Luce!

Freeman gloomily realized, moreover, that he could hardly hope to hide from his new boss, commodious as were the embassy quarters in Rome. He was special assistant for mutual defense assistance programs, which meant that he was intimately involved in high-level military matters and had to have direct access to and daily contact with the ambassador. When he heard the news, he surmised that—even if he managed not to lose his head—he'd be lucky to salvage any remaining fragment of his stomach from this predicament. He was proved wrong. Mrs. Luce came to respect him and like him, and an unstated détente developed between them: They would never discuss China. When somebody else once brought up the subject in their presence, the ambassador turned to her deputy and said teasingly, "Why don't you talk to Harry about this?"

Freeman had been routinely, even rapidly, promoted during the early phases of his career, but by 1954 had become uncomfortably aware that he had been twice passed over for further advancement. A friend in Washington tipped him off that the reason was that State was disinclined to send his name along to the White House, where the Old China Hands were in as much disrepute as if they had taken the Long March with Mao Tse-tung. The secretary of state could leave an otherwise deserving individual's name off a promotion list only if there was some question of his being a security risk, and Freeman had never been informed that any such allegation had been made about him. He had some home leave coming in 1954 and thought he might stop in Washington on his way back to Italy from California to try to clear up the baffling matter.

While he was still in Europe, though, Mrs. Luce received a copy of a promotion list, noticed that his name wasn't on it, and asked him why.

[5]Mrs. Vincent, whose lifelong cause was to uphold her husband's reputation, complained to Luce about *Time*'s shabby treatment of him. Luce ponderously replied that "progress is not made without the heavy counterpoint of pain and suffering."

Freeman shrugged diplomatically. "Now don't be cute," the ambassador said. "Is there any reason at all that you can think of? Could it have to do with the China business?" Freeman allowed that it probably could. "That's all I want to know," said Mrs. Luce. The next day, without telling Freeman, she fired off letters to President Eisenhower and Secretary Dulles, using all her considerable literary skills to praise her subordinate and damn whoever it was who might be thwarting him.

During his home leave, Freeman did not have to initiate any inquiries at the department. Instead, he was formally summoned to Washington and ordered to present himself in the office of Otto F. Otepka, a State security man. In 1973, nearly twenty years later, Freeman, by then securely ensconced back in California as president of the Monterey Institute of Foreign Studies, the nation's only graduate-level school for translators and interpreters, could still vividly recall the four and a half hours he spent in a small room containing Otepka, one of the security officer's henchmen, a young woman stenotypist, and a six-inch-thick *curriculum vitae* that the inquisitors had prepared for the occasion. The very first question put to Freeman, asked in the tones one might use in inquiring of a person when he had last kicked his mother, was, "When did you last see John Stewart Service?"

"This morning, when he picked me up at the airport and drove me over here," Freeman replied cheerfully. By then he had heard of Mrs. Luce's two letters, as Otepka might or might not have, and he felt that his ambassador was standing, at least figuratively, alongside him.

Otepka frowned, pawed through the stack of papers, and came upon a past acquaintanceship that he apparently hoped his adversary could not so glibly dismiss. Was it true, he demanded, that one of Freeman's best friends in Peking in 1946 had been a Russian named Tichvinsky? Freeman said that he had been secretary of the Legation Club in Peking then, and that Tichvinsky had been vice-president. They lived close to one another and would often walk home together after the club officers had business meetings. Yes, they had established a casual relationship and once or twice had dined together with their respective wives.

Ah, then, so Tichvinsky had been one of his closest friends! Freeman smiled and recounted his last meeting with the Russian. The American had been walking along Legation Street one day late in 1947 or early in 1948 and had espied a familiar figure approaching him. But to his surprise, the man, Tichvinsky, had stridden straight past him without a sign of recognition. What could this mean? Freeman deduced that it had to mean something and shot off a wire to Washington recounting the peculiar incident; sure enough, this was one of the first inklings the department had had that the Russians were heating up a particular phase of the cold war.

Otepka frowned again and tried another tack. What about Anna Louise Strong, the notorious radical writer? Was *she* not a close friend, and had not Freeman entertained her at his home in China? Well, yes and no. She had been one of the first Americans to visit Chinese Communist headquarters at Yenan, Freeman patiently recounted, and on her return to Peking, through a missionary who was a mutual acquaintance, he had been lucky enough to be able to arrange for her to come to his house one evening and talk about Mao and Chou En-lai and Chu Teh and the others; afterward he had put every fascinating tidbit she disclosed into a dispatch for Washington. But close friend? That night had been the only time he had ever laid eyes on the woman.

(The "Do-you-know?" game was popular among all security investigators. Arthur Ringwalt recalled that while he was at Washington in China affairs, after the war, the FBI would keep coming around and asking him, "Do you know James K. Penfield?" or whomever, and he would always say "Of course," and the next question would always be, "Is he a Communist?" Once when asked this last question about someone else, Ringwalt's response was "No, but I suspect he's a Fascist." The FBI had said, "We're not interested in anything like that. We want to know if he's a *Communist.*" Whether or not an individual was acquainted with Anna Louise Strong seemed to people like Otepka of particular significance. An informant with a grudge against Penfield once triumphantly identified her as a friend of *his;* it happened to be the case that, somewhat to his regret, Penfield had never met her.)

Freeman waited for Otepka's next move. Pointing to the fat dossier, the security man said that there was a curious gap in it. "It's a funny thing, but we seem to have lost you for a year of your life," Otepka said. He knew that Freeman had been an exchange student at Lingnan in 1934 and 1935, and that he had returned to Pomona in 1936, but where, Otepka asked sternly, had he been in between? Freeman told him: At the end of his year at Lingnan, he and two other American students there had traveled by bicycle from Canton to India. It had been an austere trek; they carried sleeping bags, and on the back of each bike was a brass box bearing the legend, in Chinese, "Around the world on a bicycle."

"How do you say that in Chinese?" Otepka asked.

"Waan yao sai gai daap dan ch'ieh," Freeman rattled off.

The interrogatory finally sputtered out. Freeman asked if there was anything else anyone wanted to know. Then the stenotypist spoke up for the first time. "How do you spell *'Waan yao sai gai daap dan ch'ieh'?"* she asked.

Freeman was flabbergasted. She was a Caucasian Occidental, but she had a flawless Cantonese accent.

"How come you speak Cantonese?" he asked.

The stenotypist said she was married to a Cantonese.

"Is he an American citizen?" Freeman asked.

"No," she said, "but we never discuss secret information."

Freeman could not refrain from remarking that it seemed curious to have had the wife of an alien there at all, in view of the fact that he *had* discussed some secrets at the session; but Otepka said there was nothing to worry about: it had just been a coincidence that she'd been picked for this chore.

Whatever Otepka's conclusions about the interview may have been, Mrs. Luce's views apparently carried more weight, for Freeman was never interrogated again. He ultimately got his promotions in due order, and indeed got a couple of embassies of his own—first the middling one at Colombia and then the prestigious one at Mexico. But he was lucky all the way along the line. To begin with, there had been Mrs. Luce's firm backing. Then when he was nominated for the Bogotá post, Mike Mansfield had made one of his rare personal appearances before the Senate Foreign Relations Committee, which had to pass on the appointment. Mansfield told his fellow senators that he didn't want to ask any questions, he wanted to tell them a couple of things. First, he was a friend of Mr. Freeman's father, and second, he had been a friend of Mr. Freeman's for twenty-five years. Now, was there any further discussion? There was not —no need for it after Mansfield had shown where he stood—and the committee voted unanimously in Freeman's favor, without, so far as could be ascertained, any senator's even mentioning China. It may have been the only time in recent history that an Old China Hand from the Foreign Service came up before a Senate group without having his Old-China-Handedness elaborately pursued.

Freeman never did make it back to the Far East. He inquired every now and then whether there wasn't some Asian diplomatic slot that he could fill, and in February 1961, just after President Kennedy's inauguration, he thought he had a shot at Bangkok, where he could have put his Chinese to some use. But nothing came of that. "Whenever I brought up the subject, I found myself against an impermeable wall," he would say later. "Every time I talked about going to the Far East, somebody would tell me to forget it."

Like some others among the Old China Hands, Freeman had imagined that when Eisenhower left the White House and Kennedy came in, the clouds that had hung so long over most of them would finally be dispersed. The combination of John Kennedy as president and Dean Rusk as secretary of state seemed almost too good to be true. Rusk was a personal friend of many of the men involved. He had been a colonel in the China-Burma-India theater of operations during the war, had moved to State under General George Marshall in 1946, had become Acheson's assistant secretary for Far Eastern affairs in 1950, and after that had been president of the Rockefeller Foundation, an organization established to aid the oppressed. When John Service, in the course of trying to rent an apartment in New York after Senator McCarthy had hounded him out of the State Department, needed some character references, Rusk had agreed to provide one of them.

(Service did not get the apartment notwithstanding; the owners of the building, more impressed with what McCarthy had been saying about him publicly than with what Rusk's private assessment might have been, had rejected him, even after accepting a down payment, on the ground that his neighbors might not like the kind of visitors—presumably, shady ones—that he might attract. "I began to realize how some of the German refugees I knew in Shanghai in 1940 must have felt when *they* were looking for a place to live," Service said afterward. On subsequently hearing of this shabby persecution of Service, George D. Aiken, the senator from Vermont, who did not share the view of some of his Republican colleagues that the Old China Hands deserved whatever they got, observed, "He received cruel and unusual punishment.")

Rusk was to be a disappointment, although he began his tenure as head of State auspiciously. Not long after he had been installed, he told a gathering of Foreign Service officers how highly he esteemed them; in his remarks he singled out John Davies as more or less the embodiment of all the virtues a Foreign Service officer should have. Davies, who by now had become, in his own wry words, an "unfrocked diplomat," was far from the scene of this encomium; he was in Peru, where he was trying to get his furniture business reorganized after a partner had absconded with the firm's money. James Penfield was present, and a couple of days later ran into Rusk in a corridor, congratulated him on his heartening words, and said he hoped they were a harbinger of better things to come for the Old China Hands and particularly for Davies. "It's high time something was done about this," Rusk replied.

But the time never ripened, in part, presumably, because of the secretary's stiff feelings about the Chinese Communists, whom he tended to appraise as a monolithic aggressive horde. "We do not recognize the authorities in Peiping for what they pretend to be," Rusk had declared in 1951, when he was assistant secretary for Far Eastern affairs. "The Peiping regime may be a colonial Russian government—a Slavic Manchukuo on a larger scale. It is not the Government of China."[6] There was little to indicate a decade later that anything had taken place to alter Rusk's rigid evaluation, and indeed as late as 1965 he would be describing as "gullible" the Old China Hands who clung to the belief that the Chinese Communists, whatever else they might or might not be, were indisputably Chinese. A few months after the Kennedy administration took office, Edgar Snow turned up in Washington. He had been to the People's Republic in 1960, had discerned that Mao and Chou seemed interested in exploring normalization of relations with the United States, and felt he should transmit this intelligence, to which probably no other American was privy, to the State Department. To Snow's dismay, Secretary Rusk had only ten unreceptive minutes to spare for him.

As for Kennedy, as far as the general public was concerned, he came to the White House with shining liberal credentials. The Old China Hands were not so sure. After all, in 1948 and 1949, while a member of the House, Kennedy had made speeches endorsing some of General Hurley's fulminations against them; and his brother Robert had in his political infancy actually worked for Joe McCarthy. And what was more, had not the new young president referred to the whole State Department as a bowl of jelly? It was uncertain, too, to what extent Kennedy dared to attempt to make any substantial changes in the nation's hands-off China policy. Unless he had that in mind, he was not likely to do much

[6]For most of the time that the United States government was not on speaking terms with the Chinese government, it insisted on referring to Mao's capital city as "Peiping," which was the name Chiang Kai-shek preferred; it was considered gauche, if not traitorous, for anyone around Washington to use "Peking." In this book, for simplicity's sake, "Peking" is used throughout.

for or about men who could not be restored to good governmental standing without at least an implicit admission by the government that the things for which they had been punished were no longer considered wrong.

For a while, Kennedy hoped to initiate a dialogue with the People's Republic by means of a humanitarian food program; surely nobody could complain too loudly, his advisers reasoned, about the president's seeking to keep anyone from starving to death. But nothing came of that plan, nor, for that matter, of the deliberations of a special study group that Kennedy set up in the summer of 1963 to make recommendations to him about possible changes in Sino-American relations. He died before the group could report back to him.

Kennedy, of course, had many more things to worry about than the feelings of a handful of aggrieved individuals. He had been elected by a slim margin, and he needed every bit of congressional support he could muster if he had any hope of putting across any of his programs. To place in Congress's consciousness the name of anyone who had been in China in the Hurley era was as chancy as trying to slip a foreign ingredient into the bean soup at the Senate restaurant.

Not long after Kennedy's inauguration, for example, Tanganyika became independent. John Emmerson, then in Rhodesia, was elated to be informed by telegram from the State Department that he was finally going to become a full-fledged ambassador. He had been designated chief of the first American mission to the newly sovereign capital of Dar es Salaam. The appointment could not take effect, naturally, until the Senate confirmed him, but word got around Salisbury, and there were an appropriate number of congratulatory and farewell parties, in between which Emmerson immersed himself in the collected works of Julius Nyerere. Then there was a second message from the States. It seemed that a couple of key Senators who would have to approve the nomination were coming up for reelection soon, and they did not want to chance offending any of their constituents with long memories by seeming to take unpopular sides on anything relating to China. So, regretfully, the appointment had been rescinded. Emmerson never got to be ambassador to anywhere.

From Kennedy's point of view, there was a broad spectrum of bygone wrongs to be righted. The Old China Hands were far from being the only individuals who had suffered during the national hysteria. The president had his staff draw up a list of names for him of all sorts of people who seemed to deserve exoneration or resurrection. J. Robert Oppenheimer and Charles Chaplin were high on this list. Oppenheimer had been branded a security risk by the Eisenhower administration in 1954; when, early in 1963, he was picked to receive the Enrico Fermi Award, Kennedy announced his intention of presenting it himself at a White House ceremony, thereby provoking clanging protests from such diehard security-risk analysts as Senator Bourke B. Hickenlooper of Iowa. These things take time: Kennedy was assassinated before the scheduled event, and President Lyndon Johnson did the honors for Oppenheimer. Chaplin fell by the wayside.

As for the Old China Hands, it had already been more or less agreed by Kennedy and his staff that whatever might be done for them would have to wait until his second term. This pokiness angered some of their friends, who could not understand how it was that John Davies, for instance, could not be redeemed during Kennedy's thousand-day incumbency. Had not Kennedy's mother, the friends argued, moved in the same high Catholic social circles as Davies's mother-in-law? Could the reason, some of Davies's more gossipy acquaintances speculated, be found at another level of family parallels? Had not Davies's wife been a society reporter for the Washington *Post*, whereas Kennedy's wife was a mere photographer for the much less genteel *Times-Herald?*

John Service, it will be recalled, was in Liverpool when the Democrats took over. Liverpool had been considered a desirable diplomatic post when it was a thriving seaport. Along with Canton, Cherbourg, and LeHavre, it had been one of the earliest spots where consulates had been set up. In the old days, the Liverpool consul had got 50 per cent of the fees his office collected; indeed, Nathaniel Hawthorne had once sought the job for that pecuniary reason. But now American shipping matters that arose at Liverpool were handled by the Coast Guard in London, and the Liverpool consulate was largely a pasture post—one earmarked for bypassed Foreign Service officers killing time before retirement. Their principal function was to issue visas to applicants from the north of England and perform similar routine consular functions, with no fee splitting. Still, it was a pleasant post, and during the three years Service held it, he did have ten agreeable weeks in London as acting supervisory consul general when the incumbent was on leave. The free time also gave him a chance to resume collecting Chinese postage stamps—something he had begun doing as a boy in Shanghai. He became a member of the

China Philatelic Society of London. It was his only connection with Chinese affairs.[7]

Service had not had a promotion since 1948. After he was restored to good standing by the Supreme Court in 1957 and reported back for duty with State, he suspected he would never have another. But then he began getting good efficiency reports, and following the Democratic victory in 1960 his hopes stirred. They were quickly dashed. The department let him know that he could stay at Liverpool until mandatory retirement, but could not expect any transfer or elevation in status. He had not even the solace of being named consul general, though that had been the rank of the person in charge at Liverpool ever since the office was established. Some senator, once again, might have objected. People like Dean Acheson and Dean Rusk were talking among themselves about what could be done for Service, but no one felt up to talking to the crusty James Eastland, now chairman of the Senate Internal Security Subcommittee that had once been the fiefdom of the ineffable McCarran.

At the end of 1962 the civil-liberties lawyer Joseph L. Rauh, Jr., wrote to Attorney General Robert Kennedy, "The liberal Democratic Administration brought nothing new for Jack Service. . . . His restoration to the Foreign Service proved to have been only an illusion of rectitude, and a career that might yet have become one of the brightest in our contempo-

[7]In 1960 Service was visited in Liverpool by an old friend, Laurence E. Salisbury, who had quit the Foreign Service in 1944. The son of a Chicago lawyer, Salisbury had had a peculiar introduction to the Far East. Early in the First World War he had got himself commissioned a second lieutenant in the British army and had been sent to Tsingtao to shepherd to France five hundred Chinese coolies who were paid sixty cents a day each to dig ditches, which they regarded as splendid pay. They all sported queues, and the first Chinese words that Salisbury learned, accordingly, were those for "Duck head," an order he felt constrained to issue when they took a bath. Salisbury subsequently became a Japanese-language Foreign Service officer; not long after Japan invaded Manchuria, he was sent to China and spent five years there. In Liverpool he wandered into the consulate's library one day, where the librarian, a gentle old lady, confided to him that she had a problem: The embassy in London had sent over, she said, "a horrible book containing all sorts of dreadful statements about Mr. Service." It was Freda Utley's *The China Story*, and it had some disparaging comments about Salisbury, too. "I wish I could get rid of it," the librarian said, "but it's government property, and I don't dare." Salisbury offered to help her. "Leave it out and I'll steal it," he said. Ever afterwards, he kept the book—with its United States of America bookplate and the legend "Library of the ——— of the U.S. of A., Class 951"—in his own library. On the flyleaf was also inscribed in ink, "Discarded in 1960," a gallant attempt by the lady librarian to keep her problem solver out of trouble in case he got caught with the stolen goods.

rary diplomatic corps finally ended . . . ruined by a combination of venality and supineness." As a friend of Service's remarked during the Kennedy years, few men had ever been so mightily defamed by nasty people and so meagerly defended by nice ones.

2

"We have no one like them today."

President Kennedy said in his first State of the Union message that his administration "recognizes the value of daring and dissent among government employees." This statement of policy was applauded by the *Foreign Service Journal*, a semiofficial publication of the American Foreign Service Association, which declared in an April 1961 editorial that the State Department "should protect the officer against having labels put on him by outsiders who may disagree with his political views." It warned that "Unless this is done, only orthodox views will be ventilated, and our policy formulation process will suffer." The journal went on to say:

> Let there be . . . within the limits of loyal service to the United States, a free play of ideas in the Foreign Service. Such a free play of ideas is only possible, however, if the President and the Secretary of State will actually defend those of their subordinates who may some day, with the benefit of hindsight, prove to have been wrong. . . . The Foreign Service consists not only of geniuses. We are fallible human beings, but we are less likely to give bad advice to those in positions of ultimate responsibility if we are free from inhibitions about the limits of what is "safe" to say. Let this be understood also by Congress, lest there be a new tendency to penalize those who have in good faith advocated the taking of risks.

By then quite a few of the Foreign Service officers who were China specialists had been penalized after demonstrating their willingness to take risks beyond the call of most duties. These were men who along with their colleagues in other areas were often mocked as effete cookie pushers. General Hurley's official biographer, Don Lohbeck (whom Hurley had chosen for that honor despite the writer's dubious credentials; he had earlier edited Gerald L. K. Smith's rabid *The Cross and the Flag*), described the China Hands, further, as "a sort of commissars-in-striped-pants outfit."

John Service was aspersed in 1950 by Congresswoman Edith Nourse Rogers of Massachusetts as a "young man who has never served his country in uniform." Actually, Service *was* in uniform during much of the war, though, being a civilian attached to the armed forces, he sported no insignia of rank. As far as the congresswoman's implications were concerned, in China, in July 1937, after the Japanese had isolated Peking, Service volunteered to escort a party of American tourists out of the city toward the relative safety of Tientsin. (The next year, John Davies, armed only with an American flag, walked into the mountain resort of Kuling to rescue some Americans stranded *there.*) During the war Service offered —though nothing came of the gesture—to make a parachute jump behind Japanese lines to obtain military intelligence; and toward the end of 1943, while surveying roads near the border between China and Indo-China, up to within a few hundred feet of Japanese troops, he had briefly engaged in a fire fight with the enemy. When some Japanese Zeros strafed a remote air base where he was spending the night, Service blazed away at them, ineffectively but self-satisfyingly, with a carbine; a few days later, some Nationalist troops in the vicinity stole his carbine.

John Davies *had* made a parachute jump, involuntarily. He was one of seventeen passengers, most of them GIs, on a C-46 transport plane that left Chabua, in Assam, on August 2, 1943, on a flight across the Hump. Eric Sevareid, then a war correspondent, was also on the plane. (Sevareid had run into Davies not long before at the Khartoum airport and had been impressed by his aplomb; while nearly everyone else was sweating out his travel plans or just plain sweating, Davies was standing composedly in what shade was provided by the wing of an airplane, reading Harold Laski's *Reflections.*) Now, in 1943, over the Patkoi mountain range, the plane's port engine conked out. The pilot ordered all hands to don parachutes and jettison their baggage. Davies did keep his attaché case, which contained a number of confidential military and diplomatic papers and also five twenty-dollar bills, which he had undertaken to deliver on behalf of the editors of *Foreign Affairs* to a Chinese in Kunming who'd written an article for the magazine but couldn't be reached through the mails.

Lightening the load didn't help. The plane kept losing altitude, and finally the pilot gave the order to bail out. No one aboard had ever jumped before, and nobody wanted to be first man out. Davies stuffed his attaché case in his shirt front, moved to the door, and showed the way. The party spent a month in the jungle, in a wild area between Burma and India known to be inhabited by headhunters, and Sevareid, who subsequently reported on the ordeal, recalled how impressed he had been by Davies's "great reserves of moral courage" (and also by his apparent imperviousness to fleas). When the group heard that Japanese patrols were nearby, Sevareid recounted, a colonel, the senior officer among them, said that if an enemy patrol spotted them the civilians should attempt to flee while the soldiers stood their ground and fought it out. Davies demurred, saying, "In the first place, this would be dishonorable. In the second place, we'd never get out."

No patrol materialized, and in due course all the men made it to safety, with Davies conspicuous as chief morale builder. As Sevareid told it on the air eleven years later:

> There were moments when another step seemed quite impossible. In such moments, it was generally the diplomat who would sing out with something like "Onward and upward with the arts," and we would laugh and gasp and keep on climbing. I began to faint with heat and thirst on one suffocating slope; the man who left his half pint of water with me—all he had—was, of course, the diplomat.
>
> After we emerged into India and the military reports were in, there was a move in the Air Force to decorate our diplomat for his outstanding personal conduct. I do not know if he ever received the decoration. [He did not.] But none of us in the strange party, I think, would have disputed the choice. For I thought then, as I think now, that if ever again I were in deep trouble, the man I would want to be with would be this particular man. I have known a great number of men around the world, under all manner of circumstances. I have known none who seemed more the whole man; none more finished a civilized product, in all that a man should be—in modesty and thoughtfulness, in resourcefulness and steady strength of character.

What prompted that testimonial reminiscence was Secretary Dulles's dismissal of Davies, after twenty-three years of service in the Foreign Service, for alleged *weakness* of character—for, in Dulles's view, Davies's lack of sufficient judgment, discretion, and reliability. "Sufficient, one may ask, unto *what?*" Sevareid concluded with unrestrained emotion. "Their [a State Department Board that recommended Davies's ouster] test can only have been of supernatural design. I saw their victim measured against the most severe tests that mortal man can design. Those, he passed. At the head of the class."

Davies himself never talked much about the incident. Exhibiting self-control and exercising leadership in stressful situations were, in his view, part of his job. So was exposure to physical suffering, and many of his colleagues had experienced that. Culver B. Chamberlain, a consul in Mukden in 1932, had been badly beaten up by Japanese sentries there. George Atcheson and J. Hall Paxton had been aboard the *Panay* when the Japanese sank it on the Yangtze River, twenty miles from Nanking, on December 12, 1937. Paxton, a missionary son less addicted to understatement than most of his China colleagues, had returned to Washington waving a hard-earned bloody shirt.

Earlier that year, Edmund Clubb had been on the scene when the United States suffered what may have been its first casualty of the war in Asia. This happened in July 1937, soon after the Japanese attacked the Marco Polo Bridge twelve miles northwest of Peking. The city gates were at once shut, and some Chinese troops erected a barricade in case the invaders should breach the walls. Clubb was at the barricade, helping Americans to get past it, when a detachment of United States Marine cavalrymen drew near, ignoring the Chinese soldiers' shouts to halt. Sensing that the Americans didn't understand the shouts and that the edgy Chinese at the barricade had taken the marines for Japanese, Clubb rushed between the two armed groups, yelling in his best and loudest Chinese that the horsemen were friends, not foes; but before he could straighten things out, one marine had been shot in the leg. After finally engineering a cease-fire, Clubb took the wounded marine to a doctor.

Arthur Ringwalt, for his part, had first tangled with the Japanese when they attacked Shanghai in 1932. He was a vice-consul there, and the place was full of Americans, or at any rate of people who held American citizenship even though, as in the case of some retired merchant seamen, they couldn't speak English. No matter; it was the duty of the United States consulate to look after them and to try to extricate them from whatever jams they might get into. A number of such folk were living in Japanese-held portions of Shanghai, and Ringwalt, who was on fairly good terms with the Japanese consul, could usually wangle a pass to enter these areas and escort the Americans out to the international settlement. But one day, trying to lead to this haven a Chinese woman who had had a baby by an American father, Ringwalt ran into a bunch of Korean thugs employed by the Japanese; they were looking for somebody to thrash and when Ringwalt obligingly appeared, they fell upon him and beat him up.

John Carter Vincent also could not have been accused of shirking military duty. Toward the end of the First World War, he had tried, at the age of eighteen, to enlist in the army. He was ridiculously underweight; though of normal height, he weighed only ninety-one pounds. He was quickly rejected, whereupon he went on a crash chocolate-malt diet, gained sixteen pounds, and was accepted. (He got in too late, however, to have had a chance to perform any battlefield heroics.) By 1927 Vincent had been accepted by the Foreign Service and was a vice-consul at Changsha, which had a substantial American population. Yale-in-China, the biggest educational institution in Hunan province, was there. Aggressive xenophobia was rife, and all outlanders were being subjected to harassment. This time it was Vincent's responsibility to shepherd the Americans on hand to safety at Hankow.[1] He got four hundred of them out aboard the U.S.S. *Palos*, a shallow-draft gunboat built by the navy specifically for service on the rapids-racked Yangtze River.[2] Among the evacuees was Vincent's sister Margaret, who was then acting as his official hostess. After Vincent had got everybody under way, he dutifully went back to his office at Changsha to collect his files and his code books, and barely had time afterward to evacuate himself.

Yale University subsequently gave Vincent a gold watch for his humanitarian pains. Vincent was pleased with the gift, but like Ringwalt, Clubb, Davies, Service, and all the others who had calmly faced up to perils, he felt that he hadn't done much that wasn't all in a diplomat's day's work. What pleased him most about the Changsha evacuation was that his sister subsequently married the naval officer commanding the *Palos*.

Benjamin Franklin, who went to Paris in 1778 as the first minister plenipotentiary of Congress, is usually regarded as the founder of the Foreign Service. Three years before that, he had been chairman of the Committee of Secret Correspondence, established by the colonies to try to ascertain how various European powers would react to American independence. For more than a century after Franklin's plenipotentiary trail-

---

[1] Since then, Hankow has been merged with the adjacent cities of Hangyang and Wuchang to become Wuhan, the capital of Hupeh province.
[2] One of the *Palos*'s sister ships was the *Panay*, which the Japanese sank in 1937. Another, the *Tutuila*, was turned over to China during the war and, in honor of Mme. Chiang, rechristened the *Mei Ling*.

blazing, the United States made a distinction between its diplomatic and consular services. Most individuals in the former category got there by being wealthy, most of those in the latter by means of political patronage.

It was not until 1924, when Congress passed the Rogers Act, named after Congressman John Jacob Rogers of Massachusetts, (Congresswoman Edith Rogers, who disparaged Service, was his widow), that the two groups were merged into a career foreign service, more or less patterned after the British career service. From then on promotions were to be made on merit and appointments to be subject to confirmation by the Senate. Ever since, the commissions given to Foreign Service officers have stipulated that the country reposed "special trust and confidence" in their "integrity, prudence, and ability."

Prudence thus was always in the forefront of a professional diplomat's consciousness. When John Davies was cashiered, he observed tartly, "I think a prudent young man would enter the Foreign Service knowing another trade." Unfortunately for Davies, he had to learn the furniture business at the advanced age of forty-eight.

The lack of trust and confidence that the superiors in government exhibited toward the Old China Hands had a perhaps permanently debilitating effect on the morale of the Foreign Service. Perceiving what had happened to some diplomats for putting on paper their best judgments based on their integrity, prudence, and ability, other diplomats took great pains to put as little in writing as possible. In 1974 one career officer revealed that over the previous eighteen years he had exchanged just three circumspect letters with a very close friend whose assignments had happened to take him to other parts of the world. Edward Rice had never got into any particular jam himself, but when in 1973 an historian asked if he had any memorabilia around from the McCarthy era, Rice informed the inquirer that he couldn't know much about that period if he thought any Foreign Service officer would have kept notes on it.

By 1953 it was George Kennan's view that the Foreign Service had been "weakened beyond real hope of recovery"—this gloomy appraisal coming from a man who had won a prize seventeen years before for an essay entitled "The Utility of a Trained and Permanent Foreign Service." He had presciently declared therein that "without this [permanent] basis as an incentive, the Foreign Service would not often attract men endowed by nature with the ability to succeed in life and therefore able to choose their own careers. No matter how alluring the opportunities of the service might be for the achievement of glory and fame, few young men would desire to enter it if their careers might be blasted at any moment by a dismissal having no connection with efficiency and depending upon the capricious winds of politics."

By 1954 so many careers had been so capriciously blasted that five senior American diplomats—Norman Armour, Robert Woods Bliss, Joseph C. Grew, William Phillips, and G. Howland Shaw—felt constrained to write a joint letter to *The New York Times* in which they declared that the recent attacks on the Foreign Service were "laying the foundations of a Foreign Service competent to serve a totalitarian government rather than the Government of the United States as we have heretofore known it." The letter concluded:

> Fear is playing an important part in American life at the present time. As a result, the self-confidence, the confidence in others, the sense of fair play and the instinct to protect the rights of the nonconformist are—temporarily, it is to be hoped—in abeyance. But it would be tragic if this fear, expressing itself in an exaggerated emphasis on security, should lead us to cripple the Foreign Service, our first line of national defense, at the very time when its effectiveness is essential to our filling the place which history has assigned to us.

A follow-up *Times* editorial said the letter "ought to be read by every citizen concerned with the security of our country." But, of course, not every citizen reads all the letters that that paper prints, nor even all its editorials. Indeed, there was good reason to believe that by 1954 a good many citizens were probably oblivious of what one of the five letter writers, Howland Shaw, had plaintively expressed in the *Foreign Service Journal* twenty-two years earlier:

> Who but the individualist will help us eventually to get rid of this rigidity and modify our views so as to bring them into greater harmony with the world ...? Who but the individualist can carry on the experiments which will insure our development? We must have him and we must be careful that there is always in the Foreign Service a place for him.

The State Department published a history of the Foreign Service in 1961, *The Foreign Service of the United States* by William Barnes (with John Heath Morgan). Nowhere in its more than four hundred pages was there any allusion to the questions of loyalty and security, which had done more to affect the course of American diplomatic history than anything else since Ben Franklin set sail for Europe. The history was compiled while John Foster Dulles was secretary of state, and he was perhaps no more eager to have this seamy aspect of government enshrined in the permanent record than had been his immediate predecessor; only once did Dean Acheson mention John S. Service in his lengthy memoirs.

Acheson, however, had a loftier outlook on individualism in the Foreign Service than Dulles. On turning over the department to him, Acheson had said, "If disagreements on policy were to be equated with disloyalty, the Foreign Service would be destroyed." Dulles was more pragmatic than philosophical. He demanded what he called "positive loyalty" from Foreign Service officers, by which he apparently meant loyalty toward whatever his position happened to be at any given moment.

The Old China Hands, no more than three dozen or so of whom were ever on active duty at any given moment, represented, of course, only a small fraction of the Foreign Service. At the start of the Second World War there were some seven hundred Foreign Service officers stationed around the world. But the China men were special among specialists; in those days China was the only spot on earth where career diplomats were not normally assigned to consulates unless they spoke the local language. Even apart from their linguistic uniqueness, the China men were a singular group; Eric Sevareid, who got to know a good many of them in less unsettling surroundings than the Patkoi Mountains, once called them "the ablest group of young diplomats I had ever seen in a single American mission abroad." In 1967, long after most of them had left government service or had been dispersed to remote missions where their language skills were worthless, Professor Fairbank wrote, "These men were true China specialists and we have no one like them today. . . . In our lifetime we shall never again get this much of a grasp of the Chinese scene."

These China specialists were extraordinarily noncompetitive. There was no single star, no Kennan, among them; they considered themselves, and probably were, a collective elite, with a shared pride comparable to that often found among United States Marines, and a shared élan stemming from their shared concern for intellectual inquiry, from their deep immersion into and understanding of Chinese ethnocentricity, and from the peculiar challenge of the problems that faced them in their work. And further, they had in common a shared awareness of how challenging it had been merely to get where they were; it was generally conceded that it took a minimum of about ten years in China before anyone could rightly be termed, in the nonpejorative sense, an Old China Hand.

They were by no means all paragons. There were human frailties in abundance among them. One memorable member of the group—a huge man with a huge thirst—once fell down the White House steps at a diplomatic reception, but survived the incident; what surprised his colleagues in the Foreign Service more was that once during the Japanese occupation of Manchuria he had thrown an officious Japanese officer down a flight of steps in Mukden and survived *that.* There was another man, one of the ablest linguists in the prewar group of Old China Hands, who had to be dismissed for exceptionally erratic behavior. The kind of thing he liked to do was to wait until a good bomb scare had got under way and then hide ticking alarm·clocks in colleagues' closets. Following his involuntary retirement, he hung around Shanghai for a few years performing various chores for the Chinese government, before he perished from a self-inflicted overdose of developing fluid.

As Robert Barnett was to observe after leaving the Foreign Service to find shelter under the more hospitable umbrella of the Asia Society, "Although the China specialists were by no means all outstandingly gifted people, the tragedy was that, however good the good men among them were, the possibility of their becoming better was largely denied them because of a system that questioned their right to be honest and decent people. The social cost of that denial has got to be a big one."

It was largely by chance that the Old China Hands came together. Asked one time why he had enlisted in the Foreign Service and gone to the not inconsiderable trouble of learning Chinese, the bluff Ludden— who not only had the esprit de corps and stamina of career marines but some of their other rugged characteristics as well—replied, "I'm damned if I know."

Most of the men were born around the turn of the twentieth century (five of them in China) and reached young adulthood during the depths of the Depression. For some of them, then, a Foreign Service career represented security; it naturally never occurred to them at the outset that "security" in a different connotation would loom so large in their professional lives.

To be commissioned a Foreign Service officer in the Depression years was not all that easy; the State Department was trimming its budget like everybody else, and it was difficult to get an appointment even after fulfilling the admissions requirements, which consisted of both written and oral examinations.

What lured some of the men to the Far East, understandably, was the heady prospect of adventure in an exotic land. Many of the Old China Hands were young and single when they first went to Asia, and in one or two instances they got more adventure than they bargained for. One bachelor, while at language school in Peking, fell in love with a Mongolian princess who was uncharacteristically blonde; her tribe had got mixed up with some Russians. The diplomat wanted to marry her, but was dissuaded when a colleague making delicate inquiries back in Washington was informed that to marry an Oriental would be so ruinous to a career that anyone contemplating such action would be better off resigning.[3]

Actually, Raymond Ludden had a pretty fair idea of why he had joined up. A native of Fall River, Massachusetts, whence many ships had sailed to remote ports and brought back romantic legends, he had finished his education at Georgetown University in Washington, D.C., and while there had been seduced by an alluring Foreign Service recruiting brochure. He took the written examination in Boston and then went to Washington for the oral. While waiting to be informed of the results, he got a job with the FBI, as a fingerprint classifier. One day he was asked to go over to the State Department to clarify some detail in his dossier, conceivably a smudged fingerprint. He asked for permission to be excused from poring over other people's whorls and loops long enough to respond to this summons, but the request was so frostily rejected by J. Edgar Hoover that Ludden excused himself from the agency for good and got a job driving a taxi.

Ludden arrived in China just before Christmas in 1932 and in due course found himself posted, as would so many of his colleagues, to Japanese-occupied Manchuria. It was one of the rules of that occupation that as a sign of respect to the conqueror any person had to take off his hat whenever he passed a Japanese sentry. Ludden indignantly stopped wearing hats, even in the dead of Manchurian winter, and he never wore one again for the rest of his life.

Everett Drumright had less cause than most of his contemporaries to be concerned about the Depression; the site of his birth in 1906, Drum-

---

[3]George Kennan, Charles Bohlen, and some of the other more prominent Old Russian Hands were periodically accused by left-wing critics in the United States of having got themselves married to White Russian princesses. They had not; indeed, the American in Moscow who came closest to fitting the description was the left-leaning Joseph E. Davies, whose wife, the celebrated General Foods heiress Marjorie Merriwether Post, lived about as regally as any American can.

right, Oklahoma, was named after his father, who struck oil in the vicinity. The son's first Foreign Service assignment was to the consulate at Ciudad Juárez, Mexico; this was in keeping with a State Department practice of shipping young officers to a border post—Windsor, Ontario, was another favorite—so they could get about a year's experience in a technically foreign city that was still within hailing distance of home.

Drumright was a model of efficiency and a stickler for protocol; a bachelor until fairly late in life, he was thought by some of his colleagues up to then to be married to his career. During the war Edward Rice once journeyed from Lanchow, far off in Northwest China, to Sian, where Drumright was stationed. It was a terrible trip for Rice, with trucks breaking down and baggage disappearing. Arriving dejectedly in Sian, Rice was cheered by the sight of a stack of mail awaiting him in Drumright's office—the first word he had had from his family for months. There were six letters from his wife, and as he began to arrange them in chronological order, he heard the faithful Drumright say, "Aren't you going to read the Departmental instructions first?"

Nicknamed "Drum," Drumright became a collector of drums; when he eventually became an ambassador, he filled his embassy at Taipei with them. Because he was, as a rule, more conservative politically than the other China specialists (it was a small joke among some of them that the second syllable of his surname would have been an apter nickname than the first), he could get away with things that could have put their careers in jeopardy. In the old days Drumright, like any other American constantly seeking information about Chinese political developments, would seize every opportunity to share a meal with Chou En-lai, often the most accessible to them of Chinese Communist spokesmen. Whereas men like Service and Vincent would later be regarded with suspicion because of their early chopsticking with Chou, the same ground rules did not apply to Drumright.

When he was having lunch with Chou one day in 1944, Chou was complaining both about the Nationalist government and about the lack of military progress against the Japanese on the Asian mainland. "I finally said to Chou, 'Why in hell, if things are as serious as you say they are, don't you people get together and fight the Japanese?' and he got mad and walked out on me," Drumright recalled. Trying to get all Chinese to cooperate in battle against the Japanese was the main purpose of just about every American in China at that time, but not every one, when his accusers brought him to bay after the war, was lucky enough to be able to say he had had a falling-out with Chou En-lai.

It was an oft-mouthed cliché about career diplomats that they were unrepresentative of the people they served or indeed of anything except the Ivy League, and there were statistics to support the allegation. Between 1946 and 1952, for instance, 25 per cent of all newly appointed Foreign Service officers had done their undergraduate studies at Harvard, Yale, and Princeton, and 10 per cent of the total at Harvard alone. In the case of the Old China Hands, the stereotype did not apply. There was not a Harvard graduate among them, and a surprisingly large number of them were exported to China from Middle America.

Edward Rice, a native of Saginaw, Michigan, received his bachelor's degree in 1930 from the University of Illinois, where he roomed for a spell with a chap who later became a member of the Communist party, a potentially crippling association that to Rice's surprise and relief never found its way into his personnel file at State.

When Rice had home leave in the United States in 1945, a cousin asked him, "What's the future in China?" Rice replied, "Within four years, the Communists will be in control of the mainland." He had grabbed the figures more or less out of the air, and indeed had forgotten the prophecy entirely when, in 1949, the cousin reminded him of his pinpoint prescience. The following year one after another of Rice's fellow China Hands came under suspicion for predictions *they* had made; he was grateful that no government investigator ever subpoenaed his cousin.

Even in high school in Milwaukee, Rice had been thinking of applying for the Foreign Service, largely because of the influence on him of a civics teacher who kept regretting in class that he had never done so. Young Rice found a book about the Foreign Service in the municipal public library and read it eagerly. Then one day in the Milwaukee *Journal* he saw a photograph of George Kennan, a local boy who had just made good by being appointed to his first Foreign Service post and was on a visit home.

Rice phoned Kennan, who invited him over after supper and gave him some succinct counseling: He should take courses in college that would help him abroad, he should brush up on a foreign language, he should become a regular reader of *Time*, and so forth. After a couple of years at the University of Wisconsin, Rice switched to Illinois and concentrated on history, political science, and international law; he also became chairman of an International Friendship Committee sponsored by the campus branch of the YMCA, and in that way got to meet a lot of foreign students.

Kennan had also advised Rice to try to have a year's business experience, and his disciple obediently got a job in the export division of a firm that made earth-moving equipment. As the national economy began to sputter, the company had to lay him off, but it agreed to underwrite his train fare to Mexico in gratitude for his having persuaded a Mexican customer who owed the company $10,000 to at least sign a promissory note.

The following year Rice returned north. He took and passed the Foreign Service exams, only to be informed that because of the state of the nation he couldn't expect an appointment for a couple of years. He held various odd jobs, and finally landed back at the University of Illinois as associate secretary of the YMCA and a principal factotum of the Cosmopolitan Club, a residence for foreign students that was in something of a slump of its own, being only half occupied. Rice managed to fill it to capacity, and the Cosmopolitan would in his view have won a coveted campus prize for high academic standing had its average not been pulled down by a young Chinese graduate student with strong Nationalist leanings but no inclination to work.

Finally the State Department notified Rice that he could have his appointment, and it was proposed that he become a Japanese-language trainee. But by the time he had found a successor at the Cosmopolitan and had got to Washington, the Japanese quota had been filled, and he was asked if he would consider switching to Chinese.

Rice had mixed feelings about that. His experiences with Chinese had been limited to the young man who wouldn't pull his academic oar, and to a quondam Chinese roommate with the unsettling habit of spitting on the floor.[4] But the $2500 a year that went with the job looked awfully good compared to the $80 a month Rice had been earning, so he agreed to go to China. He arrived in Peking on a bright sunny day, and the air, he would always remember, was like wine.

Peking was less likely, then and now, to be noted on normal days for

[4]In a report Rice wrote from Sian on October 2, 1944, about the morale of American servicemen he had encountered, he said they were bitterly critical of the Nationalists because Chiang Kai-shek's people kept airplanes in warehouses instead of on airfields, because it was possible for the GIs to buy American gasoline from the wives of Chinese government officials, because the government officials refused to take any action against other Chinese suspected of being Japanese espionage agents, and, finally, because of the Americans' annoyance at certain Chinese personal habits, "such as those of constantly hawking and spitting."

the wine in its air than for the dust, and it took Rice a while to adjust to that; but he was soon overwhelmed by the place and made fast and lifelong friends. (Rice had to survive a rather shaky start; some of his more sophisticated peers took a dim view of his resolute Middle Americanism, as evidenced by his commissioning a Chinese carpenter to fabricate, for his temple rooms at San Kuan Miao, some exact replicas of Grand Rapids furniture.) Philip Sprouse was there as a code clerk, John Davies would stop by from Mukden, Jack Service turned up a few weeks after Rice's arrival, and Jim Penfield was halfway through his two-year language course. The officer in charge of language studies was Edmund Clubb.

Rice's first post, after completing language school, was Canton, where he arrived not long before the Japanese did. As soon as they landed on the coast of Kwangtung province, Rice bet his superior counsular officer that they would quickly take Canton; to make such a bet was a cheeky thing for a junior officer to do, and to win it was cheekier yet. The senior officer was further put out when Rice, shepherding refugees across the Pearl River Bridge from Japanese-occupied territory to the relative sanctuary of Lingnan University, which stood on American property, insisted on including in his flock the Chinese husband of an American woman.[5]

Rice, it will be recalled, never got into any serious difficulties for being an Old China Hand; still, he never got an embassy of his own, either. "Those of us who survived the purge survived largely by being lucky," he would say years afterward. "I once asked Ambassador Clarence Gauss if I couldn't go into Chinese Communist territory to get information, like Jack Service and John Davies. Gauss told me to stay in Sian and work the Kuomintang side of the street. So that's what I did and that's how I kept out of trouble, and as things began happening to Jack and John and some of the others I realized that there but for the grace of Gauss went I. Nevertheless, to see so many colleagues chopped down was traumatic even if you never got the axe yourself."

[5]Rice had a consistent belief that rightness was not inevitably a concomitant of rank. After the war he was a political officer in the Philippines when Elpidio Quirino won a questionably conducted presidential election. Rice had just persuaded the American embassy at Manila to be wary of extending formal congratulations, when in came winging a telegram from General Douglas MacArthur that Rice was supposed to pass along to Quirino. MacArthur had embodied in his message something about new laurels being added to Quirino's reputation, and Rice pointed out to his superiors there that this seemed especially unfelicitous, inasmuch as the defeated contestant had been José Laurel. The message was never delivered, and MacArthur, who began making inquiries when he never received thanks for it, had one more grievance in his longstanding feud with the State Department.

John Emmerson was another Middle American, the son of a postmaster at Canyon City, Colorado. A 1929 Colorado College graduate, he never left his home state while growing up, but he had long had a hankering for travel. At the age of ten he had fallen in love with France, and his two youthful passions were a French flag he owned and a French girl pen pal. As a college freshman, he saw an announcement about some traveling scholarships being offered by the Institute of International Education, and to his delight he won one and spent his junior year abroad, mostly at the Sorbonne.

Back at Colorado for his senior year, Emmerson fell in with a political scientist who, on learning he planned to become a French teacher, talked him out of that and into trying to join the Foreign Service. Convinced, Emmerson waited two years, getting an M.A. at NYU and teaching in Nebraska, and then took the Foreign Service exams, expecting to return to Paris any day. But this was 1932, and he had to wait three years for an appointment. For part of this time he worked for the Berlitz School in Chicago, teaching something called Effective English. He had met U. Alexis Johnson in Washington, while preparing for the Foreign Service exams, and when in September 1935 he had good news from the State Department, he also heard from Johnson, who had received his appointment and was going to Japan. Why didn't Emmerson come along? So he did. Except for one home leave in 1939, Emmerson was in Asia, mostly in Japan, from 1936 to 1941. He left Tokyo, by chance, in October 1941, two months before Pearl Harbor.[6]

Philip Sprouse, another Francophile, came from Tennessee. His father made snuff and chewing tobacco. After graduating from Washington and Lee in 1928, the son saved enough money from a two-year stint at a military academy, teaching French and Latin, for two years in France. He was en route to a Ph.D. at Princeton when the Depression struck his father's business, so he quit school and got a job as a bookkeeper in a factory. While there, he heard about a friend who wanted to become a career diplomat but, since no appointments were being granted, had

[6]Emmerson's wife and their two small children had been evacuated, like most American dependents, the year before. Emmerson thereupon shared his Tokyo residence with Charles E. Bohlen, the Russian-language specialist, who, with the other diplomats who stayed in Japan, was interned after Pearl Harbor. In the fall of 1945 Emmerson was one of the first Americans to return to Tokyo. He rushed around to inspect his old house. The buildings on both sides of it had been flattened, but his house was untouched. All the Emmersons' furniture, though, had disappeared.

instead taken a clerical position in the Foreign Service, as secretary to the American minister to Tegucigalpa. Following suit, Sprouse applied for a similar clerical job, hoping to wind up behind a desk back in Paris.

He was offered Peking instead. All he knew about China was that in elementary school he had been asked to give pennies for missionaries, and the climate sounded uninviting. But he went, and what he would later call the lotus-eating quality of the place got to him. After two years as a code clerk, he took the written exams for the career service, squeaked by, went back to Washington for his orals, and returned to Peking and the code room—this time as a third secretary. Meanwhile, he had got to know Davies and Penfield, Service and Rice, and they struck him as the kind of people he'd like to be associated with for the rest of his life. He applied for the two-year Chinese-language course, and his own die was cast.

When Sprouse took home leave early in 1941, he left most of his possessions with his Number One Boy and his cook, who were soon relieved of them by the Japanese. Nearly two years later, hearing that Sprouse had returned and was in Chungking, the two loyal servants, by then in Hankow, managed to make their way through the Japanese lines and report back for domestic duty. They had no possessions of their own by then that would not fit into a handkerchief, and as it was considered infra dig for a proper Chinese manservant not to have a long gown, Sprouse set out to have some made. Material was hard to come by in Chungking, so Sprouse asked John Davies to bring some to him on one of Davies's periodic flights across the Hump from India. Sprouse also suggested that Davies might bring along a couple of wristwatches; if the servants got stranded again, they'd have something to barter. Davies duly executed his mission, but had to throw away the cloth and the watches just before he bailed out of the airplane he'd stowed them on.

James Penfield was a coastal American—born in New York, educated at Stanford. There he fell under the sway of Graham Stuart, a political-science professor who had missionary origins and had been in the diplomatic field himself; he was the author of *The International Status of Tangier.* Stuart suggested that Penfield have a go at the Foreign Service, and he did; after attending a cram school in Washington, he took all the necessary exams, passed, and was sent to Ciudad Juárez for the customary seasoning. After that he returned to Washington, was invited to state his preferences for further regional assignment, and asked for another Latin-American post.

At the same time a friend of his put in a bid for the Far East. Their preference cards got switched in a file; the friend received travel orders for Montevideo, and Penfield for Canton. Observing the Chinese scene, he noticed that the lowliest career officer could, in the mid-thirties, live very nicely; that with a $2500-a-year salary, a person could anticipate, and in fact have, a house, two polo ponies, four servants, and as many concubines as he fancied. Penfield signed up for Chinese-language school.

Oliver Edmund Clubb, who happened to be in charge of language training at that time, though only slightly older than many of the men undergoing it, was sometimes thought of as a bureaucrat's bureaucrat, a scholar's scholar. He was celebrated in Peking in the mid-thirties for a question he had devised for the exhaustive examination given to language students after their two-year course: "Trace the relations between China and Japan. Do not be brief."

Clubb was occasionally gently chided by his colleagues for uttering professorial platitudes, but like many platitudes his were not without a certain basic profundity; nobody could fault him for having declared way back in 1934, "China's problems are not easy of solution." And he had a clear idea of how Foreign Service officers should operate. "They are criticized sometimes for being pro this and anti that," he said in 1951 when he himself had come under harsh critical attack, "when all they are is pro-United States and are working for the United States, and they have offered certain judgments to the Department of State, which judgments may sometimes be right or may sometimes be wrong, but that was my function. My function wasn't to further the Chinese revolution or to stop the Chinese revolution, either one."

Clubb came from the rural Midwest. He was born at South Park, Minnesota, on February 16, 1901, the son of a rancher who raised cattle in Montana and North Dakota and brought them to a farm ten miles south of Saint Paul for fattening. The father died when the boy was only five, and the family barely made ends meet. After graduating from high school in South Saint Paul, Clubb drifted around for a bit, did a short hitch in the army (he was only seventeen when he enlisted), briefly took an engineering course at the University of Washington, and soon switched to the University of Minnesota, where he became interested in international law. Concurrently, he worked part-time as a railroad hand and a postoffice clerk.

At the university Clubb became acquainted with a resident Sinologue, who urged him to look into the Foreign Service. He did, was attracted to it, took the customary exams, and arrived in Peking in the spring of 1929. The Chinese government was then operating out of Nanking, but Peking remained the cultural and intellectual hub of the country. Among notable foreigners were the explorer Roy Chapman Andrews and the Jesuit paleontologist Teilhard de Chardin, who had helped to identify the Peking Man. "The city was sort of a little Florence or a very little Paris," John Davies once said. "Anybody who traveled beyond the Middle East seemed to end up in Peking."

Clubb quickly made himself known as an unusual young diplomat. Not only did he excel in learning Chinese, but he decided simultaneously to learn Russian; he had concluded that the destinies of China and Russia were going to be closely meshed in his lifetime, and he aspired to a closer understanding of both nations.

As a junior officer, he elected to make a month-long inspection trip to Inner Mongolia, where there had been a dreadful famine. Under the auspices of the International Famine Relief Commission, a vast irrigation project was under way, its objective being nothing less than the diversion of the Yellow River. Thousands and thousands of Chinese workers were moving thousands of tons of earth by shoulder pole, spurred on by a legendary American engineer named Oliver J. Todd, a man of such energy and drive that he became known in China as Todd Almighty.[7] Much of the land that their efforts made arable was not long afterward diverted itself—into poppy cultivation for the opium trade—but that was hardly Todd's fault, and it is doubtful whether any Almighty could have prevented it.

In March 1931 Clubb was posted to Hankow, arriving just in time for another catastrophe, a mammoth flood of the Yangtze River, which rose more than forty feet above its normal levels and left some two million dead in its wake. Cholera and dysentery were epidemic, and bandits were taking advantage of the all-around confusion; Clubb prudently left his wife and their two young children in Peking. As things settled down more or less to normal, he joined the Hankow Race Club, was elected to the board of the local YMCA, and became a leading member of something called the Monday Evening Club, a small group of intellectuals who sponsored

---

[7]Todd was also the commander of a small private army, which he found useful for fighting off bandits. He is remembered in China as a man who spoke of the Yellow River in terms some men might reserve for their mistresses, and who could drive a car with his eyes closed.

lectures and held readings of Shakespeare.

Most important, Clubb set out to make as many acquaintances as he could among the Chinese population, a practice that was not then widely emulated; the majority of foreigners in Hankow, as in the rest of China, principally tended to cultivate each other. Out of Clubb's diligent pursuit of the indigenes came a 123-page report, "Communism in China." Issued on April 30, 1932, it was the first detailed study of the Chinese Communist movement by an American—it preceded by five years Edgar Snow's *Red Star over China*.

In 1928 the Communists had gone underground in the big cities controlled by the Kuomintang, and most of what the United States knew of their activities and aspirations came from the random observations of missionaries or from what little was said about them in the Russian press. In 1930 American Foreign Service officers in China were reporting back to Washington that the few remaining Communists in China were of no account militarily, being a mere handful of intellectuals. Clubb thought otherwise. From his readings in Chinese and Russian and from his unique contacts with Chinese across the political spectrum, he suggested that the Communists, though not terribly visible, were a force very much to be reckoned with. Indeed, he appended a map to the report crediting them with control of one-sixth of all of China.

Clubb's revelations were by no means gospel. He wrongly passed along the news that Chou En-lai had been executed on June 23, 1931, on direct orders from Chiang Kai-shih,[8] and he predicted that Chiang would fall from power within a year. But his reports were far and away the most comprehensive news the United States government had yet received from any of its operatives about the Communists. In his pedantic prose Clubb wrote:

> A social revolution, such as China is now going through, is frustrated unless it has its roots in the great body of the people. The development that suffered a break in 1927 has now, five years later, evidently reached another nodule in the progression from an Imperial federalism to democratic institutions more

---

[8]Clubb, a linguist not lightly to be argued with, has long insisted that "Chiang Kai-shih" is a romanization preferable to "Chiang Kai-shek." In retirement, living on the Upper West Side of New York City, *he* would gently chide the proprietors of his favorite neighborhood Chinese restaurant because they called the establishment "Chun Cha Fu" ("everybody is happy") whereas he maintained that the correct romanization would be "Chuan Chia Fu."

consonant with the times. The development will apparently be slowly toward a form of State socialism. . . . It is to be expected that the actual pressure of economic circumstances will make requisite an attitude on the part of the new Chinese nation that will not be characterized generally by open hostility toward other countries. But that may not be said certainly.

Clubb's attempt to shed new light on what had been at best a dimly perceived area was not universally welcomed. When his report reached the legation at Peking, a senior officer there was heard to exclaim, "We don't want to have any more of *this.*" In Washington the Far Eastern division of the State Department was about to rate the memorandum "Excellent," but on representations from the East European division, which handled Russia and was unimpressed with interlopers' views of communism, the rating was downgraded to "Good."[9]

Nonetheless Clubb pressed on, gathering, analyzing, and forwarding everything he could find out about the Chinese Communists. It was he, in April 1934, who first informed Washington of a policy statement by Mao Tse-tung at a national congress of Chinese soviets convened three months earlier. A Far Eastern man in Washington, after scanning Mao's pronouncement, commented that it "would be of interest to a student of Soviet propaganda but is of no particular interest to F.E." So much for Chairman Mao.

[9]Clubb's 1932 report was reprinted in book form in 1968. Before that, however, so chary was anyone in the China field of linking anyone else, even as an observer, to communism, that when in 1964—ten years *after* the censure of Senator Joe McCarthy—the scholar Dorothy Borg treated the historic incident in her *The United States and the Far Eastern Crisis of 1933–1938,* she avoided naming Clubb as the author of the ancient report and identified him merely as a young vice-consul in Hankow.

3

"It is not only a duty to serve others, but an honor."

On the death of John Carter Vincent in December 1972, Clubb, who had earlier become one of his successors as director of Chinese affairs for the State Department, declared that Vincent had "battled strenuously and courageously, under adverse domestic political conditions, to give intelligent direction to our China policy." Vincent was anything but bellicose in appearance or manner. For one thing, he was so thin. Vincent was, every lean inch of him, a cultured Southern gentleman—low-keyed, knowledgeable, shrewd but not especially intellectual—who found the rough-and-tumble aspects of negotiation distasteful. He developed into almost a stereotype of the ideal polished diplomat, though there was little in his background to account for this.

Born on August 19, 1900, in Seneca, Kansas, he grew up in Macon, Georgia, where his family moved when he was six. His father was in the real-estate business and was a pillar of the Baptist church. The son, known throughout his life, according to Southern custom, as "John Carter," had a stern religious upbringing, and in later life would often—with a polite, Georgian smile—correct people who knew less than he did about the Bible.

After a brief matriculation at Clemson College in South Carolina, he came back to Georgia and to Mercer University in Macon, where he thought for a while he might concentrate in agriculture.[1] (John Foster Dulles eventually made it possible for him to devote much of the last twenty years of his life to his garden.) Before his graduation in 1923, he had resolved instead to become a diplomat, because he wanted to travel. He took the Foreign Service examinations soon after commencement.

[1] Another of China's Johns who went to Macon was John Birch.

48

The men who presided over his orals seemed worried when he confessed to a liking for eighteenth-century English verse. Had they inquired further and learned that he also liked classical music, he might have been rejected as overly effete.

Vincent hoped, from what little he knew of the world, to be sent to Copenhagen. Instead he got Changsha, and set off for there with his then nearly permanent accoutrements—Shakespeare's sonnets and a flute. In due course he was sent to Peking for language training, and while there met a young Chicago woman, Elizabeth Slagle, who had dropped out of college to travel to Asia with the sculptor Lucille Swan, who had commissions to do busts of some government officials. After a courtship in the romantic environs of the Forbidden City, John Carter and Elizabeth were married in 1931. They soon found themselves stationed up in Mukden, where the young woman, pregnant with the first of their two children, was barely saved by her husband from being bayoneted by a Japanese soldier who tried to expropriate her rickshaw.

The Vincents spent most of their early married life in China. In 1940 they were in Switzerland for a while, as the war was starting in Europe, and early in 1941 Vincent was sent back, *sans famille*, to China. Among the fellow passengers on his ship was the textile importer Alfred Kohlberg, who in later years was the tireless spearhead of a loosely organized confederation of supporters of Chiang Kai-shek that became known as the China Lobby. There was never any such officially designated group, but the name was convenient for describing the concerted activities of American legislators, publishers, writers, businessmen, religious leaders, crackpots, and plain folk who exerted their efforts and expended their funds on behalf of Nationalist China, and who worked in harness with such emissaries of Chiang as his peripatetic in-laws T. V. Soong and H. H. Kung. Whatever the China Lobby was, it had plenty of money—some of this dispensed through public-relations firms—and it was cohesive enough for its more strident members ultimately to render it the flattery of imitation: They were later fond of denouncing its adversaries as the "Red China Lobby."

Kohlberg—in part through enterprises he dominated, like the American China Policy Association and the *China Monthly*—was the cement that principally held all the diverse elements of the emphatically non-Red China Lobby together, and although he represented no formal constituency he wielded considerable influence and was a man not to be crossed lightly.[2] For his pains, Chiang Kai-shek awarded him the Order of the Auspicious Star after the war. There was no doubt that in Kohlberg's mind the China Lobby existed; indeed, he liked to be called "The China Lobby Man."[3]

Kohlberg, from 1916 on, had been in China many times. He would provide Chinese children with cloth and thread and needles so they could make embroidery for him, at subcoolie wages, when they were not working in the fields; his detractors claimed that a number of Chinese children had gone blind while thus in his remote employ. Kohlberg continued in this business even after being served with a cease-and-desist order by the Federal Trade Commission, which claimed he was selling Chinese lace falsely labeled "European."

On board ship Kohlberg and Vincent fell into casual conversation. As they got to exchanging reminiscences, Vincent happened to mention an incident that had taken place years back, when he'd been a freshman at Clemson: He had joined some students in a protest to demonstrate sympathy with several busboys who thought *they* were working for coolie wages; he and the other demonstrators, Vincent recalled with a chuckle, had referred to themselves as Bolsheviks.

Kohlberg had a good memory; he is believed to have passed along Vincent's confession of original sin to people like Senator McCarthy, whom he was happy to provide with supposedly incriminating facts about the Old China Hands. There was no doubt that Kohlberg always rated Vincent high among the China-losers; he once wrote, "A small group, including Alger Hiss, Owen Lattimore, Lauchlin Currie, Edgar Snow and later John Carter Vincent, planned to slowly choke to death and destroy the government of the Republic of China and build up the Chinese Communists for post-war success."

All that Vincent could recall of what Kohlberg had confided to *him* was that when the ideological Armageddon finally arrived, fascism would inevitably triumph over socialism. Kohlberg had not seemed disturbed by the prospect.

---

[2]When Raymond Ludden and John Service testified before the Senate Foreign Relations Committee in February 1972, Ludden paused at one point and asked, "Is Kohlberg still alive?" "No," said Service, "you can say what you want to."

[3]Joseph C. Keeley, a former employee of the American Legion, wrote a friendly biography of Kohlberg entitled *The China Lobby Man.* In it, among a passel of fairly hard-core right-wingers whose assistance he particularly wished to acknowledge, he listed the name of Richard M. Nixon.

Still another Midwesterner was Arthur Ringwalt, a Nebraskan who was a year older than Vincent. His father was an insurance man in Omaha who had four sons and hoped they would all follow his occupational footsteps; Arthur tried it for a few years but got bored, and after a brief fling at department-store management and a year in France, courtesy of a rich aunt, he decided when he was twenty-nine to join the Foreign Service. He was quite fluent by then in French, the language of diplomacy. He agreed, however, to be sent to China. He had just started at language school when he ran into Lucille Swan, and the sculptor, pleased at having introduced John Carter Vincent to his bride, tried a new matchmaking tack. She wondered if Ringwalt would care to meet a beautiful young Chinese woman fairly fresh from a warlord's harem. The young woman arrived in due course for dinner, escorted by a tough-looking older woman in a colonel's uniform. The evening went badly; the beauty knew no English, and Ringwalt's Chinese was still limited to such basics as "Tomorrow I'll go to church and say my prayers." The girl was disgusted, and the colonel marched her off and out of his life.

Ringwalt's bad luck with women continued to plague him and almost wrecked his diplomatic career near its inception. When he had become somewhat more fluent in Chinese, he had a male language teacher who felt that the only accent with any true class was a Soochow accent. It happened that the best-looking women in Peking's brothels were from Soochow, so the teacher would take his student there to bask in their inflections. Ringwalt decided it would further his studies if he had a sweet-talking young woman around all the time, so he placed an ad in a local paper to the effect that a serious language student desired to find a genteel young lady companion for conversational exchanges. Applicants were invited to present themselves forthwith at San Kuan Miao.

At seven o'clock the next morning, Ringwalt's Number One Boy rushed agitatedly into his bedroom. "Master, there are a great many people outside waiting to see you," he said. Ringwalt peered through a window and saw a seemingly endless line of rickshaws, each occupied by a young woman and an amah. The procession had been spotted, too, by Nelson T. Johnson, the chief of the American mission to China.

Johnson was an old Old China Hand. He had gone there as a student interpreter in 1907 and had been in Asia for most of his life; he was celebrated as the first American to make his way to Yokohama and Tokyo after the disastrous 1923 earthquake. A devotee of doing all things right, Johnson insisted that whenever he was away from his office for more than twenty-four hours he be welcomed back by his staff with ceremonial honors. He was a portly, amiable man with orange hair, who played the guitar passably and liked to sing "Frankie and Johnny" at parties. He also carried around with him a piece of calligraphy, a bit of Taoist philosophy that went *"Wu wei erh wu pu wei"*—"Through not-doing, all things are done." One thing Johnson had never done, to his embarrassment, was to pass his Chinese-language exam. Even after long years in the country he had never really got the hang of that pesky tongue; he would tell a story in Chinese at some social affair and the Chinese present would laugh politely, even though they couldn't grasp more than a couple of words of it.[4]

Johnson was, on the whole, genuinely considerate of his subordinates and reasonably flexible about their behavior, but he felt Ringwalt had gone a bit too far. He sternly summoned the young diplomat to him and pointed to the armada of waiting rickshaws. "What *is* this?" Johnson sputtered. "What does this *mean?*" The stricken Ringwalt said he would undertake to disperse the mob swiftly, but he was able to do so only by sharing among it all the money he could lay his sweating palms on.

On completing his language training, Ringwalt was horrified to learn that Johnson was to be one of his examiners. He knew about Johnson's having failed this test himself, and he suspected that the ambassador would not be averse to enabling others to share his unenviable distinction. Johnson had just returned to Peking from an international conference on sealing in the Bering Sea. He mischievously asked Ringwalt to express his views on that subject. The younger man knew absolutely nothing about it, but pluckily delivered a three-minute discourse. "So you think you're an expert, do you?" Johnson went on. "Well, tell me, what was the value of the Japanese seal catch there in 1923?" Ringwalt said he had no idea. What about the Canadian catch in 1929? his interrogator demanded.

[4]Johnson retired in 1946, but five years later returned to the State Department briefly as John Service's first defense witness in one of Service's loyalty-security hearings. "Now, I'd like to say that I don't necessarily agree with the judgment of my young men," the veteran ambassador began paternally. "I don't necessarily agree with Mr. Service's judgment in interpreting some of the things he reports at times. And I would think, at least I hope I would have exercised my right to express my disagreement with that judgment, but I would not have considered that it was my duty or my right in my relationship with the Department of State to suppress views which young men who have been trained in the service to see and try to see honestly and I have always believed that Mr. Service was honest intellectually, and I don't remember any of my young men that I didn't consider honest intellectually. And I have never been known consciously to have been deceived by them."

Ringwalt shook his head dumbly. "You don't know anything, Ringwalt, do you?" Johnson said, but then, having had his sport, gave Ringwalt a passing grade.

Back in the United States in 1938, Ringwalt got himself more acceptably involved, this time with Mildred Teusler, the daughter of a medical missionary who had founded a hospital in Tokyo in the nineteenth century. The doctor was a cousin of Mrs. Woodrow Wilson, who attended the ceremony when Ringwalt married his daughter. The president's widow had first checked with Secretary of State Cordell Hull to find out if the young Foreign Service officer was a suitable match for her kin. Hull knew nothing about Ringwalt and passed the inquiry along to Stanley K. Hornbeck, who in turn bucked it down to John Carter Vincent. Normally, in the bureaucratic tradition, Vincent would have passed it along one step lower to *his* deputy, but his principal subordinate was Ringwalt himself; after briefly considering letting Ringwalt appraise his own character, Vincent sent appropriate words of approval back up the line for Secretary Hull to submit to Mrs. Wilson.

John Carter Vincent was so steeped in the history and culture of the Far East that it was sometimes wrongly thought that, like Henry Luce and others with a passionate interest in China, he must have been born there to a missionary family. The misconception may have stemmed from the fact that two of the other most prominent Johns of his time—John Davies and John Service—*were* missionary sons.[5] Both these men were of an independent turn of mind, standing less in awe of their superiors than most members of the diplomatic hierarchy. This forthright attitude was sometimes taken as a rebellion on their part against their missionary fathers' unquestioning obedience to a higher authority. At the same time, however, the equanimity displayed by Davies and Service in the face of adversity may have been a direct patrimonial inheritance; Service's father had not complained when, at the end of a long, hard career selflessly devoted to the YMCA, that organization invoked a technicality to deprive him of a small pension he had expected.

Davies's father, John Paton Davies, Sr., who died in 1972 in retirement

[5] In H. Bradford Westerfield's *Foreign Policy and Party Politics*, published in 1955, the author, who was on the whole critical of the China specialists in the Foreign Service, said that "their fatal flaw seems to have been an extreme missionary humanitarianism, a virtue dangerously excessive for the framers of a nation's foreign policy." American policy was in actuality far more shaped by men with views diametrically opposed to theirs, some of whom, like John Foster Dulles, also had missionary forebears.

in Alexandria, Virginia, at ninety-three, was a Baptist minister whose progenitors had come from Wales. The senior Davies had gone to Oberlin College, which spawned many missionaries to Asia and had a motto that seemed apt for them: "Learning and Labor." After his seminary studies and ordination, he married a Canadian farm girl who had migrated from Manitoba to New York to embark on a singing career and had become a soloist with a church choir. In 1906 the young couple sailed for China to convert the heathen.

For many years the Reverend Mr. Davies was a rather unbending clergyman. He was furious when John Junior married a Catholic. But he thawed in later life. When a daughter of that heretical alliance informed her grandfather, by then well into his eighties and given to wearing turtlenecks and love beads alternately with his clerical collar, that she was going to marry a Jew, the old man presented the newlyweds with a Bible, accompanying the gift with the sensible suggestion that the bridegroom could read the Old Testament and the bride the New. By then the retired minister could even tell jokes about his working life; his favorite had to do with a hotel proprietor who, when asked why he always gave Baptists cheaper rates than worthies from other denominations, said, "The Baptists are so narrow I can fit three of them into a double room."

John Davies, the older of the missionary's two sons, was born in Kiating, in the far western province of Szechwan, on April 6, 1908. Four years later the family moved to Chengtu, the capital of Szechwan. Chengtu was somewhat closer to the outside world than Kiating but was still fifteen hundred miles from the coast. Chengtu and Chungking were only two hundred and fifty miles apart, but it could take ten days to travel between them by overland safari or by river junk. One usually allowed three months for a round trip between Chengtu and Shanghai, depending on the condition of the rapids that roiled the waters.

Chengtu was laid out like Peking, with a sacrosanct inner city and stout exterior walls. It boasted a resident viceroy of the emperor, an arsenal, and a mint, but as it had never been designated a treaty port, it harbored almost no Western businessmen. There were British and French consuls, however, a French army doctor, and a number of warlords. Mrs. Davies, her singing career now forsaken for higher-priority business, once single-handedly broke up a battle between two minor warlords by striding between their marshaled forces and demanding an immediate cease-fire.

Of Chengtu's total population of half a million, there were only about one hundred and fifty foreigners. Of these, one-third of whom were

American, nearly all belonged to missionary families, and most of the Americans were affiliated with a local institution, the West China Union University.[6] (There were also some Catholic missionaries, mainly French, but they kept pretty much to themselves.) Chengtu, situated on a flat plain and ringed by paddy fields, was disagreeably humid in summer, and all the foreigners would take to the surrounding hills, traveling, as a rule, by sedan chair. A few wheelbarrows excepted, Chengtu had no wheeled vehicles. There was no household electricity (those were the days of oil for the lamps of China), and it took about two and a half months for a letter to arrive from the United States. There was a telegraph office, however, and in a few government buildings there were telephones. Local businessmen wishing to sneak a midmorning opium pipe would say, "Out to telephone," and take off.

The Davies household not only attended church services every Sunday, but held morning prayers daily. Davies *père* must have drawn comfort from his resident flock, because, as in the case of most missionaries in China, the number of conversions he brought about was unimpressive. It was hard to tell sometimes just how firmly he had implanted the seeds of Christianity in any Chinese minds. After he had been in Chengtu for about a decade, for instance, he set off on a trip one day aboard a thirty-foot houseboat that belonged to the mission. (It was called a wuban, because it was five boards wide, in contrast to the more common three-board-wide sampan.) By then Davies, in addition to his pastoral duties, had become principal of a boys' school and was teaching at West China Union. Quite a crowd assembled at the river bank, accordingly, to wish him Godspeed. But while his church members were piously praying to his God for the safety of his journey, they were simultaneously sacrificing a chicken and spilling its blood into the Yangtze to pacify its waters, and were shooting off firecrackers to dispel any evil spirits that might be lurking around. The Chinese, being addicted to gambling, knew how to hedge bets.

After the Chinese revolution of 1911, when the Manchu dynasty was overthrown and the republic was being established, most of the inland missionaries had fled toward the coast; the trip was especially harrowing

---

[6]It was customary for all the Americans to get together for Thanksgiving dinner. One November they noticed that, including infants, there were forty-eight of them present— precisely one, they reflected with pride and patriotism, for each of the then forty-eight states of the Union.

for the Davies family because their second son, Donald, had been born just five days before they felt they had to board their wuban and decamp. Donald Davies eventually became a Foreign Service officer himself, but he did not join up until after serving in the war as a naval intelligence officer; before that, he had been an Associated Press reporter in China. When he did follow his brother's footsteps, he would go only so far; he felt, unlike the Service brothers, that one China specialist was enough for any one family.

But Donald Davies did feel a strong urge to represent the United States abroad. "This frightful missionary complex really does things to a person," he would say after his retirement in 1963. "I had a strong feeling of wanting to be of service to my nation. Perhaps it's because when you're born abroad, and brought up largely with foreign children, you tend to become a super-patriot. You are convinced that your country has to be the best place there ever was. And then there was also the ethical feeling that a missionary son has: It is not only a duty to serve others, but an honor. John felt that way, too."

Like many missionary children of their generation, the Davies boys were shipped off in their teens to the Shanghai American School, supported by the American missionaries in China. The majority of the day students came from business or diplomatic families, the majority of the boarders from missionary ones. The sole purpose of the school was to prepare its students to attend college back in the States; there were no courses in Chinese history or culture. Donald Davies eventually went to Davidson College in North Carolina; John to Alexander Meiklejohn College, an experimental two-year academy that was part of the University of Wisconsin. (Meiklejohn, its founder, believed that the twentieth century was overemphasized in most undergraduate programs; he never let his students get that far, confining them to Athens their first year and to nineteenth-century America their second.)

For his third year of college, John Davies returned to China—working his way back across the Pacific as an ordinary seaman—and enrolled at the Yenching University, on the outskirts of Peking; John Leighton Stuart, who in later years would become American ambassador to China, was president. Davies had had no particular career in mind up to then, but after becoming acquainted with Edmund Clubb in Peking at that time, he decided Clubb would be an ideal man to emulate. First, though, he set out once more for the United States and finished college at Columbia. On graduating, he quickly took the Foreign Service exams and was notified that he had passed on November 19, 1931—the same day, as it happened, that Secretary of State Henry L. Stimson notified Japan that its invasion of Manchuria was deemed by the United States to be in violation of both the Kellogg Pact and the Nine-Power Treaty of 1922.

Davies was soon packed off by the State Department, for seasoning, to Windsor, Ontario. That worked out nicely for him. Just across the Michigan border lived his maiden aunt, Florence Davies, who was women's editor of the Detroit News and happy to pamper a stray nephew. She, too, had gone to Oberlin, where among her classmates was Anna Louise Strong, whose preacher father had met her mother while both were attending Oberlin.[7]

Then Davies was off to China again, his fare this time paid by his new employer, and he ended up with the American consulate at Yunnan-fu (now Kunming), high in the southwest mountains. This was one of a dozen or so consulates that the United States then maintained, from Harbin south to Canton, and the younger diplomats would regularly be shuttled from one to the other. John Service, for instance, was Davies's replacement at Yunnan-fu.

Yunnan-fu was notable for, among other things, the kinds of missionaries it attracted—men and women far less stable, on the whole, than those with whom Davies and Service had grown up. It was a way station, for one thing, for religious workers heading toward the most remote missionary post in China, at Batang in the Tibetan foothills, where emissaries from the Assembly of God had established a precarious presence. American missionaries were supposed to fill out a consular form every year if they wanted to keep enjoying the protection of their government. While Arthur Ringwalt was stationed at Yunnan-fu, he received the forms from the Assembly of God contingent, two nurses and two doctors. There was a note appended. One of the nurses had had a baby and wanted it registered as a United States citizen. Ringwalt wrote back and said he'd have to have the name of the father first. The mother wrote back that she really couldn't tell; it could have been either of the doctors. Ringwalt dubiously forwarded this explanation of the situation to Washington and, to his surprise, the baby was declared in good standing despite its cloudy

[7]Thanks to an introduction from his Aunt Florence, Davies once stayed in the radical writer's Moscow apartment, at the end of a westbound trip on the trans-Siberian railroad. Miss Strong wasn't there at the time, but the fact that Davies had slept under her red roof would later be brought up as evidence of his alleged Communist leanings.

lineage. There was another missionary couple in Yunnan-fu who earned their living by begging in the streets, abetted by their twelve pathetic children. They were late in filling out *their* annual forms, and Ringwalt finally went to see them and said they would really have to come around and register, or he couldn't guarantee them any further consular services. "Can't you wait until tomorrow?" they asked him. "We're having another baby tonight."

In 1933 Davies went to Peking for the usual two-year language course. Among the new friends he met there was John Fairbank, who was working on a Ph.D. dissertation about the Chinese Customs Service. Davies could already speak Chinese fluently, of course, but he had what his mentors considered coarse Szechwanese intonations. He perfected a more elegant Mandarin accent, which was not especially difficult because he was a natural linguist (in later years he would master Russian, German, and Spanish, and he could get by passably in French and Japanese).

Davies would soon have considerable first-hand experience with the Japanese at Mukden, their principal rail and commercial center in Manchuria. He was assigned there in 1935 and spent a couple of years intently watching the Japanese try to fashion a working satellite government.[8] Soon after the Sino-Japanese War began in 1937, Davies was transferred to Hankow, where Chiang Kai-shek had his seat of government. Nelson Johnson was on hand, as were a number of others who would play leading roles in the unfolding China story—among them Chou En-lai, Joseph W. Stilwell, Claire L. Chennault, Evans Carlson, Agnes Smedley, and Freda Utley.

---

[8]Joseph Ballantine, a Japanese-language Foreign Service officer, was the consul general in Mukden. During one of his absences, he left Davies in charge, and the young diplomat had to send a monthly political report back to the State Department. One day when he had nothing better to do he composed a parody of a conventional political report and sent it to Arthur Ringwalt, who was then in Washington on the China desk. "The government of Manchukuo has announced the decoration of 1,423 virtuous widows," Davies wrote. "This is an interesting statistic. Last year, the Manchukuo government recognized 1,456 virtuous widows. Whether the standards of the Manchukuo government have tightened or those of the widows have slackened is not known." Ringwalt was amused and passed the spoof along to John Carter Vincent, who also liked it and forwarded it up the line to *his* superiors, until it reached Stanley K. Hornbeck, the man in charge of Far Eastern affairs, who was not easy to amuse. Hornbeck sent it back down the chain of command with the frosty annotation that such frivolity was not to be condoned and that the author of the offending document should be admonished. It was up to Ringwalt to write the rebuke, and he composed a suitably stern one, but at the same time that he transmitted it officially he appended a personal note: "I can't help it."

In *The China Story*, Mrs. Utley had a chapter, "How the Communists Captured the Diplomats," in which she told how Miss Smedley had sinisterly influenced Stilwell and said that Davies "became one of the most potent influences in the Department furthering the cause of the Chinese Communists." In his own reminiscent book *Dragon by the Tail*, Davies reproduced a photograph of a dinner party he'd given in Hankow in 1938. A Communist editor named Chang Han-fu was present. So were Miss Smedley and Mrs. Utley, the only ladies in attendance. Davies resisted the temptation to point out in a caption, as he could have, that while everybody else in the picture was conversing openly, Mrs. Utley was in an apparently conspiratorial tête-à-tête with Chang Han-fu.

By the fall of 1941 both Davies and Ringwalt were back in Peking, cultivating any Japanese they could talk to, in the hope of ascertaining what Japan's intentions were toward the United States. The two Americans gave a party for some Japanese they knew, including a second secretary and a naval attaché from Tokyo, and as the convivial evening progressed the guests announced that they wanted to wrestle. The naval attaché pinned Davies down and then said gigglingly, "One of these days —ha ha—the *whole* Japanese Navy—ha ha—is going to take all of you to task." Everybody laughed uproariously.

Davies was a man singularly free of bitterness, but he had little good to say about missionaries, whom he chided in *Dragon by the Tail* as members of "a righteous and consecrated crusade that strove with love to win China to Christ and, in so doing, did much to shatter a civilization that had endured for millennia." He concluded the book with the dour statement, "The truth of the matter is that China has been since the fall of the Empire a huge and seductive practical joke. The western businessmen, missionaries, and educators who had tried to modernize and Christianize it failed. The Japanese militarists who tried to conquer it failed. The American government which tried to democratize and unify it failed. The Soviet rulers who tried to insinuate control over it failed. Chiang failed. Mao failed."

John Service was more tolerant of missionaries, perhaps because his father was an administrator rather than an ordained minister. Even so, Robert Roy Service was a straitlaced man. He himself would sip Chinese tea on ceremonial occasions; otherwise, he abstained from tea, coffee, tobacco, and liquor. It was one of those mysterious ironies that afflict good men's lives that he nonetheless died of cirrhosis of the liver, probably because of a vitamin deficiency. He and his wife, Grace Boggs, had both graduated from the University of California at Berkeley in 1902, at a time when the YMCA had something of the appeal to young people that the Peace Corps was to have sixty years later. For much of their long stay in China, the Services were supported by the campus Y, which was then an extracurricular institution of substance. The Y was very big in China then, too. It built swimming pools and conducted night classes; it sought to improve labor conditions and create a more wholesome life for everybody; there was a time when a good many Kuomintang officials came out of the Y. Its emissaries not only tried to teach the Chinese about the Western world and (sometimes no more than incidentally) about Christianity but also, with much greater success, taught them Ping-Pong and basketball.

Robert Roy and Grace Service arrived in China in 1905, just ahead of the Davieses, and they proceeded to establish the first branch of the YMCA in Chengtu. The Services lived in a rambling house with walls of bamboo, mud, and plaster. They filled it with Tibetan art, which was then quite easy to obtain in Chengtu. The father, owing in part no doubt to his abstemious habits, was a fine athlete; he liked to run and he liked to ride horseback. His wife weighed only one hundred pounds and was constantly sick, but she had formidable inner strength. She would arise every morning at 6:30 because, although there were plenty of servants around, she wanted to make sure that her husband's collars were properly starched. She was also a meticulous diarist; she once reminded herself that in the previous year she had written 405 letters and read 64 books. An entry for October 1908 noted that "Mr. and Mrs. J. P. Davies of Kiating visited us . . . with their young John."

Robert Roy Service was, like the Reverend Mr. Davies, a Baptist, but Grace was a Presbyterian, and as it happened most of their good friends in Chengtu, even after the Davieses moved there in 1912, were Methodists. The two American families lived on opposite sides of the city, and the only ways of getting across town were by sedan chair or on foot. The Services had four children—a girl, who died in infancy, and three boys. John was the oldest of the sons. His birth, in the summer of 1909, had been a source of considerable annoyance to the family doctor. The baby was due in June, but didn't arrive until August 3, which meant that the doctor had to hang around sweltering Chengtu instead of moving up into the cooler Kwanhsien Hills. Next came Robert, who eventually went into forestry and was killed in a lumbering accident. The third son was Richard.

There had been an earlier tragedy, too, the sort of experience to which missionaries had to become inured if they were to retain their sanity and which made others marvel at their perseverance and endurance. This was the death of their infant daughter, Virginia. Robert Roy and Grace Service had arrived in Shanghai at the end of 1905 with the six-month-old child. As they were traveling up the Yangtze toward Chengtu, on the twenty-one-day stretch to Chungking, the infant contracted dysentery and died. They buried her in a foreigners' cemetery at Chungking and proceeded determinedly toward their destination. Following the 1911 revolution, when the Services, like the Davieses, moved precipitously to the east (flying from their boat an American flag that Jack had received on his first birthday), they interrupted their journey at Chungking long enough to visit their daughter's grave.[9]

Jack Service had a sheltered childhood. There were hardly any Chinese among his playmates. The missionaries, understandably fearful of disease, tried to keep their children away from both unwashed foods and unwashed natives. (The boy kept being chased by water buffalo and nipped at by dogs—unlike his young Chinese peers, he noticed enviably. He concluded that foreigners like himself smelled peculiar, probably because of all the meat they ate.) When Robert Service first agreed to go to Chengtu, he was told he'd be getting to Shanghai every year for a YMCA conference and that his wife could accompany him on every other trip. They were also theoretically entitled to home leave every six years. But it was nine-and-a-half years before the family left remote Chengtu and, in 1915, came back to the States, to spend a year in Cleveland. There the parents worked for the Y, and Jack attended first grade.[10]

When the Services returned to China—it took two years for their trunks to arrive from Cleveland, and when they did the one containing

[9]When Robert Roy Service died in 1935, he was buried in Chungking alongside his daughter. In 1971 John, returning to the land of his birth for the first time in twenty-six years, made a pilgrimage to the cemetery, but the graves had been removed in consonance with the Maoist belief that all arable land should be used for growing crops. Service observed philosophically that the transformation of the scene was indicative both that the Chinese had abandoned ancestor worship and had abandoned a favored status for foreigners.

[10]Some of the boy's Ohio acquaintances couldn't understand why he didn't regard chicken-on-Sunday as a gustatory treat. The reason was that in Chengtu the Services had no refrigeration and accordingly ate freshly killed chicken nearly every day. The acquaintances also couldn't understand why, when in deference to Jack's upbringing they gave him chopsticks to eat with instead of silverware, he seemed quite clumsy. The reason for *that* was that in Chengtu he was accustomed to a bowl, and he didn't know how to cope with a flat plate.

their best Bible was missing—Grace Service continued her young sons' schooling by means of the system of education by correspondence run by the Calvert School of Baltimore, which families like the Davieses also employed; as a teacher, she was so demanding that by the time Jack was eleven he was ready for high school, which in those days meant the American School in far-off Shanghai.

John Service had become fairly fluent in Chinese in Chengtu, but it was hard for him to keep up with the language in Shanghai; the majority of the people he was with spoke English and their servants spoke pidgin English, considering it infra dig to use their native tongue. (Years later, when he was bringing up his own children in Shanghai, he had to cajole their amah into talking Chinese to them.) Still, a boy could not help being affected by the life around him, and by his teens he had ingrained in him the Chinese esteem of sensitivity to the feelings of others; *kuan-hsi* was the word for it. How useful for an incipient diplomat to be constantly reminded of the virtues of saving face, of not throwing one's weight around, of putting propositions in the form of suggestions instead of being crude or blatant! Service also learned patience: the kind that made his own subsequent ordeal tolerable; the kind that sustained Mao Tse-tung while waiting for his revolution to take hold; the kind, indeed, that on Taiwan sustained Chiang Kai-shek's hope of someday retaking the Chinese mainland. Service's friends would later also attribute to him a trait called *hsüeh-wen*, roughly translatable as "learning and culture." (It was a word that some educated Chinese in Taipei would use—discreetly—in putting down Chiang; he had no intellectual legitimacy, they would say, never having acquired *hsüeh-wen*.)

In a characteristically self-deprecatory gesture, Service, whose Chinese always remained fluent, would speak in later years of "his sadly eroded command of the language." When he retired to Berkeley, it had a sizable Chinese colony and a commensurate number of Chinese restaurants, and he became a faithful patron of most of them (excluding the few he dismissed as chop-suey joints). He would fascinate the waiters with his mastery of their tongue as he engaged in earnest colloquy as to whether he should order the potstickers (a pork appetizer much fancied in Szechwan) or the black mushrooms with bamboo shoots. Diffident as Service might be of his own command of Chinese, other Americans who had long grappled with the slippery language stood in awe of it. One of them who taught the language once observed admiringly, "Jack is such a paragon of bilinguality that he doesn't think there's any difference between English and Chinese."

The Services had a second home leave in 1924, and during the stay Jack finished high school, at the age of fifteen, in Berkeley. That year, while taking a mechanical-drawing course, he was falsely accused of stealing a T-square; it was his first taste of harassment, though but a sip compared to the heavy doses he would later swallow. Being so young, he decided to wait two years before going to college; thus when the family returned to China he apprenticed himself—the T-square episode notwithstanding— to a Shanghai architectural firm that designed buildings for the YMCA. Then he took off, alone, for the States. He had thought he might follow his parents to the university at Berkeley, but after attending summer school there to obtain a few credits missing from his record, he decided to go instead to Oberlin.

There Service became absorbed in art history; in fact, it interested him so much that he stayed on for a year of postgraduate work devoted mainly to that subject. Another missionary son, Edwin O. Reischauer, was in his college class. They were boyhood acquaintances, having once crossed the Pacific on the same ship (Reischauer had beaten Service in the finals of the junior deck-tennis championship), and for three years at Oberlin they lived in the same rooming house. Still another classmate was Caroline Schulz, the daughter of a Regular Army officer. Service married her in Haiphong two years after their graduation. They had three children—two sons and a daughter named Virginia, after Service's sister who died in infancy—the first two of whom were born in China.

At Oberlin Service, who had always been tall and thin—he stood five feet, eleven and a half inches, and weighed 126—blossomed as a long-distance runner. He was captain of both the track team and the cross-country team his senior year. Later he became the half-mile champion of Shanghai. In Peking there was a cinder bridle path at the far edge of a broad strip of grass surrounding the legation quarter. While other youthful diplomats would trot around it on horseback for exercise, Service ran around. Later, during the war, Service, Davies, Ludden, and Emmerson worked out a code to use among themselves and to perplex any Japanese who might intercept their messages. They used "Snow White" for "Mme. Chiang Kai-shek" and "Harvard" for "Communist," not anticipating how this might be construed during the McCarthy era; "Asylum" stood for for "Washington," a reasonable enough selection in any era; Service himself, because of his passion for running, was known as "Hare."

Robert Roy Service never had much use for the diplomatic corps; like most missionaries, he looked askance at its people because they had a rough-and-tumble, hard-drinking, worldly reputation; some of the Foreign Service corpsmen he knew in China were particularly noted for their devil-may-care ways. The elder Service would therefore have preferred some gentler métier for his son, but when Jack left Oberlin in 1932, he decided to take the Foreign Service exam. (He was encouraged by the news that John Davies had not long before taken and passed it.) Service passed it, too, but again there were no vacancies. An old hand in Washington advised him to go back to China and apply for a job there as a Foreign Service clerk, on the theory that the government might look favorably on an applicant whose transportation abroad it didn't have to pay for. So he went to China, and in 1933 at the age of twenty-four, after an interim job as a $50-a-month clerk at the Bank of Shanghai, he got a clerk's job at the consulate at Yunnan-fu.

Two years afterward Service was finally commissioned a Foreign Service officer, and after passing his language examination, he was sent to the consulate at Shanghai. There his boss was Clarence E. Gauss, a China-coast type who had never bothered to learn Chinese since one did not much need the language at treaty ports. (He had the peculiar notion that the study of Chinese could have a corrosive effect on a non-Chinese brain, though he was willing to concede there could be exceptions.) Later, when Gauss became ambassador, he seemed amazed to learn that there were inland indigenes at Chungking who spoke Chinese but no English. His mastery of the vernacular was limited to a few phrases like K'ai fan! ("Boy, bring dinner!"), and owing to his linguistic shortcomings, he was greatly taken by young Service's glibness.

Gauss was a native of Washington, D.C., where he had been largely educated by private tutors. Later trained as a court reporter, he had begun his diplomatic career in 1906 as a $900-a-year clerk. He arrived in China for the first time as a deputy consul general at Shanghai in 1907, and except for brief tours of duty long afterward in Paris and Australia, he spent the bulk of his adult life in China, being stationed at one time or another in Tientsin, Tsinan, Shantung, Mukden, Amoy, and Peking. He had a precise, orderly mind and had once drawn up a legal manual for consuls that the Foreign Service highly prized. He also could be sour and brusque. Early in the Second World War a young diplomat arrived in

China after a hair-raising voyage across the Indian Ocean in a convoy; he had been pressed into service as an ammunition bearer during a set-to with a Japanese submarine, and he had grown a beard. He reported to Gauss and asked what his instructions were. "Get a shave," Gauss said.

But Gauss understood the responsibility of a superior to his juniors in a crunch; scoffing once at the idea that Edmund Clubb could have been won over by the Communists he was trying to learn about in the early thirties, Gauss had declared, "Mr. Clubb is sufficiently strong-minded that he could pick a clock to pieces to see how it ticks without being influenced." Gauss's own nickname was The Honest Buddha. He liked to play pinochle with John Carter Vincent, and one evening while they were discussing some of the difficulties they were having with Chiang Kai-shek and his sycophants, Gauss said wearily, "Well, I think it's about time they cleared us out of here. I'm considered a sourpuss and you're looked on as a leftist."

Gauss grew fond of Service, of whom he would subsequently say to a State Department Loyalty Security Board inquiry in 1950:

He was outstanding. I don't know of any officer in my whole thirty-nine years of service who impressed me more favorably than Jack Service, and I have had an awful lot of young officers with me. . . . One of the first things that impressed me most about Mr. Service was this: He was born and raised abroad. . . . In the case of many American boys born and raised abroad they become international in their outlook; they get away from their American side, and you find them in China, and it is particularly true . . . of language officers in Japan and China and in the Orient—first thing you know they are pro this or pro that; anti this or anti that. Jack Service impressed me particularly during my whole period of contact with him of going right down the middle of the road as an American. He was objective in his approach to all of the political problems that we had. Now, I don't mean to say he was ostentatiously American, but he thought in his whole analysis, his political information and everything else, he thought as an American. And, to me, that was one of the most refreshing things that I could have had in my whole service. For instance, at Chungking I had an officer who was so pro-Chiang Kai-shek that he would just go red in the face when anybody said anything in criticism of the existing government. You couldn't deal—you couldn't use an officer like that. But Jack Service impressed me at Shanghai and at Chungking as one of that type of Americans that could go right down the middle of the road as an American who recognized that he was abroad to recognize American interests and look at things from the American standpoint. There was no suggestion in any case of pro or anti anybody.

Service's brother Richard graduated from Pomona in 1935, and he too came back to China hoping for a Foreign Service clerkship. While his application was pending, he got a job with the export branch of the Philco company. He also contracted appendicitis, pneumonia, and intestinal tuberculosis—the last, apparently, from drinking untreated milk not in China but in California. He recuperated at his brother's home, and while convalescing tried to improve his own Chinese, which was a cut below Jack's. Scholarly Sinologists are expected to know about five thousand Chinese characters, and a political analyst trying to extricate nuances from newspapers to know about fifteen hundred. Jack Service had climbed comfortably above the latter plateau; Dick Service came close but never quite made it.[11]

By the autumn of 1940, the war between China and Japan had heated up to a point where dependents of Americans in the area—among them Jack Service's wife and their two small children—were ordered home. At the same time, Jewish refugees were swarming in from Europe, seeking visas to the United States. These sad, drifting people were often the butt of jokes, some of them cruel and some anti-Semitic, made by the American diplomats on the scene, a few of whom were larking it up in the absence of their families. Service was remembered by his Shanghai contemporaries as a man who stayed aloof from all the jokes at the expense of the hapless newcomers, and—what was more important—succeeded in somewhat ameliorating their haplessness by almost single-handedly raising the daily quota of visas granted from two to twenty.

As the Japanese moved farther and farther into China, occupying large areas of the north, the east, and the south, Chiang Kai-shek transferred his Nationalist government headquarters from Nanking to Hankow and

[11]John King Fairbank was the king of this particular mountain. His Chinese nickname was *Fei Wan-tzu*, which means "ten thousand characters." One aid in learning Chinese is the use of cards with an English word on one side and the appropriate Chinese characters on the back. As a young man, Fairbank was almost never seen without a pocketful of cards, and he knew hundreds of characters that most Chinese never used. After a while Fairbank began using cards that had *only* Chinese on them, and on spotting an educated Chinese would flash one of them—bearing, like as not, some obscure word —and ask what it meant. Among some Chinese, who did not take well to the notion of being beaten by a foreigner at their own game, Fairbank became known as The Terror of Peking, too.

finally, in 1938, to Chungking, at the confluence of the Yangtze and Chialing rivers. (The United States embassy was across the Yangtze from most Chinese government offices, and in conducting diplomatic business it was necessary to climb long flights of steps up the river's steep banks. This was particularly hard on John Carter Vincent, who was chronically plagued by a bad back; on occasion, he had to be carried up and down in sedan chairs.) The Communists, their Long March of 1934–1935 well behind them, had dug in solidly in the northwest and the north, with their headquarters at Yenan. In May 1941, on the recommendation of, oddly, Everett Drumright, who had felt Service could be more valuable writing political reports in Chungking than handling visas in Shanghai, Service flew to join the staff of the embassy, where Gauss was soon to succeed Nelson Johnson as ambassador. On the plane were Henry and Clare Luce, en route to a visit with Chiang Kai-shek. Service himself first met the Generalissimo and his lady a few days later at a reception for the Luces. "Service—what a lovely name!" said Mme. Chiang when he was introduced. "I hope you'll be of service to China." Whether or not he was, it was characteristic of the Kuomintang attitude that Mme. Chiang had a concept of his job that was backward. Service was not supposed to be of service to China, or to any faction in China; his obligations and his loyalties were to the United States.

In China at that time, Chiang's Kuomintang and Mao Tse-tung's Communists were, as Theodore H. White put it, "two frozen entities"; they had been briefly, if not warmly, united against Japan but now were pursuing their separate ends. After Pearl Harbor the United States's highest priority out there would be the defeat of Japan, and to *that* end just about all the Americans in China were united, hoping to persuade all Chinese forces, Nationalist and Communist alike, to prosecute the war vigorously and, if possible, in view of the demonstrated corruptibility of some of them, virtuously.

But the United States scarcely knew anything about the Communists; nobody had paid much attention to what Edmund Clubb had dredged up nearly a decade earlier. Quite apart from the possibility of learning more about Mao's long-range plans, there were certain immediate advantages to be gained from striking up an acquaintance with the Communists: They could supply intelligence about the Japanese forces confronting them, and they could help bomber crews who might have to bail out in their area. Ambassador Gauss assigned Service to find out all he could about the Communists.

Service didn't know anybody in Chungking especially well, except the embassy crowd and a few old friends of his parents. One of the first things he did, to get better acquainted, was to join the local Rotary Club; later he helped to organize a Masonic group. (He soon felt very much at home in Chungking. Edward Rice recalled that one day when he was taking a stroll there with Service and Philip Sprouse, Service sniffed the existence of a tiny restaurant in a side alley, ran ahead of them, bought a bowl of meatballs and broth, slurped it down, sprinted back, and caught up with them before they'd covered a block.) And he spent a great deal of time with journalists. The exchange of information and ideas between the Foreign Service and the press is a time-honored practice that has long been engaged in, to the profit of both, by responsible diplomats and responsible journalists everywhere. Representatives of both groups who were in Chungking in 1941 felt uncommonly interdependent. The city's normal population of half a million had been swollen by an influx of refugees to more than a million.

In this sea of milling Chinese, thousands of whom seemed concerned almost obsessively with strange Oriental politics, there were only a few hundred foreigners. Among these were a half-dozen resident American correspondents and ten junior diplomats. It was natural for them all to become close friends. The United States was not yet at war, and its diplomats were behaving circumspectly; the journalists, though, would visit Chinese troops at the front. They freely told the diplomats what they saw and heard up there, and the diplomats in turn told the journalists, whom they trusted without reservation, just about everything *they* knew.

It was the company he kept that would eventually get Service into trouble, and the principal accusation leveled against him was that he had associated with Communists. Of *course* he had in China, Gauss would testify before the Loyalty Security Board in 1950:

Now, I would like to go very positively into that particular question because the only thing that I know about of Mr. Service—of complaint against him —is the McCarthy statement that he associated with Communists. In Chungking Mr. Service was a political officer of the Embassy. His job was to cover the waterfront. His job was to get every bit of information that he possibly could. . . . Now, it was difficult to get information in those days. We had a censorship. They had all those wonderful stories about Chinese victories which never proved to be true. . . . Jack Service's job was to go over to the other side of the river and to see everybody that he could. He would see the foreign press people. He saw the Chinese press people. He saw anybody in any of the embassies or legations that were over there that were supposed to know anything. He saw any people in the Foreign Office or any of the other ministries. He went to the Kuomintang Headquarters and talked with whoever he could see there. He went to the *Ta Kung Pao,* which was the independent newspaper. He went to this independent newspaper, he was in touch with those people. He went to Communist Headquarters. He associated with everybody and anybody in Chungking that could give him information, and he pieced together this puzzle that we had constantly before us as to what was going on in China, and he did a magnificent job. . . . [His contact with the Communists was] strictly in accordance with his official duties. I didn't tell him to go there, but I expected him to go there; that was his job; and you didn't have to tell Jack Service what his job was, or how to do it. He did it.

It was as simple as that. Reporting was the job of the Old China Hands. John Davies stressed the point in 1954 in a letter to the chairman of a State Department board that was scrutinizing *his* career: "On the question of my reporting about China, I was asked whether some of my estimates were based on insufficient evidence. I agreed that they were. In so answering, I was applying perfectionist standards to myself. I was harsher toward myself than I think I would be toward others. It is true that, ideally, a Foreign Service officer should wait until all of the evidence is in before making a judgment. But it is often the case, as in a battle, that to wait for all the intelligence to come in is to be paralyzed while decisive events pass one by."

There was no reason to believe that anyone paid much more attention to Davies's apologia than had been paid to many of his reports that occasioned it. When Clubb appeared at one of *his* loyalty-security hearings, he submitted in his defense more than three hundred documents that he had written across two decades on China and on Sino-Soviet relations. In a five-month hearing, none of the men who passed judgment on Clubb questioned the substance of any of these dry memoranda, although the papers represented what Clubb's government career had been all about. One judge, presumably of the opinion that Clubb's unobjectionable reports might not accurately reflect objectionable beliefs, did ask him if it wasn't possible for a person to write one way and think another. Not for twenty years it wasn't, Clubb replied.

But at least before the boom fell, the Old China Hands reported freely what they saw and heard and thought. Perhaps no Foreign Service officer will ever report again with like candor. Soon after Chiang Kai-shek moved his government to Taiwan, Robert Barnett turned up. He saw a good deal of a very high-ranking American diplomat stationed there. After they got to be friends, the diplomat began confiding to Barnett some quite critical views about the Generalissimo, none of which Barnett, knowledgeable old China Hand though he was, had seen encompassed in any official message to Washington. "I said to him," Barnett recalled, " 'Why don't you put some of these things in writing and send them back to the Department? This is important intelligence and could help shape policy.' And he looked at me and said, 'Bob, that may be so, but what if I wrote a report and somebody like Senator Knowland[12] saw it?' And then I realized that the China Lobby had succeeded in its mission of aborting the primary mission of the Foreign Service."

As John Davies had suggested, nobody is perfect. For instance, there was Stanley K. Hornbeck, a rigid, dogmatic, domineering bureaucrat whom no one ever accused of losing China—even though for some time Alger Hiss was his right-hand assistant. Hornbeck was an uncommon State Department man—one who had come into diplomacy full-blown from the academic world. He had a pedantic approach to language; he was forever bombarding his underlings with directives that said things like "It would be appreciated if officers whose duties involve drafting would make sure that they understand the difference in meaning between the word 'particularly' and the word 'especially'; also between the phrase 'in regard to' and the phrase 'in respect to'—and be guided accordingly."

Hornbeck was born in Franklin, Massachusetts, in 1883, had studied at Oxford, and, after getting his Ph.D. at the University of Wisconsin in 1911, had taught there and at Harvard. He had been in charge of Chinese affairs for the State Department on and off since 1928 and had run them with a heavy hand. He liked to summon assistants by means of a loud buzzer; there was one poor functionary so terrified of him that his face would become suffused with blood even when somebody else was buzzed.

Hornbeck was the ranking administrator, the big departmental cheese, the evaluator of field reports supreme. Thus it could be understood why people gave credence to a memorandum of his own that he issued on November 27, 1941, a fortnight before Pearl Harbor: "In the opinion of the undersigned, the Japanese Government does not desire or intend or

[12]William F. Knowland, a senator from California, was often called "the Senator from Formosa."

expect to have forthwith armed conflict with the United States . . . the undersigned does not believe that this country is now on the immediate verge of 'war' in the Pacific."

In regard to, or in respect to, that particular, or especial, misjudgment, Hornbeck was, quite properly, never castigated. It was conceded in his case, as it should have been, that a man has a perfect right to make a mistake. Hornbeck was never accused, for instance, of losing Pearl Harbor.[13]

At the same time that Hornbeck was committing his gaffe, Clubb was en route to Indo-China. He had been in Shanghai and was now about to start in on a sensitive consular job—manning a listening post at Hanoi. French Indo-China was in a peculiar fix then; it was under the Vichy government, but the Japanese had arrived in some strength as uninvited, though perforce tolerated, guests. Clubb took a French ship from Manila to Haiphong. Off the mainland coast, shortly before landing, he was told by a crewman that the night before he'd seen a blacked-out Japanese naval convoy cruising nearby.

As soon as Clubb got ashore and was in a position to send a coded message, he shot off a telegram to the American naval base at Cavite in the Philippines, with a request that it be forwarded apace to Washington. By then he was able to report that a convoy of Japanese troop transports had been reliably said to be off northern Borneo and that a whole division of Japanese troops, not to mention a flock of Japanese aircraft, were supposed to be in the vicinity of Camranh Bay. What this meant Clubb didn't profess to know, but it seemed indicative of Japanese martial activity, and he thought somebody in Washington who could interpret it or tie it in with other intelligence should know about it posthaste. Clubb's alert was forwarded from Cavite to Washington and was received by the State Department there, he was later to ascertain, at 5:21 a.m. on December 6—more than twenty-four hours before the attack on Pearl Harbor. However, there was no evidence that anyone in Washington chose to take any action with respect to the report beyond filing it.

Early in December 1941 most of the consequential Old China Hands were in the Far East, with the notable exception of Davies, in Washing-

---

[13]No man had a monopoly on myopia. At a dinner party in Manila in September 1941, Laurence Salisbury heard General Douglas MacArthur, after the ladies had left the table, pound it and declaim, "Japan will never join the Axis!" The next day's papers said it had.

ton, and Penfield, in Greenland. John Service and John Vincent, his land legs restored after his crossing with Alfred Kohlberg, were in Chungking. There Vincent would soon become concerned about America's helping the Russians at Stalingrad, a battle he overoptimistically viewed as decisive. "If they lose," he wrote a government official back in Washington, "there won't be much sense or need in sending things to England and China; if they win it won't be necessary." Vincent had little hope from the start of his new tour of duty that the Chinese would be able to contribute much to the struggle unless a great deal was sent. Just a week after Pearl Harbor, he composed a message for Ambassador Gauss to transmit to Secretary of State Cordell Hull: "Chiang may be intentionally misleading in his statement on the part that China may be counted on to play in the struggle. . . . The Chinese army does not possess the aggressive spirit, training, equipment, or supplies for any major offensive or expedition."

Philip Sprouse, that fateful December, was also in the United States. He had been supposed to ship out to Shanghai the month before, but his sailing had been canceled; his new departure date—which, of course, became meaningless—was set for December 8. John Emmerson had been aboard the last passenger ship out of Shanghai and Tokyo. A good many of the other men, however, fell all at once into Japanese hands. Ludden was grabbed at Canton; Freeman at Peking (along with two old-timers, Hungerford B. Howard and Troy L. Perkins); Drumright and Stanton (and another old-timer, Charles S. Millet) at Shanghai; Robert S. Ward[14] at Hong Kong; Harry E. Stevens at Tientsin. Most of the men, like Freeman, had irksome but not overly uncomfortable internments.

Clubb was not quite so lucky. He took over the consulate at Hanoi on a Saturday morning, and early the next morning the Japanese took him over. Clubb was in his pajamas when his captors arrived. They ordered him to leave with them as he was. Clubb, though, had been in the Foreign Service long enough to believe that there were right ways and wrong ways

---

[14]Ward, born in Canada of American parents, went to Peking as a language officer in 1931. He spoke Chinese beautifully; Chou En-lai liked to sit next to him at international dinner parties because he was so easy to chat with. Ward got into trouble in an odd fashion. Falling seriously ill at Urumchi, in Sinkiang province, where there were no American medical facilities of consequence, he was taken by some Russian diplomatic acquaintances to a Soviet hospital for surgery. The operation was a success, but Ward was later criticized in Washington for having let himself thus be manipulated by Communist hands. He was also the English translator of the celebrated Chinese book *Rickshaw Boy*.

of doing things, even of being taken prisoner. He insisted on getting dressed and packing a bag with some books and toilet articles. The Japanese raiding party acquiesced. Things got a bit more complicated, however, when the Japanese asked for the keys to the consular safe. It was an old safe, and, as Clubb knew, could easily be broken into, but he refused the demand. The senior Japanese said he assumed Clubb did not have the keys. "But I do have them," Clubb replied. "I just won't give them to you." He retained the keys, symbolic of his sense of duty, until some two months later when he was visited by a diplomat from Switzerland, at which time he ceremonially yielded them up to this neutral personage.

The Japanese were not at all pleased by Clubb's protocolary intransigence. They never beat him or anything like that during the eight months he was their prisoner, but for two months they kept him in solitary confinement, in an unheated room with no furniture other than a bare plank that served as a bed. The Japanese didn't really know what to make of their imperturbable prisoner, especially when, reflecting on his own tutorial days in Peking, he asked to have a language school set up in his cell. "I was interested in making the best possible use of my time," he said years afterward, "so I asked for a language teacher. I figured as long as they were holding me I might as well learn their language. But they said no. Fortunately, I had the history of the Sung dynasty with me to read."

When in mid-1942, through the offices of the International Red Cross, an exchange of diplomats was finally arranged between Japan and the United States, Clubb's captors at first threatened—unless he would sign a statement attesting to their good treatment of him—to take his name off the list of those who were to board the liner *Asama Maru* at Saigon and sail to the neutral port of Lourenço Marques, in Portuguese-owned Mozambique, where the actual exchange of internees was to take place. Clubb refused to sign anything of the sort, and the Japanese, who by then may have come grudgingly to admire his high-principled behavior, pursued the matter no further.

As the *Asama Maru* was approaching Lourenço Marques, a radio message came in from the State Department; there was such a shortage of trained Chinese-language men in China that although all those who were being repatriated could, if they wished, return to their families in the United States before further assignment, the department would certainly appreciate anyone's agreeing to fly at once up through Africa and across Asia and back to Chungking. There were two volunteers: Raymond Ludden and Edmund Clubb.

4

"Where I am, the consulate is."

With the outbreak of war on a global scale, there was a quick shuttling and shuffling of those relatively few American troops available and of the senior officers qualified to lead them. Among the latter was Joseph W. Stilwell, then a fifty-eight-year-old major general commanding the Third Corps on the West Coast. A native of Florida who had graduated from the United States Military Academy in 1904, a year after Douglas MacArthur, Stilwell knew China well. He had gone there first in 1911, on leave from his post in the Philippines; he had no idea when he made his holiday plans that he'd be arriving just after the historic October revolution of that year.

As a junior officer, Stilwell had demonstrated an uncommon interest in and mastery of languages. After teaching English and Spanish at West Point, he was sent to China in 1920 to take a linguistic course for military men similar to that set up for the Foreign Service officers. Afterward, like many other army officers of his generation, he served a three-year stint with the Fifteenth Infantry, the "Can Do" regiment based from the 1911 revolution on at Tientsin, sixty miles up the Hai Ho River from the China Sea. The regiment's principal mission was to keep open the rail line between Tientsin and Peking, seventy-five miles further inland. During the Boxer Rebellion of 1900, quite a few Americans had, with other foreigners, been besieged far from a seaport, and the United States wanted its nationals to have a fair chance of making it safely to the coast in case of similar trouble. What the Fifteenth Infantry was supposed to do was to make their getaway possible.

Stilwell joined the outfit in 1926 as a major and battalion commander; the regiment's executive officer was Lieutenant Colonel George C. Marshall. Their tours of duty overlapped for eight months, and the two men became well acquainted. One difference between them was that whereas

Marshall, like most of the other officers at Tientsin, regarded his stay there as merely one more fairly routine assignment in the long climb up the career ladder, Stilwell's language training put him in another category. He was the military version of an Old China Hand. He had four additional years in China, during the 1930s, as American military attaché.

Another "Can Do" alumnus who had become fluent in Chinese was David D. Barrett, who at the time of the Japanese march on the Marco Polo Bridge in July 1937 was an army captain serving under Stilwell as an assistant attaché.

One difference between Stilwell and Barrett was that Barrett was not a West Pointer. He had joined the army during the First World War after teaching high school in his native state of Colorado. He had got to China by accident. After the war he had volunteered for service in Siberia, but the ship that was taking him out was diverted by a bad storm to the Philippines. Once there, he volunteered to proceed to the Asian mainland, with which he soon became enchanted.

Barrett had two longstanding ambitions. One of these he shared with almost every Regular Army officer: He hoped before he retired to become a general. The other goal was fairly esoteric: He hoped that whenever he retired and whatever his rank he would be able to spend the rest of his life in China. For that, he was well equipped. He had a better grasp of the language than Stilwell or, for that matter, of any other army officer of his time. John Fairbank once observed of him that "Speaking Pekinese indeed could diminish a foreigner's foreignness, and Dave Barrett spoke it with an obvious love of every tone and phrase." It was not unusual for officers sequestered at remote and tranquil posts to divert themselves by memorizing poetry; another literate Fifteenth Infantry veteran, Major General Edwin Forrest Harding, knew great chunks of verse and at parties would cheerfully recite them. Barrett, though, was renowned for his specialty—reciting long passages from Shakespeare, in Chinese.

Barrett had other envied social graces. He could rattle off Chinese proverbs, for instance, in a glib fashion that confounded many Chinese. Early in the war he attended a dinner in Kweilin that an American general was giving for his Chinese counterpart, General Chang Fa-kuei, who had a legendary capacity for drink. Chang's nickname was Old Ironsides, because he supposedly had the capacity and imperviousness of a tank. It amused him to display his prowess by drinking his peers into a coma. Colonel Barrett, loyally doing what he could to protect his superior officer, started off the evening by plying Old Ironsides with bourbon, which he proffered by the tumblerful. The tactic was effective; halfway through dinner, Chang began to nod and sway. Summoning his last reserves of consciousness, he counterattacked. He tapped on his glass for attention and demanded that each of the many Chinese officers in the room drink a large and separate toast with the American general. Before this conceivably lethal directive could be executed, Barrett sprang to his feet, and, by spouting a string of diversionary Chinese proverbs, deftly turned about the ominous situation, so that while the American general was going through his ordeal General Chang would simultaneously have to swap individual toasts with every foreigner present. Old Ironsides had enough wits left to rescind his order.

After the hostilities at the Marco Polo Bridge, neither Captain Barrett nor Colonel Stilwell was in a literary or celebratory mood as they headed together toward the scene to try to assess for themselves what was going on. Toward the end of their reconnaissance, some Japanese in the area took a few shots at them. It was the only time in Barrett's whole illustrious military career, as it happened, that he heard a shot fired in the traditional anger. "I said, 'Colonel, let's get the hell out of here,' " Barrett recalled years later, when he had retired, without receiving his general's star, to San Francisco, "and we piled into our car with no needless delay and no fussing about who outranked whom and who should climb in first or last. We did have time to observe a dead Japanese soldier lying alongside the road, and I said, 'Colonel, there's going to be trouble over all this.' I look back on that remark as a masterpiece of understatement."

Right after Pearl Harbor Stilwell was summoned to Washington for reassignment. He thought he was going to be sent to North Africa, to Casablanca or Dakar, to command some of the troops that were to be massed there in long-range preparations for the invasion of Europe. On December 27, 1941, he had dinner with John Davies, who was at that moment on the China desk in the State Department. Knowing that whatever job Stilwell got would be important and interesting, and having no idea what his own wartime lot might prove to be, Davies proposed that he accompany the general as a diplomatic aide. With the French political situation as complex and delicate as it was—Admiral Darlan and General de Gaulle were both pursuing their different ends from their respective headquarters—Davies felt that it might be helpful for a military commander to have at his beck someone with a background in diplomacy.

Stilwell liked the idea. But then on January 1 he met with General Marshall. The chief of staff said the government was looking for a man to head up the newly created China-Burma-India theater of operations (CBI). Stilwell, sensing what was coming next, tried to beg off. "They remember me as a small-fry colonel that they kicked around," he said with his characteristic bluntness. But on January 14 he received word that Secretary of War Henry L. Stimson had picked him for the post—an assignment that still another former Fifteenth Infantry officer, Haydon L. Boatner, would later appraise as the "most difficult task assigned any American in the entire war."

Once the die had been cast, it seemed to Stilwell that it would be more desirable than ever to have some civilian political officers on his staff. His area of jurisdiction was vast, and of its components China was the largest, the most formidable, and the most involved. A war against Japan had been under way there for more than four years, but the Chinese government forces had not acquitted themselves with particular distinction. The Japanese controlled all the big coastal cities. Chiang Kai-shek, operating out of inland Chungking, seemed less preoccupied with Japanese than with Mao's Communists, who had been operating out of Yenan in the northwest since their Long March of 1934–1935, and who indeed were in exclusive control of an area comprising 150,000 square miles and containing over fifty million people. Ever since the Generalissimo had been kidnapped at the end of 1936, just outside Sian, by some of his own supporters who were determined to force him into effecting a common front against the Japanese between his Nationalists and the Communists, an uneasy coalition had existed. Most of the available evidence, however, seemed to indicate that Chiang was less concerned about making the world safe from the Axis nations than making China secure for himself.

Two weeks before Stilwell learned of Stimson's decision, for instance, on December 30, 1941, Ambassador Gauss, accompanied by John Carter Vincent, had his first meeting with Chiang since Pearl Harbor. Chiang asked for a billion dollars from the United States. Gauss said the Generalissimo would have to spell out what he wanted it for before he could expect to get it from Washington. Chiang said no, he'd like the money first and would provide the rationale for it after he had it. The strong implication was that if he didn't get what he wanted he might just go ahead and make a separate peace with Japan, and where would that leave the then hard-pressed United States? Whatever Chiang might or might not do was hardly a high-priority consideration in Washington. The war in Europe against the Axis stood first, and then came General MacArthur and Admiral Chester W. Nimitz, both starting to battle the Japanese—

and often each other—for control of the Pacific. The CBI, however, could not be overlooked. There were the British to worry about, with their stake in Burma and India, and under optimum conditions the Chinese were at least theoretically capable of keeping a lot of Japanese occupied in China who might otherwise have been fighting elsewhere.

Gauss and Vincent had been so depressed by Chiang's intransigence that they skipped H. H. Kung's New Year's Eve party. It turned out that the Generalissimo had a perhaps better reading of Washington's frame of mind than did the two Americans in Chungking. Chiang did not get everything he wanted, but he got a half billion, no strings attached.

Davies left Washington for Asia on February 25. He was to work mainly out of Stilwell's Indian headquarters, at New Delhi. It was not long before Stilwell began looking around for additional civilian assistants. One of the myths propagated by the China Lobby and its adherents was that John Service was whispering into General Stilwell's ear practically from the start. In fact, both Service and Ludden did not join Stilwell's staff until the summer of 1943, more than a year after the general embarked on his new job. Even after Service went to work for Stilwell, the two men—the one had graduated from West Point five years before the other was born —were, though friendly, far from intimate; Stilwell spent little time at his Chungking headquarters, where Service was based, and when the General did turn up there some of his assistants shared his quarters, but not Service. He did not even attend Stilwell's staff meetings.

Inasmuch as Stilwell's principal enemy, in his own logical view, was Japan, the general, who received a third star when he went to Asia, thought it would make sense to have an expert on Japanese affairs on his advisory staff. Davies proposed John Emmerson, and arrangements were shortly made to have the army borrow him from the State Department. Emmerson turned out to be in Lima, Peru, where he had begun to think he'd be a long time in ever getting back to any part of Asia. During the furor that accompanied the internment of Japanese on the West Coast of the United States, somebody in Washington remembered that there were some thirty thousand Japanese in Peru. Imported years earlier as indentured laborers for cotton plantations, some of them had saved their pay and opened *bodegas* and *cantinas*, which had incurred for them, among Peruvians, the same kind of resentment that many East Africans traditionally felt for Indian shopkeepers in their midst.

When Peru declared war on the Axis nations, the Japanese became enemy aliens and the South Americans had a chance to settle old scores.

This was calculated not to set well with the Japanese, and Washington believed that the American embassy in Lima should have a Japanese-speaking man around to be on the lookout for sabotage and espionage. (There were sixteen FBI agents already on hand, called "legal attachés," but none could speak Japanese.) So Emmerson had been dispatched south. He could discover no seditious behavior on the part of any of the Japanese in Peru—partly because the thousand or so purportedly most dangerous ones had already been rounded up and shipped to internment camps in the United States—but he figured he'd probably be stuck down there for the remainder of the war; he was beginning to have second thoughts about having abandoned his career as a French teacher. There was nothing intrinsically wrong with Spanish, but it was by now, after all, his fourth language. While he was earnestly applying himself to quadrilinguality, he was ordered to prepare to join Stilwell in Asia.[1]

Perhaps Stilwell, outspoken and impatient, was not the ideal choice for China. He had a generally low opinion of Chiang Kai-shek, and the feeling was mutual; as far back as 1938 the Generalissimo had declined to talk to him. But as the head of any state can refuse to accept an ambassador tentatively designated to serve in his country, so could Chiang doubtless have vetoed Stilwell's appointment; that he chose not to was, in the retrospective view of Everett Drumright, whom he did later accept as an envoy, a gesture of gracious accommodation to Franklin Roosevelt.

From the larger American point of view, in any event, Stilwell seemed a logical choice for the CBI command. Whatever his sentiments toward Chiang, he knew and loved China and its people, he knew the terrain and the language, and he was a senior officer of proven capability and responsibility. Moreover, General Marshall was behind him, and the fact that Marshall himself had done a tour in China lent further weight to *his* views. The Chinese aspect of the three-way job seemed, early in 1942, a not overly complicated one. It was, basically, to get as many Chinese as possible, politics notwithstanding, to engage as many Japanese as possible in battle. Stilwell visualized the role of the Americans under him as chiefly one of training Nationalist Chinese soldiers, who by nearly all accounts could stand any amount of improvement in skills, supplies, and morale;

---

[1] All four of the Foreign Service officers assigned to Stilwell were subsequently accused of exercising a baleful influence over him. John Davies was the only one, in fact, who had any kind of regular—though benign—access to the general; Emmerson only laid eyes on Stilwell three times while under his jurisdiction.

it was characteristic of him that early on he issued a directive that all officers and enlisted men working directly with Chinese counterparts should at least try to learn their language.

Stilwell had precious few ground troops of his own, nor could he realistically hope to receive any consequential numbers of them while the war in Europe was on. There were too many higher-priority manpower demands from too many higher-priority theaters of operation. And what American air strength there was in China when he arrived was notably independent of him. It was the private fiefdom of a crusty, crafty fighter pilot, Claire Chennault, who had been retired from the army air corps for deafness in 1936. As Douglas MacArthur, upon his first retirement from the American army, had found a professional haven in the Philippines, so did Chennault, in 1937, gladly become Chiang Kai-shek's chief aerial adviser. On July 4, 1942, he was welcomed back into United States uniform. He had retired as a captain and was now a brigadier general, but it was evident all along that in his particular chain of command there was only one link that counted—the one attaching him to Chiang Kai-shek. When John Davies flew to Asia early in 1942, among the messages he carried was one from Roosevelt's then principal adviser on Chinese affairs, Lauchlin Currie, expressing the hope that Chennault would cooperate with General H. H. Arnold, the overall American air commander. General Arnold eventually made a personal reconnaissance of China in February 1943 and concluded that it would be almost impossible to fly in everything that Chennault said he needed to defeat the Japanese.

Back under Washington's jurisdiction, Chennault became commander of the United States Fourteenth Air Force, but he continued to operate in maverick fashion. He himself would complain of the strange setup at Stilwell's headquarters; he once said that Stilwell had his own foreign policy, with John Davies officiating as his secretary of state. Chennault's operation, though, was equally peculiar. For one thing, unlike most generals fairly far down the chain of command, he enjoyed direct access to President Roosevelt, with whom, from Chennault's headquarters in Kunming, the general would exchange letters that he did not bother to forward through conventional military channels. "My men have worked miracles," Chennault once wrote the president. (In their accomplishments, his men were notably abetted by Chiang Kai-shek, whose response to requests from Chennault was, by contrast to those from Stilwell, miraculous. If Chennault told the Generalissimo he needed three new air fields and had to have them built within two months, he could usually count on getting them.) In just about every exchange, Chennault would urge upon Roosevelt his passionate belief that, Stilwell's concerns on the ground notwithstanding, the war against the Japanese in China could be best waged in the air.

In 1948, long after the Japanese had surrendered and not long before Chiang Kai-shek's own military downfall, Chennault enthusiastically supported the last-ditch proposal that twenty thousand American *ground* troops be sent to China to try to salvage the sinking Nationalist government. But earlier the veteran pilot, like so many others involved in the tangle of China, had felt that some sort of rapprochement between the Nationalists and the Communists was essential. He had written Roosevelt on September 21, 1944, for instance, saying he favored "thorough political reconstruction at Chungking, followed by true unification between Chungking and Yenan. Only in that way can we insure a strong, united, and above all, independent China, such as our interests in the Pacific require."

The persuasiveness and eloquence of many of Chennault's wartime messages to Roosevelt was attributable in part to his having a gifted amanuensis, Joseph W. Alsop, who, though a mere captain in the armed forces, also enjoyed direct access to his distant commander-in-chief. Captain Alsop would now and then journey from Kunming to Chungking to share his views with the top embassy people there; John Service recalled that one time Alsop cheerfully proposed that American generals who—like Stilwell—didn't share his views be drawn and quartered, and also flogged, which for a talented writer seemed a mite tautological. Yet Alsop's loyalty to Chennault and antipathy to Stilwell were more strategic than ideological; the writer declared after the war that while he felt that Stilwell, Davies, and Service had contributed to the loss of China, they were nonetheless "passionately loyal but mistaken Americans."[2]

Stilwell, preoccupied with the arduous land war in Burma for much of his early months in the CBI theater, did not spend too much time in China himself. Chungking was a headquarters town, and he was not a headquarters man. He had comfortable enough quarters there—he had

---

[2] In January 1950 Alsop contributed a three-part why-we-lost-China article to the *Saturday Evening Post* in which the Old China Hands were rather severely taken to task. But when the men he had criticized came under further attack for being allegedly soft on communism, he sprang to their defense. Somewhere along the line all three acerb articles were ripped out—conceivably, in contrition, by the author himself—of the bound volumes of the *Post* at the New York Public Library.

been given a house belonging to T. V. Soong, one of the Generalissimo's high-powered brothers-in-law—but he found the atmosphere starchy and frustrating; he preferred to be in New Delhi or in the bush.

And, of course, the more time he spent in Chungking the more personal contact he was bound to have with Chiang Kai-shek, for whom, among a number of other concurrent titles, Stilwell had been designated chief of staff. The longstanding hostility between the two men has already been mentioned; hardly ever did either one have a good word for the other. Nevertheless, in a 1942 *Handbook on China* distributed by Stilwell's headquarters to his troops (John Davies was instrumental in preparing it), a section on the government of China was, though grammatically impeachable, markedly deferential toward the Generalissimo. It said, "The National Military Council is often spoken of as the Military Affairs Commission. It exercises absolute control over the armies and citizens in time of war. Its chairman, Chiang Kai-shek, is Commander-in-Chief of all China's armed forces. As Director-General of the Kuomintang Party and Chairman of the Supreme National Defense Council as well as the National Military Council one can see what an important official he is." When Theodore H. White, for instance, once asked Stilwell for an explanation of the debacle his meager forces had undergone in Burma, the general replied, "We are allied to an ignorant, illiterate, peasant son of a bitch called Chiang Kai-shek." Chiang, of course, was familiar with Stilwell's low opinion cf his character and capabilities, and his view of the American was not dissimilar. A few of the Generalissimo's own partisans, in their versions of the period when the two antagonists were thrown together, have subsequently ascribed to Chiang a defensive reason for his attitude toward Stilwell; they have asserted that the Generalissimo believed the general had it in mind from time to time to have him assassinated.

For the first few months of 1942, one of the principal Allied goals in the Pacific was itself defensive—this being merely to stop the series of Japanese conquests before they became overwhelming. MacArthur had dramatically vowed he would return to the Philippines, but long before he could even start thinking about that he had to concentrate on stopping the Japanese advance in Papua, New Guinea, lest otherwise Australia soon be engorged in the Greater East Asia Coprosperity Sphere. In China Stilwell's modest aim was to nibble away at the Japanese wherever he could make contact with them with whatever resources he could muster.

The Americans in China were momentarily cheered by the Doolittle raid on Tokyo in April 1942, but their elation was to be short-lived. In retaliation, the Japanese overran a large Nationalist air base at Chuchou, in the northeastern province of Chekiang, Chiang's very home province; according to Chennault's headquarters, a quarter of a million Chinese died in that avenging attack.[3]

That was only one of the disastrous aftermaths of the raid. All of the sixteen B-25s under Doolittle were to have flown to China after dropping their bombs on Tokyo and to have joined Chennault's slim fleet of aircraft; not a single one of the planes reached its Chinese destination. And what planes did get through at other times did not always help much. In 1943, for instance, the United States sent Chiang Kai-shek thirty A-29s for the use of his Nationalist air force. Eighteen months later, James Penfield, in Chengtu, checked up on the twenty that had arrived. They had been used for only two or three missions apiece; but even so, only twelve remained and five of those had been converted into transports.

On the diplomatic front that April there had also been activity. John Davies, for instance, had delivered a pair of shoes to Mme. Chiang Kai-shek, for which he would later have to answer questions. There was nothing sinister about the gift or the recipient, but the donor back home had been Mme. Chiang's old friend, Mrs. Owen Lattimore. A few weeks later John Carter Vincent would get even more complexly involved with the Soong sisters. He had dinner with the Madame at the home of her sister, Mme. Sun Yat-sen; the third famous sister, Mme. H. H. Kung, was also present. "I am literally encompassed by Soong sisters," Vincent wrote home. The fact that Vincent was at all acquainted with Mme. Sun would later be held against him by his inquisitors, who were not put off by the fact that the evening at her home had been largely devoted to playing bridge and that at the dinner table, as it happened, the American had sat not where he could exchange conspiratorial confidences, if any, with the suspect Soong, but had been sandwiched between her two unexceptionable sisters.

[3]David Barrett, by this time a colonel, went to Chuchou afterward to evaluate the Japanese assault and concluded that the Chinese on the scene had put up feeble resistance. The pro-Chiang historian Chintung Liang, on the other hand, has argued that the United States was so tardy in notifying Chiang that the Doolittle raid was to take place that he had no time adequately to protect the air base, which he suspected would be attacked; and that when he asked that Doolittle's planes be held back until he could beef up his forces at Chuchou, his request was denied.

At another dinner at that time, Mme. Chiang told Vincent how much she admired Claire Chennault and suggested that if Vincent had any confidential communications he wished to send back to Washington without going through all the bother of using diplomatic channels, why didn't he just send them through her? She may have been twitting him. The Nationalist Chinese knew just about everything the Americans were up to anyway. On June 5, 1943, when John Davies was back in the States, he ran into T. V. Soong, who told him, "There are no secrets in Washington. Rest assured, Mr. Davies, that no conference takes place regarding which I do not have accurate and complete information."

Vincent, in any event, did not succumb to Mme. Chiang's blandishments. Instead, the following month he notified Secretary of State Hull, through conventional channels, that the United States should not become overly concerned about the Generalissimo's threats to pull out of the war if his requests—in this instance, for three American combat divisions operating out of India, for five hundred more combat aircraft, and for five thousand tons of airlifted supplies a month over the Himalayas—were not granted; he also counseled that "assistance should not be given because of a fear that the failure to do so would result in the Chinese authorities' ceasing resistance and making peace with Japan."

Vincent was working for Ambassador Gauss, Davies for General Stilwell. In that capacity Davies three times visited Chou En-lai in the early summer of 1942; the thrust of Chou's remarks to him was that the Chinese Communists were ready to fight the Japanese and that the Communist leaders would welcome official American representatives at their headquarters up in Yenan. Gauss was getting copies of the memoranda written by Davies, who regarded himself as "a thin binding tie" between the ambassador and Stilwell, but Gauss wasn't especially happy about the arrangement whereby one of his most reliable political reporters was not directly responsible to him.

The ambassador did not even have Service at his immediate beck. This must have represented a considerable loss to Gauss, for in an efficiency report he prepared about Service at that time he declared, "Mr. Service in my opinion is one of the best equipped and most able of the younger officers of the service; head and shoulders over most of his colleagues of equal seniority in the service. I could ask for no more efficient or satisfactory staff officer. He is the outstanding younger officer who served with me over my thirty-six years of service. I rate him: Excellent."

Unaware at the time of this head-turning encomium, and oblivious of the verbal skirmishing that was going on in China far from any formal battlefields, Service was doing the kind of thing he fancied and to which he would indeed devote about half his four wartime years. He was ranging far into the Chinese countryside, seeking information that might be useful to the policy-makers superior to him. On one such expedition, not long after Pearl Harbor, he had been dispatched to Rangoon to pick up a new car for the embassy and drive it back to Chungking before the Japanese cut off all overland routes. Having a car to drive, even one way, had been an unaccustomed luxury for Service. He had habitually got around as a "yellow fish"—someone who cadged rides (after haggling over the price) from truck drivers. Service carried a sleeping bag with him during these times and put up at small Chinese inns, sharing the bedbugs with the indigenes and subsisting, if necessary, on dried garlic and hot steamed bread, which were sometimes the only food available. "Jack had uncanny instincts," said one junior diplomat who often observed him in action. "He could walk along a Chinese street and by the kind of matches sold or clothing worn or food being cooked could analyze the structure of the local society."

Midway through 1942 Service was sent to Lanchow, in the northwestern province of Kansu. Lying between the snowcapped mountains of Tibet and the Gobi Desert of Mongolia, Lanchow had been an historic stopping place for the camel caravans that plied the old east-west silk route. It was still a trading mart of consequence, and the United States had no idea what sort of stuff the Russians might be shipping in in exchange for the sheepskins and tea that the Chinese had traditionally shipped out.[4] No Foreign Service officer had been there since China and Japan had gone to war. Now an opportunity presented itself for a firsthand look. There had been an oil strike in the area, and the Chinese govern-

[4]Lanchow was far removed from the outside world in time and space and comprehension. While Edward Rice was United States consul there in April 1944, in the midst of a war characterized in so many other areas by austerity, a Chinese provincial official treated him to an eighteen-course meal, including fourteen meat courses. The host said merrily that he doubted the Germans ate as well. Rice said he doubted any Americans did, then, either. "But America is largely an agricultural country," the host replied. The social life at Lanchow was on such a scale that after leaving there Rice never again drank vodka. He had consumed what he judged to be a lifetime's quota in drinking bouts with the resident Soviet consul general, a man of high competitive bent. Rice scored his most memorable victory when on one occasion his tottering rival offered to send him home in a waiting limousine. Rice had the triumphant last word. "I'll take my bicycle," he said. "Only Communists can afford limousines."

ment was sending a party of engineers northwest. Having some vague notion that the United States might be disposed to fly in a batch of modern refinery equipment, piece by piece, across the Himalayas, Chiang's government invited the American embassy to send an emissary along. Yellow-fish Service seemed a logical choice. He was delighted, not knowing much about petroleum products but feeling he could learn something about political conditions in that remote and often troubled corner of the country.

Although the Yellow River flowed through Lanchow, it was an arid place. There were practically no trees, and the residents customarily used rafts made of skins; they would be inflated to float with the river as it coursed northward, then deflated and hand-carried back south. Because of the shortage of wood, the oil flow was being captured in earthen reservoirs dug below the wells. (As wary as prospectors anywhere of disclosing too much about their treasure, the Chinese at Lanchow confiscated all cameras; Service was able to come up with a fairly accurate map of the area by counting and memorizing his footsteps as he walked from point to point.) Awakened one night by a rainstorm while sleeping in an earth-walled schoolhouse still further downhill from the reservoirs, Service wandered outside, looked uphill, and saw a stream of fire. The rain had crumbled the earth dams, and oil had flowed into some workers' shelters and had been ignited by their wood fires. Now it was pouring ablaze down a drainage ditch that led to the schoolyard. Service sounded the alarm in his loudest and most urgent Szechwanese, and the engineers just barely made it away safely to higher ground.

Service then journeyed eastward on beyond Chungking, to Loyang in the Honan province, where there was a severe famine. Its consequences would, naturally, affect Chinese manpower and Chinese military potential. Among other observers of that dire scene was Thomas M. Megan, a Catholic missionary from Iowa who, in the topsy-turvy world that was China during the war, would later find himself a brigadier general on Chiang's intelligence staff.[5] He had impressed the Kuomintang when,

[5]The Generalissimo was generous in dispensing high rank to foreigners whose services pleased him. He conferred a major generalship upon an American procurement officer, Burton E. Vaughan, who was a mere colonel in his own army, as Megan was a mere bishop in his. Vaughan's promotion stemmed from the circumstance that he was handling rations for thirty-nine Chinese divisions being supplied by the United States. Inasmuch as his principal Chinese assistant was a brigadier general, he had to be given two-star rank to save military face all around.

after being trapped at his previous post by the Japanese, he calmly made his way through enemy lines on a bicycle.

Some of the suffering that Service witnessed he was soon able to discuss, back in Chungking in November, with John Carter Vincent and Chou En-lai. For the Americans, a meeting with Chou, while usually productive of some illumination about Communist thinking, was by now fairly routine and on the whole less eventful than a trip out of town; but this time Chou had with him Lin Piao, who had recently been posted to the capital to help try to work out some kind of accommodation between Mao and Chiang. Service came away from the meeting more worried than ever that China was less likely to experience rapprochement than rebellion. He reported soon afterward:

> It is now no longer wondered whether civil war can be avoided, but rather whether it can be delayed at least until after a victory over Japan. . . . Even if a conflict is averted, the continuance or, as is probable in such an event, the worsening of the already serious economic strains within the country may result in economic collapse. If there is civil war, the likelihood of such an economic collapse is of course greater.
>
> There is also the possibility that economic difficulties may make the war-weary, overconscripted and overtaxed farmers fertile ground for Communist propaganda and thus bring about a revolution going beyond the moderate democracy which the Chinese Communists now claim to be seeking. Such a Communist government would probably not be democratic in the American sense. And it is probable, even if the United States did not incur the enmity of the Communists for alleged material or diplomatic support of the Kuomintang, that this Communist government would be more inclined toward friendship and cooperation with Russia than with Great Britain and America.
>
> For these reasons it would therefore appear to be in the interest of the United States to make efforts to prevent a deterioration of the internal political situation in China and, if possible, to bring about an improvement.
>
> The Communists themselves (Chou En-lai and Lin Piao in a conversation with John Carter Vincent and the undersigned . . .) consider that foreign influence (obviously American) with the Kuomintang is the only force that may be able to improve the situation. They admit the difficulty of successful foreign suggestions regarding China's internal affairs, no matter how tactfully made. But they believe that the reflection of a better-informed foreign opinion, official and public, would have some effect on the more far-sighted elements of leadership in the Kuomintang, such as the Generalissimo.

Service was in Washington late in January 1943 when he delivered himself of these and other views. He had been summoned home because Washington had had little contact with anyone who had lately been out in the Chinese hustings; in fact, no Foreign Service officer had been back from Chungking for consultation since before Pearl Harbor. As soon as he reached Washington, he was asked by, among others, General William J. Donovan, the head of the Office of Strategic Services, to write the memo and to put in it his overall assessment of the Chinese political scene. In it he also said that some *non*-Communist Chinese of his acquaintance, among them "the nephew of the well-known late editor of the *Ta Kung Pao*," considered "the likelihood of civil war the greatest problem facing China." It might be helpful, Service added, if the United States could persuade Chiang to let American observers visit Mao's secluded headquarters at Yenan. Up to then, the only Americans to go there had been a few correspondents, and while secondhand information relayed by journalists was always useful, Service felt that most who had made the trip "appear to have a bias favorable to the Communists." He added, "I suggest that the American representatives best suited to visit the Communist area are Foreign Service officers of the China language service. One or two men might be sent. They should combine moderately long-term residence at Yenan or its vicinity with fairly extensive travel in the guerrilla area. It is important that they not be required to base a report on a brief visit during which they would be under the influence of official guides. . . ."

It was characteristic of Service to use the first person singular. Unlike some other China Hands, who carefully couched their observations and opinions in the third person, he had no compunctions about identifying himself as the source of a fact or an interpretation. Accordingly, when it later became fashionable for people seeking explanations of what had gone wrong in China to seek scapegoats as well, it was easy to focus on him; there was no doubt of his involvement.

At the time that Service wrote that memorandum about Yenan, nobody objected strenuously to it except Stanley Hornbeck, who was then a senior advisor to the State Department on Far Eastern affairs and then and always had a bureaucratic fondness for the status quo. Service's report, as it happened, was submitted on the eve of the Casablanca Conference, and most of the decision-makers in Washington were far too preoccupied with that potentially momentous gathering to care much what a single thirty-year-old Foreign Service officer thought about the Chinese Communists one way or another. But Hornbeck, among others, cared, and his reaction was practically apoplectic. In 1971, reflecting on how the document he had composed twenty-eight years earlier had been received, Service would write, "It is almost laughable, after intervening events, to recall the waves of consternation and disapproval that were caused by this memorandum. . . . My views were dismissed as rash, exaggerated, and 'immature.' "

Although certain twentieth-century presidents of the United States have tended to use football metaphors to describe great affairs of state, none have been publicly fond of the old standby, "When in doubt, punt." Franklin Roosevelt preferred the lateral pass. On being confronted with a difficult situation abroad, he liked to avoid meeting it head on through his formally designated agents—an ambassador or military commander; rather, he would send a special emissary, whose function presumably was to cut through red tape but who often ended up ensnarling all existing lines of communication.

Few senior American officials abroad had to cope with as many Roosevelt legates as did Ambassador Gauss and General Stilwell. In July 1942, for instance, the same month in which Mme. Chiang Kai-shek told a surprised Stilwell that she and her husband, apparently intending to bypass conventional American military channels, would see to it that he got the fourth star of a full general, Roosevelt sent Lauchlin Currie, a confusing personage even at home, to China as a special envoy.[6] Currie's advice to Roosevelt on returning to Washington was to get rid of Gauss, Stilwell, and T. V. Soong all at once—a sort of standoff, inasmuch as the president had no more direct authority to demote Chiang's brother-in-law than Chiang had to promote Roosevelt's general-in-charge.

But Currie at least had by then become a fairly familiar figure in China and was as conversant with what was going on there as anybody around the White House. The arrival in October of another Roosevelt emissary was something else again. This one was Wendell Willkie, who knew nothing about China but was immersed in a course of self-education in one-worldliness. As was so often the case where China was involved,

[6]An economist born in Nova Scotia, Currie had a Ph.D. from Harvard and taught there briefly before the war. He moved up through various government jobs into the White House, and after the war was accused of having had a malign, left-wing influence there. Eventually, he left the country for South America.

domestic American politics was a prime consideration in the Willkie mission; Roosevelt, concerned about solid backing for his conduct of the war and with the possibility of running for a fourth term already looming, was trying to get in the good graces, or at least blunt the sharp opposition, of the man from whom he had wrested his third term. Willkie, that strange amalgam of Indiana rusticity and corporate finance, had never been to China before, and he was overwhelmed by it. He particularly enjoyed a street demonstration that the Kuomintang carefully staged for him in Sian on October 10, 1942—Double-Tenth Day (the tenth day of the tenth month), the Chinese equivalent of the Fourth of July; Willkie thought the outpouring was spontaneous. He was no less overwhelmed in Chungking by Mme. Chiang Kai-shek.

Ambassador Gauss, who was understandably sensitive about his position and the prerogatives that went with it, felt from the moment of Willkie's arrival that this transient representative of Roosevelt wasn't paying due deference to the president's *in situ* one. So he pretty well ignored Willkie, and let the peregrinating plenipotentiary be escorted around by Philip Sprouse and Colonel Barrett. It fell to Vincent to usher the visitor to the principal audience arranged for him with Chiang Kai-shek. Willkie may or may not have been briefed beforehand on what some of the Foreign Service officers on the scene had been reporting at every opportunity: Vincent's assertion to Gauss, for instance, three months earlier, that "the Kuomintang is a congeries of conservative political cliques whose only common denominator and common objective is desire to maintain the Kuomintang in control of the Government." But he had been told that the Generalissimo knew no English. Willkie spent most of his time flirting in that language with Mme. Chiang, who was usually present on such ritual occasions. While Vincent, who had no clear idea why Willkie was out there in the first place, was trying to explain to the eminent husband what the call was all about, Willkie was murmuring into the eminent wife's attentive ear.

Vincent said afterward that the only tangible result of the Willkie mission—aside from his having kissed a few Chinese babies, perhaps under the impression that he would soon be running for world office— was that a bicycle store had impulsively renamed itself the Willkie Shop. (Another result was that Mme. Chiang took off for the United States the next month and didn't return to China until the following July.) When his *One World* was published shortly thereafter, Willkie burbled in it, "Military China is united; its leaders are trained and able generals; its new armies are tough, fighting organizations of men who know both what they are fighting for and how to fight for it. . . . [T]his is truly a people's war." (Paying some belated attention to Mme. Chiang's husband, Willkie described him as scholarly, reflective, poised, and sincere.) This was, of course, almost exactly the opposite of what the experienced Foreign Service officers had been reporting to the home folks. The trouble was that while not even many people in the State Department were bothering to read what the diplomats wrote, practically everybody in the country was reading *One World.*

As the war progressed, there was considerable travel back and forth between the United States and China. In August 1943, for instance, Generals Stilwell and Chennault were both in Washington conferring with General Marshall; according to General Wedemeyer, who was also present, Chennault described Chiang Kai-shek to the chief of staff as a great democratic leader, a devout Christian, and a man of absolute integrity, whereas Stilwell characterized him as an arrogant, untrustworthy member of the coolie class. How hard to be chief of staff and receive two such diverse appraisals of the same person from two high-ranking field commanders!

John Service, meanwhile, accompanied by Arthur Ringwalt, had returned to China, taking the long way there across Africa and Asia. At the embassy in Chungking, Service was pleased at the appearance of an old friend and missionary son, Robert Barnett,[7] who had come up from Kunming. Not yet in the Foreign Service, Barnett, after working in China early in the war for United China Relief, had been commissioned in the air force and assigned to Chennault's headquarters as a combat intelligence officer. Now, in the fall of 1943, Chennault was anticipating an acceleration of his aerial war and an influx of men, and he had instructed Barnett to prepare a tract called *An Orientation Booklet for United States Military Personnel in China.* There was one chapter in it on the political scene, in which, to avoid giving offense to anyone at all connected with that scene, Barnett had dwelt largely upon Sun Yat-sen and his three principles of San Min Chu I (Nationalism, Democracy, and People's Livelihood), which just about everybody in China professed to be in favor of. The text was approved by Chennault and his staff, and then by Stilwell's G-2, but the military thought the embassy should look it over as well, and that had brought Barnett to Service's office in Chungking.

[7]His father had been head of the YMCA in China.

What amused Barnett about the visit, in the light of subsequent allegations of pro-communism against Service, was that when the Foreign Service officer read his manuscript, already endorsed by the archconservative Chennault, he suggested that certain passages in the bland political chapter be amended or deleted because they could be interpreted as alluding too favorably to the Chinese Communists.[8]

In May of that year John Carter Vincent, who had been in China for twenty-four months, returned to Washington to serve under Stanley Hornbeck. It cannot have been the most congenial of associations, if the recollections of Alfred Kohlberg are to be believed; Vincent largely admired the Foreign Service officers who were reporting from abroad to him at the State Department, but Hornbeck said of them at that time, according to the importer, "When I see the people that this Department is sending to China, I shake in my shoes."

The men were scattered all over the giant distant country. Everett Drumright, who probably did not give Hornbeck tremors, was in Sian—the only American, except for a handful of missionaries, in that ancient inland city. Arthur Ringwalt and Richard Service were manning the consulate at Kweilin. For a while the only quarters they could find were in a rundown hotel. They had one bathtub and would take turns every sweltering afternoon sitting in it to cool off. The Chinese had an outdoor movie screen that practically touched their window; they saw Chaplin's *Great Dictator*, in reverse, every night for a couple of weeks.

The place was also overrun with rats, but Service resourcefully rigged up a contraption, fashioned from a dry-cell battery and some wires, that shocked their whiskers whenever they started through the principal rathole in the consuls' room. After a bit, the two men found an apartment that was more comfortable, and there they gave a banquet one night for Chiang Ching-kuo, the Generalissimo's son and presumptive successor, who was passing through Kweilin.

It was perhaps inevitable during a war, when practically each day

[8]When Barnett was ultimately called up before the McCarran committee and asked the usual questions about what he had done and whom he had seen in China on such and such a day years earlier, he confounded his questioners by giving crisp, explicit replies. What they did not know was that he had written his wife a letter every single day he was abroad, detailing his activities, and that she had saved the correspondence. "These sessions were generally Dostoyevskian attacks not only on a man's mind but also his memory," Barnett said. "I was lucky enough to be able to throw their whole absurd scenario back at them."

brought a new crisis and everything had to be done in a hurry, that a proliferation of government agencies and agents should arise. Secretary of State Hull wondered once if Gauss couldn't do something about coordinating all those in China. There were a dozen or more different United States organizations represented in Kweilin, for example—the Treasury, the Office of War Information, the Office of Strategic Services, the armed forces, and whatnot—all of whose operatives were scrambling about seeking intelligence, to the despair of the Foreign Service professionals. When Ringwalt went to talk to one Chinese about tungsten ore, the fellow said he had no time for him; he had already been interviewed exhaustively on that score by a couple of Americans representing something or other and had no more to say on the subject. There was one army man around, a former shoe salesman, who let it be known that he thought Ringwalt and Service should leave all political reporting up to him. They were not much pleased with that, but they could not help admiring his acrobatic social graces; he had the knack of being able to squeeze himself through a wire coat hanger.

James Penfield was also back in Asia, having been reassigned from Greenland and having made his way to China via the Trans-Siberian railway. His new post was Chengtu, where Davies and Service had been raised. The Szechwanese provincial capital was then bustling with wartime activity. Hundreds of thousands of coolies were constructing B-29 bases for General Curtis LeMay, along with three supporting fighter-plane fields. Penfield was, among other things, supposed to keep tabs on the local warlords who—John Davies's mother's earlier pacifying efforts notwithstanding—were still aggressively in business; they would come around to his residence at night to cajole American arms, with which, they assured him, they would speedily dispose of the Communists and, when it came to that, of the Nationalists to boot.[9]

On his way to Chengtu, Penfield stopped off at the farflung northwest

---

[9]When Penfield left Chengtu, he was succeeded as consul by Richard Service, who had to evacuate Kweilin in September 1944 when the Japanese took it over. It was the first time that Service, then thirty-one, had been back to his boyhood home in twenty-five years. He was pleased to find that one of the three resident warlords, Marshal Teng Hsi-hou, remembered his father and felt hospitable toward the missionary's son. Marshal Teng had a problem. His life had been saved not long before by an American air force surgeon, who had warned him that if he ever took another drink no medical skills of any origin could help. For a high-ranking Chinese military man not to drink was socially difficult, if not impossible; the only solution was to appoint a surrogate drinker to take one's place and swap one's toasts. The marshal elected to confer this high honor on Dick Service.

outpost of Urumchi (also known as Tihwa), in the province of Sinkiang, where Edmund Clubb was holed up—the only American in a region of 500,000 square miles. Urumchi was within the borders of China, but 90 per cent of its population was non-Chinese—mostly Turki. There were two minority groups, Chinese and Russian, and since Clubb knew both languages, it was a logical spot for him to be in. He had had some difficulty getting there, however. The area had not long before switched from domination by a then Soviet-leaning warlord to Nationalist control, and Chiang Kai-shek's finance people were flooding it with their own currency; Clubb was bumped off his scheduled flight by a load of banknotes. He finally got through by hitching rides on trucks along a route that had been set up between China and the Soviet Union as part of their 1937 treaty of friendship. One truck he was yellow-fishing on had run out of water in the middle of the Taklamakan Desert. Penfield was touched by the intellectual Clubb's earnestness; in the best *mens-sana-in-corpore-sano* tradition, he was trying to keep fit by exercising at 5:00 a.m. every morning on some parallel bars in his backyard, but, in the long run, it was to no avail. Clubb had to be evacuated the following December with an aggravated case of dysentery.

Clubb had a very special warlord to deal with at Urumchi—the legendary Sheng Shih Ts'ai, a Manchurian soldier who had seized power there in 1933, not long after a regional White Russian coup. Sheng had imprisoned *its* leader and in 1935 made a deal with the Soviet Union. It provided him with arms and money; he in turn adopted a six-pointed red star as his regional emblem and put his political enemies of the moment on trial as Trotskyites. Once he even joined the Soviet Communist party. In a ten-year reign he was estimated to have imprisoned one hundred thousand of his neighbors. Any American there had to be extremely circumspect about his associations, for anybody he talked to on the street might come under suspicion of disloyalty to Sheng and be imprisoned or tortured or both as a result.

Early in Sheng's rule there had been Russian policemen and agronomists and mining engineers and medical advisers swarming all over Urumchi. But when the Nazis attacked Stalingrad, Sheng decided the Russians had had it and he began to shift his allegiance to Chiang Kai-shek. (He never had much to do with the Chinese Communists at all.) Then after Stalingrad held, he started to shift back, but the Russians pulled most of their people out of his bailiwick and he reversed tracks again. By the time he irrevocably threw in his lot with Chiang, his followers were so accustomed to being on the side of the Russians, or just plain confused, that they objected and revolted; Sheng, his fiercely beating wings sorely clipped, ended up as a functionary in the Ministry of Forestry and Agriculture in Chungking.

The following year John Service would get involved in the bizarre political situation out in Sinkiang. The Nationalists, as if they didn't have a war with Japan on their hands, sent several infantry divisions there, conceivably to take over Tibet or Outer Mongolia, conceivably to cow the Kazakhs who lived on both sides of the Mongolian-Chinese border. There was some skirmishing between the Chinese forces and the Kazakhs, who were thought to be under Soviet domination. Asked to analyze the conflict from back in Chungking, Service strongly advised that the United States, whatever else it did, steer clear of it and, when it came to that, of all matters affecting relations between the Russians and the Nationalist government. "Neither now, nor in the immediately foreseeable future," he reported on April 7, 1944, "does the United States want to find itself in direct opposition to Russia in Asia; nor does it want to see Russia have undisputed dominance over a part or all of China. The best way to cause both of these possibilities to become realities is to give, in either fact or appearance, support to the present reactionary government of China beyond carefully regulated and controlled aid directed solely toward the military prosecution of the war against Japan." Seven years later, the Internal Security Subcommittee of the United States Senate used this memorandum to try to demonstrate that Service was issuing a warning to America "that she had better see what Russia wanted in Asia and go along with Russia's desires rather than what was well for America or the world."

General Sheng did not exactly roll out a red carpet for Clubb. When the American reached Urumchi, the warlord said he had received no advance word that anyone was coming to establish a consulate and would require some official communication to that effect before he would decide whether or not to recognize Clubb's presence. Clubb had been unfazed by the Japanese at Hanoi in 1941, and he was not disposed to bow to a petty tyrant. "It doesn't matter whether you have confirmation of my presence or not," he stiffly informed Sheng. "Where I am, the consulate is." It was a lonely consulate. Clubb had a local watchman, a cook, and a messenger; that was his entire staff. His safe consisted of a leather box his wife had made for him years earlier in Peking. He did his own typing, a not inconsiderable task, inasmuch as he averaged close to ten reports a month. Since he never knew when the next plane might be coming along, he dispatched most of his prose by telegraph. There was plenty to report on; it had been the American hope that supplies for China, instead of having to be flown over the Hump, could be shipped from the Soviet Union by way of Urumchi, and it was important to know which way at any moment the volatile warlord might be leaning.

As Clubb was diligently churning out intelligence from Urumchi, so were his Foreign Service colleagues submitting reports from other parts of China, nearly all of them emphasizing the need for internal changes to expedite the war against Japan:

Ringwalt from Kweilin:

> As far as the Chinese are concerned, the Nationalist military appear to be only too pleased to continue the truce [with the Japanese] indefinitely, as they control the [smuggling] trade with occupied territory and are growing comfortably rich.

John Service from Chungking, quoting a reporter on the staff of *Ta Kung Pao:*

> A first essential of a real effort to continue the struggle against Japan and improve conditions in the country is resurrection of the United Front, cooperation with the Communists and utilization of Communist methods of mass mobilization coupled with better economic controls. But this is a hurdle which the unrelenting anti-Communist leaders of the present government can never get over.[10]

Drumright from Sian, lamenting that the Nationalist armies didn't seem to be able to organize the local people so they could live off them:

> The Chinese Communists have been able to, hence they continue to operate in north China. . . . There are no indications that the Chinese are capable or desirous of offensive operations against the Japanese in north China. The Chinese strategy is entirely defensive in character; in spirit and morale the Chinese soldier is absolutely defense-minded without any conception of offen-

[10]As Foreign Service officers often got information from journalists, so, reciprocally, did they often provide it to them. *Ta Kung Pao* had not long before been suspended for an article on the Honan province famine that the Nationalist government did not like; some of the unacceptable details may well have come, in the course of normal *quid pro quo,* from Service, who had observed the famine close up.

sive operations; in training, equipment, physical condition and medical care
the Chinese soldier suffers such serious deficiencies that from an offensive
standpoint he has no value. . . . [T]he Japanese are the secondary enemy and
the Communists the primary one. . . . Chinese military officers are content
to leave the defeat of Japan to the United States and Great Britain. . . .[11]

Davies from Chungking:

The Kuomintang and Chiang Kai-shek recognize that the Communists,
with the popular support which they enjoy and their reputation for administrative reform and honesty, represent a challenge to the Central Government and
its spoils system. The Generalissimo cannot admit the seemingly innocent
demands of the Communists that their party be legalized and democratic
processes be put into practice. To do so would probably mean the abdication
of the Kuomintang and the provincial satraps.

The Communists, on the other hand, dare not accept the Central Government's invitation that they disband their armies and be absorbed in the
national body politic. To do so would be to invite extinction.

This impasse will probably be resolved, American and other foreign observers in Chungking agree, by an attempt by the Central Government to liquidate the Communists. This action may be expected to precipitate a civil war
from which one of the two contending factions will emerge dominant. . . .

Chiang Kai-shek and his Kuomintang lieutenants fully realize the risks of
an attack on the Communists. This may explain the reported statements of
high officials in Chungking that they must prepare not only for the coming
civil war but also for the coming war with Russia. Chiang and his Central
Government recognize that they cannot defeat the Communists and the
Soviet Union without foreign aid. Such aid would naturally be sought from
the United States and possibly from Great Britain.

. . . we may anticipate that Chiang Kai-shek will exert every effort and resort
to every stratagem to involve us in active support of the Central Government.
We will probably be told that if fresh American aid is not forthcoming all of

---

[11]By early 1944 Drumright, for all that he was predisposed to be sympathetic to Chiang
Kai-shek, would be reporting that the Communist troops in his area were "well-fed,
well-led, and well-disciplined," and that some Nationalist troops he'd spotted on a highway
between Paocheng and Paoki were "the most tattered, torn, tired, and famished group
of soldiers he had ever seen, many of whom were literally skin and bones and some of
whom would perhaps die before reaching Paoki—troops who are not now and probably
never will be in a condition to fight either the Japanese or the Communists."

China and eventually all of Asia will be swept by communism. It will be difficult for us to resist such appeals, especially in view of our moral commitments to continued assistance to China during the post-war period.

It is therefore not inconceivable that, should Chiang attempt to liquidate the Communists, we would find ourselves entangled not only in a civil war in China but also drawn into conflict with the Soviet Union.

By 1943 still another experienced Old China Hand, George Atcheson, Jr.,[12] was adding his own tried ingredients to the ever-bubbling stew of Foreign Service reports. A doctor's son from Denver, Atcheson had gone to college at Berkeley, worked briefly as a journalist, and joined the Foreign Service in 1920. He had had his share of adventure in China. In December 1934 some Communist bandits had made off with a young American missionary couple and their infant child at Tsingteh, in the Anhwei province, and murdered the parents. Atcheson had been sent to investigate the gruesome tragedy and, since diplomats were expected to be jacks-of-all-trades, had been deputized a coroner for the occasion. When the two bodies were recovered, twenty-two days after the kidnapping, it was rumored around Tsingteh that the victims had been not merely decapitated but otherwise mutilated; Atcheson and a Chinese doctor jointly examined the corpses, and the diplomat was able to report, not that it offered much solace to the families of the deceased, that they had been merely beheaded.

Atcheson, who would himself suffer an untimely death, perishing when a military plane went down off Honolulu in August 1947, arrived at Chungking in the spring of 1943 to replace Vincent as counsellor at the embassy. Ambassador Gauss thought him an estimable substitute, though he was not much of a man for pinochle; Gauss later called him "the senior officer in whom I had the greatest confidence and trust and in my opinion was one of the outstanding senior officers in the Service." The ambassador had such a high opinion of him, indeed, that when he himself left China the following year to be replaced by Patrick Hurley, he gave Atcheson one of his most cherished Chungking possessions—an innerspring mattress. Someone tipped Hurley off to this luxury, and at one of his first staff meetings he announced to all hands, Atcheson included, that among many other underhanded deviltries being perpetrated against him had

[12]In view of the widespread nomenclatural confusion that enveloped all these men, it was inevitable that George Atcheson was often taken for Dean Acheson, and vice versa.

been the theft of the ambassadorial mattress. Atcheson resignedly yielded it up.

Atcheson was a careful, conscientious man who believed that almost any report could be improved by revision. One of his younger assistants once mischievously handed him a document that Atcheson himself had laboriously polished and honed several months before. As the junior man had surmised, Atcheson promptly sat down and again rewrote it. But he was just as interested in content as in style. He had been back in China not more than three weeks when, on May 28, 1943, he sent a memorandum to the secretary of state saying that conservative Chinese were telling him that morale there had seriously deteriorated, and that unless there was some effective military action soon by the Nationalists, the status quo would probably last less than a year. "Foreign loans will no longer help," Atcheson declared. "Political gestures are limited in usefulness to their effect upon leaders, who for the most part actually lead only in a negative way; political gestures do not help the troops or the people."

John Service attained the rank of consul in July 1943. A month later, after his return from still another trip to Lanchow, he and Ludden joined Davies as civilian members of General Stilwell's staff. It was a transfer arranged on a high level—carried out by the secretary of state at the request of the secretary of war. Gauss did not much like losing two more of his more experienced reporters, but he was in a hospital in California at the time and in no position to raise much of a fuss.[13] Stilwell was hopeful then, as were Roosevelt and Marshall, that Chiang could be persuaded to put all ground troops in China under the American's command. But Chiang was loath to cede that much authority. Pending a resolution of that sticky jurisdictional point, Stilwell, who was trying to organize a joint Nationalist-Communist military operation in North China the object of which was to deter any thrust the Japanese might have had in mind up the Yangtze toward Chungking, would not permit his

[13]Several months later, in good health and back in Chungking, Gauss would complain to Secretary of State Hull that the reassignment of the Foreign Service officers had been made without his embassy's acquiescence or, for that matter, awareness; moreover, Gauss stated, Service and Ludden had never been properly briefed on their new duties, and their wandering around the theater of operations as civilians in uniform was confusing to military police. The novel setup, Gauss added, was proving to be wasteful of scarce trained specialists; not long before, he had dispatched Jim Penfield to Chengtu, only to learn that Stilwell had concurrently sent Ray Ludden there.

military staff people any direct contact with the Communists lest the sensitive Chiang Kai-shek take umbrage at such fraternizing.

The Foreign Service officers, however, were under no such wraps; after all, their job had been to sound out the Communists at every opportunity. In fact, although now technically subservient to the military rather than to the State Department, the men still felt a strong sense of obligation to their career employers; whatever observations or reflections they put down on paper for Stilwell, they sent copies, as Davies had done from the start, to the embassy at Chungking. Stilwell was glad to have them aboard. "I was lucky to find old friends in the Chungking Embassy who were disposed to help me in a job that their experience had proved to them held little hope of accomplishment, whatever their opinion as to the choice of an instrument," he confided to his diary at the time. "We have a lot of good boys in our Foreign Service: if they could only make themselves heard and get to positions of responsibility a little more quickly, we'd be all right, but as long as we go on paying off political debts with the top posts, we handicap ourselves out of the race."

The pro-Chiang historian Chin-tung Liang took a dim view of this new liaison. He wrote in 1972:

> Another significant aspect of the Stilwell Mission was the fact [he used the word loosely] that the political advisers to Stilwell had been in collusion with the Chinese Communists. . . . What may perhaps interest historians is that all these clandestine activities were aggressively carried out after Moscow had issued the order in May 1943 to "make positive attack on the Chiang Kai-shek line." [His source for this appeared to be the notoriously unreliable ex-Communist informer Louis F. Budenz.] . . . The arrangement gave Davies and his cohorts the opportunity to collude with Chinese Communist elements in Chungking in a scheme to undermine the United States confidence in China. Time and again the Davies-Service group fed Washington with materials claiming that political groups were opposed to the National Government. Other reports grossly exaggerated the critical condition in China and distorted facts. These activities did serious damage to Sino-American relations.

By contrast, the American historian Claude A. Buss, who had been a China-language officer in the Foreign Service himself, had written in 1962:

For the United States, Mao had only the strongest distrust. He never took the attitude that an American could be considered pro-Communist just because he seemed to be anti-Kuomintang. Ambassador Gauss often criticized Chiang Kai-shek, but he had no use whatsoever for communism or Communists. General Stilwell's attitudes towards the Chinese Communists—often interpreted as sympathetic—were based on the cold-blooded logic of military expediency. He had no liking for communism, and both Mao Tse-tung and Chou En-lai knew it. The Foreign Service Officers on Stilwell's staff were interested in the Communists only because they wanted the strongest possible Chinese effort against Japan.

This Foreign Service point of view was what later critics of the Old China Hands could never comprehend; they believed, instead, the China Lobby argument that if you weren't wholeheartedly for Chiang you had to be against him. John Service once explained it this way: "You have to remember, I think, that a man who is a strong conservative in the American terms, and on American affairs generally, finds himself in China or has found himself during the past few years in China being sympathetic toward what might normally be called a much more liberal point of view. Practically all of the Foreign Service officers and even men such as George Atcheson and former Ambassador Gauss were all extremely conservative men in American terms. But the conditions in China of inadequacy and inefficiency, corruption if you wish, the failure of the Kuomintang, and the aspects of the Communists which produced better government was winning popular appeal, made these people recognize that whether one liked the Communists or not they were doing a better job than the Kuomintang. They were not Communists or pro-Communists."

In early November 1943, soon after Service and Ludden went on temporary duty with the military, Stilwell was summoned to the Cairo Conference. He took Davies along with him. It was at Cairo that Davies heard President Roosevelt, his publicly expressed confidence in Chiang now apparently tempered by private misgivings, say to Stilwell that if Chiang Kai-shek failed, "we should look for some other man or group of men to carry on." The next month John Emmerson finally arrived in New Delhi—where Stilwell had established his basic headquarters so as to be not too close to Chiang—to round out the political foursome. There Emmerson ran into Stilwell's marauding combat commander, Brigadier General Frank Merrill, who invited him to accompany him on one of his forays. "You can talk Japanese in the jungle," Merrill told Emmerson. Emmerson accepted, having nothing better to do at the moment, and did indeed get a chance to practice the language, interviewing prisoners of war captured in North Burma during the Battle of Myitkyina.

When Stilwell and Davies got back to New Delhi themselves, Davies sat down and wrote to Harry Hopkins, whom Roosevelt wanted to keep an eye on the frustrating Chinese situation, "The Generalissimo is probably the only Chinese who shares the popular American misconception that Chiang Kai-shek is China." Chiang himself, as 1943 drew to a shaky close, was trying to present Owen Lattimore—conceivably in return for the pair of shoes his wife had received, courtesy of John Davies, from Lattimore's wife—with a pourboire of $5000. Lattimore declined the gift.

5

"I was prepared to contradict the ambassador, but..."

Through much of 1943, the Foreign Service officers had been telling anyone who would listen how useful they believed it would be to have some knowledgeable American observers at the Communists' headquarters at Yenan. Yes, there were Communists in Chungking to chat with, diplomats of a sort themselves, though they represented no formally recognized political entity; but it was one thing to talk to an envoy and another to be at his capital. There were a number of cogent reasons for sending a mission to Yenan. For one, there was intelligence to be gleaned, probably from Japanese prisoners of war there; the Nationalists rarely took prisoners, but the Communists were known to have quite a few in custody. What they might divulge about their country's plans could, of course, be as helpful as what Mao and his top assistants might divulge about *theirs*.

Still another reason was a practical military matter, with humane ramifications. The Twentieth Bomber Command was beginning to operate from the new B-29 bases at Chengtu, but it had precious little weather information from North China and Siberia. The Russians, though ostensibly allied with the United States, weren't sharing what they had. Raymond Ludden, Stilwell's liaison man at Chengtu, was recommending that the United States try to have a weather officer at Yenan to arrange, with the Communists' sanction, for a regional network of meteorological informants; what they passed along could probably help to save a lot of air crews' lives. And when it came to *that*, it was important to improve on methods of rescuing airmen who went down behind the Japanese lines. The Communists, having infiltrated most of the enemy-occupied areas, were in a position to lead these stranded fliers out to safety, and had already in several instances demonstrated their willingness to do that. In pointed contrast, Americans who had to bail out in Southeast China, where the Nationalists were active, could sometimes be retrieved only by paying ransom to their supposedly friendly custodians.

Davies had been pushing unremittingly to have an observer group sent to Yenan. He wrote Stilwell on January 15, 1944:

> We need to dispatch immediately, while it is still welcome, a military and political observers' mission to Communist China to collect enemy information, assist in and prepare for certain limited operations from that area, report on Russian operations in North China and Manchuria should Russia attack Japan, and assess the possibility of North China and Manchuria developing into a separate Chinese state—perhaps even a Russian satellite. Chiang's blockade of the Communists and their consequent isolation are forcing them toward dependence on Russia.[1] An American observers' mission would break this isolation, reduce the tendency toward dependence upon Russia and, at the same time, serve to check Chiang's desire to attempt liquidation of the Communists by civil war. The Generalissimo will naturally be opposed to the dispatch of American observers to Communist China. His permission cannot be obtained through ordinary diplomatic and military channels. The request should come to him directly from the President, who can overcome any initial refusal by exercise of our ample bargaining power.[2]

Davies sent copies of this proposal to Harry Hopkins and Lauchlin Currie, who he hoped would call it to the attention of the president. They did. The following month Roosevelt notified Chiang that the United States would shortly be sending a mission to North China. Chiang did not demur, but did nothing to expedite the move, although he agreed that additional American correspondents could travel to Yenan.

Chiang's foot-dragging was making Stilwell, among others, increasingly restive. Stilwell had already decided that his onetime assistant attaché, David Barrett, now a colonel and well en route to his general's star, should

---

[1] Chiang was generally thought to have some four hundred thousand of his best troops stationed in Northwest China for no discernible purpose other than to cordon off the Communists from the rest of the country.

[2] John Service, in his memorandum of April 7, 1944, which would be interpreted in 1951 as having pro-Russian implications, had chimed in, "We must be concerned with Russian plans and policies because they are bound to affect our plans in the same area. But our relations with Russia in Asia are at present only a subordinate part of our political and military relations with Russia in Europe in the over-all United Nations war effort and post-war settlement. We should make every effort to learn what the Russian aims in Asia are. A good way of gaining material relevant to this will be a careful first-hand study of the strength, attitudes, and popular support of the Chinese Communists. . . ."

head up the mission, and Barrett was transferred from Kweilin to Chung-king to get ready; but neither he nor anyone else could leave without Chiang's say-so, and Chiang was keeping mum. On March 10 Davies wrote to the secretary of state, "In this situation, which would long ago have caused a less stout-hearted and conscientious officer to ask for his own transfer, General Stilwell has persevered in attempting to carry out his mission." Davies thought appropriate to the situation a remark Woodrow Wilson had made to Secretary of War Newton D. Baker after the First World War about General William Graves's tribulations in Siberia: "I suppose it is the old story, Baker, men often get the reputation of being stubborn merely because they are everlastingly right."

In the Nationalist-controlled areas, meanwhile, things were going on as usual. Commenting from Sian on graft and corruption within Chiang's government, Drumright reported in March that "A continuation of the present practices of the officials is likely to result in the peasants' welcom-ing the Communists who went to great efforts to conciliate the populace when they were in this area in 1936 and 1937."

Stories of extravagant living in high places were legion in China during the war. A possibly apocryphal one dealt with a transport pilot who, while flying over the Hump in uncharacteristically perfect weather, told a per-plexed passenger that he was worried about all the thunder and lightning outside. The passenger said he was unaware of any, whereupon the pilot said he should go back to the cargo compartment and check things out there. He did, and found no storm but a grand piano addressed to Mme. Chiang Kai-shek. "You ever see such a terrible storm?" the pilot asked when he returned. "Don't you think we'd better turn back? And don't you think because of this awful storm we ought to lighten our load to save our plane?" The passenger was beginning to get the idea. So the two of them pushed the piano out the cargo door. It was certainly not apocryphal that the Generalissimo's wife was a highly privileged wartime character. An American major in the medical corps, sent to Chungking because he specialized in tropical diseases, found on arriving that his principal func-tion was not to minister to ailing troops but to prevent Mme. Chiang, and her husband, from catching cholera.

The Japanese, for their part, were being alarmingly active. In April 1944 they launched a massive five-month attack in East and Central China, called Operation Ichi-Go. Their sixteen divisions were outnum-bered three or four times by the Nationalist troops theoretically opposing them, but the Chinese couldn't or wouldn't put up any appreciable resistance. By the time Ichi-Go had run its destructive course, Americans in the vicinity were blowing up precious matériel that had been laboriously flown over the Hump, simply to keep it from falling into enemy hands.

On May 8, back in Washington, while all concerned were still waiting to hear what if any would be Roosevelt's response to Davies's four-month-old recommendation, John Carter Vincent was having lunch with Chiang's ambassador to the United States, Wei Tao-ming, who said that the idea of sending American military observers to Yenan was ill-advised; there was nothing the Americans needed to know about the Communists, Wei told Vincent, that they could not perfectly well find out in Chungking.

The State Department, however, was not sure that Chiang himself could learn everything *he* needed to know in Chungking; it had decided by then that American support of China did not have to be interpreted unequivocally as support of the Generalissimo, but it was hard to convey this decision to him. Messages addressed to him sometimes never seemed to get beyond his wife and her brother, T. V. Soong, who took it upon themselves to decide what Chiang should see. There was no doubt that plenty of intelligence was available to the Generalissimo in Chungking, which Brooks Atkinson described in 1943 as a "witches' fairgrounds of anxieties, suspicions, and intrigue." Policemen who were ostensibly directing traffic there would jot down notes whenever an American diplomat passed by; Mike Mansfield said after a visit the following year that "there is one detective assigned to every ten foreigners."

If what John Service was concurrently reporting from Chungking reached the Generalissimo's eyes or ears, he cannot have been pleased. On May 10, for instance, Service turned out a report entitled "Domestic Troubles in the Chiang Household," which he justified by saying, "Normally such gossip about the private lives of government leaders would not be considered as within the scope of political reporting. This is hardly the case, however, in China, where the person concerned is a dictator and where the relationship between him and his wife's family is so all-important." Thereupon Service passed along some spicy rumors about Chiang's mistresses, amply detailed: Mme. Chiang had found a pair of high-heeled shoes under the Generalissimo's bed, for instance, had flung them out of a window, and hit a guard on the head. "The guard's supposed remark on the troublesomeness of women does not translate well into English," Service dryly added. Ambassador Gauss himself, five days later, would be describing Chiang as "capricious, suspicious, and irascible"—no wonder.

Service's keyhole comments came at about the same time that he himself was attempting to become intimately involved with a Chinese family at the opposite end of the political spectrum. The editor of a Communist newspaper in Chungking, Chiao Kuan-hua, had taken ill and badly needed blood transfusions. The Chinese at that time, whatever their ideology, did not ordinarily like to give blood—they equated it with giving up part of their life—so Service, learning of Chiao's plight from his wife, Kung Peng, then Chou En-lai's secretary, volunteered as a donor. But to no avail, for dull needles, an unskilled laboratory technician, and Service's stringy veins combined to make him faint before any blood could be drawn. His example, however, had stimulated some Chinese into overcoming their scruples, and Chiao's life was saved.[3]

All these events were taking place at a time when the Allies were feverishly getting set for the invasion of Normandy, and whatever went on in China could be paid scant attention in Washington. On D Day in France, Service was having breakfast in Chungking with Marshal Feng Yü-hsiang, the famous Christian general who a couple of decades earlier had strikingly manifested his conversion by baptizing hundreds of his troops en masse—he used fire hoses. Now Feng, temporarily out of favor with Chiang, was telling Service that China's Nationalist armies would never be able to acquit themselves with distinction in battle unless they had better leadership; he felt that criticism of the Generalissimo in the United States was warranted and should be continued. Feng said that Chiang could, if he wished, bring about the necessary changes in military leadership, but that the only people who could effectively tell him what he needed to hear were the Americans.

The main event in China during that historic month of June 1944 was the arrival of another prominent emissary from President Roosevelt, who was finally getting around to putting some pressure on Chiang. This was no less than Vice-President Henry A. Wallace, who was doing some one-worlding of his own, prefacing a two-week visit to China with four

[3]Returning to China in 1971 after a twenty-six year hiatus, Service had a reunion with Chiao, by now deputy foreign minister. (He was the first official of his government to greet President Nixon in Shanghai.) Service and Chiao laughed together at the idea of how the minister might have suffered in the intervening years if he had been identifiable as a Chinese Communist with American State Department blood in his veins. Even without it, Chiao seemed to have had a singular attachment to the United States. On hearing of President Roosevelt's death, he was reported to have burst into tears and then spent a whole night writing poetry.

weeks in the Soviet Union. As Chiang Kai-shek had put on a street show
for Willkie, so did he now modify the normal outdoor scene for Wallace's
benefit; he had the police round up beggars and remove them, roped
together, from public scrutiny.

In further anticipation of Wallace's arrival, John Service was asked by
Gauss, with Stilwell's concurrence, to draw up a briefing document for the
visitor. Service finished it on June 20, just one day before Wallace turned
up. He said:

> We must seek to contribute toward the reversal of the present movement
> toward collapse and to the rousing of China from its military inactivity. This
> can be brought about only by an accelerated movement toward democratic
> political reform within China. Our part must be that of a catalytic agent in
> this process of China's democratization. It can be carried out by the careful
> exertion of our influence, which has so far not been consciously and systemati-
> cally used.
>
> This democratic reform does not necessarily mean the overthrow of the
> Generalissimo or the Kuomintang. On the contrary—if they have the vision
> to see it—their position will be improved and the stability of the Central
> Government increased. The democratic forces already existing in China will
> be strengthened, the reactionary authoritarian trends in the Kuomintang will
> be modified, and a multi-party United Front Government will probably
> emerge. It is almost certain that the Generalissimo and the Kuomintang would
> continue to play a dominant part in such a government.
>
> It goes without saying that this democratization of China must be brought
> about by, and depend on, forces within the country. It cannot be enforced by
> us—or by any other foreign nation. . . . If we come to the rescue of the
> Kuomintang on its terms we would be buttressing—but only temporarily—a
> decadent regime which by its existing composition and program is incapable
> of solving China's problems. Both China and ourselves would be gaining only
> a brief respite from the ultimate day of reckoning.

Service also warned, "The break between the Kuomintang and the
Communists not only shows no signs of being closed, but grows more
critical with the passage of time; the inevitability of civil war is now
generally accepted."

If Wallace ever read Service's memorandum, there was no evidence
that he ever discussed it with anyone in China. He seemed, in any event,
to regard that part of his journey as anticlimactic; the Iowa corn grower

had had four exhilarating weeks gabbing about agriculture with farmers in Siberia and Central Asia, and by the time he got to China, via Urumchi, he seemed a trifle bored.

Wallace was accompanied by, as an interpreter, Owen Lattimore, who well knew the vice-presidential route, and by John Carter Vincent, whom Secretary Hull had directed to go along largely to try to prevent the vice-president from making any promises to Chiang that America couldn't keep. Among the many items that Wallace was to discuss with Chiang, in three days of talks, were the status of General Stilwell and the sending of observers to Yenan. On the first point, it was agreed that sooner or later—probably sooner—Stilwell would have to go, and there was considerable discussion about a possible successor, with Vincent at one point leaning toward Chennault and Chennault's ubiquitous ambassador, Joseph Alsop, who was on the scene but not present at the high-level conversations, leaning contrarily toward Wedemeyer, the ultimate choice. (Not long afterward Vincent would tell President Roosevelt that in his opinion there was no American general anywhere who could get along with Chiang Kai-shek unless the Generalissimo and his principal associates changed their attitude.)

At the first session, on June 21, not much was accomplished beyond Wallace's conveying the information that Roosevelt would be happy to act as a mediator between the Nationalists and the Chinese Communists. That led to confusion; it developed at the second session that Chiang thought the president was talking about mediating between his forces and the *Russian* Communists. On June 22 the subject of Yenan also came up. Chiang said he couldn't permit any American observers to go there until the Chinese Communists came to terms with him—on his terms. "Please do not press," the Generalissimo said. "Please understand that the Communists are not good for the war effort against Japan."

That night Wallace and Vincent agreed that the line to pursue with Chiang was that the United States was not interested one way or another in the Communists, but rather in the prosecution of the war against Japan. And so the next morning, according to notes Vincent took, "Mr. Wallace again stressed the point that whereas he appreciated that President Chiang was faced with a very real problem in handling negotiations for a settlement with the Communists, the American Army was also faced with a very real problem with regard to obtaining intelligence by the B-29 group at Chengtu. He pointed out that the American Army had no interest whatsoever in the Communists but that it had for very urgent reasons an interest in carrying on the war against Japan from China. He urged that President Chiang's problem of reaching a settlement with the Communists and the United States Army problem of obtaining intelligence be treated as separate—as indeed they were."

Chiang reluctantly agreed the morning of June 23 that he would let American observers go to Mao's headquarters; Wallace had apparently won a significant victory. After the morning meeting the vice-president received a message from Roosevelt once more emphasizing the need for an observer group at Yenan. At another get-together with Chiang that afternoon, accordingly, Wallace asked the Generalissimo to reaffirm his approval; the rationale apparently was that if he could be made to say the same thing twice in a row he would be stuck with it.

John Service was also at the afternoon meeting. Along with composing the briefing document for Wallace, he had been otherwise involved in preparations for the visit. Stilwell had been pretty much in the dark about what Wallace was going to discuss with Chiang, and at the last minute had decided it would be helpful if the vice-president would bring up the matter of observers. Service, accordingly, had drafted a telegram from Stilwell's headquarters to General Marshall in Washington, incorporating the text of a suggested message for Roosevelt to send to Chiang via Wallace. Around noon on June 23 word had come from the War Department that the president approved the notion and the message. So Service, who knew more about all this than most people on the scene, was sent along in the afternoon. "The idea was to strike while the iron was hot and not leave the details to be waffled about after the powerful presence of Wallace had left the scene," he would say later. "The Gimo had a good poker face. The Madame's was not so good, and I well remember her expression when she came into the room for the afternoon session and found me in Wallace's entourage. The chief point in having me along was that I had been doing most of the planning on the observer group, knew best what facilities and staff we wanted, and might be able to sniff out hidden technicalities and roadblocks that the Kuomintang might try to throw in our way. Actually, Chiang had given up on this one, but my presence that afternoon associated me firmly with the scheme in Chinese eyes and was another nail in my coffin."[4]

[4]Service rode to that meeting with Wallace in a big black Cadillac belonging to Chiang. "A smallish but very happy dog came trotting down the road toward us," Service recalled, "tail wagging and not a care in the world. Chiang's chauffeur did not take his foot off the accelerator, did not swerve or hesitate, and did not blow his horn. The big car just rolled

On June 24 Wallace left Chungking for Kunming. He rode to the airport alone with the Chiangs. Years afterward one of Vincent's inquisitors would demand of him why he had allowed Wallace to drive off unescorted with the Chiangs, if he had been supposed to dog his heels. "Because the Vice-President told me to ride in the second car," Vincent replied. "Oh," was the rejoinder, "then you deliberately disobeyed orders, did you?" (Vincent did at least escape being asked about a time when, in China, he *had* disobeyed a State Department directive: to pass along to the Generalissimo a gift map from the American Geographical Society. He had taken it upon himself not to do so because China was shown on the map in white and Mongolia in green, and he knew that Chiang would find the differences in color objectionable.)

On the way to the airport the Generalissimo told the vice-president that he thought it would be desirable for President Roosevelt to have a personal representative permanently stationed in Chungking to handle both political and military matters. So much for Ambassador Gauss. As for Stilwell, both Chiangs reasserted to Wallace en route their conviction that whatever else happened, he would have to leave. Wallace cabled Roosevelt from Kunming four days later, urging a united front between the Nationalists and the Communists and the replacement of Stilwell by Wedemeyer. In a subsequent report to the president, the vice-president said:

> At this time, there appears to be no alternative to support of Chiang. There is no Chinese leader or group now apparent of sufficient strength to take over the Government. We can, however, while supporting Chiang, influence him in every possible way to adopt policies with the guidance of progressive Chinese, which will inspire popular support and instill new vitality into China's war effort. At the same time, our attitude should be flexible enough to permit utilization of any other leader or group that might come forward offering greater promise.
>
> Chiang, at best, is a short-term investment. It is not believed that he has the intelligence or political strength to run post-war China. The leaders of post-war China will be brought forward by evolution or revolution, and it now seems more likely the latter.

---

straight ahead and over the dog. There was a hard thump, but we never stopped. And the chauffeur gave no sign of knowing that anything had happened. Wallace did not look happy."

At the June 23 meeting the subject of agrarian reform had arisen. Chiang had told Wallace that the Chinese Communists were, for propaganda purposes, describing themselves as "in fact nothing more than agrarian democrats." The alert Alfred Kohlberg had somewhere picked up this stray remark, and from that apparently derived the right-wing gospel that it was the Foreign Service officers who had put out the propaganda and had "misguided American opinion with the myth that the Chinese Communists were 'agrarian reformers.'" The issue reached such ludicrous proportions that during Dulles's incumbency at State all the Old China Hands' reports were scrutinized to see where and when and how they had used the dread words. One of the few examples anybody could discover was that while assisting Wallace, Vincent had suggested to Chiang that "the best *defense against* Communism in China was agrarian reform" (italics added).

Of course the Communists were agrarian-minded; all Chinese traditionally have been and still are. But of the various accusations that were leveled against the Old China Hands, none was more persistently articulated than that instead of viewing the Communists as authentic revolutionaries, they saw them as agrarian reformers—usually put as "merely agrarian reformers."[5] The writer Geraldine Fitch, for instance, said that the agrarian-reform theory had been "put over on the American people" as a "soothing syrup to keep Americans pacified and apathetic about what the Communists were doing to China." Another chronicler in this vein, John T. Flynn, said that Stilwell "fell—as did everyone—into that busy, virulent cabal of State Department officials and news correspondents, almost all of whom had become the feverish protagonists of the 'agrarian' reformers headed by Mao Tse-tung, and the bitter, busy critics of General Chiang Kai-shek."

The accusation, in due course, was picked up by various ultraconservative congressmen. One of these was Representative John M. Ashbrook, a Republican from Ohio: "The theory propounded by [Edgar] Snow and others in the 1940's that the Communists were really only innocent

[5]Nobody bothered to consider statements like one Vincent made in a January 11, 1945, memorandum to Undersecretary of State Joseph C. Grew: "The Chinese Communists are Communists, at least the leaders are. They are not agrarian democrats although they have had the wisdom—sadly denied the Kuomintang—of adopting measures of agrarian reform. . . . [T]he only hope of preventing civil war and disunity will lie in the creation of a democratic framework within which the opposing groups can reconcile their differences on a political level."

agrarian reformers was to a great degree the cause for a shift in Sino-American policy in the late forties." Representative Walter H. Judd, addressing the Republican National Convention in 1952, had this to say: "It was not this Administration which indulged in the illusion that Communists in China are democratic agrarian reformers."[6] Neither congressman saw fit to chastise one of their own legislative colleagues, Mike Mansfield, probably because he was not the sort of man one accused of being a dupe of the Communists or of anybody else. Still, he had said of the Chinese Communists while a member of the House early in 1945, "They are not Communists in the sense that Russians are as their interests seem to focus on primarily agrarian reforms."

Curiously, nobody knows who first used "agrarian reformers," with or without the "merely," in connection with the Chinese Communists. They almost certainly did not use it themselves. Asked by Edgar Snow in 1939 whether they considered themselves mere reformists rather than social revolutionaries, Mao had replied, "We are always social revolutionaries; we are never reformists"; and Chou En-lai would consistently echo that response when the question was put to him. The coining of the phrase has been variously attributed to Lauchlin Currie and to, of all unlikely sources, Stanley Hornbeck; Geraldine Fitch, without citing chapter or verse, attributed it, even more outlandishly, to General George Marshall. Edward Rice would recall that Patrick J. Hurley once described the Communists to him in 1944 as agrarian reformers. "I was prepared to contradict the ambassador, but I never had a chance to get in a word edgewise," Rice would later declare.

The bulk of the evidence available would seem to pin the authorship, grotesquely, on one of the Foreign Service officers' bitterest enemies, Freda Utley, who in 1939 wrote in her *China at War*, "The Eighth Route Army and the partisans in the north appear to have demonstrated that today a comparatively small measure of agrarian reform is all that is necessary to induce the peasants to help the troops in every way within their power. . . . This change to a policy of agrarian reform, from one of agrarian revolution, has prevented the Japanese gaining any real control over the territories they have 'occupied.' " Mrs. Utley, to be sure, later

[6]The scholar Kenneth E. Shewmaker, who studied the agrarian-reform controversy at length, contended that Allen Dulles, while running the Central Intelligence Agency, held that the Communists had foisted the phrase upon American Democrats. It was uncontested fact, at least, that Allen Dulles was John Foster's brother.

changed her mind, but she had seemingly started all the trouble.[7]

It remained for Louis F. Budenz, the apostate former managing editor of the *Daily Worker*, to put the seeming stamp of credibility, in 1950, on the sinister implications of the agrarian-reform contretemps. Budenz, whose own credibility was moot, if not nonexistent, had by then been added to the faculty of Fordham University. He told a Senate subcommittee investigating the loyalty of State Department employees in 1950 that Owen Lattimore had been selected by the Kremlin to organize a campaign to spread the word in the United States that the Chinese Communists were merely agrarian reformers. Prodded for details, Budenz stated, "Well, the order to represent the Chinese Communists as agrarian reformers was certainly carried out, according to reports coming to me. It was carried out through the mobilization of writers in that field. Yes, it was. . . . But specifically I do not know because I did not hear the detailed report on that matter." That was the most concrete illustration he could give of the devilish plot. He also said lamely that he had never said that Lattimore said *personally* that he thought the Communists were agrarian reformers.[8]

Lattimore denounced the allegation as a "plain, unvarnished lie," and said that after visiting Yenan in *1937*, "The one thing I knew for sure, after talking with a few of the Chinese Communist leaders on that one trip, was that they were copper-riveted, brass-bottomed Communists and not 'just agrarian reformers.' " The indefatigable Utley subsequently said, "Technically, this statement may be true, because Mr. Lattimore is always very careful in his choice of words and is an expert in double talk and double think."

John Service, who like many of his confrères got saddled with the agrarian-reformer onus, uttered what was perhaps as good as any other last word about the whole tiresome business. He testified under oath that "I never called them 'merely agrarian reformers,' " and he was never gainsaid.

Regardless of what Chiang Kai-shek and Henry Wallace had agreed upon during their private ride to the airport, Roosevelt had not yet

---

[7]The year she was doing so was the same year in which Edgar Snow was quoting Mao to the effect that his people were *not* agrarian reformers.

[8]On another occasion Budenz told another Senate committee that Lattimore "was a representative of the [Communist] Party in the [Henry] Wallace mission [to China in 1944]."

decided to relieve Stilwell, and he was, after all, commander-in-chief of his own armed forces. Indeed, on July 4 the Joint Chiefs of Staff, who were rarely accused of procommunism, had recommended to the president that he obtain for Stilwell command of all Chinese ground forces, and while informing Chiang of this elevation also let him know that Stilwell would be promoted to a four-star general, and that air power alone (this meant Chennault) could thenceforth be viewed as of negligible consequence in the Asian war. Roosevelt accordingly sent Chiang, through military channels, an "eyes only" communication, which, because Stilwell was absent from Chungking, was delivered to the Generalissimo by Stilwell's chief of staff, Major General Benjamin G. Ferris. Ferris did not speak Chinese and took Service along as interpreter. It was on this occasion that Chiang aggrievedly blamed Service for what he voiced; it may have been a case of premature confusion of medium and message.

If Chiang was depressed by this turn of events, so was the bypassed Gauss. On July 12 he cabled Secretary Hull:

> I feel China situation is rapidly reaching desperate straits. . . . Chiang undoubtedly is worried, but he gives no evidence of being prepared to meet the emergency. I feel that the situation can only be held by radical measures to effect a united front in China representative of all parties and elements who should share with Chiang the responsibility of making and carrying out plans for renewed resistance and for reviving spirit of resistance of both the people and the army. This would require a complete about-face on the part of Chiang and I do not know that other elements could be brought in even if Chiang agrees. I believe, however, the step worth trying and that it should be on Presidential level through diplomatic channels.

This last may have been a mild dig at Stilwell, or else an allusion to Gauss's awareness that Roosevelt had something other than regular diplomatic channels in mind for further negotiations with the Generalissimo.

Meanwhile, word was circulating among the consular posts that the Yenan mission was shaping up. Everybody wanted to go there. From Sian Rice put in his bid to Gauss. Gauss said no; there were others who could hobnob with the Communists; he should continue gathering intelligence on the Kuomintang side of the street. "So that's what I did, and that's how, solely by being lucky, I survived the purge," Rice said after his retirement. Anyway, the observer group belonged to Stilwell, not to Gauss, and when it finally got under way on July 22, John Service was the

Foreign Service member of the party. (Ludden would join it in August, Davies and Emmerson in October.) The group called itself the Dixie Mission—all military ventures had code names, and this one was chosen because the Communists were the rebels of China—and its first contingent consisted of seven officers, one enlisted man, and Service. The doughty Colonel Barrett was in command. John Fairbank would later call its presence in Yenan "the high point of official contact between the United States and the Chinese Communist leadership."

To the missionary-son Service, Yenan had in 1944 something of the atmosphere of a religious retreat. (In later years the place would be regarded by the Chinese as a Lourdes-like shrine, full of parks and museums and memorials to the great events that were fashioned from it, as if the wounds of a nation had been healed there.) Less than a week after his arrival, Service reported: "To the skeptical, the general atmosphere at Yenan can be compared to that of a rather small sectarian college—or a religious summer conference. There is a bit of the smugness, the self-righteousness, and conscious fellowship." The visitors, like their revolutionary hosts, lived in mud structures tunneled beneath cliffs on one side of the Yen River. On the other side was a veritable galaxy of future Chinese leaders—among them Chu Teh, Yeh Chien-ying, Liu Shao-ch'i, Lin Piao, Ch'en Yi, Huang Hua (later the head of the first People's Republic of China mission to the United Nations), Chou En-lai, and Mao Tse-tung himself. The Chinese lived as austerely as their American guests —in warm weather Mao tended a small vegetable patch in which he raised his own tobacco (in cold weather everybody's water froze in drinking cups) —but the Communists were very hospitable, though restrained. "The Allies should be received warmly and modestly," said a directive of the Central Committee of the Party. "It is necessary to refrain from excessive luxury while avoiding indifference."

The Communists provided the Allies not only with food and shelter but with reasonably up-to-date captured Japanese newspapers and with Japanese prisoners, who were welcome—particularly after Emmerson arrived —for interrogation purposes, inasmuch as the few prisoners who got as far behind the lines as Chungking were, as Service later said, "shopworn." (On hearing that Emmerson, while at Yenan, hoped to learn a little Chinese to complement his Japanese, his Communist hosts arranged to have a language teacher come to his residence every morning.) Once, the Chinese presented all their guests with peaked army caps and homespun suits called *Chung-shan.*[9] The Americans lined up for a photograph thus attired and, in Colonel Barrett's view, "looked like a Welsh coalminers' choir, but not a very good one." At about that time Service, clad in the conventional American army uniform that he had mostly worn since he was assigned to Stilwell, posed for a picture with some old Szechwan acquaintances he met again in Yenan, among them Ch'en Yi, who would become Mao's foreign minister before his death in 1972 and who as a boy had gone to school briefly at the Chengtu YMCA. So, although the Communists did not much fancy old-fashioned Chinese courtesy, at Yenan Ch'en Yi would refer to Service, half in jest, half in deference, as "the son of my teacher."

For diversion at Yenan, not to mention for variety in diet, there was occasional pheasant-shooting—the Americans in their native fashion going after birds in flight with carbines; the Chinese, less sportingly in alien eyes, peppering them on the ground with 12-gauge shotguns. There were also Saturday-night parties in a pear orchard, where the pro-tem allies would eat watermelon and dance to the music of a local pickup band of limited skill but limitless spirit. Lin Piao and Chou En-lai were light of foot; Mao danced in a sort of grizzly-bear shuffle but was quite accommodating about taking a turn around the packed-earth floor with any girl who asked him. On their own the Americans played softball, being joined now and then by the famous Ma Hai-teh—the Lebanese-American doctor, né George Hatem, who had joined the Communists just after the Long March and would devote the rest of his life to their cause.[10] Service, who as a boy had had no chance to become proficient at American team sports, was exiled to right field, where, although he couldn't catch a fly, he could, as an accomplished runner, swiftly pursue balls bouncing around among the fruit trees.

On a more substantive level, Service was crucial to the Dixie Mission because of his knowledge of China and the Chinese language. (One moonless night, upon being challenged by a Communist sentry and responding in the vernacular, Service could not convince the soldier that he

[9]"Chung-shan" was the given name of Sun Yat-sen, and these garments were called Sun Yat-sen suits until they became associated with Mao.
[10]Dr. Ma would become chiefly credited with having eradicated venereal diseases from China, though, following the common practice in the People's Republic, he himself would give most of the credit to Chairman Mao.

wasn't Chinese himself.) Almost at once he began churning out a flow of reports to be ferried back to Chungking on a weekly courier plane—the Americans' only link, except for a sputtering radio, with the outside world. According to Lyman P. Van Slyke, who as head of the Center for East Asian Studies at Stanford University was generally conceded to be the foremost American authority on that period of Chinese history, the intelligence that Service furnished from Yenan was far and away the most accurate and the most revealing to which the United States had yet had access.

The access was on a high level. "Here is Mr. Jack Service's preliminary report on the Communist situation in China," Harry Hopkins wrote to President Roosevelt. "Service is a member of the State Department staff. He certainly makes some arresting observations." Among these were some rather rosy ones: ". . . the Communists base their policy toward the Kuomintang on a real desire for democracy in China under which there can be orderly economic growth through a stage of private enterprise to eventual socialism without the need of violent social upheaval and revolution. If this view is correct [he did at least recognize that it was debatable], it follows that the policies of the Chinese Communist Party will not run counter to the interests of the United States in China in the foreseeable future, and that the Party merits, so far as possible, a sympathetic and friendly attitude on our part."

That was written on July 30, 1944. Four days later Service reported that one had to look at the Communists from two standpoints—the theoretical and the practical. As for theory:

> . . . socialism, in their view, cannot be evolved at one jump from the present primitive agrarian society of China. It can come only after considerable development of the Chinese economy and after it has passed through a stage of at least modified capitalism. Their Communism, therefore, does not mean the immediate overthrow of private capital—because there is still almost no capital in China. It does not mean the dictatorship of the proletariat—because there is as yet no proletariat. It does not mean the collectivization of farms —because the political education of the peasants has not yet overcome their primitive individualistic desire to till their own land.
>
> . . . the Communist Party becomes a party seeking orderly democratic growth toward socialism—as it is being attained, for instance, in a country like England—rather than a party fomenting an immediate and violent revolution.

It becomes a party which is not seeking an early monopoly of political power but pursuing what it considers the long-term interest of China. . . .

As for the practical aspects of the matter:

Their espousal of democracy appeals to the great majority of the people of China and is a good club for beating the Kuomintang. . . . [T]heir proclamations of liberal economic policies based on private property are also useful in appealing to foreign sympathy. . . .

They can afford to sit back and wait. If things continue as they are now going, time will bring the collapse of the Kuomintang, leaving the Communists the strongest force in China. They will then be free, immediately or gradually as circumstances seem to dictate, to revert to their program of Communism.

Even the almost over-adroitness of the Communists in the field of public relations and propaganda inclines one at times to be suspicious of them. . . .[11]

Gauss was regularly getting copies of Service's reports. Passing that one along to Washington, he noted, "Mr. Service inclines toward acceptance of his first explanation of Chinese Communist policy although he admits that elements of the second probably enter into its formulation."

In late August 1944 Service had an eight-hour meeting with Mao Tse-tung—perhaps the most remarkable conversation the chairman would have with any American government official for a quarter of a century. Among Mao's remarks, as Service transmitted them to Stilwell on August 27, were the following:

It is obvious that the Kuomintang must reform itself and reorganize its government. On its present basis it cannot hope to fight an effective war. And even if the war is won for it by the United States, subsequent chaos is certain. . . .

[11]Not long afterward Service disclosed one abortive public-relations scheme. The Communists were thinking of changing their identification overseas, to get more favorable publicity, and to better juxtapose themselves against the Kuomintang, which means "National Peoples' Party." They had it in mind to use a comparable Chinese name, Kungchantang, which translates literally as "Common Property Party." "It seems questionable whether the Communists can be successful in popularizing this Chinese name," said Service, "when the term Communist Party has become so well known abroad, has so much more meaning to the average foreigner, and is so much easier for most foreigners to remember."

We Communists accepted KMT terms in 1936–37 to form the United Front because the foreign menace of Japan threatened the country. We are, first of all, Chinese. . . .

Our support of Chiang does not mean support of despotism; we support him to fight Japan. . . .

Chiang is stubborn. But fundamentally he is a gangster. That fact must be understood in order to deal with him. We have had to learn it by experience. The only way to handle him is to be hardboiled. You must not give way to his threats and bullying. . . . The United States has handled Chiang very badly. It has let him get away with blackmail—for instance, talk of being unable to keep up resistance, of having to make peace, his tactics in getting the five-hundred-million-dollar loan, and now . . . the plea for cloth. Cloth! Are we or are we not fighting the Japanese! Is cloth more important than bullets? . . .

The position of the United States now is entirely different from what it was just after Pearl Harbor. There is no longer any need or any reason to cultivate, baby, or placate Chiang. The United States can tell Chiang what he should do—in the interest of the war. American help to Chiang can be made conditional on his meeting American desires. . . .

Soviet participation either in the Far Eastern war or in China's postwar reconstruction depends entirely on the circumstances of the Soviet Union. The Russians have suffered greatly in the war and will have their hands full with their own job of rebuilding. We do not expect Russian help. . . .

But Russia will not oppose American interests in China if they are constructive and democratic. There will be no possible point of conflict. Russia only wants a friendly and democratic China. Cooperation between America and the Chinese Communist Party will be beneficial and satisfactory to all concerned. . . .

China must industrialize. This can be done—in China—only by free enterprise and with the aid of foreign capital. Chinese and American interests are correlated and similar. They fit together, economically and politically. We can and must work together. . . .

We will not be afraid of democratic American influence—we will welcome it. . . .

America does not need to fear that we will not be cooperative. We must cooperate and we must have American help. This is why it is so important to us Communists to know what you Americans are thinking and planning. We cannot risk crossing you—cannot risk any conflict with you.

This was not made public in its entirety until 1969, by which time, of course, it didn't much matter what Mao had said to Service in 1944.

Two days after that report the indefatigable Service produced another one, which went, in small part, "If the Kuomintang is actually what it claims to be—democratic and sincerely anxious to defeat the Japanese as quickly as possible—it should not oppose our insistence on giving at least proportional aid to the Communists. It is not too much to say that the strength of the Kuomintang opposition will be a measure of the desirability of support of the Communists." The day following that observation, as August was drawing to a steamy close in Chungking, Gauss met with Chiang Kai-shek, who told the ambassador that ever since the Dixie Mission had got under way the Communists had refused to negotiate with him about a unified effort against the Japanese. The Generalissimo blamed this disagreeable turn of events upon the United States presence at Yenan. Gauss disagreed.

During their ride to the airport, Chiang had suggested to Vice-President Wallace that Roosevelt send him a new eminence. The president now acted on that. The personage he chose was Major General Patrick J. Hurley. Hurley was then sixty-one years old, but he still held his six-foot-two-inch frame ramrod straight. (When, even later in his long and rambling life, he would unsuccessfully run for the Senate from New Mexico, one of the things that allegedly contributed to his defeat was the description of him by one disenchanted voter as "the only man I ever saw who can strut sitting down.") When Hurley arrived in Chungking in 1944, he had two sergeant batmen along; their principal function, the Foreign Service officers on the scene said snidely, was to lace him into his corset. His red hair had by then turned white and was complemented by a glorious white mustache, but his blue eyes were as blue as ever. He was a kind of living embodiment of the colors of patriotism, and he saw himself in a very patriotic light. So did his authorized biographer, Don Lohbeck, who suggested that Hurley belonged in the same class with George Washington and Robert E. Lee.

A hot-tempered Oklahoman, Hurley was once accused by political adversaries of having killed a mule with a two-by-four. He denied it. "I have never killed a mule," he said. "I have never even killed a career diplomat." This was true in a literal sense, but he managed in his time to kill quite a few diplomatic careers; his giddy path was strewn with their wreckage. There was certainly a tradition of violence in his family. His father, a poor Irish immigrant who had arrived in what is now Oklahoma in 1882 on an open wagon, had once badly beaten another son for coming home late; the bruised boy had tried to leave town by jumping a freight train and had been killed under its wheels. The father had been a coal miner, and the surviving son himself went into the mines at the age of eleven.[12]

After attending an Indian college, Hurley became a lawyer and by 1911 was national attorney for the Choctaw nation. It was often wrongly thought that he had some Indian blood in him—a misapprehension to which he contributed by, when the mood struck him, emitting blood-curdling Choctaw war whoops or conducting Choctaw snake dances. He became a successful oil and gas lawyer in Tulsa, and married the daughter of the admiral who commanded the Atlantic Fleet in the First World War. (Stilwell, often called "Vinegar Joe," once called Hurley the oil to his vinegar. An *un*authorized biographer of Hurley, Russel D. Buhite, wrote in his *Patrick J. Hurley and American Foreign Policy,* "He cannot be dismissed as a snake-oil salesman, though he possessed some of the traits.") In due course he became Herbert Hoover's secretary of war, and as such got Douglas MacArthur appointed chief of staff. As secretary, Hurley first visited China in 1931; so tenuous was his grasp on some of the elementary aspects of the Chinese situation that in a letter that year to Chiang Kai-shek he referred to Chiang's wife as "Madame Shek."

Hurley, one of those colorful eccentrics who now and then surface above the faceless norm of American politics, was a nonstop talker. In Chungking this proved to be unfortunate, because he was almost totally ignorant about China and his volubility made it difficult for others to enlighten him. (Chiang Kai-shek didn't mind; the Generalissimo much preferred that sort of American to the sort who could read and speak Chinese and had spent a good deal of time living among Chinese.) After a three-hour wartime call on Hurley in Chungking, Mike Mansfield said, "He talked for two hours and forty-seven minutes and I talked for thirteen minutes, which was about right." Colonel Barrett was less charitable toward Hurley's monomaniacal quirks. "His discourse," Barrett observed tartly, "was by no means connected by any readily discernible pattern of thought." When Edward Rice, who had a decade of experience in China behind him, was summoned to give Hurley a briefing, he spent forty-five

[12]On May 14, 1956, Patrick J. Hurley Day was celebrated at Coalgate, Oklahoma, the county seat of the mining district.

minutes with the general but contributed nothing to their dialogue beyond a respectful "Hello" and a dazed "Good-bye." In between, Hurley delivered himself of an all but incomprehensible monologue.

Hurley had, though, at least read two of Rice's reports, one of them an interview with some refugees from Shanghai, who said that the absence of any American planes over their city had convinced them that the Allies had abandoned them to the Japanese. There had been talk of bombing the docks in Japanese-occupied Hankow, but Chiang had demurred, saying that the Chinese there would never forgive him if he permitted it; Hurley wanted to use Rice's account of the way feelings ran in Shanghai to influence the Generalissimo to yield on Hankow. Subsequently the general wrote a flattering letter to the State Department about Rice, who evidently struck him as a good listener.[13]

Philip Sprouse had a comparable experience. During *his* initial meeting with Hurley, he was subjected to a forty-five-minute diatribe against, among others, Ambassador Gauss, John Carter Vincent, John Davies, and John Service—all of whom Sprouse held in high personal and professional esteem.[14] "I've never gone through such an ordeal in my life," Sprouse later commented. "Hurley didn't know anything about me except that I was a China specialist, and that *per se* made me bad."

In some high quarters of the State Department, Hurley was actually viewed as a madman; one plan he put forward was dismissed there as "hysterical messianic globaloney." Hurley in turn felt that the department was dominated by men espousing three philosophies that were anathema to him: pro-imperialism, pro-communism, and pro-Zionism. "Hurley may not have been insane," Sprouse once said, "but at routine staff meetings he would invoke the Magna Carta, the Declaration of Independence, and the Gettysburg Address, with such passion that at the end of his spiel you always felt like saying, 'All right, I'll vote for you.' " Known in Chungking

[13]When John T. Flynn later erroneously included Rice's name on a roster of Foreign Service officers whom Hurley had scalped, Rice complained. Flynn replied that he had talked to Hurley at great length and that "I have no record of General Hurley having made any exception which would include you." With some difficulty, Rice extracted a copy of the Hurley testimonial from his personnel file and sent Flynn a photostat. Flynn then replied that he would eliminate Rice's name from the next printing of the book in question. Rice never found out whether he did.

[14]Asked after the war specifically about Hurley's allegation that John Service was a pro-Communist dedicated to bringing about the downfall of Chiang Kai-shek, the normally placid Gauss replied, "I am sorry General Hurley isn't here because I would call him a liar to his face."

as "The Big Wind," Hurley, when he ultimately got to be known in Yenan as well, was described by Mao Tse-tung to Chu Teh as "The Clown." Chiang Kai-shek, in pointed contrast, told Roosevelt he regarded Hurley as a man with "rare knowledge of human nature."

Just why Roosevelt was so tolerant of Hurley is hard to fathom. Perhaps Buhite had the answer: "In his association with foreign statesmen . . . [Hurley] seems to have believed that handshakes, smiles, anecdote swapping and other forms of personal camaraderie would sweep away divisive and long-standing issues; in this sense he resembled Franklin Roosevelt." In any event, Roosevelt, even though he slightingly referred to Hurley as one of "a great many make-believe generals," kept assigning him to one high-sounding mission after another.[15] Early in 1942 Hurley was sent to Australia, though he was officially designated minister to New Zealand, to try to expedite the running of supplies to the beleaguered MacArthur, not yet out of the Philippines. He hadn't accomplished much, except to try in vain to get himself named minister to Australia, to succeed Nelson Johnson. There had been further errands to run for Roosevelt in the Soviet Union and the Middle East, and at the end of 1943 Hurley had been instrumental—to precisely what extent was moot—in drawing up a Declaration on Iran, one of those avowals of purpose that in times of stress seem more important than they often turn out to be.

Toward the end of 1944 Roosevelt had apparently decided that he needed to find still another job for good old Pat Hurley. It was an election year, and he couldn't be sent back to the Middle East because he was identified with the oil interests and was anti-Zionist. To be sure, if he failed to fulfill whatever task he got, Roosevelt could hardly suffer in domestic politics; Hurley was an out-and-out Republican. Stimson and Marshall proposed China for him, and as soon as

[15]The then Major General Stilwell wrote in his diary on January 18, 1942, "So they make Mr. [William S.] Knudsen a lieutenant general. How ducky. Why not Shirley Temple? And for Christ's sake, why not an admiral for once?" The next day he wrote, "So they make Pat Hurley a brigadier general. For Christ's sake again." (The fact that his diaries, edited by Theodore H. White, were published as The Stilwell Papers in 1948, cannot have been of much help to the Foreign Service officers who had long since been branded as friends of Stilwell and foes of Hurley and Chiang Kai-shek; to the China Lobby, Stilwell's candid, derogatory remarks about the Generalissimo, whom he called "Peanut," did not constitute insouciance or even irreverence —they were downright blasphemy.)

The Big Wind got wind of this, he asked to be named ambassador. That was politely ignored.

On August 18 Roosevelt instructed Hurley, "You are hereby designated as my personal representative with Generalissimo Chiang Kai-shek, reporting directly to me. Your principal mission is to promote efficient and harmonious relations between the Generalissimo and General Stilwell, to facilitate General Stilwell's exercise of command over the Chinese armies placed under his direction." (When Hurley restated his understanding of his responsibilities a few months later, the two top-priority items were "to prevent the collapse of the National Government" and "to sustain Chiang Kai-shek as President of the Republic and Generalissimo of the Armies.")

While Hurley was packing for his journey, John Service was continuing to grind out reports from Yenan. On September 4, 1944, he said of the Communists:

> None seem soft, flabby, or indolent. [Mao was younger then.] This vitality is not only physical; it is also intellectual. . . . Communism, especially in China it seems to me, is chiefly an intellectual cause. And in its development in China it has passed through many stages without being completely dominated by a single man or dogma—like Sun Yat-sen and his San Min Chu I.

The Communists, he went on, were proud, tough, frank, self-critical, unified, incorruptible, and democratic. But among their negative traits were effacement of individuality, uniformity of thinking and expression, and lack of humor. He added:

> It might be argued that the Communists have the advantage of a "cause," that they use such direct appeals as distributing the land of the landlords to the peasants, that they spread a rabble-rousing Communism, or that they have found an equivalent of the fervor which gave such impetus to the Taipings or the Boxers. But, in fact, this argument is never heard. Even the Kuomintang does not bother to advance it. . . . The conclusion . . . seems justified that the peasants support, join and fight with the Communist armies because they have been convinced that the Communists are fighting for their interests, and because the Communists have created this conviction by producing some tangible benefits for the peasants. These benefits must be improvement of the social, political, and economic condition of the peasants. Whatever the exact nature of this improvement, it must be—in the broader sense of the term as

the serving of the interests of the majority of the people—toward democracy. . . . We cannot yet say with certainty that the Communist claims of democratic policies are true. But that they are at least partially true is the only reasonable explanation of the popular appeal which the Communist armies have shown.

Two days later, on September 6, Hurley blew into Chungking, accompanied by Donald M. Nelson, whom Roosevelt had asked to check up on economic conditions in China. At Hurley's first meeting with Chiang, on September 7, the Generalissimo told him, to Hurley's delight, that Stilwell could, after all, have command of all Chinese armies, but Chiang swiftly backed off from that commitment when he saw a reorganizational plan proposed by Stilwell.

On September 19 another fateful message reached Chungking—this time from Quebec, where Roosevelt and Marshall were conferring with Winston Churchill. (According to a message from Secretary Hull to Gauss a fortnight earlier, Roosevelt had already perceived "a discouraging lack of progress in Chiang's thinking, in view of his own [Roosevelt's] professed desire to reach a settlement with the Communists and in view of reported dissident developments in other areas not under Communist influence.") In the message from Canada, which Stilwell, who happened to be in Chungking, was to deliver in person, a sharply critical Roosevelt told Chiang, "Only drastic and immediate action on your part alone can be in time to preserve the fruits of your long years of struggle and the efforts we have been able to make to support you. Otherwise political and military considerations alike are going to be swallowed in military disaster." The message also contained a request that Stilwell be given "unrestricted command" of all Chinese armies to avoid that disaster. Hurley saw the communication as soon as it came in and was opposed to delivering it. He sensed accurately that that "unrestricted," for one thing, would make Chiang's hackles rise; why, his very title of "Generalissimo" hung in the balance.

But Stilwell had had it by now with Chiang, and he was eager to proceed with the harpooning, as he put it, of his longtime adversary. He delivered the message, and its effect was even worse than anticipated because Chiang got the impression that Stilwell had also drafted it. (In all likelihood, Marshall had.) Chiang's reply to Roosevelt, sent via Hurley, said that all previous arrangements about Stilwell and an enhanced command were off. "All this ended," the Generalissimo declared, "when it was made manifest to me that General Stilwell had no intention of cooperating with me but believed in fact that he was appointed to command over me." Chiang later told Hurley that he believed Stilwell "was in conspiracy with the Communists to overthrow the government," and Hurley, who himself believed that there was a Communist conspiracy operating in Washington, probably believed him. In any event, aside from the formalities attendant to a change in command, Stilwell was through.

Up in Yenan very little was known about the discussions that were taking place in Chungking or back in Washington. There was far more concern, at the start of October, about getting Ray Ludden under way for his arduous four-and-a-half-month trek through the terra incognita of North China, where the Japanese were theoretically in occupation though the Communists were actively opposing the outside enemy. Ludden left Yenan on October 6 with three American army officers and a Signal Corps sergeant. Two of his four companions never made it back alive. They traveled, sometimes by mule but mainly on foot, for some two thousand miles, always escorted by Communist troops, sometimes nearly a thousand strong. The Americans wore Chinese Communist uniforms, and they knew that if they fell into Japanese hands *none* of them would return.

They had a threefold objective: to determine the military capabilities of the Communists; to distribute fairly primitive meteorological equipment at crucial points to help get weather information to the bombers operating out of Chengtu (the people who got the equipment, cyclometers and barometers for the most part, were to make daily reports by radio back to Yenan); and to scatter around medical supplies, to be used by any airmen who might be forced down behind the lines. It was a tough journey, made in the dead of a bleak Chinese winter, but Ludden felt a vital one. "What we wanted to do was to get out into the bush and see whether or not this thing actually worked on the ground the way they said, the way they told us in Yenan," he explained later. "And when we sent this party out, it was for the purpose of doing exactly that, to find out if it worked as they said it was working, and we found that it did." Recapitulating his trek, Ludden wrote:

> The peasant has been trained to protect that which is his. In the face of repeated Japanese offensives the Communists have taught the north China peasant the secret of survival. . . . Visual evidence of popular support of the Communists in north China is so widespread and obvious that it is impossible

longer to believe that it is a stage setting for the deception of foreign visitors. For the first time in modern Chinese history a purely Chinese administration extending over wide areas has positive popular support and popular participation in developing. . . . The basic premise for all political indoctrination work with which I came into contact was that government should be for the benefit of the governed. Decent treatment, honest taxation, fundamental civil rights, a warm back, and a full belly constitute the simple formula whereby the Communist armies and governments are genuinely united with the people. . . . The Communists have survived more than seven years of Japanese offensives and ten years of prior civil war. They have consistently maintained the right of self-preservation and perhaps their most important contribution in the north China area is the fact that they have taught the peasant the technique of survival.

Commenting on what Ludden reported, Everett Drumright, by then back in Washington in Chinese affairs, said that "there is no similar organization (the People's Militia) in Kuomintang-controlled China where, it is generally acknowledged, less use has been made of the collective power of the masses than in Communist-controlled China. The Kuomintang would probably be well advised to adopt and put into practice some of the measures carried out by the Communists in organizing the masses."

On October 9, on the eve of the celebration of the Chinese Independence Day, John Service routinely reported to Stilwell, "From the basic fact that the Communists have built up popular support of a magnitude and depth which makes their elimination impossible, we must draw the conclusion that the Communists will have a certain and important share in China's future. . . . I suggest the further conclusion that unless the Kuomintang goes as far as the Communists in political and economic reform, and otherwise proves itself able to contest this leadership of the people (none of which it yet shows signs of being willing or able to do), the Communists will be the dominant force in China within a comparatively few years."

That same day Service had had another talk with Mao Tse-tung, who had shown himself sophisticatedly aware of American political nuances and had "suggested that if there was going to be any direct pressure on the Kuomintang it would be delayed until after the President's reelection since, inasmuch as the President had built Chiang up, he would do nothing to discredit him—thus perhaps stirring up the 'friends of China' and making China policy a political football—until after the election was safely over." Mao was also concerned that he had had no response to an invitation he had sent to General Hurley to come to Yenan and personally appraise the Communists.

A few hours later the weekly courier plane showed up from Chungking and out stepped an army colonel, E. J. McNally, whom Service had known when they both were language students in Peking. There was little time for nostalgic chitchat, for McNally had several items of hard sobering news to convey. To begin with, it seemed that Hurley hadn't replied to Mao because he had reckoned that even to acknowledge such an invitation would have constituted implicit recognition of the Communists as a political entity, and at least before Election Day back home the president's personal representative was reluctant to take that potentially vote-swinging step. Moreover, McNally went on, ever since Hurley's arrival in China there had been far less talk about giving Stilwell command of all Chinese armies than about Chiang's demand that Stilwell be relieved.

To Service and the other Americans at Yenan, it seemed incredible that the removal of the man who was trying hardest to prod Chiang into effective resistance against the invaders of his land could be an item on anybody's agenda. On October 10, Double-Tenth Day, the Generalissimo made a holiday speech in which he said he would fight on a double front —against Japan and to maintain his leadership. He suggested pointedly that foreign powers stop meddling in internal Chinese affairs, and there was of course but one such power enmeshed in them. It was at this moment that Chiang, in private, told Hurley that he thought Stilwell was conspiring with the Communists to overthrow his government, which was a charge of grave meddling indeed. Hurley at once informed Roosevelt, "There is no other Chinese known to me who possesses as many of the elements of leadership as Chiang Kai-shek. Chiang Kai-shek and Stilwell are fundamentally incompatible. Today you are confronted by a choice between Chiang Kai-shek and Stilwell. There is no other issue between you and Chiang Kai-shek. Chiang Kai-shek has agreed to every request, every suggestion made by you except the Stilwell appointment."

On October 10 the dumbfounded Service, largely ignorant of far-off declarations, sat down and wrote a lengthy memorandum to Stilwell, hoping thereby to shore up his general's sagging prospects. It was a forthright document composed, Service would later concede, in "some haste and heat." "Although in Yenan I am only a distant observer of recent developments in Chungking and Washington," he said in a covering note, "I trust that you will permit the continued frankness which I have assumed in the attached memorandum regarding the stronger policy which I think it is now time for us to adopt toward Chiang Kai-shek and the Central Government." Among the points that Service made were:

> Our dealings with Chiang Kai-shek apparently continue on the basis of the unrealistic assumption that he is China and that he is necessary to our cause. It is time, for the sake of the war and also for our future interests in China, that we take a more realistic line.
>
> The Kuomintang Government is in crisis. Recent defeats have exposed its military ineffectiveness[16] and will hasten the approaching economic disaster. . . . With the glaring exposure of the Kuomintang's failure, dissatisfaction within China is growing rapidly. The prestige of the Party was never lower, and Chiang is losing the respect he once enjoyed as a leader. . . .
>
> *We need not support Chiang in the belief that he represents pro-American or democratic groups.* All the people and all other political groups of importance in China are friendly to the United States and look to it for the salvation of the country, now and after the war.
>
> . . . *we need feel no ties of gratitude to Chiang.* The men he has kept around him have proved selfish and corrupt, incapable and obstructive. Chiang's own dealings with us have been an opportunist's combination of extravagant demands and unfilled promises, wheedling and bargaining, bluff and blackmail. Chiang did not resist Japan until forced by his own people. He has sought to have us save him—so that he can continue his conquest of his own country. . . .
>
> Our policy toward China should be guided by two facts. First, *we cannot hope to deal successfully with Chiang without being hard-boiled.* Second, *we cannot hope to solve China's problems* (which are now our problems) *without consideration of the opposition forces*—Communist, provincial and liberal.
>
> The parallel with Yugoslavia has been drawn before but is becoming more and more apt. It is as impractical to seek Chinese unity, the use of the Communist forces, and the mobilization of the population in the rapidly growing areas by discussion in Chungking with the Kuomintang alone as it was

---

[16]Rice, obediently working the Kuomintang side of the street in Sian, was concurrently reporting that in Honan province one hundred and twenty Nationalist troops armed with machine guns had fled in disarray on being approached by twenty bandits armed only with rifles. "A foreigner who recently arrived at Sian reports that the Communists apparently expect that with the expulsion of the Japanese from China they will themselves be found in possession of most of north China's countryside," Rice added; "viewing conditions in Honan, it would not seem strange if they turned out to be correct in such expectation."

to seek the solution of these problems through Mikhailovitch and King Peter's government in London, ignoring Tito.

. . . *The crisis is the time to push—not to relax.*

We should not let Chiang divert us from the important questions by wasting time in futile discussions as to who is to be American commander. This is an obvious subterfuge.

There is only one man qualified by experience for the job. And the fact is that *no one who knows anything about China and is concerned over American rather than Chiang's interests will satisfy Chiang.*

We should end the hollow pretense that China is unified and that we can talk only to Chiang. This puts the trump card in Chiang's hands. . . .

More than ever, we hold all the aces in Chiang's poker game. It is time we started playing them. [Emphases are Service's.]

Stilwell never laid eyes on this attempt at last-ditch support of his cause until he had left China and was back in Washington, sitting uncomfortably at a desk. (Stilwell later told Service that while he agreed with every word of the memorandum, he was afraid that the time its author had put into writing it had been wasted.) Service had sent copies of it, though, as he did with all his communications, to the American embassy in Chungking; and, as so often happened with the Foreign Service officers' messages to their American associates, T. V. Soong got to see this one: Hurley gave it to him. Hurley, for his part, accused Service of giving another copy to the Communists at Yenan, which Service flatly denied. Hurley eventually had the document made public and charged that it constituted evidence of Service's insubordination to him—though in fact, Service was never his subordinate. According to Secretary of State James Byrnes, Service was quite within his rights in sending the message to Stilwell. But Service was never to be forgiven by the China Lobby for his sharp indictment of Chiang. That vocal and influential collection of politicians and businessmen, Chinese and American, believed that the United States should do everything within its power to guarantee Chiang's continuing control of China, or at the very least, regardless of the cost, save face for him.[17]

Service's Double-Tenth Day document was ultimately inserted in the

[17]"I did not advocate throwing Chiang out," Service said five years later, when making exegeses of his wartime comments had become a popular indoor sport in China Lobby circles. "What I did say was that we could and should make our own terms."

Congressional Record by Representative Walter H. Judd of Minnesota, a onetime medical missionary in China who was practically an honorary member of the Kuomintang. Before his election in 1942, Judd had had some kind things to say about the Chinese Communists, but like Freda Utley he had undergone a profound conversion. When he put the memorandum in the *Record*, he added that it "illustrates the conniving against highest officials of the Government of China, being carried on even during the war by representatives of our Government. The Chinese Government had the right to expect that the representatives of the United States, its ally, would do their best to help it with its overwhelming problems, which it knew better than anyone else it could not possibly solve without sympathetic understanding and support from us. Instead, officials of the United States were insisting that our Government intervene to coerce the responsible heads of the Chinese Government into so-called cooperation with a Communist rebellion."

Judd had been visiting China just before Service wrote to Stilwell. The congressman was not much liked by some of the Foreign Service officers then in Chungking, and they spread the story that he arrived with his mouth open, and left with his mouth open, and never opened his ears in between. When he turned up, a State Department functionary detailed to look after him begged all the American officials on the scene to be nice to him, but the more the diplomats thought about that the madder they got. One night when a few of them were supposed to have dinner with him, they stood him up; convening instead in a room just above *his* room, they sang, in what they hoped was a carrying voice, "Poor Jud is dead." Returning to Washington, Judd told John Carter Vincent that a knowledgeable friend in Chungking had informed him that the Kuomintang was too weak to rule but too strong to be overthrown, but that he himself thought Chiang could probably muddle through. It was hardly a vote of full confidence.[18]

Service was summoned back to Washington, ostensibly for routine

[18]Vincent was aware that he was among the diplomats in whom Judd had little confidence; he was thus startled to learn in postwar Washington that his daughter Sheila had a brand-new best friend, Mary Lou Judd, the congressman's daughter. The girls had the same piano teacher. "My God, that I should live to see this day!" Vincent exclaimed when his daughter broke the news. But he was a proper diplomat, and on hearing further that Sheila was going to Mary Lou's for lunch, he pulled himself together and said, "Give my greetings to her father." At lunch, Judd, not to be outdone, returned the greetings. After that there were a good many more shared sonatas, but no more socializing.

reassignment, at the end of the month. It was a time of flux: Stilwell was being removed from the chilly atmosphere of Chungking to the United States; Davies, who had been back home not long before, was moving, along with Emmerson, up to Yenan. ("Mao is big and plump," Davies told his diary after he got there, "with a round, bland, almost feminine face. . . . There is an immense smooth calm and sureness to him. Chou has leaner facial architecture. . . . He is the one of quick, deft gestures. He will make a photogenic foreign minister.") En route to the States, Service had stopped over at Chungking and spent an hour with Hurley, who allowed him to speak for three minutes. In that brief period of grace Service managed to reiterate something else he had put into his agitated Double-Tenth Day document—his conviction that Hurley himself should go to Yenan to seek rapprochement between the Central Government and the Communists. Hurley said the two opposing forces put him in mind of Oklahoma politics: the Nationalists were akin to the Democrats there, and the Communists to the Republicans. On a broader scale, Hurley told Service, if he, a Republican, and Roosevelt, a Democrat, could work together, there was no reason why the forces of Chiang and Mao couldn't work together against the Japanese. "God damn it, Service, I'm going to see that the Communists get arms!" he whooped. Service thought that was great; he was for having *anybody* get arms who would use them against the enemy.

On October 28 President Roosevelt made it official. Stilwell was recalled. Ludden got word of this several days late, hearing of it from a Communist regimental newspaper far off the beaten communications track. The paper carried the additional shocking news that Ambassador Gauss had resigned. Ludden was so discouraged he was of half a mind to abandon his weary mission then and there and walk back to Yenan.

Gauss's own discouragement by then was of such proportions that he would soon be telling Wedemeyer, "We should pull up the plug and let the whole Chinese government go down the drain." Gauss would probably not have hung on much longer in any event, but he had not meant to give up his post so precipitously. He had merely asked Service to convey informally to the State Department his intention of soon retiring, since he had about had it with Hurley. Gauss's resignation was forthwith announced by the White House before he could proffer it formally. Among the people Service talked with in the capital at that time was Harry Hopkins, who told him that Roosevelt planned to make Hurley the new ambassador to Chungking and asked what he thought of that idea. "A disaster," Service said. Hurley was appointed notwithstanding. So much for the often repeated theory that John S. Service was one of that era's principal architects of foreign policy in China.

It was left to Vincent to reassure the inquiring press that the departures of Stilwell and Gauss from the Asian scene were just coincidental. "When Chinese Communist-Kuomintang relations have been mentioned," Vincent informed Undersecretary of State Grew, "I have endeavored to direct the attention of correspondents along the following lines: We have been for years and are now vitally interested in the achievement of unity in China. Our interest at present focusses on effective prosecution of the war in China. Where it is clearly indicated that changes, reforms, and other action might result in a more effective prosecution of the war we have favored them." It sounded like the sort of optimistic communiqué that a general issues after a particularly bad setback on the battlefield.

6

"Hit him on the other side, Charlie!"

Franklin Roosevelt was elected to a fourth term on November 7. The day before, without advance notification to anyone at Yenan, Chinese or American, the courier flight had arrived there with General Hurley aboard. Hurley had notified President Roosevelt, whom he evidently wished to believe he was going to act the part of an authentic daredevil general. "Today I am going into territory held by Communist troops," he said. Colonel Barrett went to the airstrip to meet the plane, as he usually did, and so did Chou En-lai. When Hurley appeared in the plane's doorway, aglitter with decorations, Chou asked, "Who's that?"

"That is Major General Patrick Joseph Hurley, and he is a special emissary of President Roosevelt," replied Barrett.

"Keep him here until I can find Chairman Mao," said Chou, and he dashed off to town.

Barrett was wearing a plain padded Chinese uniform. While he was waiting for the Chinese to return and tender their unexpected guest a proper reception, the colonel gazed at Hurley's dazzling chest and said "General, you've got a ribbon for everything except Shays's Rebellion." If Barrett had been better acquainted with Hurley, he would have known that that sort of banter was not likely to amuse him, and that the general's star Barrett coveted had at that instant probably begun to slip from his grasp.

A few minutes later Chou returned with Chairman Mao in a battered truck, followed by a hastily mustered battalion of Communist troops, and an impromptu review was staged for the distinguished visitor. Hurley was not to be outperformed. He favored his reception committee with an ear-shattering Choctaw war whoop. Then Mao, Chou, Hurley, and Barrett climbed on the truck for the ride back to town. There was no conversation, merely a typical Hurley monologue, which Barrett did his best to translate as they jolted along the dusty road. The task was not easy; noticing a farmer beating a mule off in a field, Hurley yelled, "Hit him on the other side, Charlie!"

John Davies was also at Yenan, and Hurley told him soon after he was settled into his cave that he had brought along the draft of an agreement that he expected the Communists would sign and that he would get the Nationalists to sign on his return to Chungking. Davies ventured the suggestion that the Communists might not be quite as easy to deal with as Hurley apparently anticipated. This piqued Hurley, who packed Davies off on the plane's return trip to Chungking. With Stilwell's days on the scene clearly numbered, Davies sensed that he wouldn't be very comfortable in China, although for a while Hurley seemed disposed to have him stay there; the same thought had occurred to John Carter Vincent back in Washington, and he began taking initial steps, never completed, to have Davies transferred to the American consulate at Colombo, Ceylon, where not even Hurley's voice could carry unamplified.

That November 7 had been a memorable day for Davies even before Hurley materialized, for he had set forth some of his observations and conclusions about the situation in China:

> The United States is the greatest hope and the greatest fear of the Chinese Communists. They recognize that if they receive American aid, even if only on an equal basis with Chiang, they can quickly establish control over most if not all of China, perhaps without civil war. For most of Chiang's troops and bureaucrats are opportunists who will desert the Generalissimo if the Communists appear to be stronger than the Central Government.
>
> We are the greatest fear of the Communists because the more aid we give Chiang exclusively the greater the likelihood of his precipitating a civil war and the more protracted and costly will be the Communist unification of China.
>
> So the Chinese Communists watch us with mixed feelings. If we continue to reject them and support an unreconstructed Chiang, they see us becoming their enemy. But they would prefer to be friends. Not only because of the help we can give them but also because they recognize that our strategic aims of a strong, independent and democratic China can jibe with their nationalist objectives. . . .
>
> The Chinese Communists are backsliders. . . . Yenan is no Marxist New Jerusalem. The saints and prophets of Chinese Communism, living in the austere comfort of caves scooped out of loess cliffs, lust after the strange gods

of class compromise and party coalition, rather shamefacedly worshipping the Golden Calf of foreign investments, and yearn to be considered respectable by worldly standards. . . .

Only if he is able to enlist foreign intervention on a scale equal to the Japanese invasion of China will Chiang probably be able to crush the Communists. But foreign intervention on such a scale would seem to be unlikely. Relying upon his dispirited shambling legions, his decadent corrupt bureaucracy, his sterile political moralisms and such nervous foreign support as he can muster, the Generalissimo may nevertheless plunge China into civil war. He cannot succeed, however, where the Japanese in more than seven years of determined striving have failed. The Communists are already too strong for him.[1]

Civil war would probably end in a mutually exhausted stalemate. China would be divided into at least two camps with Chiang reduced to the position of a regional warlord. The possibility should not be overlooked of the Communists—certainly if they receive foreign aid—emerging from a civil war swiftly and decisively victorious, in control of all China. . . .

If the Generalissimo neither precipitates a civil war nor reaches an understanding with the Communists, he is still confronted with defeat. Chiang's feudal China can not long co-exist alongside a modern dynamic popular government in North China.

The Communists are in China to stay. And China's destiny is not Chiang's but theirs

With Davies sent to Chungking, there was no Chinese-speaking Foreign Service officer in Yenan to sit in on the talks Hurley began to have with Mao and Chou the following day. Barrett was there, however, and was amazed at Hurley's expansiveness. "He told the Communists that if they weren't satisfied with the terms for unification he was offering, what then would they like?" Barrett recalled. "At their second meeting, Mao and Chou presented their terms, and Hurley examined them and said, 'Gentlemen, I think this is fair, but it doesn't go quite far enough.' He suggested additions, practically giving the Communists the moon on a

---

[1]Mike Mansfield was in China at about this time. Reporting to Congress on his trip, he said, "On the basis of information which I have been able to gather, it appears to me that both the Communists and the Kuomintang are more interested in preserving their respective Parties at this time and have been for the past two years than they are in carrying on the war against Japan. Each Party is more interested in its own status because both feel that America will guarantee victory."

silver platter. I was astounded, because up to then Hurley had always struck me as a pretty shrewd negotiator, and Mao and Chou seemed flabbergasted by his proposals, too. They were beside themselves with joy that Hurley had made what seemed to me to go far beyond any reasonable offer."

Hurley ended up with a five-point proposition: (1) The Nationalists and Communists would "work together for the unification of all military forces in China for the immediate defeat of Japan and the reconstruction of China"; (2) a coalition government and coalition National Military Council would be formed; (3) there would be in China "a government of the people, for the people, and by the people . . . to establish justice, freedom of conscience, freedom of press, freedom of speech, freedom of assembly," etc.; (4) all anti-Japanese forces in China would be recognized by the new government and council, and foreign aid would be distributed equitably among them; and (5) "The coalition National Government of China recognizes the legality of the Kuomintang of China, the Chinese Communist Party and all anti-Japanese parties."

The five-point plan was laid out on a flat stone at the Yenan airstrip on November 10 while Hurley's plane was revving up, and it was ceremoniously signed by Mao, Chou, and Hurley, who had no doubt that he would soon have Chiang's name on it, too. Chou, who was to accompany the general back to Chungking, was not so certain. "General, be sure to show this first to Chiang Kai-shek himself," Chou told Hurley. "Don't let T. V. Soong see it. He'll put roadblocks in its path." Hurley concurred, but as soon as he reached Chungking, he showed the document to T. V. Soong, and that was the end of it. Hurley probably truly felt that the Nationalists would fall into line; what he did not know—what, being loath to listen, he perhaps *could* not know—was something that practically any American around could have told him: Professions of good will from Chinese at any level could not always be taken at face value.

In Chungking Hurley told Davies that if there was a breakdown in the unification negotiations, the fault would lie not with the Communists but with Chiang. Hurley could be almost paranoiac on the question of a leader being traduced by his followers; now it was Chiang's people, presumably including Soong, who were sabotaging the Generalissimo. But Davies himself was not prepared yet to give up faith in Chiang Kai-shek. While he felt that "we must not indefinitely underwrite a politically bankrupt regime," he also said on November 15, "We should not now abandon Chiang Kai-shek. To do so at this juncture would be to lose more than we could gain. We must for the time being continue recognition of Chiang's government and give him nominal support. . . . A coalition government in which the Communists find a satisfactory place is the solution of this impasse most desirable to us. . . ."

Chiang forthwith produced a three-point plan to replace Hurley's five-pointer.[2] The Kuomintang was proposing that the Communists be subordinate to, rather than coequal with, the Nationalists. Chou En-lai took it back to Yenan with him. Hurley still hoped for some kind of rapprochement, though his grounds for optimism were few. "The defeat of Japan is, of course, the primary objective," he soon wrote Roosevelt, "but we should all understand that if an agreement is not reached between the two great military establishments of China, civil war will in all probability ensue." That was the best news Hurley could send the president; Roosevelt, however, had some very good news indeed for *him*—a message sent on November 17 that the president wanted to appoint him ambassador to China. Hurley accepted the same day.

In Yenan the Communists were furious. They had accepted Hurley's terms, and now they were being presented with a quite different set, which Hurley evidently also endorsed. "General Hurley says we will gain the approbation of the world if we give in," Mao and Chou told Colonel Barrett. "The approbation of the world will do us little good if we submit to being tied hand and foot by the Generalissimo. . . ." Mao flew into a violent rage. Barrett was astonished. For a Chinese to lose his temper was the equivalent of losing face, and here was Mao storming and fuming and actually coming close to being rude. When Barrett dutifully reported back to Hurley what had happened, Hurley flew into a rage, much of it, Barrett recalled, "against me simply because I made the report.[3] In fact, I felt impelled to remind him that I was not Mao, only poor old Dave Barrett. But that was the beginning of the end with me." (The real beginning had probably been when he facetiously admired Hurley's beribboned blouse.)

So General Hurley was now Ambassador Hurley, and in mock honor of his new status some of his underlings at once conferred a new nickname

---

[2]Hurley believed that T. V. Soong and Wang Shih-chieh, a Nationalist chief information officer, had drafted the three-pointer. Wang complicated matters by saying that Hurley had drafted it. Hurley, who ordinarily liked to be invested with the authorship of high-level documents, flatly denied that.

[3]It was thus that Barrett had the fairly unique experience of, in a very short span of time, hearing Mao call Chiang a "turtle's egg" and hearing Hurley call Mao a "motherfucker" —vilifications that in those days were, by Sino-American yardsticks, just about equal.

upon him: the Genbassador. With Stilwell's departure, the old unwieldy CBI theater had been dissolved, and the American military presence in China had become a command unto itself. In accordance with the conversations Chiang Kai-shek had had with Henry Wallace, General Wedemeyer, who had been working under Admiral Lord Louis Mountbatten in India, was brought in to take charge. Wedemeyer was a noncombat officer, a very senior staff man, of lofty intellectual pretensions and few fixed convictions. "He had such an open mind it was like a tube," Fulton Freeman remarked once he had safely retired from the Foreign Service. Wedemeyer's nickname was Barefoot Al (which he acquired because of his habit of pretending to be humble and uninformed; "I'm just a farm boy from Nebraska," he would say); and he earned a certain amount of real respect in Chungking after demonstrating his knack of being able to do stunts on a bicycle. He received some of his staff training at the German War College in Berlin between 1936 and 1938, where, although only a junior officer, he had been entertained by General Ludwig Beck, chief of Hitler's general staff. Wedemeyer had admired a good deal of what the Nazis were up to then, though not, he said in his memoirs, their treatment of the Jews.

Wedemeyer had known China since he had served a tour in Tientsin before his German caper, and he admired Chiang Kai-shek. "Once Al and I were staying overnight at the Gimo's house," Colonel Barrett recalled, "and after we had retired to our bedrooms Chiang came along and tucked Wedemeyer in. Al was deeply affected. No man who could do a thing like that, he thought, could be a bad man. As a matter of fact, Chiang was not a bad man but a good man. After I myself left Yenan for the last time, Chiang invited me to dinner and said, 'Colonel Barrett, do you still love the Chinese Republic?' and I replied, 'Generalissimo, I have applied to the War Department of the United States to be allowed to retire in China and live the rest of my life under your command.'" It didn't work out that way. Barrett did go along to Formosa with Chiang as military attaché at the American embassy, but Chiang turned down his request for permanent residence there, giving no reason. (It was generally believed in Taipei that Barrett had undone himself by a chance remark at a dinner party. He was asked by an attractive Chinese woman seated next to him how soon he thought the Generalissimo would recapture the mainland. Not one to mask his opinions, Barrett said he thought that would never come to pass. The woman turned out to be the wife of T. V. Soong's brother.)

By then the Communists had also shown themselves callously indifferent (though they later expressed their regrets for their attitude) to the soldier who had devoted twenty-three of his thirty years of military service to China. While Barrett was in Taipei, in the summer of 1951, Mao's Peking Military Control Committee professed to have uncovered a dastardly American spy ring that was bent on assassinating the chairman, and it singled out "a certain David Dean Barrett" as having "played a leading and particularly sinister role in this ring." In comic-book form, the Communists dramatically related how Barrett had arranged to have Mao killed by mortar fire while celebrating the previous Double-Tenth Day at Tien An Men Square, the spacious central plaza of Peking. A number of alleged accomplices were executed. "The charges were fantastic and utterly without foundation," Barrett said, "and had they not had such tragic results for the seven persons convicted, would have been laughable. In all sincerity, I never in my life plotted to assassinate anyone, in line of duty or otherwise. . . . The only part of this fantastic and insulting libel which gets under my skin is that it depicts me smoking cigars and wearing spats."

Ever since the Old China Hands had been assigned to Stilwell, there had been grumbling—from Gauss, from the State Department, and from Hurley, among others—about their peculiar half-military, half-diplomatic status, and they suspected at first that Wedemeyer would dispense with their services. But Wedemeyer, though he would come to have ambivalent feelings about them, was initially quite happy to have them around. On November 22, 1944, Secretary of War Stimson wrote to Edward R. Stettinius, Jr., the newly designated secretary of state, "General Wedemeyer indicates that it is his conviction that unless [Davies, Emmerson, and Service] are retained, military activities will be hampered." By the time he got around to his memoirs in 1958, however, Wedemeyer was saying, or permitting Freda Utley to say for him, "Their sympathy for the Chinese Communists is obvious in their reports and in their recommendations that we back the Communists instead of the Nationalist Government." Then the talented bicyclist backpedaled a bit:

> Whatever their motives, which may have been dictated by a number of reasons ranging from misplaced idealism to naked careerism or worse, their activities were actually not out of line with the policy that both Hurley and Marshall vainly endeavored to implement: namely, collaboration between the Nationalist Government and the Communists.

Another twist of the handlebars:

> Today . . . it seems obvious not only that their sympathies lay with the Chinese
> Communists, but also that they were either consciously or unwittingly dis-
> seminating exaggerated or false, Communist-inspired reports concerning the
> Nationalist Government designed to stir up all manner of Sino-American
> distrust—as, for instance, when John Davies sent me long accounts or rumors
> or unsubstantiated reports that the Generalissimo was collaborating with the
> Japanese or had reached a tacit nonaggression pact with them. . . . I should
> have realized that it was strange, if not positive proof of John Davies' Commu-
> nist sympathies, that in his report of his visit to Yenan, December 15–17,
> 1944, he should have been so concerned that a leading Chinese Communist
> general, Peng Teh-huai,[4] had "little faith in what the United States will do
> to help the Communists."

But wait:

> On many occasions I was questioned by FBI agents and Congressional com-
> mittees concerning my views about the loyalty of the four political advisers on
> my staff. I could understand more fully the feelings of those individuals toward
> whom the finger of suspicion was pointed as the result of their associations,
> actions, and philosophy of life, for I had been suspected of being pro-Nazi in
> 1941. [But this had not hindered his army career at all; he had been constantly
> promoted; there had been no public demand for his scalp in spite of the fact
> that he had been accused of being partial to an enemy, rather than an ally.]
> . . . Because of my own experiences I was on all occasions meticulous about
> Davies, Service, and others in China. But it was no exaggeration to say that
> they were hypercritical of the Nationalists and commendatory with reference
> to the Communists.

On May 10, 1945, after John Service had finished his wartime stint in
China, General Wedemeyer sent a letter to the secretary of state in which
Service was "highly commended" for outstanding performance of duty.
The testimonial, to which Wedemeyer did not allude in his 1958 recollec-
tions, said further of Service, "His thorough knowledge of Chinese cus-
toms and language enabled him to develop and maintain cordial relations

---

[4]The general, whose name was more commonly romanized as P'eng Te-huai, was vice-
commander of the Eighteenth Group Army.

with Mao Tse-tung, Chu Teh, and other Communist leaders. During his extended residence in Yenan he wrote a great number of detailed reports on military, economic, and political conditions in areas under Communist control, a field in which the American Government had previously had almost no reliable information. He prepared valuable analyses of the political situation as it affected the war potential of the Chinese Government and by correlation that of the United States Forces in China."

John Emmerson, whose name Wedemeyer never could spell right, had gone to Yenan just about the time that Barefoot Al had taken over his command, and when Emmerson was next in Chungking, he went to the general with an idea that had been brewing in his mind up north. The Communists had shown themselves quite adept at inculcating Japanese prisoners with their ideology. They had been helped in this propagandistic pursuit by the presence in Yenan of a leading Japanese Communist variously known as Susumu Okano and Sanzo Nosaka. While staying with the Chinese Communists, Nosaka was ostensibly in charge of a Party front called the Japanese People's Emancipation League. It was Emmerson's feeling that if Japanese prisoners could be swerved from their hardcore allegiance to the emperor toward communism, why could similar techniques not be employed, when and if the war was over and the United States was occupying Japan, to swerve all Japanese toward democracy? Perhaps after watching how Nosaka and his associates turned the trick, Emmerson and his associates could travel around American prisoner-of-war camps and try to indoctrinate the Japanese there; whatever success they had would surely benefit the subsequent United States military government in Japan.

Wedemeyer and Hurley both felt the notion had merit, and Emmerson was soon sent to Washington to explore it further. But after a while, with the crazy logic that would prevail in some quarters of Washington, it came to be believed that because Emmerson had studied Communist methods he must be partial to communism, and that was the end of his brainwashing brainstorm.[5]

[5]In 1946 Nosaka managed to make his way from Yenan through Soviet-occupied North China into North Korea and then to South Korea and, on an American army ship, from Pusan to Japan, where he became head of the Japanese Communist party. Emmerson would later be accused of having engineered this journey, though he had nothing to do with it. (Neither did John Service, though he was similarly accused. When Nosaka, making his way south through Korea, had been stopped at the Thirty-eighth Parallel, he told the American army sentries there that he knew both Emmerson and Service; Service, then

Hurley had left China for a spell after the breakdown in negotiations, and he returned early in January 1945 to present his credentials as full-fledged ambassador. He brought with him the only air-conditioning unit in Chungking, as well as a Cadillac that he would sometimes say had had to be cut in two to be flown over the Hump and then spliced together. In any event, the car kept coming apart. One time while it was being reassembled, he had to make do with an ancient Mercury with half the windows missing. (Had he known the Mercury was the selfsame car that John Service had driven up the Burma Road, he might have refused to ride in it altogether.) After a diplomatic reception one day, General Wedemeyer asked Hurley, teasingly, "Pat, how'd you like a lift in my brand-new vehicle, that just came in over the Hump?" Hurley accepted the invitation with alacrity, unaware that the vehicle was a jeep with no windshield. The fastidious ambassador ate dust all the way home, and Wedemeyer, who was used to that, laughed all the way. Hurley was staying with Wedemeyer then; the ambassadorial residence was temporarily out of commission because during a heavy rainstorm a large boulder had rolled downhill and smashed into it.[6]

---

in Japan, had been asked by American occupation headquarters whether this was true. Of course, he said; he had known Nosaka in Yenan, as a Japanese Communist.) "It makes one shudder to recall to what ridiculous lengths we all had to go trying to remember what we did and said years previous," Emmerson said in 1972. "Why should I have had to prove my innocence about all this? One of the charges against me was that my reports were slanted toward Communism, and that was fairly easy to disprove; I simply dug out everything from the archives and plunked them down and said here they are. But how could I prove I *didn't* bring Nosaka back? To demand of anyone that he try to prove anything like that was, at the very least, an undignified procedure."

[6]Hurley's biographers had the impression, probably conveyed by their subject himself, that a Japanese air raid had dislodged the boulder. One of them told of Hurley's catching a bad cold in Chungking "because of long hours spent in damp and chilly air raid shelters"; and another, of a Japanese bombing attack on Yenan while Hurley was there. There was no such air raid, nor were there any raids at Chungking while Hurley was there.

One night not long after Hurley returned, George Atcheson, Fulton Freeman, and some of the other Foreign Service officers were playing poker when they got a phone message: The building in which the embassy offices were located was on fire. They rushed to the scene, pulled out a few crucial safes and filing cabinets, and then watched the place burn to the ground. "Have you notified the Ambassador?" Freeman asked Atcheson. "No sense worrying him about bad news," Atcheson replied. The next morning Hurley and Wedemeyer were at breakfast when their Number One Boy asked them in pidgin English what they thought about the big fire the previous evening. Hurley was put out at being

Hurley may have meant well, and he may have felt that he, single-handed, could unravel the complex political, ideological, and economic knots into which wartime China was all but inextricably tied; but however noble his motives, his actions were often the despair of the individuals with whom he had to deal. One of the first things he did as ambassador was to issue a spoken order to the effect that nothing unfavorable to Chiang Kai-shek was to be transmitted to Washington through diplomatic channels. Arthur Ringwalt was the head of his political section, and when reports came in from the field that, in nearly everyone's view but Hurley's, gave an accurate picture of what the Nationalists were up to, Ringwalt sent them along notwithstanding.

Hurley then decreed that nothing was to be forwarded unless he himself had initialed it. (Hurley subsequently denied having imposed any restrictions on Foreign Service officers' reports. Ringwalt insisted that he did.) Ringwalt argued that Washington would be confused if it received nothing but intelligence favorable to the Kuomintang. Indeed, he himself, Ringwalt confessed, had not long before passed along to Washington some intelligence quite unflattering to Chiang. He had a copy with him and showed it to the ambassador. "You mean to say you sent them *that?*" Hurley bellowed. "Why, I've killed men for less than that." And he actually drew a pistol. Ringwalt never knew whether it was loaded. When the ambassador had more or less simmered down and sheathed his weapon, he stated flatly that from then on United States policy would be whatever he said it was and that his policy was against sending anything derogatory. Ringwalt said that in that case it would be difficult to send anything at all, and for a couple of weeks that was what happened: The State Department got nothing from China except Hurley's own messages. According to John Davies, "By December 1944, as I remember, General Hurley began to assert, without confirmation from Washington, that American policy was one of unqualified support of the National Government of China and the Generalissimo. This was a policy which, as I have said, seemed to me to be full of danger to American interests. In a sense, General Hurley was simply articulating a hitherto accepted assumption. On the other hand, it could be said that he was enunciating a policy just at the time its validity, its basis in the realities

so tardily and informally let in on the news, and he concluded then—not without justification—that he couldn't rely on his staff to tell him everything it knew. Freeman was put out, too; he had had aces back to back and never got to finish the hand.

of a rapidly shifting situation, had become questionable."

Just what policy *really* was nobody knew for sure. A State Department policy paper issued in May 1944 had declared that the United States "is not committed to support the National Government in any and all circumstances." General Wedemeyer was told by Washington the following January, "It does not necessarily follow that China should be unified under Chiang Kai-shek." This was quite consonant with what Vincent would be telling the secretary of state at the end of that month: "One long-term objective in China is to assist in the development of a united, democratically progressive, and cooperative China which will be capable of contributing to security and prosperity in the Far East. . . . It does not necessarily follow that China should be unified under Chiang Kai-shek. However, with regard to the short-term objective, Chiang appears to be the only leader who now offers a hope for unification. The alternative . . . might be chaos."

In the light of his debate with Hurley, Ringwalt himself wrote a report to the effect that there was good reason to believe that United States money and arms designated for the Nationalists were being conveyed by their intended recipients, presumably for a good price, to the Communists. Ringwalt, who had no wish to test the ambassador's marksmanship, sent it to Hurley with a covering note asking him to read it and send it on if he cared to. There was no response from Hurley for a couple of weeks. Then Ringwalt was summoned to the ambassador's office, where he found T. V. Soong reading his report. Soong was clearly irritated and told Hurley, "There's nothing to it, General."

"*See*, Arthur, there's nothing to it," parroted Hurley. He never sent the message to Washington.

Soong gazed penetratingly at Ringwalt and asked him, "Exactly how do you spell your name?" Some months later in Washington, Ringwalt ran into a Chinese he had known from his school days back in Nebraska. "Hello, hello," said the Chinese, and then he burst into laughter. "I've heard the funniest thing about you. Ha ha ha! You're in T. V. Soong's black book."

Edmund Clubb by then was stationed in Vladivostok, from where he was submitting *his* reports through the American embassy in Moscow. It was not an easy assignment. Food was scarce, and the Russians barred random visitors because of a naval base there. The United States, however, deemed it useful to have someone on that austere scene, partly because provincial Soviet newspapers were obtainable that could not be acquired in Moscow; Clubb, of course, was an especially useful choice for the job in view of his command of Russian.[7] Though far removed from his China-language colleagues, Clubb was not entirely out of touch with Chungking. "Hurley has given out directions that only favorable reports of the National government be sent in and those who think unfavorably in regard to the subject are classified as 'Communists,' " he noted in his diary on July 1, 1945. "Yes, it is just as well that I am not there at the present time."

Hurley subsequently modified his stand; he would forward reports of his subordinates with a covering message indicating his nonconcurrence. Typical was his addendum to a memorandum composed by Ringwalt and a Foreign Service colleague, Robert Lacy Smyth, who felt obliged to let Washington know that according to sources of information they thought reliable the Nationalists and Communists were already fighting each other in six-division-strength battles, and that all the Chinese they knew were pessimistic about the prospects of internal peace as long as the United States continued to give "unlimited support" to Chiang. Hurley refused to believe it, and his caveat was this: "For my part I believe that the Communist controversy can be settled satisfactorily and without civil war if some of our American ideological crusaders will permit the American Government policy to become effective." To this Undersecretary Grew responded dryly, "We have read with interest your telegram . . . and find helpful the information reported by you and by members of your staff in making our estimate of developments in China."

Davies had made a quick two-day trip back to Yenan in mid-December.[8] He rode up there with Colonel Barrett and a lieutenant colonel, Willis H. Bird, who was working for the OSS. Davies had no idea of the nature of their mission. It was to sound out the Communists, on behalf of Wedemeyer's chief of staff, Major General Robert B. McClure, another alumnus of the Fifteenth Infantry at Tientsin, as to what kind of

[7] The NKVD evidently considered him of some consequence; it set up observation posts across from his office and his home, and like other consular officers he was followed wherever he went. (When Clubb arrived, the Soviet Union and Japan were not at war with each other, so there were Japanese in the city; at the local theater, the Russians carefully put the Japanese in one section and the few Americans around in another. After the USSR declared war on Japan, Clubb was allowed to sit wherever he liked.)
[8] It was then that he had upset Wedemeyer by conferring with the Communist general P'eng Te-huai. Wedemeyer also took a dim view of a report Davies had written a couple of days earlier in which he had described the Chinese Communists as "the most coherent, progressive, and powerful force in China."

support they could be expected to provide should the United States drop several thousand airborne troops into Northeast China. There was, and perhaps will forever be, considerable doubt as to just who knew or did not know about this scheme in advance. In any event, Barrett and Bird discussed it with Mao, Chou, Chu Teh, and Yeh Chien-ying, then returned to Chungking to talk further with General McClure, and then went back to Yenan with an amplified proposal—this one involving more than twenty-five thousand American paratroops. The Communists were puzzled by this sudden fraternal development, and Mao told Barrett and Bird that perhaps he and Chou ought to go to the United States to talk over something of this magnitude with President Roosevelt. They never got the invitation they were seeking.

More importantly, although Barrett had gathered from McClure that the plan had been cleared with the highest Americans in China—that meant Hurley and Wedemeyer—it turned out that Hurley claimed to know nothing at all about it. The ambassador felt that he had once again been given the runaround. Someone would have to suffer for the slight. The victim in this instance was Colonel Barrett, whose long wished-for promotion to brigadier general had not long before been recommended by Wedemeyer to the War Department. When T. V. Soong complained to Hurley about what the two American officers had been doing behind the ambassador's back in Yenan, Hurley managed to have Barrett's promotion vetoed.

Barrett, doomed to stay a colonel forever, was exiled to Kunming, and his place as chief of the Dixie Mission was taken by Colonel Ivan Yeaton, an officer who was much more to Hurley's and Wedemeyer's liking; as military attaché in Moscow he had achieved the reputation of being stiffly anti-Communist. In Yenan, Wedemeyer said, Yeaton "was supplying me with excellent first-hand reports concerning Communist machinations and their subversive operations among the Chinese people in the areas they controlled."

As a further result of General McClure's activities, Wedemeyer had a falling-out with Hurley. Wedemeyer had been out on the Burma Road when Barrett and Bird went to Yenan; the first *he* evidently knew about their mission was when he happened to see a copy of a message from Hurley to Roosevelt saying that members of Wedemeyer's staff were undermining Hurley's ongoing attempts to unify the Nationalists and the Communists. Wedemeyer was peeved that Hurley hadn't told him that directly, and when he returned to Chungking and the quarters he shared with Hurley, the two men did not speak for quite a while. The ambassador and the commanding general would eat breakfast together every morning without exchanging a word. For Hurley, that was uncommonly restrained behavior; having subsequently encountered General McClure at a cocktail party, he challenged him to a fist fight.

At about this time John Davies, much to his relief, had finally been transferred to Moscow, and he went to say good-bye to the ambassador at breakfast time. By then Hurley and Wedemeyer were communicating face-to-face again; one thing they had agreed on was that the Foreign Service officers attached to the military should soon be returned to the State Department. Hurley, according to the eye-witness Wedemeyer, "accused Davies of being a Communist and of failing to support the directive of his country in support of the Chinese Nationalists." Hurley had been incensed at a recent Davies memorandum, one of those sent on to Washington by Ringwalt without the ambassador's concurrence, in which Davies had written, "The negotiations between the Generalissimo and the Chinese Communists have failed. . . . [I]t is time that we un-equivocally told Chiang Kai-shek that we will work with and, within our discretion, supply whatever Chinese forces we believe can contribute most to the war against Japan." Wedemeyer added, "Tears came to the eyes of Mr. Davies as he heatedly denied Hurley's accusations.[9] Hurley said that he was going to have him kicked out of the State Department. Davies begged the ambassador not to ruin his reputation and his career. I endeavored to calm them down."

Hurley was becoming increasingly disenchanted with the professional diplomats no matter whom they were working for. When Ray Ludden returned from his winter in the wilds, he naturally reported in to the ambassador. Instead of inquiring after Ludden's health or requesting an account of the highlights of his singular journey, Hurley demanded right off to know what his directive had been. "I told him I didn't have any directive," Ludden said. "I said I had a set of military orders; I was to do whatever Dave Barrett told me to do. Well, then, Hurley next wanted to know, what was *Barrett's* directive? How the hell was I supposed to know? All I knew was that Dave Barrett was running the Dixie Mission and that when he told me to get my ass in the saddle I got it there."

[9]In one of Davies's last reports before leaving China he urged that the United States "make a determined effort to capture politically the Chinese Communists rather than allow them to go by default to the Russians."

John Service, in Washington at the start of 1945, had expected to be sent to Moscow himself; but now that Davies was going there, Wedemeyer, who had not yet taken steps to implement his understanding with Hurley that he would give up his political advisers, asked to have Service back. Service was hesitant to comply. He told the chief of personnel for the Foreign Service, Nathaniel P. Davis, that he was worried about Hurley's attitude toward him. Davis told him not to be concerned; he would still be working for the army, not for the embassy. Service hadn't been back in Chungking forty-eight hours when Hurley called him in and said that if he confined himself to accurate reporting everything would be all right, but that if he did anything to get in Hurley's way, the ambassador would destroy him. Service mentioned this to Wedemeyer, who said to forget it, that was just the way Hurley talked. So Service betook himself once more to Yenan, where an American observer with whom he was sharing a billet was astounded to see Mao Tse-tung stop by after supper one evening to shoot the breeze with his American friend.

On February 11, 1945, the Yalta Agreement was signed, and its provisions, though not immediately made public, would have grave implications for China—particularly the acceptance of the Soviet Union as a major Pacific force on condition that it entered the war against Japan and reaffirmed its friendship with Chiang Kai-shek. While Roosevelt, Churchill, and Stalin were arriving at their shrouded decisions, Ludden was finally finding it possible to deliver a report on his journey. With Service in attendance, he related his adventures in the field to Wedemeyer, and the two Foreign Service officers also took the opportunity to expand on their current views in general. Wedemeyer was impressed with what Service and Ludden had to say, and he asked them to put their thoughts in writing. The general, along with Hurley and Emmerson, was about to take off for the United States. Major General Mervin E. Gross, his chief of staff, would be temporarily in command of the military end of things; the embassy would be run by George Atcheson, with Ringwalt and Freeman as his principal assistants.

On February 14, Service and Ludden produced their report. "American policy in the Far East can have but one immediate objective," it began, "the defeat of Japan in the shortest possible time with the least expenditure of American lives. To the attainment of this objective, all other considerations should be subordinate." Drawing an analogy to Yugoslavia, they quoted Churchill on Tito: " 'The sanest and safest course for us to follow is to judge all parties and factions dispassionately by the test of their readiness to fight the Germans and thus lighten the burden of Allied troops. This is not a time for ideological preferences for one side or the other.' " They added:

> A similar public statement issued by the Commander in Chief with regard to China would not mean the withdrawal of recognition or the cessation of military aid to the Central Government. That would be both unnecessary and unwise. It would serve notice, however, of our preparation to make use of all available means to achieve our primary objective. . . . We cannot hope for any improvement in this situation unless we understand the objectives of the Kuomintang government and throw our considerable influence upon it in the direction of internal unity. We should be convinced by this time that the effort to solve the Kuomintang-Communist differences by diplomatic means has failed; we should not be deceived by any "face-saving" formula resulting from the discussions because neither side is willing to bear the onus of failure. We should also realize that no Government can survive in China without American support. . . .
>
> Whether we like it or not, by our very presence here we have become a force in the internal politics of China and that force should be used to accomplish our primary mission. . . . Support of the Generalissimo is but one means to an end; it is not an end in itself, but by present statements of policy we show a tendency to confuse the means with the end. There should be an immediate adjustment of our position in order that flexibility of approach to our primary objective may be restored.

Just two weeks later, on February 28—concurrent with the Teheran Conference, to which John Davies had been ordered from Moscow (where because of his knowledge of China he had quickly become, George Kennan declared, "a rock of strength to us [at the embassy]")—a further report was transmitted from Chungking that was to have more repercussions than anything any Foreign Service officers put on paper during the entire war. In those two weeks, it had seemed to the diplomats who were trying to keep abreast of events in Hurley's absence that the turbulent situation in China was swiftly deteriorating. Both the Nationalists and the Communists were stiffening in their attitude vis-à-vis each other; there were hints of imminent civil war around; the major war against Japan seemed, by everyone but the troubled Americans, to have been all but forgotten.

Most of the diplomats were living in the same Chungking house. There were no women around, and they spent their evenings in desultory addiction to bridge or darts or crossword puzzles, or in analyzing and reanalyzing the gloomy condition of China. Time was running out on them, they had reached a point of no return; if they didn't do something fast, everything the United States had tried to do in and for China up to then might go down the drain.

After one such downcast soirée, they decided to pool their thoughts in an urgent message to the State Department, which Atcheson felt had not been getting, from Hurley, anything like an objective view of existing conditions. Service was its principal author, and its principal substance was the recommendation "that the President inform the Generalissimo in definite terms that military necessity requires that we supply and cooperate with the Communists and other suitable groups who can assist the war against Japan . . . and that we are taking direct steps to accomplish this end."[10]

This was a bold suggestion; it would have amounted, if carried through, to a near ultimatum to Chiang. Because of the possible importance of the communication, the junior Foreign Service officers cleared it with General Gross. Then they took it to Atcheson. He looked it over and, knowing how sensitive Hurley could be when he thought he was being slighted, said it couldn't go out. "It'll never work," Atcheson said. "They'll say we're all traitors, that when the cats were away the mice began to play." *But*, he added, inasmuch as Hurley and Wedemeyer were both in Washington, there was a solution; they would insert in it a request that the two generals be consulted before any action was taken on it. So a sentence was added: "The presence of General Wedemeyer in Washington as well as General Hurley should be a favorable opportunity for discussion of this matter."[11]

At 1:00 p.m. in Chungking on February 28, Atcheson thereupon trans-

---

[10]Vincent, in Washington, was of like mind. "The prospects for early political and military unity in China are discouraging," he said in a March 1 memorandum. "There should be no question of choosing between Chiang and the Communists; or withdrawal of support from Chiang. But likewise there should be no question of an exercise of our prerogative, dictated by military necessity, to utilize all forces in China capable of cooperating with us in the fight against Japan. Chiang, having failed to effect military unity, should be told that he has forfeited any claim to exclusive support."

[11]Hurley no doubt resented being listed second.

mitted the message. It was duly received and sent along to the White House. Hurley first laid eyes on it on March 4 at Vincent's office in the State Department, and he immediately exploded. He first blamed Vincent for receiving it and then he turned to the senders. "I know who drafted that telegram: Service," he yelled. "I'll get that son of a bitch if it's the last thing I do." He was equally mad at Atcheson for having signed it. Atcheson later said, "I regard his attacks upon those officers as well as upon me as completely unfounded, as based in the minimum on long-standing prejudice, and as incomprehensible for any reasonable purpose especially in the light of our arduous efforts, against overwhelming odds, to assist him, to work for and with him and to please him."

The following day Hurley lodged a protest with Joseph Ballantine, then director of Far Eastern affairs, who recalled that Hurley "said he regarded the sending of the telegram as an act of disloyalty to him on the part of his staff [Service was not on it, of course], and that it reopened a question which he thought had already been decided, that it revived the question of the recognition of the Communists as armed belligerents, and that it was over that issue that General Stilwell had been recalled."

The animadversions leveled at some of the China specialists must have stemmed as much from clashes of personality as from conflicts in policy. Hurley and his supporters never had an unkind word to say, for instance, about Everett Drumright; yet there was really very little different in substance between what Atcheson et al. had proposed in Chungking on February 28 and what Drumright said in Washington on March 2:

> The most formidable barrier to the achievement of American policy with respect to China lies in the continuation of political and military disunity in China. . . . Internal unity is essential if China is to put its maximum effort into the war and if internecine strife and grave international complications are to be avoided. . . . A commitment on the part of the Kuomintang to relinquish one-party government at an early date would, it is believed, contribute materially to the attainment of internal unity. . . . To the extent that Chiang Kai-shek is sincerely willing (1) to accept American counsel, (2) to cooperate whole-heartedly with the United States in bringing about the defeat of Japan, and (3) to carry out measures designed to achieve internal reform and the promotion of national unity, it would appear to be in the interests of the United States to support him and his Kuomintang-sponsored government. But it is clear that it would be in the American interest to maintain a flexible policy in this respect vis-à-vis Chiang in the event that his government and adminis-

tration deteriorate to a point reaching impotence; and, second, the United States appears to possess, in its discretion to grant or withhold support and assistance, a weapon which may be used to induce Chiang to cooperate, reform the administration of his government, and put China's maximum effort into the prosecution of the war. . . . We should constantly bear in mind the possibility that Allied forces may land on the China coast, and that we may find it essential in the conduct of our military operations in such areas to cooperate with and grant assistance to such Chinese military forces, including Communist and other non-Kuomintang forces, as may be present there.

Inasmuch as the suggestions embodied in the February 28 telegram were rejected by the White House, the State Department tended to regard the document as just another Foreign Service straw tossed into the wind and blown away. But Hurley would forever regard it as an act of sabotage and betrayal. When James F. Byrnes became secretary of state and the whole sorry business was dumped in his lap, he told the Foreign Relations Committee:

The officer in charge of an American mission in a foreign country bears the responsibility for full and accurate reporting of the factors and events which are necessary for the intelligent formulation and execution of United States foreign policy. . . . It is difficult to understand how Mr. Atcheson failed in any way to observe the letter or the spirit of these rules and traditions. His telegram of February 28 was a full and free report of the current situation in China as he saw it. His recommendation was an honest effort to assist the Department of State in the formulation of its future policy in China. There is nothing to indicate that he sought to circumvent his superior in making this report and recommendation. On the contrary, the telegram expressly suggested that this was a matter upon which the views of Ambassador Hurley should be sought by the Department in Washington. . . . In my opinion, based upon the information which has thus far been presented to me, there is nothing . . . to support the charge that either Mr. Atcheson or Mr. Service was guilty of the slightest disloyalty to his superior officers.

Service made another visit to Yenan in March. Wedemeyer had wanted to keep all four of the Foreign Service officers who'd been assigned to Stilwell, but there had been a good deal of dispute about this arrangement between the War and State departments; it was finally agreed that there would be only one person, whose main function would be to maintain liaison with the Communists in their own territory. Service was the one selected, and there was a good reason for his going back north at that moment: The Communists were about to have their first party congress in ten years, and this would be an event well worth taking in. Wedemeyer was worried that Hurley might look askance at the journey—whatever the Communist congress proposed, Hurley might conclude, on the basis of past performances, that Service had proposed, and Wedemeyer simply didn't want any more altercations with the touchy Genbassador—but his headquarters gave the necessary authorization, and Service flew north on March 8. He found the Communists more intransigent toward Chiang Kai-shek than they had ever been before, partly in resentment toward an intransigent speech he had made about them a week before. "The Communists regard the Generalissimo's March 1 statement as a virtual declaration of war," Service reported back to Chungking.

Mao invited Service in for a long talk on March 13. The chairman expressed his bewilderment at the backing and filling that in his view characterized United States policy; he still hoped to discuss all of this man-to-man with Roosevelt, who, as Mao could no more anticipate than anyone else, was in the last month of his life.

Wedemeyer turned out to be right about Hurley. The ambassador got it into his head that the purpose of Service's trip to Yenan was to deliver some secret plan to the Communists relating to American landings in China—presumably a bastard offspring of the abortive McClure plan that Barrett and Bird had ferried up in December. In Washington Hurley stormed and raged and, Vincent's efforts to the contrary notwithstanding, Service received orders on March 30 to leave Yenan and return to the States. He had one last meeting with Mao, Chou En-lai, and Chu Teh on April 1; the Communists hoped that perhaps his recall meant that their forces were actually going to get some American aid after all, but they were willing to settle, in the case of civil war that seemed increasingly inevitable, for a hands-off American policy toward both sides. Service said in paraphrase of Mao's remarks:

Communist policy toward the United States is, and will remain, to seek friendly American support of democracy in China and cooperation in fighting Japan. But regardless of American action, whether or not they receive a single gun or bullet, the Communists will continue to offer and practice cooperation in any manner possible to them. Anything they can do—such as intelligence, weather reporting and rescue of airmen—the Communists consider an obligation and duty because it helps the Allied war effort and brings closer the defeat of Japan. If Americans land in or enter Communist territory, they will find an army and people thoroughly organized and eager to fight the enemy. . . .

Whether or not America extends cooperation to the Communists is, of course, a matter for only America to decide. But the Communists see only advantages for the United States—in winning the war as rapidly as possible, in helping the cause of unity and democracy in China, in promoting healthy economic development of China through industrialization based on solution of the agrarian problem, and in winning the undying friendship of the overwhelming majority of China's people, the peasants and liberals.[12]

Service left Yenan for the last time (until he returned for a nostalgic look in 1971) on April 4, 1945. He paused in Chungking to pack his things and then, to his surprise, was spirited to Washington in VIP style—from China to Africa, in fact, on a plane with no other passengers. He arrived in Washington on April 12, the day of Franklin Roosevelt's death.

Back in Washington, meanwhile, the unflagging Hurley had conferred with the failing president and had persuaded Roosevelt to go along with

[12]At about the same time, the Military Intelligence Division of the War Department was gathering material for a covert study, finally completed in June 1945, entitled *The Chinese Communist Movement*, which concluded that the Communists were incapable of driving the Japanese out of China on their own, but could provide strong support, if themselves supported, to any Allied operation against the invaders. The existence of the report was not made known until 1951. Colonel Barrett, who was probably more familiar with the subject than any other military man, did not hear of the document until 1968, when it was edited for publication by Lyman Van Slyke, who said in his preface, "It scored the Nationalist Government as an inefficient dictatorship that had alienated nearly every sector in society, but at the same time vigorously acknowledged the regime's formal legitimacy, impeccable international status, and overwhelming material superiority. It reproached the Communists for their continuing commitment to Communism, their aggressive expansionism, and their cynical use of the united front sanction, but went on to recognize the excellence of their leadership, their effective use of limited resources against Japan, and their ability to win genuine mass support. This ambiguity—rooted in Chinese reality, and not simply in the language of the report—is clear, for example, in the following statement . . . : 'Here the matter rested. Chiang Kai-shek spoke from the point of view of a traditionalist who insists on his legal rights. The Communists insisted on their revolutionary right to question the moral value of the Government's legal rights.' . . . Ironically, one thing that made *The Chinese Communist Movement* unsuitable to critics of the Truman Administration was that its political assessments of both the Nationalists and the Communists were drawn largely from the reports of the very men the critics were attacking: the State Department's most experienced China hands and such independent observers as Edgar Snow."

his views on Chiang's unimpeachable sovereignty. (There was some ambivalence to Roosevelt's thinking on the subject of who was running China. He had told Edgar Snow that same month, the journalist said, "Well, I've been working with two governments there. I intend to go on doing so until we can get them together.") On March 27, moreover, Hurley and Wedemeyer had met with the joint chiefs of staff, who according to Admiral William D. Leahy, Roosevelt's personal chief of staff, emerged from that session with the incredible "opinion that the rebellion in China could be put down by comparatively small assistance to Chiang's central government." If that conclusion was based on what the joint chiefs learned from the two Chungking-based generals, it had all the earmarks of a case of the blind leading the halt.

Having put in, by his lights, a pretty fair month's work—Atcheson's telegram's recommendations rejected, Atcheson and Service both approved for recall from his bailiwick, and, above all, his beliefs endorsed by President Roosevelt—Hurley held a triumphal press conference in Washington, announcing that the differences between the Nationalists and Communists were dwindling. Then he set forth again for Chungking, by way of London[13] and Moscow, where he hoped to give Stalin the benefit of some of his Far East expertise and to discuss the influence of the Russians on the Communists in China.[14]

Hurley behaved like Hurley wherever he was. Averell Harriman was American ambassador to Moscow when he arrived, and George Kennan his deputy chief of mission. Hurley was overjoyed after talking to the Soviet leader, who gave him the impression that the Russians were full square behind Chiang Kai-shek and would prefer to see the United States take the same unfaltering stand. Hurley may have been correct in judging that Stalin would rather have had a postwar China governed by Chiang than by Mao Tse-tung, but the ambassador was laboring under two basic misconceptions: first, that the Generalissimo was stronger than he really

[13]At the airport in London, Hurley had a cordial gabfest with "Wild Bill" Donovan, the OSS chief. Among the subjects they discussed was John Carter Vincent, who, Donovan had heard from a State Department security man, was suspected of leaking documents from the department to a left-wing journalist. Donovan, as he may or may not have disclosed to Hurley in London, had a few days earlier inquired of that security man if *Mrs.* Vincent was not a Communist. She was not.

[14]John Service had been interested in that, too. At Yenan, during his terminal visit, he had found only three Russians on hand, two journalists and a doctor, and they had discernibly lower standing in the Chinese Communists' eyes than the Japanese Communist Nosaka.

was; and second, that the Chinese Communists would have to kowtow to Chiang, sooner or later, because the Russian Communists were in his corner.

The American embassy in Moscow was less certain. Kennan said that "there was ample advice available to [Hurley] which he showed no desire to tap. . . . I mean, it is not surprising to me that Hurley didn't know that he was being given the usual run-around and the usual patter by Stalin and Molotov, but I think that if he had been a wiser and more thoughtful man he would have asked some people who would be familiar with those conditions for some years for commentary. . . ." By then, among the diplomats in Moscow to whom Hurley would not—or by nature could not —listen was, ironically, John Davies.

In a laudatory commentary on Davies in his *Memoirs*, Kennan wrote, "He was a man of broad, sophisticated, and skeptical political understanding, without an ounce of pro-Communist sympathies, and second to no one in his devotion to the interests of our government. To reflect that here, trying to bring some element of realism and sobriety into the views of General Hurley on the subject of Soviet intentions, was a man who only shortly thereafter would have to suffer years of harassment and humiliation . . . largely because of the charges, inspired largely by this same General Hurley, to the effect that he was naive or pro-Communist in his sympathies—to realize this is to recognize the nightmarish quality of that world of fancy into which official Washington, and much of our public opinion, can be carried in those times when fear, anger, and emotionalism take over from reason in the conduct of our public life."

Kennan was so worried that Washington would get the wrong impression from Hurley of how the Russians really felt about China that he shortly sent the State Department a copy of a Moscow article in which —although Chiang personally got off rather lightly—his government and his Kuomintang were roundly criticized. Hurley simply could not believe that his enemies were not ceaselessly plotting against him. When he heard about this development in Chungking, he said, with dubious piety, "There are also rumors afloat here, that we do not credit, to the effect that John Davies is responsible for news items in Moscow papers that appear to be adverse to the Chinese government." Ambassador Harriman laughed when he first heard of this absurd allegation; later he reflected that it was a snide attack on one of his subordinates, and he became angry.

Subsequently, Edwin F. Stanton, then the deputy director of the Bureau of Far Eastern Affairs, felt it necessary to send up through department channels a memorandum about Hurley, who at a time, he said, when the United States especially needed flexibility in dealing with China, was pushing Chiang into intransigence. "Hurley is conducting this Government's relations with China along lines which we do not approve and which we fear will lead China toward internal chaos and serious external complications," Stanton wrote. He added, "During General Hurley's visit here, it was very evident from his remarks that he is extremely suspicious of and entertains a dislike for Foreign Service officers in China. This antipathy has been confirmed by officers returning from Chungking, who have indicated the serious effect it has had upon their morale. . . . In consequence, it is becoming increasingly difficult to persuade Foreign Service officers who gave service under General Hurley to return to China.[15] Of equally serious nature are the severe restrictions imposed by General Hurley upon political reporting by officers in China."

Hurley didn't much care what was being said about him in the State Department. Harry Truman—the presidency, the war, and the atom bomb all suddenly thrust upon him—had little time to reflect on the intricacies of Chinese politics or the specter of Chinese civil war; he knew that Roosevelt had given Hurley a good deal of responsibility, and he himself, for the time being, was glad to give Hurley free rein. The ambassador took the opportunity to have Atcheson, whom he finally shanghaied out of China on April 19, replaced by a noncareer diplomat more congenial to him, the Richmond, Virginia, banker Walter S. Robertson, a man of solid Southern conservatism. (Edward Rice recalled that when

[15]Philip Sprouse was supposed to have ridden back to Chungking on Hurley's plane. He dreaded the prospect: The closer Hurley got to any career Foreign Service officer, the less he seemed to like the person. Sprouse was spared the ordeal of prolonged intimacy when at the last moment he was pulled off the flight and sent instead to California to help the Nationalist Chinese delegation to the founding conference of the United Nations with baggage and laundry and do whatever else he could to keep its members in good humor. The party paused at Los Angeles so it could be suitably entertained by the Chinese community there, which arranged sight-seeing trips to Hollywood studios, Forest Lawn, and other local shrines. A high spot of the stopover was a banquet at a Chinese restaurant, in the course of which Sprouse briefly wished he had gone with Hurley after all; the fanciest floor of the establishment had been reserved for the special party, and just as the eminent statesman Wellington Koo was proposing a toast to global amity and undying friendship between Nationalist China and the United States, the horrified diplomat heard a loud American voice braying outside the door, "No God damn Chink's going to keep me out of this place." With the aid of a couple of policemen, Sprouse managed to hustle the intruder out of earshot before an international incident took place for which he, as an escort officer and, worse still, as a Chinese-speaking Foreign Service officer, would eventually no doubt have suffered the major blame.

Robertson walked into Hurley's office, he would be greeted with a jovial "What can I do for you, Walter?"—a marked contrast to the earlier frosty "What seems to be the trouble now, Atcheson?")

The day Atcheson departed, Ringwalt, in Chungking, wrote of him to Service, in Washington, "Maybe he can get us home soon. I hope so as 'Small Whiskers' is due in at any moment." As substitutes went, Ringwalt, for one, was rather pleased with the choice of Robertson; the newcomer, who had been in charge of lend-lease in Australia, was a good friend of Ringwalt's wife's aunt. But Ringwalt quickly became disenchanted. In an attempt to make Robertson *au courant* with the prickly situation in China, he had introduced the new deputy chief of mission to three men, one of them an air force officer, who were quite knowledgeable about the Communists and could brief Robertson about them in considerable detail. When they had left, Robertson turned to Ringwalt and said, "I can't stand any more of this. Those Communists shouldn't be allowed inside the embassy *at all.*"[16]

[16]Robertson, who on the recommendation of Walter Judd was selected by Eisenhower and Dulles to be their first assistant secretary of state for Far Eastern affairs, saw everything in terms of unimpeachable good and intractable evil. "No regime as malevolent as the Chinese Communists could ever produce five million tons of steel," he once said. However, during the 1952 presidential campaign, Robertson refused to sit back quietly when the Republican party distributed among fat-cat contributors, including himself, a booklet written by Robert Welch, the head of the John Birch Society. It had a foreword by General Wedemeyer. What upset Robertson was the statement in it that Hurley had thrown Philip Sprouse out of the embassy in Chungking because of supposed left-wing associations. Hurley hadn't thrown Sprouse out of anywhere for any reason, and Robertson wrote Welch asking for proof of the slander. Welch eventually admitted he had no proof. After Eisenhower was elected and Robertson was named assistant secretary, the Virginian insisted that a copy of Welch's confession be put in Sprouse's personnel file, just in case, as seemed not unlikely in that era, that particular point was raised again. (For a while, Wedemeyer permitted his name to be used as an adviser to the Birch Society's publication *American Opinion,* but he quit because, of all things, of John Birch himself. A Baptist missionary in China, Birch was serving under Wedemeyer, as a junior intelligence officer, when he was killed by Chinese Communists on August 24, 1945, just after the end of the war. One widely believed version of the incident had it that Birch was leading a small party to collect some Japanese files at Suchow when his group ran into some Communist soldiers, whom Birch infuriated by calling them "bandits." Wedemeyer broke with the Birch Society, reportedly because he didn't like its trying to make a martyr of a man who had supposedly suffered a quite unnecessary and self-provoked death.)

7

"The Foreign Service is not an exhilarating business."

In the United States most of the career State Department officials concerned with Far Eastern affairs—among them Joseph Grew, Stanley Hornbeck, and Nelson Johnson—had been either occasional or regular readers of a small-circulation fortnightly, started in 1937, called *Amerasia*, which almost exclusively ran articles about their special sphere of interest. They accepted it as routine, as most of them accepted membership in the Institute of Pacific Relations, an organization that had been founded in Honolulu, chiefly by YMCA officials, in 1925. The IPR had been chiefly supported by the Rockefeller Foundation and the Carnegie Corporation, and in the heyday of red-baiting would come under blistering attack.[1] There were certainly left-wing—or at any rate non-right-wing—influences active in the IPR; but one Senate report on the contributions it received from the trustees of its American Council during that allegedly subversive period showed that John Carter Vincent had given nothing, John Fairbank five dollars, Owen Lattimore ten dollars, and Henry Luce twenty-five hundred.

By 1945 the principal proprietor of *Amerasia*, which at its zenith never attained a circulation as high as two thousand, was a man named Philip Jaffe. A greeting-card manufacturer by trade, Jaffe was born in Russia in 1897, migrated to the United States eleven years later, and graduated from Columbia University. In appearances before Congressional committees he was partial to the Fifth Amendment, but off that particular stage he would describe himself as not a Communist but a Utopian. He was

---

[1]The conclusion of a report by the McCarran committee, which investigated the IPR at extensive and ludicrous length in 1950 and 1951, was that "a group of persons associated with the IPR attempted, between 1941 and 1945, to change United States policy so as to accommodate Communist ends and to set the stage for a major United States policy change, favorable to Soviet interests, in 1945."

well known in decidely left-wing circles, in any event, as a patron of certain of their arts. Jaffe had visited Yenan in 1937, traveling there by road from Sian with his wife Agnes, Owen Lattimore, and T. A. Bisson, who was both an educator in China and a writer about the country. Bisson recalled of their trip to Mao Tse-tung's headquarters that when the chairman was introduced to Jaffe at Yenan, he was inspired to say, "God bless the Christmas-card business."

In Shanghai, in the summer of 1937, Jaffe spent some time with the American radical Max Granich and his wife, Grace Maul, who had been publishing there an English-language, pro-Communist journal called the *Voice of China*. Born in 1896 in New York City, Granich had been variously an office boy, cow-puncher, orange-picker, and shipyard worker until, in his thirties, he turned up in Russia as a construction engineer. His brother was Mike Gold, a writer for the *Daily Worker*. The *Voice of China* was published in the international settlement of Shanghai, and its proprietors, like all other Americans, were covered by the rules of extraterritoriality. When the Chinese postal authorities seized a batch of Granich's journal in 1937, Clarence Gauss, then American consul general in Shanghai, didn't object, he believed, for one thing, that "the activities of Granich are being conducted in the interest of the Third International." The State Department, though, in instructions bearing John Carter Vincent's initials, overruled Gauss, on the ground that under extraterritoriality *all* Americans, whoever and whatever they might be, were entitled in such circumstances to the return of their property. Fifteen years later the House Un-American Activities Committee would get after Vincent for his unwillingness to bend the law, although as it happened Vincent did not like the law. "I regarded the system from the commercial angle as exploitative and from the missionary angle as presumptuous," he said.[2]

[2]As for Granich, he retired, more or less, from politics and with his wife ran a summer camp in New England; among his campers were Bobby Fischer (who Granich said was a real handful) and the offspring of such special families as the Paul Robesons. In the fall of 1971 the Graniches were among the first Americans to be welcomed to the People's Republic of China after the ping-pong players had broken the visa barrier. They were in Peking at the same time as John Service and his wife. Chou En-lai gave a reception for the sixty or seventy foreigners in his capital at the time. Service was impressed, when the guests were about to have their picture taken with their host, by Chou's insistence that the Graniches sit in the place of honor on either side of him.

In the spring of 1973 the Chinese invited Granich, by then a widower, back again, and gave him carte blanche to bring along any fifteen traveling companions of his choice. The seventy-seven-year-old radical was treated like a VIP wherever he went in the People's

In the January 26, 1945, issue of *Amerasia,* one of the more alert of its handful of readers espied in it an article on Thailand that was oddly similar to a report put out not long before by the OSS. It was not the plagiarism that mattered so much as the fact that the government document was a classified one. Early in the morning of March 11, accordingly, a secret and, no warrants having been issued, conceivably illegal raid was conducted at the *Amerasia* offices in New York, under the leadership of an OSS security man named Frank Bielaski.[3] There were three more such raids, in the course of which many government documents that apparently shouldn't have been there were found there. Then the FBI launched a sweeping investigation of Jaffe and a few of his associates, principally among them the writers Kate Louise Mitchell and Mark Gayn, a navy lieutenant named Andrew Roth who was assigned to the Office of Naval Intelligence in Washington, and a low-ranking State Department functionary named Emmanuel S. Larsen. On April 18, at a strategic conference with the State Department and the navy, the FBI said it had its case nearly wrapped up and that it wanted to arrest its five suspects at once and charge them with, among other crimes, espionage on behalf of the Soviet Union. James Forrestal was secretary of the navy, and he demurred; if a naval intelligence officer was then publicly accused of such an offense, Forrestal argued, the news might upset the delicate balance of negotiations being carried on in Moscow between Harry Hopkins and Premier Stalin. The FBI agreed to wait.

April 18: John Service had been in the United States just six days —six days of national grief and confusion, inasmuch as Franklin Roosevelt had died on the first of them. Service was occupying a vacant desk at the State Department in the Office of Chinese Affairs, while awaiting a new assignment after the Hurley purge.

Republic, and among those who took great pains to make his journey comfortable was Ma Hai-teh, the American doctor long converted to the new Chinese way of life. It was a sentimental reunion for both men; it was Granich who had first told Ma, forty years earlier in China, that the Red army needed physicians, and when the doctor had asked what the pay was, Granich had replied that just doing the job should be reward enough. Dr. Ma had been doing it ever since.
[3]Bielaski came from a family with a high level of security-consciousness. His sister was Ruth Shipley, who for many years presided hawklike over the Passport Division of the State Department. Bielaski was proud of his role in American security history; he once declared that the Hiss-Chambers contretemps was chicken feed compared to the *Amerasia* case.

Back in China, Stilwell and, to a lesser degree, Wedemeyer had often been too preoccupied with other matters to meet regularly with the press. That job had as a result often been delegated to Davies, Ludden, or Service, whoever was around headquarters at any given time. It had thus become matter-of-fact for Service to brief the press, to help it transmit from China, in spite of Chiang Kai-shek's censorship, what the knowledgeable Foreign Service officer perceived to be the truth; indeed, there was such a dearth of information forthcoming from or transmittable through official Chinese channels that no word about the rupture between the Generalissimo and Stilwell had leaked out of China until Brooks Atkinson had hand-carried an account of the general's ouster across the Himalayas to *The New York Times.* Many journalists in China *expected* men like Service to furnish them with news. When F. McCracken Fisher was running the Office of War Information in China during the war, he would have felt let down if Service, off, say, to Szechwan with a road-survey crew, had not returned with some detailed notes and some photographs for Fisher to distribute to the often fact-starved press corps in the area.[4]

[4]Another Oklahoman (his father was in the gas business and frequently visited Drumright, Oklahoma), Fisher had first gone to China on a student tour, had then run student tours, and had finally become a student himself at Yenching in Peking. He was there in 1932 when the Japanese arrived and shut down the *Peking Chronicle,* the city's only English-language newspaper. Fisher and another student began to reissue it on their own. Fisher became a United Press correspondent, and an invaluable one, for he was fluent in both Chinese and Japanese. The UP had had nobody representing it in Nanking during its rape; when in 1938 the Japanese were closing in on Hankow, Fisher was sent there, and during the enemy occupation of the city he filed dispatches by means of a tiny radio that he kept concealed in a cigar box behind the bar in a French saloon. Fisher was an extremely religious man. His wife was the daughter of a missionary, and had another for a maternal grandmother. All their lives, the Fishers said grace before every meal.

During the war, he spent a good deal of time in Yenan, and because of his command of Japanese saw a good deal of Sanzo Nosaka. After the war, working in Washington for State, Fisher was subjected to the usual interrogatory; the security men in charge of his inquisition, perhaps luckily for him, seemed unfamiliar with Nosaka. Even so, he was transferred from a fairly responsible position to a near-menial one, and during his last eleven years as an information officer with State, until he retired in 1961, he was never consulted about any information having to do with Japan or China. "There was a good deal of trauma in not being made use of," he said, "when so much of your life had been devoted to something."

At one point in the early 1950s, some security investigators demanded of Fisher that he denounce some of his wartime associates in Asia. When he got to his home in Arlington, Virginia, he beckoned his wife to join him in the yard and hang up some diapers; he was afraid to talk to her indoors, thinking that perhaps their house had been bugged. He told her that he had just declined to say anything damaging about any of his friends and as a result might be out of a job the next day. "If you'd denounced anybody,

In Washington Service saw no reason not to continue trying to be helpful to journalists. He had called on Harry Hopkins just before that gray eminence departed for Russia, and Hopkins had remarked that it was too bad the only Chinese person any American seemed to know about or care about was Chiang Kai-shek. "I thought, damn it, that somebody ought to do something about getting more information out," Service would say years afterward. "I probably should have quit the Foreign Service then and there and spoken up. When the business about Daniel Ellsberg and the Pentagon Papers came out, I had some inkling as to how he must have felt."

On April 18, the very day that the FBI was conferring with the navy and State, there began to be spun a web that Service would be trying to brush away for the rest of his life. He had a phone call from Mark Gayn, whom he had never met but knew as a writer on China for *Collier's*. It seemed Gayn was preparing some articles for the *Saturday Evening Post*, and would Service have lunch with him? Of course; it was the sort of informal briefing session that Service construed to be practically part of his job. At lunch Gayn remarked that if Service happened to be in New York, he would be glad to put him up at his apartment. Service was delighted; he was at loose ends, socially, with his six-months-pregnant wife and two children out in California; he had friends in New York and no regular stopping place there.

Next came a phone call from the navy intelligence officer Andrew Roth. Service *had* met him—briefly, the previous November, when the State Department had asked him to talk about China at the Washington branch of the Institute of Pacific Relations. Roth invited Service to his house in Washington for dinner the following night, April 19. Splendid! Being a bachelor in Washington at that time could lead to lonely evenings. Roth called back: One of the other dinner guests was to be Philip Jaffe, the editor of *Amerasia*, whom Service had never met before. Jaffe, Roth said, was eager to chat with Service about Chinese developments, but there would probably be little chance for serious conversation at dinner; perhaps they could meet in the course of the afternoon. Why not? How could one Asian expert just back from Yenan not be interested in

---

you wouldn't have a wife tomorrow," she replied. The Fishers were not without grounds for being circumspect in their conversations. A naval officer up for promotion lived next door, and the FBI had been around checking up on him; one agent had asked Mrs. Fisher if she had ever seen any liquor bottles in her neighbor's trash, and she had thrown the G-Man out of her house.

getting together with another who had also been there?

As for Emmanuel Larsen, Service met *him* under impeccable auspices: They were introduced that fateful April by Joseph Ballantine—rather, reintroduced, in a sense, for when Service had been an infant in Chengtu, Larsen had lived in his house. Larsen was the son of a teacher who had left San Francisco after the 1906 earthquake and, lured by an advertisement that promised free saddle horses and other heady exotic perquisites, got a job at the Imperial University in Chengtu. Flooded out of their home there in another vexing catastrophe, the Larsens had taken temporary shelter in the Service residence while the Services were away for the summer; when the missionary family returned in the fall they found their unexpected guests solidly entrenched, along with a scattering of dogs, goats, cats, rabbits, and a couple of ponies.

Emmanuel Larsen, on growing up, had stayed in China as a businessman, then became a civilian employee of the navy, and switched to State in 1944. Service had bumped into him once or twice in Washington in the spring of 1945—one time, Larsen would later contend before a House Judiciary subcommittee, at a lunch at the Tally-Ho Restaurant where, he claimed, John Carter Vincent had denounced General Hurley. Larsen changed his mind often.[5] Of that lunch, Service could not even remember that Vincent was present and thought it highly unlikely: Vincent would be far less apt to have lunch at the Tally-Ho, Service said, than at the Cosmos Club.

Service made no effort to conceal from his confrères at State his new associations with journalists who were flatteringly eager to hear about recent happenings in China. Indeed, some of the department people he saw daily must have known that the naval lieutenant and the magazine writer and the newspaper editor had been under round-the-clock surveillance for a month, but no one saw fit to warn Service. (Service was supposed to have been given a liaison job in Intelligence, representing the State Department in some of its dealings with the army and the navy, but the assignment was canceled, without anyone's telling him why, the day after he first met Jaffe.) The then senior legal officer at State, Adrian Fisher, reflected years afterward, "It was like a scene out of *Heaven's My Destination.* Jack Service went into a bawdy house thinking it was still a girls' boarding school." Being just about as nonideological a person as any

---

[5]Larsen once swore that Philip Jaffe had told him he'd been a frequent house guest of the John Fairbank family. Professor Fairbank categorically denied it, also under oath.

government could hope to have in its employ, and never suspecting that some of his new friends might have ulterior motives in soliciting his company, Service spent a good deal of time with them in Washington and New York that spring. He was considerably less concerned about what they were up to than about where he would be assigned; meanwhile in May he was pleased to be notified that he had received a two-grade Foreign Service promotion, from FSO-6 up to FSO-4. (Service was the youngest of twenty-two career men who were then jumped upward. By 1957 all of the fifteen men in this group who were still in the Foreign Service, except for John Service, had reached FSO-1, and nine of them had attained the next and highest grade of career minister. Service was still a Class 2 officer—the only one extant with more than ten years' service in that grade.)

In all, Service saw Jaffe seven times between April 19 and May 29, and had no compunction about lending the editor, for background use, his own personal copies of several reports he had filed from China. These were technically classified, but mainly because Service had classified them himself. According to a Loyalty Review Board that would find reasonable doubt of Service's loyalty at the end of 1951, the contents of the documents were largely of a journalistic nature:

> We have examined the 18 reports copies of which Service concedes were or may have been lent by him to Jaffe. Some of these are not classified; others are classified "secret" or "confidential." Service testified, and the evidence indicates, that these were his own classifications and that, in many cases at least, before he showed them to Jaffe by reason of lapse of time or otherwise they were no longer secret or confidential.
>
> From our examination of these reports, it appears to us that they were for the most part such as a newspaper reporter on the spot might transmit to his newspaper. Some of them, however, appear to us to be of a nature which no discreet person would disseminate without express authority, and some of them were dated within four to six weeks of the time they were lent to Jaffe, and the originals had not been in the hands of the State Department for more than a week. These recent reports therefore might be considered as "hot news."

On May 8, at Jaffe's request, Service visited the editor's room at the Statler Hotel in Washington. Service did not know that the room was bugged. The actual tape recording of the Service-Jaffe dialogue of that day has never been revealed; a transcript that was ultimately provided by the FBI seemed in parts to be garbled (i.e., Jaffe's allegedly saying to Service, "Hurley's fighting Chungking then," and Service's replying "Oh yes"; Chungking was just about the only thing Hurley *wasn't* fighting). The crucial reported sentence had Service saying to Jaffe, "Well, what I said about the military plans is, of course, very secret," an apparent allusion to the McClure-Barrett-Bird proposals that had got nowhere the previous December. Service would later swear under oath that he could not recall having said precisely that, and that in any event he had never disclosed any "secret plans" to Jaffe because he wasn't privy to the details of any.

By now, of course, Service was hopelessly enmeshed in the net that was being tightened around Jaffe, Gayn, Roth, Larsen, and Kate Mitchell, whom Service met once during the spring; she was writing a book, he was informed, on Confucianism. On June 5 Maurice Thorez, the leader of the French Communist party, evidently speaking on behalf of Moscow, launched an attack on Earl Browder and the American Communist party. The next day, John Carter Vincent, then still chief of Chinese affairs at State, asked Service what effect he thought the split within the ranks might have on the Chinese Communists. Service dutifully prepared a memorandum (he thought the effect, if any, would be negligible) and took it in to Vincent himself.

As he left his own office, Service noticed a couple of men lounging outside and asked if he could help them; no, they said, they were waiting for somebody. They were still around when he went out to lunch. At 7:30 that evening, they appeared at the door of his apartment, identified themselves as FBI agents, and told him he was under arrest for violation of the Espionage Act.[6] The navy had withdrawn its objections to a swoop; Roth, Jaffe, Mitchell, Larsen, and Gayn were arrested simultaneously. Ray Ludden, who was celebrating his birthday in New York, had expected to hear from Service that night about an anniversary drink they were scheduled to have together, and he was miffed when he never even got a phone call from his old friend.[7]

---

[6]The Kuomintang press, learning at first only that Service had been picked up on that charge, informed its readers that he was a Japanese spy.
[7]Ludden was home on leave, and expected to return to China under Wedemeyer. But just before he was supposed to go back, Wedemeyer said that Hurley was putting too much pressure on him not to permit any of Stilwell's old advisory gang to resume their previous operations, so he would have to give Ludden back to the State Department. "That was the day I started hunting around for my foxhole," Ludden recalled. In the weeks immedi-

By the time the accused persons were arraigned before a United States commissioner, the FBI had alerted the newspapers and had prepared tidy press releases that were distributed as the six were booked. Larsen, with whom Service had exchanged no more than a few dozen words in any language throughout their lives, began talking to him in Chinese. Reporters were watching, and Service felt that there had already been enough intimations of conspiracy. "Let's speak English," he said brusquely. Larsen seemingly had never much liked Service, and this rejection did nothing to enhance his amiability; he soon became convinced, moreover, that Service had somehow made him a scapegoat in the *Amerasia* incident. Larsen also developed a grudge against John Carter Vincent, which stemmed from his having called Vincent's office after his arrest. Drumright had taken the call, and Larsen had heard him say "This is Larsen," to which Vincent replied, "What does he want?" Drumright had further said, "He wants to know . . . are you going to do anything for him?," and after a moment had reported to Larsen, "John Carter Vincent says he wouldn't touch you with a ten-foot pole."

In the FBI press releases, Service was identified as "John Stewart Service"; that was the start of his quinquesyllabic identity. (His wife was in California, and got a call from a friend. "Say, is your husband Jack's name 'John Stewart Service?' " the friend asked. Caroline said it was indeed. "Well, you better get to a radio quick," was the startling response. "He's just been arrested as an international Communist spy.") Service stayed in prison overnight before he was bailed out. "Nowadays, being arrested has a sort of cachet," he told a friend in 1972. "It was different then. I was overwhelmed with disgrace and shame. I remember some guy in another cell, booked for car theft or rape, or whatever, asking me, 'What are *you* in for?' I said, 'Conspiracy to violate the Espionage Act,' and he said 'I don't know what that is, but it sounds like something real big!' "

Meanwhile, the FBI had searched Service's State Department office and confiscated all his papers, some of which he would never see again; it developed later that the bureau's operatives thought there was some-

---

ately following Service's arrest, Ludden himself was hunted down wherever he went by the FBI, which, unimpressed by his having once worked for the agency himself, kept nagging at him to say something detrimental to Service. Ludden finally found temporary sanctuary at an army post, where the commanding general told him that if Ludden did not want to be pestered by J. Edgar Hoover's people he simply wouldn't permit them to set foot in his territory.

thing sinister about his having a lot of material on hand about Chinese Communists—the very people he was supposed to be keeping tabs on for his government. While they were at it, the FBI men made off with a copy of a letter Service had just written to the authors Theodore H. White and Annalee Jacoby, in which he had speculated (with, understandably, the future of General Hurley in mind) about the hiring practices of the fledgling Truman administration. "There is a feeling that good jobs should go to good party members," Service had said. The word *party* triggered the imaginations of the Communist-hunters on the staff of the McCarran committee; its chief counsel, Robert Morris, seemed disappointed to learn that Service had been referring to the Democratic party.

The apprehension of six alleged Communist spies, three of whom were actually employed by the federal government, set off a veritable barrage of fireworks in the right-wing press. The Scripps-Howard chain's chief expert on communism, Frederick Woltman, averred on June 8 that the stolen documents had helped turn the United States against Chiang and toward Mao, that the key man in this purloined-papers drama was Service, "the State Department's principal adviser to our embassy in China [which Service, of course, was not]," and that the dirty work had begun after his return in 1944 from "a highly secret military strategic commission to Yenan"—a flattering, if not exactly foolproof, description of Colonel Barrett's Dixie Mission. "It was after the commission returned that sharp disagreements arose between Chiang Kai-shek and General Joseph Stilwell," Woltman went on, "as a result of which the latter was returned to this country." If the Scripps-Howard man had been better briefed by, say, a China-language Foreign Service officer familiar with the events he was writing about, he might have made fewer errors.[8]

In Chungking the Nationalist press was rather pleased with Service's detention, but in Yenan the reaction was altogether different. Mao and Chou hadn't expected Service's recall to lead to anything like *that.* The Communist *Liberation Daily* on June 25 carried an editorial—generally believed to have been written by Chairman Mao himself—in which Service's arrest was termed a watershed in American-Chinese relations.

[8]A Hearst reporter, Ray Richards, had it two days later that Service had gone to Moscow to help some Communists on the American embassy staff there undercut Chiang in resisting Chinese Communist demands. Richards's source was an "important attaché of the Chinese delegation" at San Francisco, a description that could fit the Chinese priest Yu-pin, who never could tell Service and Davies apart and who wasn't correct about either of them.

And in that editorial, just when phrases like "the Davies-Service clique" were beginning to achieve currency in the United States, there appeared for the first time the ominous-sounding "Hurley and his ilk." A leading biographer of Mao's would subsequently state, "The editorial, which was written throughout in a sharp and almost aggressive tone, concluded with a warning that, if the American authorities chose to support the Chinese reactionaries, they would receive from the Chinese people the lesson they deserved."

Service hadn't thought much about getting a lawyer. He didn't really think he needed one; after all, the *Amerasia* plot, if it was a plot, had been hatched and discovered while he was still in Yenan, a pretty remote place to conspire from. Even so, on the advice of friends in Washington, he went to see a few attorneys in the city, among them John C. Reid, with whom he had gone to Oberlin. They had barely known each other there; Reid was a mere freshman when Service was a big-shot senior. Reid was the ideal kind of counsel for a man in Service's dreadful circumstances. He was a lawyer of unassailable respectability; he specialized in tax law and his principal clients were du Ponts.[9] This was not his kind of case, however, and for the moment there seemed to be nothing he could do.

At the beginning of August the Department of Justice submitted the *Amerasia* case to a twenty-member federal grand jury. It took twelve votes to indict. The jury voted, 14-to-6, to indict Jaffe and Larsen. There was a 13-to-7 vote against Roth. By votes of 15-to-5 and 18-to-2, respectively, Gayn and Mitchell were let off. By a vote of 20-to-0, the grand jury refused to indict Service—who freely acknowledged then, and has acknowledged ever since to anyone who would listen, that he was indiscreet in his dealings with the Jaffe crowd. Jaffe pleaded guilty and Larsen *nolo contendere;* both received modest fines. The government eventually dropped its case against Roth.

[9] A few years later, when Eisenhower became president, Reid was invited by Attorney General William Rogers to be his assistant attorney general in charge of the Tax Division. Reid didn't really want the job; he was just beginning to make some big money in private practice; but it was hard to resist that kind of beguiling summons. He finally figured out a way to beg off: He said that if he were nominated he would have to be approved by the Senate, and that because he had stood up for Jack Service surely Joe McCarthy or some like-minded Senator would raise hell with the administration during his confirmation hearings.

Service assumed, wrongly, that he was in the clear, although there were some rough edges to be smoothed over at State. Undersecretary Grew, for instance, had impulsively declared after the arrests that the department had "caught some thieves in its chicken coop." Grew also thought, mistakenly, that Service had held a press conference on China at the Institute of Pacific Relations. Service had not, as it happened; he had merely turned up at one of the IPR's periodic sherry parties as had also, on one occasion or another, Stanley K. Hornbeck, Joseph C. Grew, and Wang Shih-chieh.

Grew resigned as undersecretary not long afterward, being replaced by Dean Acheson, and Acheson's enemy Joe McCarthy wasted no time in saying that Grew was "forced to resign" because he had wanted Service more severely prosecuted than he had been.[10] Grew actually quit for two quite different reasons: He had had forty-one years in diplomacy and was tired, and he had a policy disagreement with some of his colleagues, involving not John Service, but the American position toward the postwar status of the emperor of Japan.

Service's exoneration by the grand jury came on August 10, and it got far less publicity than his arrest, because it coincided with the dropping of the atomic bomb on Nagasaki. He had been on leave status pending disposition of his case, and on August 12 he was summoned to appear before the Foreign Service Personnel Board, which gave him a clean bill of health the following day and restored him to active duty. The department indicated that he would probably be assigned next to some post in Europe, but then someone reflected that this could be interpreted by the Chinese Nationalists as evidence that a man who was *persona non grata* to them could be dislodged from the Asian orbit. So in September—the Democrats still having some guts—just after the Japanese surrender, Service was sent to Tokyo, as George Atcheson's executive officer, to work in the diplomatic section of General MacArthur's newly formed occupation headquarters.

John Emmerson was also sent to Japan—logically enough, because of his linguistic prowess—at the start of the American occupation of the country. He had been playing another round of diplomatic musical chairs. James Penfield, who had been attached to Admiral Chester Nimitz's staff

---

[10]Walter Judd reacted to the outbreak of the Korean War, in part, by calling for the reinstatement of Grew, whom he characterized as one of the "men whom the left-wing boys pushed out of the Department."

at Guam, had been summoned to Washington to work in the Office of Chinese Affairs. Emmerson, his idea of indoctrinating Japanese prisoners having been turned down, was sent to fill Penfield's slot. He was flying across the Pacific when the Japanese surrender was signed; on reaching Guam he found orders to proceed to Yokohama and join MacArthur's staff. Japan had never allowed political parties much freedom before, but now they were fully tolerated, and even encouraged, and MacArthur wanted a weekly report on what each was up to. Emmerson was assigned to that task—a rather formidable one, since as few as three individuals could form a new party and several triumvirates were in fact indulging in the heady privilege.

On October 4 MacArthur decreed a Japanese Bill of Rights and followed that within a week by releasing thousands of political prisoners whom the imperial government had stashed away. Some of these had been locked up for eighteen years. Emmerson had already interviewed several of them at the Fuchu Prison—Communists, Koreans, members of obscure underground sects—in connection with his new assignment; they had a lot of information about the operations of the secret police, and what they could disclose was expected to be useful when the Americans began to hold war trials of Japanese militarists. Emmerson recommended that a few men with substantial stories to tell be further interrogated by MacArthur's counterintelligence experts, and three of them were duly removed from jail for one day, ahead of the general amnesty, and taken by jeep to headquarters for questioning. From this evolved a subsequent accusation that Emmerson himself had released some Communists and driven them around Tokyo in a staff car to the applause of a crowd of half a million, thereby, the allegation continued, contributing greatly to the renaissance of the Japanese Communist party.

Emmerson never laid eyes on MacArthur while working for him in Japan. Atcheson and Service had not much more contact than he with the supreme commander. But that was not the way Hurley saw it from Chungking. Still trying in his bumbling way to unify disintegrating China, the ambassador had persuaded Mao to accompany him from Yenan to Chungking on August 28—the first airplane ride the chairman had ever taken and his first face-to-face encounter with the Generalissimo since 1927. The reunion had been unproductive, however, and Hurley somehow concluded that it was because Atcheson and Service had been posted to Japan. Hurley forwarded to President Truman a protest from Chiang (which Hurley himself had drafted) against the two "pro-Communist"

Old China Hands' being permitted to "direct" United States policy in Asia. Direct policy! MacArthur had never had much use for the State Department in any circumstances, and Atcheson and Service, though they lived with the rest of the American brass at the old Imperial Hotel, were assigned offices in the Mitsui Bank building; they could hardly get into the Dai Ichi building, where the general was enthroned. Chiang also informed Truman, ventriloquially, that neither Atcheson nor Service would be permitted to set foot again on the Chinese mainland; when Mac-Arthur was informed of that ultimatum, he seemed to find it amusing.

Hurley made another trip back to the United States in late September to rest up from his Atlas-like labors and to air his complaints in his own name. He was encouraged by Alfred Kohlberg, who kept him supplied with clippings from the Communist *Daily Worker*, which had got hold of some of Hurley's own reports and was lambasting him for them. At Santa Fe, New Mexico, on November 15, Hurley, whom President Truman and Secretary of State Byrnes expected to return to Chungking to represent them as soon as he'd had a home leave, grumbled in a speech that no one in the State Department had made a public declaration of United States policy toward China in nearly four years; he added that he himself had been defeated in China by Foreign Service men who asserted that he was not upholding the policy of his country.

By November 26 Hurley was in Washington, and that evening he learned of a speech made on the floor of the House a few hours earlier by Representative Hugh DeLacy, a radical Democrat from the state of Washington. DeLacy and five other West-Coast congressmen—among them Helen Gahagan Douglas, who had not yet been unseated by Richard Nixon—were attempting to get the United States to make a drastic policy change indeed: specifically to pull out of China lock, stock, and barrel. DeLacy said that Hurley and Wedemeyer "have now committed us to armed intervention" in China's internal affairs; in discussing "the rotten Hurley policy in China," he chastised the ambassador for his rough treatment of the Foreign Service officers who had been there.

Hurley's response was to fire off a letter of resignation to Truman. The ambassador, who may have hoped that the president would come stoutly to his defense and prevail upon him—with a suitable public show of confidence—to change his mind, had a lot to get off his mind:

> . . . it is no secret that the American policy in China did not have the support of all the career men in the State Department. The professional

foreign service men sided with the Chinese Communist armed party and the imperialist bloc of nations whose policy it was to keep China divided against herself. Our professional diplomats continuously advised the Communists that my efforts in preventing the collapse of the National Government did not represent the policy of the United States. These same professionals openly advised the Communist armed party to decline unification of the Chinese Communist Army with the National Army unless the Chinese Communists were given control.

Despite these handicaps we did make progress toward unification of the armed forces of China. We did prevent civil war between the rival factions, at least until after I had left China. We did bring the leaders of the rival parties together for peaceful discussions. Throughout this period the chief opposition to the accomplishment of our mission came from the American career diplomats in the Embassy at Chungking and in the Chinese and Far Eastern Divisions of the State Department.

I requested the relief of the career men who were opposing the American policy in the Chinese Theatre of war. These professional diplomats were returned to Washington and placed in the Chinese and Far Eastern Divisions of the State Department as my supervisors.[11] Some of these same career men whom I relieved have been assigned as advisors to the Supreme Commander in Asia. In such positions most of them have continued to side with the Communist armed party and at times with the imperialistic bloc against American policy.[12] This, Mr. President, is an outline of one of the reasons why American foreign policy announced by the highest authority is rendered ineffective by another section of diplomatic officials. . . .

The Hydra-headed direction and confusion of our foreign policy in Washington during the late war is chargeable to the weakness of our Foreign Service. If our Foreign Service had been capable of understanding and sympathetic effectuation of our announced war aims it would not have failed so completely to obtain commitments to the principles for which we claimed to be fighting from the nations to which we gave the strength of our productivity and manpower.

[11]It was hard to figure out just whom he was thinking of. Drumright, with whom Hurley had no argument, was then running the Office of Chinese Affairs, directly under Vincent, who had never served under Hurley. Ringwalt and Freeman were working under Drumright, but it was laughable to suggest that they had any supervisory powers over Hurley, and anyway, they were far from his principal *bêtes noirs*.

[12]Hurley kept carrying on about "imperialistic blocs," but it was hard to figure out whom or what he was thinking of here also.

Once again Hurley was defused. Truman accepted his resignation the very next day, and appointed General Marshall to be his special envoy to China. The official ambassador's hat would in due course be handed to John Leighton Stuart, the missionary educator who had spent most of the war interned by the Japanese in Peking.

When the bare bones of the news of Hurley's resignation reached Tokyo, Atcheson and Service began to celebrate. The occupation of Japan was officially austere. General MacArthur had ruled that all available shipping space was to be reserved for essential supplies, and whiskey for the occupiers was not among these. The navy, however, did not feel bound by the army's strictures, and an admiral had given Atcheson a whole case of bourbon, which he and Service had deposited in a Mitsui Bank safe-deposit vault. Now, hearing about Hurley, they broke out a precious bottle. Their jubilation was interrupted on their learning from some journalists who stopped by their office that Hurley was blaming "career men in the State Department" for his leave-taking. They had no doubt whom he meant. Atcheson, who hadn't much liked his Japanese assignment to begin with ("Come take my place," he had written to the retired Laurence Salisbury; "I can't stand it any more"), sent a telegram to Secretary of State Byrnes saying that Service and he "very much regret that we have become the objects of this publicity and we certainly have no desire to enter into any public dispute. However," he continued, "if these ridiculous contentions have actually been made by Mr. Hurley, it is our suggestion that the best means of dispelling them would be to produce the record. . . ."

At just about that time General Wedemeyer had arrived in Tokyo, en route to the United States, to confer with General MacArthur and Admiral Raymond P. Spruance about how the United States should handle the defeated Japanese troops who were still in northern China. The three high-ranking officers reported to the Pentagon that they concurred that the situation in China afforded an excellent opportunity for the United States to bring about a compromise between the Nationalists and Communists there. Later, when it became unpopular to have seemed to advocate any such unification, all three authors of the joint statement reacted in their characteristic fashion: MacArthur denied having signed it, Wedemeyer straddled the issue, and Spruance declared, "We meant exactly what we said." During the Tokyo stopover Wedemeyer had a cordial chat with Service, in which the general said that the Foreign Service officer was being recommended for a medal awarded to civilians for exemplary work during the war. In Washington, Service later heard, Wedemeyer saw J. Edgar Hoover, and afterward there were no more cordial meetings and no further talk of a decoration.

Hurley was producing a new record of sorts in Washington, making an emotional and sometimes distraught appearance before Senator Tom Connally's Foreign Relations Committee, which wanted some elaboration of his broadside indictments.[13] Hurley wasted no time in bringing up Service's own emotional memorandum to Stilwell of October 10, 1944, which he regarded as evidence of the "sabotage" being waged against him by the Foreign Service. (That led Senator Styles Bridges, the rock-ribbed conservative from the granite state of New Hampshire, to rehash the *Amerasia* case.) A good deal of what Hurley had to say to the senators was more confusing than illuminating. He seemed to be telling them at one point that the way the world was set up, the Russians and he were on one side, and the British and French and other "imperialist" nations on the other. And he mentioned—with atypical modesty he did not credit himself with the inspiration—that the Chinese Nationalists and Communists had both adopted as their slogan "a government of the people, by the people, and for the people." Hurley added darkly that when a letter had come into the State Department attacking him, and Drumright had drafted a response in his defense, Vincent had stricken the pro-Hurley comments from the version that ultimately went out, thereby leaving the ambassador "naked to my enemies, and to the enemies of America."

And just who were his enemies?, the puzzled senators kept demanding. One by one the names came out—Service, of course, then Atcheson, Vincent, and on to Davies, Freeman, Ringwalt, and Emmerson.[14] (Ludden's name was somehow omitted; perhaps Hurley had momentarily forgotten him.) These men, Hurley went on, "were disloyal to the American policy," but despite their efforts to undermine the Nationalist government by, in part, disclosing secret Allied plans to the Communists, under

[13]The verbatim proceedings of Hurley's appearance were not printed until Senator J. W. Fulbright, a later chairman of the committee, put them out in 1971, "in the belief that an understanding of the history of the period of our involvement on mainland China is important to our expectations of more normal relations with the People's Republic of China."

[14]Freeman and Ringwalt were sitting among the spectators when they heard Hurley say of them, according to Ringwalt's recollection (though the transcript of the hearings does not contain the words), "If they're not Communists, they're pro-Communists"; then he looked toward them and shouted, as if he had caught them red-handed, "There they are!"

Chiang Kai-shek China had been "fighting like a wounded tiger." As for the telegram that Atcheson et al. had dispatched on February 28 (the text was not yet publicly known), Hurley sputtered, ". . . as soon as I left, George Atcheson and everybody attempted what they had been trying to do when the President sent me to China, and that was to destroy the Government of the Republic of China."

"He [Atcheson] said that in the letter?" asked Connally.

"No, he did not, but . . ." said Hurley, veering off on a new tack.

The Foreign Relations Committee hearings had been not long under way when Secretary of State Byrnes instructed his legal adviser, Green H. Hackworth, as follows:

> "I desire you to determine to the best of your ability whether there is any evidence within the Department, or available to the Department, that any of the officers named by General Hurley in his recent testimony, or any other employees of the State Department, ever communicated to the Communist faction in China any information concerning allied military plans for landings or operations in China. I also desire you to determine to the best of your ability whether any of the officers . . . advised the Communists in China that Ambassador Hurley's efforts to prevent the collapse of the National Government did not represent the policy of the United States, or openly or privately advised the Communist faction to decline unification of the Chinese Communist Army with the Nationalist Army unless the Chinese Communists were given control. . . . I desire you to acquaint yourself with any information which may reach the Department from time to time concerning allegations against the personnel of the Department on the grounds of disloyalty to the Government of the United States.

It took Hackworth three months to come up with a reply. He found "no evidence that any of the Foreign Service officers referred to by General Hurley or other employees of the Department ever communicated to the Communist faction in China any information concerning Allied military plans for landings or operations in China," no evidence that they were saying behind Hurley's back that he was working against American policy, and no evidence that they had urged the Communists to reject unification unless they were given control of the Nationalist army. "The officers in question deny that they ever made any such suggestion or that they ever entertained any such view," Hackworth told Byrnes.

"They felt that unification of the Chinese forces was desirable but none ever suggested, so far as is disclosed by the record, that the Communists should be given control." By the time Hackworth responded, the Senate hearings had long since been terminated—cut short rather abruptly, indeed, when the committee itself concluded that Hurley had no basis for his freewheeling charges.[15]

On the other side of Capitol Hill, the House of Representatives was concurrently demonstrating its unwillingness to let the Senate have a monopoly on arguing about China. Representative George A. Dondero, a Republican from Michigan and one of the less illustrious statesmen of modern times, gave a floor speech on December 10 entitled "General Hurley Is Right."[16] What Dondero had to say was largely drawn from a Washington *Times-Herald* interview with Paul Yu-pin, the perambulating vicar apostolic of Nanking. Said Dondero:

> The prelate said there was every indication that Service was working in the interests of the Communist Party and that it was upon his advice that General Stilwell approached Chiang Kai-shek in person no less than three times to ask that the Chinese Communists be armed with American lend-lease supplies . . . "Vinegar Joe," playing into Service's hands, the bishop continued, appointed Service himself to the job. The report Service submitted to Stilwell, the prelate said, "lauded the Communist soldiers in glowing terms." . . . Following his report to Stilwell, Service kept urging him to go to the Chinese Generalissimo with the demand that the Communists be armed. Cognizant of the situation in China, Vinegar Joe hesitated to do so, the bishop said, but finally consented when his political advisor insisted.

[15]At one nerve-jangled point Hurley complained that the committee—with the supportive Republicans Bridges and Arthur Vandenberg notably excepted—was treating him like a bootlegger. Having said that, he then asked to have the remark stricken from the record. Connally refused.

[16]According to the by no means always accurate Emmanuel Larsen, there could be cooperative interplay between the upper and lower branches of the Congress. Larsen once testified that Dondero, seeking some dirt on Owen Lattimore, had sent him over to see Senator Kenneth A. Wherry of Nebraska, and that Wherry had explained why, telling Larsen, "You know, I am the expert on homosexualism." But Larsen had had nothing to contribute to Wherry's expertise in that line. "I may mention," Larsen also said, "that Mr. Dondero, undoubtedly a very excellent man and good lawyer, and so on, is totally blank when it comes to Far Eastern affairs and knowledge of what went on. He doesn't know the slightest about it."

After a while—Dondero went on, still citing Yu-pin—Service repeated his insistence, and Stilwell meekly·complied. Then:

> Again the Chinese leader refused. And it was then, the prelate said, that Stilwell was informed that if the demand was repeated, there was no other alternative but to ask that President Roosevelt recall him from China. . . . Undismayed, Service kept hammering at Stilwell that the Chinese Communists were getting a raw deal, and again insisted that the demand be resubmitted for the Generalissimo's reconsideration. And it was on this third visit to his good friend, with whom he had broken bread on many an occasion, that Stilwell was informed by the Generalissimo he was asking Roosevelt to relieve him of his duties in China. Service, the bishop said, was a definite detrimental influence during his assignment in China.

The House of Representatives reacted to Dondero's restatement of Yu-pin's blather by instructing its Judiciary Committee to reexamine the *Amerasia* case all over again.

In Japan, while Hurley was daily favoring the Foreign Relations Committee with potshots against them, Atcheson and Service were doing their best to defend themselves. On December 8, for instance, Service wrote a long letter to the secretary of state that went, in part:

> I am not a Communist. This can be verified by anyone who knows me well.
>
> I did not "sabotage" American policy in China. On the contrary, in answer to unavoidable questions by Communists I explained the impossibility of American intervention in favor of a political party forcefully opposing a recognized government.
>
> I did not tell the Communists that Mr. Hurley's statements did not represent American policy. On the contrary I never left doubt that they were the policy.
>
> I did not send messages of any kind to the Communists; nor did I show my reports or other official reports to Communists or any other Chinese; nor did I give the Communists, orally or otherwise, any classified American military information. Officers who were members of the Observer Group can confirm that we took all possible precautions to safeguard our reports.
>
> I did not advocate the collapse or overthrow of the Central Government. On the contrary, my reports will show that I consistently took the view that the Central Government could (and should) strengthen itself by liberalization

which would promote unification of the country on a democratic basis, and that American influence should be exerted to that end.

Atcheson, too, was making himself heard from Tokyo. In a telegram to the secretary of state on December 6, he said:

> Mr. Hurley's continuous assaults together with the falsity and apparent vindictiveness of his statements seem at this distance to place us in a position where a statement of some kind in refutation appears increasingly unavoidable. I am most reluctant to make a statement which might prolong the matter or which might raise for public discussion any question of past or present policy. But continuous replies of "no comment" to press inquiries lend themselves to the implication that by avoiding comment we give credence to Mr. Hurley's charges. My reputation in the service generally after 25 years is of importance to me. My reputation in China where I spent some 17 years is of importance to me. My reputation in my present position is of importance to me. Mr. Service feels the same way. . . .
>
> Early this year, while I was awaiting promised replacement, after the normal tour of duty, Mr. Hurley returned to the United States and, under the Department's instructions, I assumed charge of the Embassy and remained until after the middle of April, when my successor arrived. The Ambassador's absence was not designed to stop the work of the Embassy. During that period I sent the Department a telegram [the February 28 one] in the light of the current situation, submitting for consideration some thoughts which we felt might assist in furthering Chinese unity in the war against Japan. The telegram specifically requested that its contents be discussed with Ambassador Hurley in Washington. I do not know Mr. Hurley's purpose in implying that this was done behind his back.
>
> Mr. Hurley's statements, in regard to "Communism" and to "European Imperialism" are so empty as regards Foreign Service Officers as to merit no further comment.

The following day Atcheson decided they merited some comment after all:

> From conversations in Chungking with Mr. Hurley, it is my impression that his ideas on this subject flowed from some oral instructions from the late President to keep an eye on European imperialistic activities in southeast Asia,

with especial reference to French Indo-China and Siam and which were not intended to have reference to China itself. I remember commenting to Mr. Hurley in Chungking last autumn that it would be difficult to assume that Great Britain, in the light of her hopes to restoration of her large commercial interests in China, would wish anything but a peaceful and stable China and that the same consideration would logically apply to French policy, as a disturbed China would not be conducive to revival of French trade or to the benefit of Indo-China.

I am positive from my two years in Chungking that there was no "alignment" by any Foreign Service Officer with any European imperialistic activities as mentioned by General Hurley. I myself saw no evidence of any activities on the part of British, French or Dutch diplomatic representatives seeking any derogation of the authority of the Chinese National Government or of any desire that China should emerge from the war anything but a stable and unified nation.

On December 8 Atcheson again wired the secretary:

General Hurley began his assignment in Chungking with a strong prejudice against the Department and the Foreign Service and especially officers who had served with his predecessor. Even before his appointment was definite, I assured him that if he should become Ambassador, he would find that he had a competent professional staff of officers thoroughly devoted to the service and to their jobs, that they were making a life work of the service, that most of them had served under a number of chiefs, that they would be loyal to him as their new chief. I urged him to show confidence in them. I called the staff together and told them of these comments and all were in complete agreement that they would do their best for him. It was, however, a fixed idea with him that there were officers in the Foreign Service and American military officers who were in opposition to him. For a long time he did not show us his telegrams to the President in regard to his negotiations with the Chinese Communists and did not in fact even report to the Department in the matter but sent all his messages by channels other than the Embassy to the White House. When we finally persuaded him that an Ambassador had an obligation to report also to the Secretary of State, he called upon several officers to assist in putting into shape a series of telegrams to the Department in regard to his activities.

In his first drafts of these telegrams he inserted unwarranted and unbecoming references to his predecessor and also references to the "opposition" of

Foreign Service and military officers. I pointed out to him that as we in the Embassy had not known the details of his activities, no officers there could very well be in opposition to them; and that now that we knew what was in progress, no officer in the Embassy was in opposition to his activities or objectives but on the contrary all were staunchly in favor thereof. . . .

From Moscow that rancorous December, John Davies, on hearing that he was on Hurley's list of saboteurs, wrote home, "Our foreign relations are in a fantastic state—wishful thinking, vacillation, secret skeletons, and pervasive confusion. For these reasons the Foreign Service is not an exhilarating business. To get out of it and be able to speak the truth would be a refreshing experience. On the other hand, somebody has to carry on with the job. We can stay on hoping that things will be better, that our experience can be productive of some good."[17]

[17]At a reception in the Soviet Union, Secretary Byrnes took Davies over to Foreign Minister Molotov, and told the Russian, jokingly, "Pat Hurley says he's a Communist, so when he comes knocking at your door, you let him in, hear?"

8

"Sticking to verified and documented facts."

Marshall left for China just before Christmas. Vincent and his ten-year-old boy saw the general off. "Son, there goes the bravest man in the world," Vincent said as the plane taxied away. "He's going out to try to unify China." At least Marshall's approach to that Sisyphean task was certain to be different from Hurley's. Marshall's personal reputation was secure; he had no interest in self-glorification; years earlier in China his wife had asked him if he had any objection to her publishing an account of their stay there, and he had told her to go ahead; but first he deleted all the laudatory references to himself.

Marshall left with some bargaining power; Truman had authorized him to offer China a loan of a half billion dollars, but only on condition that a coalition government could be established to receive and administer it. Philip Sprouse, then consul general at Kunming, was preparing to play Christmas-dinner host to the twenty or so Americans there when he received word to proceed posthaste to Chungking and put himself at Marshall's disposal. (Marshall had no holiday meal problems. He had already been invited to Christmas dinner by the Christianized Chiang Kai-sheks.) Sprouse figured he'd be back at his post in three weeks, but he spent nearly a year working for Marshall.[1]

Nobody thought there was much hope that Marshall could accomplish very much. It would later be charged that all the China-losers in the State Department had burdened him with demands to be made upon Chiang Kai-shek that they knew the Generalissimo could not possibly accept. But in fact the directive he carried with him was a compilation of proposals

[1]When in 1947 Marshall became secretary of state, Sprouse would again be working under him, this time as head of Chinese affairs, a job he detested. "Everything you did, you did in the sheer agony of defending the past," he said, "instead of thinking about the future."

drawn up by State and by the Pentagon, and the two branches had differed very little in what they suggested. They both agreed that any further American aid to China had to be preceded by unification of its government, and that was a condition that neither the Nationalists nor the Communists were particularly minded to accept.

Marshall wanted to impress all Chinese with the significance of his mission, and inasmuch as the Second World War was over, there were many senior military men at loose ends who were available to accompany him and by their very glittering presence to lend weight to his efforts.[2] He deposited them at the Peking Union Medical College. There was a place nearby sometimes called the Temple of One Thousand Sleeping Buddhas. The Chinese living in the vicinity promptly began calling the new American enclave the Temple of One Thousand Sleeping Colonels.

In mediating between the rival Chinese factions, Marshall appeared to be off to a very fine start indeed. He had been in China scarcely two weeks when, on January 10, he was able to announce a cease-fire in the civil war. A tripartite authority—consisting of one Nationalist, one Communist, and one American—was set up to administer the welcome truce. But when Marshall went home in March to give Truman a personal report on his activities, the whole thing fell apart. The Soviet Union was pulling out of Manchuria, and both Chinese factions began scrambling to fill the vacuum. The Communists violated the cease-fire by moving into the crucial northern city of Changchun on April 15, and this provoked the Nationalists into retaliatory action. They took Changchun on May 23. Marshall, who had departed believing that the fighting had stopped, was back by then; he had returned to find an almost all-out war in seemingly unstoppable progress.

To the Old China Hands still around, this grim turn of events was not especially surprising. Raymond Ludden told Marshall one evening that,

---

[2]Wedemeyer, in his memoirs, had Marshall surrounded by a quite different coterie of henchmen, asserting that "by the time he arrived in China on his fatal mission, George Marshall was physically and mentally too worn out to appraise the situation correctly. . . . [H]e became an easy prey to crypto-Communists, or Communist-sympathizing syco-phants, who played on his vanity to accomplish their own ends." Just about *everybody*, Wedemeyer by then had been led to believe, was part of a conspiratorial apparatus; he said of Marshall's earlier career, "Marshall also had to contend with the vagaries of President Roosevelt who, even before his faculties failed during his fourth term, had been surrounded by intriguers and the soft-on-communism eggheads who enjoyed his wife's patronage and were given formidable power by Harry Hopkins and others in the President's confidence."

although he hated to say so, it seemed to him the general was in the same sorry position that Stilwell had been in two years earlier. "The only time we ever got anything out of Chiang Kai-shek," Ludden said to Marshall, "was when we backed him into a corner and beat it out of him."

"That's just what Chou En-lai told me," Marshall replied.

The Generalissimo, indeed, had changed so little that in August 1946 President Truman, at Marshall's suggestion, sent him a stiff note chiding him for permitting the "cruel murders" of Chinese liberals and his associates' "resort to force, military or secret police" to achieve their partisan* ends. Truman said that the influence in Chiang's China of militarists and political reactionaries was "violently repugnant" to the American people and that unless Chiang cleaned up his own house "American opinion will not continue in its generous attitude toward your nation."

Marshall gamely continued trying to patch up the unraveling situation; but the only hope for China's serenity was that its two major forces could see eye to eye, and each was so hostile toward the other and so suspicious of what the American representative was doing as he shuttled between them, that the Marshall Mission soon became mission impossible. In January 1947 the United States gave up trying. "The salvation of the situation," said Marshall in a plague-on-both-your-houses report largely drafted for him by Sprouse, "would be the assumption of leadership by the liberals in the Government and in the minority parties and successful action on their part under the leadership of the Generalissimo would lead to unity through good government."

At least no one could directly blame the Foreign Service officers for this latest Chinese debacle. Sprouse was the only one of them intimately involved with the Marshall Mission; and even there he was subordinate to Walter Robertson, who was the general's chief civilian adviser and the American member of the ill-fated tripartite supervisory body. Most of the other Old China Hands were far from the scene of inaction. John Service, for example, had been hospitalized in Tokyo with infectious hepatitis in April 1946. By the time he was pronounced fit in August, the State Department decided that he needed a change of scene, preferably a relatively tranquil one, and he was posted, following a brief home leave, to Wellington, New Zealand.[3] For one eight-month stretch, between

[3]The right-wing historian Anthony Kubek, who pursued Service as tenaciously as did any flea any dog, had this version of that period: "MacArthur flatly refused to have Service, so he was brought back home and—after Dean Acheson succeeded George Marshall as Secretary of State—was put in charge of placements and promotions in the Department.

ambassadors, he was in charge of the United States embassy there. In 1948 Service got another promotion: at thirty-nine, he became the youngest Class 2 officer—the diplomatic equivalent of a brigadier general—in the Foreign Service. ("It was an event of considerable satisfaction to me since I felt that in a sense it put a seal on the events of 1945," he would say later.) It appeared that his single indiscretion had been firmly consigned to the past and that he could look ahead to a promising career. In reality, however, that was Service's last Pacific post and his last advancement in rank. Never again would the government see fit to avail itself of his Asian expertise.

Remote from Washington though Service physically was during his New Zealand stint, his celebrity—more accurately, notoriety—was being vigorously sustained in the Capitol. Some of what was going on there was unknown to him: Between 1946 and 1948 the State Department four times investigated him, largely on the basis of information provided by the FBI, and four times found him guiltless of any wrongdoing. More publicly, the House Judiciary Committee had turned over its reexamination of the *Amerasia* case to a three-man subcommittee chaired by Representative Samuel F. Hobbs of Alabama. The subcommittee reported in October 1946 that it had found nothing objectionable in the way the prosecution of Jaffe and the rest of his crowd had been handled, although it did feel that the handling of the government files to which they had obtained access had been slipshod.

One of the principal witnesses before the Hobbs subcommittee was Emmanuel Larsen, who had been fined $500 in the purloined-papers affair. Larsen had had a hard time since then. Feeling understandably unwelcome at State, he had sought a job with the War Department, on whose behalf he hoped to serve in Korea; but then Ray Richards, the same Hearst man who had been nagging at Service, had written a story wondering why the United States would be thinking of sending a "Communist spy" out there. Larsen had gone to see Congressman Dondero, who

---

Astonishingly . . . ," Service spent two years in New Zealand after being invalided out of Japan. In 1950, in the course of one of Service's hearings before a State Department Loyalty Security Board, Sir Patrick Duff, who had been Great Britain's high commissioner for New Zealand, recalled that he had dined at the Services' residence in Wellington on the day of the then Princess Elizabeth's birthday, and that Service had proposed a toast to her—". . . hardly the type of gesture, I should fancy," Sir Patrick said, "which anyone of Communist leanings would go out of his way to make."

offered to furnish a suitable character reference but first wanted him to tell all to the Hobbs group.

So Larsen had talked, one of his odder allegations being that Service had been surreptitiously in touch with Jaffe while the Foreign Service officer was still *in* China. Out had flowed, too, the story about the lunch with Vincent and Service at the Tally-Ho: "They went to lunch. They had their meetings. I was with them at some lunch meetings where they talked openly about defeating this crowd like Hurley, do everything to get him out. They sabotaged Hurley. You may take my word for that. They sabotaged Hurley. I have given certain little notes and evidence to Hurley that I had committed to memory and helped him with his speech. It was a pity he did not launch it more systematically. He spoiled that for me." Larsen continued: "I do not think Vincent is really pro-Communist in his heart. He is just an ambitious person."

In subsequent cross-examination about this statement, Larsen declared, under oath, that it sounded rather incoherent to him, that he didn't really know whom he meant by "they," that he could recall only one lunch, that Service hadn't said anything, that he couldn't remember what notes he had given Hurley or why he had said Hurley had spoiled things for him. "I realize your point is to gather sufficient evidence to protect Mr. Service," he told an attorney questioning him, "against very serious charges which I myself—and you may put that in the record and repeat it anywhere and quote me—I do not believe they are true. I will once more summarize what I have said at the past meeting—that I have undoubtedly, through questioning and pressure and promises, and through my personal animosity to Mr. Service, and Mr. John Carter Vincent—that stems from no personal clash with these two gentlemen, but that was fired within me by a lot of very poisonous talk that was poured into my ear and poured into my wife's ear—agreed that these two men were very much against me, and I believe that as a result of all this I have been extremely unfair to them, and have said careless things that I should not have said. . . ." This recantation was uttered in 1950, exactly four days after Larsen had repeated his nearly five-year-old charge that Service was part of a "plot to sabotage" Hurley.

Just before the Hobbs subcommittee concluded that the *Amerasia* business was a thoroughly beaten dead horse, another weapon was being forged for the arsenal gradually being stockpiled for the forthcoming all-out war against the Old China Hands. Alfred Kohlberg was its chief Vulcan, and what he produced then was a new magazine called *Plain*

Talk, which, whatever else it was, was plainly at the opposite end of the ideological spectrum from *Amerasia*. Its editor was the archconservative Isaac Don Levine, who boasted in his memoirs, "My editorial creed was to stick to verified and documented facts."

The featured article in the initial issue of *Plain Talk* was "The State Department Espionage Case." Its authorship was attributed to Emmanuel Larsen. While Larsen had been licking his wounds in Florida several months back, he had a visit from two ex-FBI men who had worked on the *Amerasia* case. On behalf of Kohlberg, they offered him $300 to write the story. He could use the money; it would cover three-fifths of his fine. He prepared an article and in August brought it to New York, where he had what for him was a shattering experience. His hotel was also the scene of a veterans' jamboree: "wild women suddenly burst into my room, threw themselves on the bed, and I had to take one and throw her out, and finally I kept my door locked all the time."

Even more unsettling was the fact that Kohlberg and Levine had reservations about his text. They didn't think it went far enough in attacking the Old China Hands and their baleful influence on the State Department, the White House, the country, and the world. So Levine, the man with the unflinching editorial creed, and Ralph de Toledano, a writer of similar ideological bent, set about revising Larsen. "They rewrote that article so I hardly recognized it," he stated later. In their version, the one that was ultimately published, they mentioned a report written by John Service that had turned up in Philip Jaffe's possession. This was one of the documents that Service was supposed to have mailed naughtily to Jaffe from Yenan even before he submitted it to the State Department. It had been called "Generalissimo Chiang Kai-shek—Decline of His Prestige and Criticism of and Opposition to His Leadership," and the very title was calculated to make *Plain Talk*'s readers tremble with outrage. The only trouble was that Service hadn't written the report; it had been written by Philip Sprouse.[4]

The *Plain Talk* exposé also dusted off the old canard that Undersecre-

---

[4] Poor Sprouse! Not only did he get confused then with Service, but, because his name was Philip, he got confused with Jaffe. In searching Service's office when he was arrested, the FBI had found a letter from a "Phil" containing two words that were suspicious because they were in Chinese—"*Kung hsi.*" Ah ha, here was a concrete link between Service and the *Amerasia* editor and their wily Oriental machinations! The letter was actually from Sprouse, who had just heard of a new assignment Service was supposed to be getting: "*Kung hsi*" meant "Congratulations."

tary Grew had been forced out of the department for his insistence that Service be punished for his *Amerasia* connections. Still another congressional committee, this a Senate one, would declare in 1950 that if Larsen's account of what had happened to his article was true (the committee had compared both versions and found that the original "contains none of the bases for charges of a plot to destroy American policy in the Far East which have greatly confused the American people"), then "the action of Levine and his associates in connection with the *Plain Talk* article is one of the most despicable instances of a deliberate effort to deceive and hoodwink the American people in our history. Such conduct is beneath contempt."

Kohlberg was merely warming up.[5] He kept a vigilant watch on his adversaries, and he was not nodding when Vincent, in charge of all Far Eastern affairs of State in the fall of 1946, accepted a speaking engagement, as government officials regularly do, at a November 11 session in New York of the Annual Foreign Trade Convention. Kohlberg presumably felt no need, one week later, to monitor the remarks of General Wedemeyer at the National War College in Washington. Wedemeyer already had his stamp of approval, and what he said was, by Kohlberg's rigid criteria, unexceptionable: He described Mao Tse-tung and Chou En-lai as men whose "loyalties are first in the interest of Stalin and his program and then in the welfare of their own countrymen"; he called Chiang Kai-shek "a real Christian gentleman" who was "weighted down by the Confucian philosophy which required loyalty to family and friends."[6]

---

[5]When he got really going, he would, in a later publication he sponsored called *China Monthly* (Bishop Yu-pin was one of its advisers), eagerly ascribe to Douglas MacArthur, "the greatest living American," the statement that the fix the United States had got itself into with Asia was attributable to "stupidity at the top—treason just below." Just below was, of course, precisely where the Foreign Service officers found themselves uncomfortably perched.

[6]Kohlberg would probably not have approved, however, of an incident that occurred just after Wedemeyer spoke. Among newly matriculating students at the War College was Fulton Freeman, assigned there by the State Department. There was nothing Freeman wanted less than a confrontation with the general, whose disagreements with the views of the Old China Hands were becoming increasingly marked. Freeman slouched down in the last row of the lecture hall, hoping he wouldn't be spotted. But then there was a coffee break; one-third of the students were commanded to clink cups with the distinguished guest of honor, and Freeman found himself, willy-nilly, in that chosen minority. Wedemeyer came right up to him, exuding cordiality. "Why, Tony, you baldheaded son of a bitch, what are you doing here?" the general exclaimed. "When these guys [mostly army colonels and navy captains] start asking me questions about China in the next period,

Talking to the trade group on "American Business and the Far East," Vincent said he believed it to be unsound practice to invest in corrupt and politically confused nations. There was no indication that any of the businessmen in the audience objected to this sound advice. But Chiang's ambassador to the United States was among the listeners, and he took umbrage, even though Vincent had not been alluding specifically to China but, rather, to the Far East as a whole. When *Plain Talk* got around to reporting on the occasion, it conveyed the impression that Vincent had been talking *only* about China and had thus insulted the ambassador. The American China Policy Association, another organizational creation of the indefatigable Kohlberg, demanded of the secretary of state that the government dissociate itself from Vincent's remarks and apologize to the ambassador. Said the association, "Mr. Vincent's sympathies with the Yenan rebellion in China, and the precision with which his statements conform to the policies laid down in the Communist press, are self-evident."

Vincent was unruffled. His thoughts were on larger and more ominous matters than Kohlberg's hurt feelings. He was deeply concerned, for one thing, about the whole future of the Far East, and in December 1946 he wrote to the secretary himself on quite a different topic: Vincent wanted the American government to ponder the future perils of getting involved in the war that was getting under way between the French and their colonial subjects in Southeast Asia. "With inadequate forces, with public opinion strongly at odds, with a government rendered largely ineffective through internal division, the French have tried to accomplish in Indochina what a strong and united Britain has found it unwise to attempt in Burma," Vincent said. "Given the present elements in the situation, guerrilla warfare may continue indefinitely." An unhonored-to-be prophet had spoken up.

A few months later, however, Kohlberg could note with satisfaction a triumph of sorts in his own continuing guerrilla warfare. Vincent was out of Far Eastern affairs, having been shifted to Switzerland as American minister in that notably peace-loving nation. In connection with the new

I'm sure I won't know the answers, so you come sit next to me and answer them." And, sure enough, when the question-and-answer time came around, Wedemeyer announced jovially to the group, "Whatever you ask me, I'm going to give you *my* answer and then ask Tony here for the *real* one." Had Kohlberg been aware of that, he would probably have later accused Freeman of infiltrating the War College so he could sabotage Wedemeyer.

assignment, Vincent was nominated for the Foreign Service rank of career minister, and that meant he would need Senate confirmation. Senator Styles Bridges lost no time in sending to his Republican colleague Arthur Vandenberg, a pillar of the Foreign Relations Committee, a list of twelve charges against Vincent. Bridges alleged, to begin with, that Vincent's "actions, advice, and recommendations" had been "coordinated with the steps outlined" in the "Program of the Communist International and its Constitution" and in a resolution adopted in 1928 by the Sixth World Congress of the Comintern. Another accusation was that Hurley's resignation had stemmed from the leaking of American diplomatic correspondence to the Chinese Communists; Vincent was supposed to have had a hand in this nefarious trickle. The speech to the Annual Foreign Trade Convention in November was the basis of still another charge. So was Vincent's 1944 trip to China with Henry Wallace; Bridges suggested that the vice-president's report of that journey "be examined for further indications of Mr. Vincent's approval of the Communist program in China, opposition to the support of the Nationalist government and furtherance of extension of the influence of Russia in China."

After a point-by-point refutation by Secretary of State Acheson of each of Bridges's twelve accusations, Vincent won confirmation, but not without a last-ditch effort by Kohlberg to gun him down. The importer informed Senator Vandenberg that a couple of years earlier Hurley had told him that he had heard from somebody that Vincent was "a secret Russian espionage agent." Vincent was at first succeeded as head of Far Eastern affairs by his then deputy, James Penfield, but Penfield was one of the Old China Hands whose mere presence in Washington was causing Truman and Acheson to get their lumps from the China Lobby and its allies. It was thus decided to put someone more or less untainted into that post, and Penfield was "exiled," as he later put it, to Czechoslovakia. The fact that Penfield's "specialized China training was never utilized after my departure for Prague in the summer of 1948" was, Penfield would say, "in itself a far from unique failure to use manpower to the optimum. Out of a forty-year career I spent twelve in or dealing with China, which is not far from par for the course in terms of post-World War II personnel management. What makes our experience unique is that the special qualifications of a whole group of officers were not used for reasons far more sinister than bureaucratic personnel mismanagement. We were the pawns of political expediency or perhaps distrust by successive administrations."

Penfield was succeeded in the department by W. Walton Butterworth, Jr., a classmate of George Kennan's at Princeton and later a Rhodes scholar, who seemed an excellent choice to the Truman administration to head up Far Eastern affairs because he had had precious little to do with them in the turbulent past, aside from a brief period of service in China at the time of the Marshall Mission; presumably, no one could find Butterworth objectionable, and that was as good a qualification as any for his appointment.

But not even Butterworth got by unchallenged. In 1949 the title of his job was changed to assistant secretary of state for Far Eastern affairs. That meant that Vandenberg's Foreign Relations Committee and the Senate proper would have to confirm him before he could continue doing what he had been doing for a year. His name was sent to the Senate on June 24, 1949, but it was three months before he passed muster; Vandenberg kept objecting to him—in all likelihood, not without some prodding by Kohlberg—on the ground that he was somehow identified with the Old China Hands crowd. When the Butterworth appointment finally came up before the full Senate, only six of its members crossed political party lines —the Democrats were for him and the Republicans against, as if Far Eastern policy was somehow akin to the distribution of postmasterships —and he might not have squeaked by had not Vandenberg been home ill in Michigan and unable, at the critical moment, to throw his considerable weight around.

General Hurley had tried vainly to unify and pacify the fragmented and fractious Chinese. General Marshall had tried. Now in the summer of 1947, with Marshall as secretary of state, it was General Wedemeyer's turn. Once again, Sprouse joined the mission. Wedemeyer largely drew up his own instructions, which were approved by Vincent and other Asian experts in Washington without any consequential demurral. The general was to "proceed to China without delay for the purpose of making an appraisal of the political, economic, psychological and military situations —current and projected":

> In the course of your survey [formally, it was Truman instructing Wedemeyer] you will maintain liaison with American diplomatic and military officials in the area. In your discussions with Chinese officials and leaders in positions of responsibility you will make it clear that you are on a fact-finding mission and that the United States Government can consider assistance in a program of

rehabilitation only if the Chinese Government presents satisfactory evidence of effective measures looking towards Chinese recovery and provided further that any aid which may be available shall be subject to the supervision of representatives of the United States Government. In making your appraisal it is desired that you proceed with detachment from any feeling of prior obligation to support or to further official Chinese programs which do not conform to sound American policy with regard to China. In presenting the findings of your mission you should endeavor to state as concisely as possible your estimate of the character, extent, and probable consequences of assistance which you may recommend, and the probable consequences in the event that assistance is not given.

Wedemeyer spent only one month on his fact-finding quest. While still in China, he reported that "the existing Central Government can win and retain the undivided, enthusiastic support of the bulk of the Chinese people by removing incompetent and/or corrupt people who now occupy many positions of responsibility in the Government, not only national but more so in provincial and municipal structures. . . . To regain and maintain the confidence of the people, the Central Government will have to effect immediately drastic, far-reaching political and economic reforms. Promises will no longer suffice. Performance is absolutely necessary. It should be accepted that military force in itself will not eliminate communism."

Wedemeyer's postmission report, which like Marshall's earlier one was largely composed by Sprouse, was delivered to the president on September 19. The general, through his amanuensis, had a number of commendable things to say about recent developments in China:

Although the Japanese offered increasingly favorable surrender terms during the course of the war, China elected to remain steadfast with her Allies. If China had accepted surrender terms, approximately a million Japanese would have been released for employment against American forces in the Pacific. . . .

I retain the conviction that the Generalissimo is sincere in his desire to attain [political and economic reforms]. I am not certain that he has today sufficient determination to do so if this requires absolute overruling of the political and military cliques surrounding him. Yet, if realistic United States aid is to prove effective in stabilizing the situation in China and in coping with the dangerous expansion of communism, that determination must be established.

All in all, however, what Wedemeyer had to say about Chiang and his government could hardly have sat well with his old Chinese friend. Nobody in Washington had any doubt that the Generalissimo would take amiss Wedemeyer's assertion that "Adoption by the United States of a policy motivated solely toward stopping the expansion of Communism without regard to the continuing existence of an unpopular and repressive government would render any aid ineffective. Further, United States prestige in the Far East would suffer heavily, and wavering elements might turn away from the existing government to Communism."

Because of unflattering statements like that, and also because one of Wedemeyer's substantive recommendations was that Manchuria be removed from Chinese sovereignty and placed under United Nations trusteeship—an arrangement that would be palatable to neither the Nationalists nor the Communists—the general's report was not made public. The China Lobby, typically, spread the word that Wedemeyer had been muzzled because what he had said was too *favorable* toward Chiang. The Generalissimo undoubtedly knew better; he, after all, had already been distressed by some of Wedemeyer's interim fact-finding while he was still *in* China; at Nanking, before taking leave of the country, the general had said, "In China today I find apathy and lethargy in many quarters. Instead of seeking solutions of problems presented, considerable time and effort are spent in blaming outside influences and seeking outside assistance."

Among the Americans in China who helped bring Wedemeyer up to date in that summer of 1947 was Edmund Clubb, who had spent the early postwar years in Manchuria—"the cockpit of Asia," he and others called it.[7] Clubb had been stationed at the Manchurian city of Changchun since the Nationalists had retaken it from the Communists (who had stepped in when the Russians decamped) in May of 1947. In June Clubb had rescued from a conceivably grim fate some White Russians who had fled

[7]Life in Manchuria was austere, but it had its ludicrous moments. Clubb was around when, just after the war, the United Nations Relief and Rehabilitation Agency arrived. UNRRA's idea of improving the Manchurian diet was to bring in shiploads of soybeans. The agency seemed unaware that Manchuria was practically the home of the soybean; the furnaces at Mukden were stoked with soybean cakes.

to Changchun from Communist-held Harbin to its north, but whom the Nationalists had inexplicably loaded onto trucks and were shipping back toward Harbin, where Russians of that hue were *personae non gratae*. Hearing about the intended deportation, Clubb commandeered a jeep, raced after the truck, and persuaded its driver to reverse his tracks. Another time—by negotiating over a radio from Changchun and then marching ceremoniously to the Nationalist-Communist border with a white flag in his hand—Clubb had succeeded in achieving the release of two American military attachés whom the Communists had been holding in a Harbin jail for several weeks. Clubb himself had been scheduled to man a United States consulate at Harbin, but the Communists didn't want him there, although they were letting a few foreign journalists in. Anna Louise Strong was among them. She had stopped off at Changchun en route and had run into Clubb, who told her he was also planning to go north to preside over a diplomatic installation. Clubb heard afterward that one of the reasons he was barred from Harbin was that Miss Strong had convinced the Communist authorities there that he wasn't the sort of person they'd like to have hanging around.

Shortly before rushing to the aid of the White Russians, Clubb—soon to be nudged out of government service because he was allegedly soft on communism—had been speculating in a diary he kept about the state of Sino-American relations. "The way that Americans continue to think that old New England courtesy is an adequate weapon to use against the hard-bitten Communists," he jotted down on March 30, 1947, "continues to be a matter of amazement." A July 1, 1949, entry in the diary went, "That Mao Tse-tung chap, with his statement re Communist policies, minces no words to make it clear whose side they are on. It is not the American side." Livingston T. Merchant, a deputy assistant secretary of state for Far Eastern affairs, appeared before a departmental Loyalty Security Board that was grilling Clubb the following year. Merchant, after extolling Clubb as "an extraordinarily well qualified, trained, disciplined Foreign Service officer of complete integrity and complete loyalty," was asked if Clubb had a pro-Communist bias. "The bias, if any, ran the other way," Merchant replied.

In September 1947 Clubb was finally transferred out of Manchuria, to be consul general at Peking. Throughout Hurley's incumbency he had been far removed from the scene of strife, and the Genbassador had accordingly no sharp bone to pick with him. But there were always new recruits available to peck away at the Old China Hands. Whittaker Chambers turned out to be one of Clubb's chief nemeses. Chambers, his appetite whetted by the taste of fame he began to enjoy in 1948 during his confrontation with Alger Hiss, remembered something that had happened in the summer of 1932. Clubb had a home leave due then and expected to spend some time on the East Coast of the United States; knowing few people there, he asked some of his acquaintances in China for letters of introduction to people he might find it interesting or instructive to talk to in New York. Agnes Smedley, whom Clubb knew principally in her capacity of correspondent for the *Frankfurter Zeitung*, obliged with a note to Walt Carmon, an editor of the *New Masses*.

At loose ends in New York one hot summer day, Clubb wandered over to the *New Masses* office and asked for Carmon. He was out, and the visitor was received by Chambers, with whom Clubb exchanged a few desultory words. Twenty years later, reflecting in his autobiographical *Witness* about the early 1930s, Chambers would refer to "an entirely new type of Communist . . . [members of a] small intellectual army . . . [who would] help to shape the country's domestic and foreign policies . . . they would, at last, in a situation unparalleled in history, enable the Soviet Government to use the American State and Treasury Departments as a terrible engine of its revolutionary purposes, by the calculated destruction of powers vital to American survival (like China). . . ."

Getting more specific, Chambers said that he had perceived the onset of that seditious tide while working for the *New Masses:* A young "messenger" had come in, bearing a sealed envelope, had been surprised not to find Carmon there, and had talked to Chambers "reluctantly." The messenger had mentioned, among other sinister-sounding things, the "Hanyang Arsenal." When Chambers was talking to the FBI about Hiss, he happened to see a picture of Clubb in a newspaper, and he felt patriotically constrained to tell about that supposedly conspiratorial meeting—their sole encounter—with the supposedly message-bearing Foreign Service officer. Chambers told, among others, the members of the House Un-American Activities Committee, and in all the government circles where dossiers were beginning to be compiled about suspect characters, red flags were soon flying alongside Clubb's name.

Clubb had no recollection at all of meeting Chambers until he consulted his diary, where he found that he had inscribed at the time that the *New Masses* was "a horrible rag" and Chambers "a shifty-eyed, unkempt creature"—scarcely the words that a true-blue Communist courier would have selected. (Chambers claimed in *Witness* that the

British authorities in Peking, with whom Clubb had left many of his personal possessions when he quit China for the last time, had read over the diary and spotted the item about the *New Masses* and had accordingly turned the incriminating document over to the appropriate United States authorities. Actually, the British had returned it to Clubb, unread, at Clubb's request; he wanted it so he could refresh his hazy memory of the incident.) Another entry that Clubb had made in the diary immediately after chatting with Chambers went, "But no, I think the parliamentary method will be of great use in politics still. I could never be a revolutionary of the Communist type—they take themselves so damned seriously!"

Between 1947 and October 1, 1949, when Mao Tse-tung exultantly hoisted his red flag over Tien An Men Square in Peking, the United States had little solid impact on China. In April 1948 Congress passed a China Aid Act in the amount of $463,000,000—far short of what Chiang Kai-shek was hoping for, but still a tidy sum, and comforting at that moment because the Communists were on the verge of recapturing the symbolic city of Yenan, which the Nationalists had grabbed the year before in the then still seesaw civil war.[8] For the Old China Hands in Washington, caught up helplessly in the national frenzy to find scapegoats for the confusing upheaval that was under way on the other side of the earth, it was a hellish time. Sprouse was running Chinese affairs, with Freeman as his deputy; they were putting in sixty or seventy hours of work a week, trying to answer questions flung at the Truman administration by irate and often ignorant congressmen; it was during this harrowing period that Freeman had to have much of his stomach cut out.

Knives were being sharpened for everybody. John Service returned to Washington from New Zealand early in 1949. The Alger Hiss probes had the public aroused,[9] the Un-American Activities Committee was stage

---

[8]Long after Hurley, long after Marshall, long after Wedemeyer, yet another American military man, Major General David Barr, made his estimate of the Chinese combat scene. On November 18, 1948, he reported that "no battle has been lost (by the Nationalists) since my arrival due to lack of ammunition or equipment. The military debacles in my opinion can all be attributed to the world's worst leadership and many other morale-destroying factors that lead to a complete loss of will to fight." It could have been Stilwell talking five years earlier—or, for that matter, almost anyone talking about South Vietnam a generation later.

[9]If Hiss could, as seemed reasonable, be believed to have been what he was alleged to have been (Good Lord, he had been Acheson's boy and Dulles's boy and even Stanley Horn-beck's boy) why, then, could past sins not be believed of *anybody?* Indeed, in 1973, at

center, and Joe McCarthy was in the wings. Service's new assignment was to be with the State Department's Division of Foreign Service Planning, an administrative, rather than policy-making, group; before he started, there was to be a brief interim job—one highly esteemed in departmental circles—on a Foreign Service Selection Board, which made recommendations on promotions of junior officers. He had sat on the board for only a week when the Scripps-Howard newspapers—in those days always eager to try to build new circulation out of old circumstances—once again took up the *Amerasia* case. Service offered to quit the board, in view of all the bad publicity the department was accruing because of him, but his superiors said no.

Still, they felt they couldn't keep him on the Planning assignment; the work would have required him to go regularly to Capitol Hill, and the halls of Congress seemed an undesirable haunt for a man whose name was being bandied about as a suspicious character, if not a downright traitorous one. "One trouble with the whole security and loyalty programs of that time," a senior State Department official said years afterward when he was more or less securely ensconced in a tenured academic post, "was that it never developed any self-protection against political exploitation. Whatever Joe McCarthy or anybody else charged against anybody, however preposterous it might be, would immediately be investigated by the FBI or some similar outfit, and then a Departmental board would have to consider the matter. Now, people who sat on that judgmental board might also be the ones who had to go up to the Hill and appear before appropriations committees, and the men sitting on those committees might include some who'd helped spread the accusations in the first place. So gradually everyone became very circumspect and began to feel insecure, the judgers themselves fearing that if they did not judge the way Congress wanted them to, they might themselves soon be judged."

So the department made Service as inconspicuous as possible, putting him in a back room of the office of the chief of personnel. (Late one Friday afternoon the chief ambled into Service's office and said, "Jack, I need some names for guys who could be Ambassador to Pakistan. Sorry to dump it on you now, but I've got to have at least three candidates by first thing Monday morning." One of Senator McCarthy's informants at State, a woman who worked in personnel, would subsequently reveal that

a meeting in Washington, Hiss would suggest that there were parallels between his experience and the experiences of the Old China Hands.

Service had been observed pawing through that office's files over weekends when nobody else was around, as indeed he had been doing, though not, considering that he'd had other weekend plans, with unmitigated pleasure.) On January 18, 1949, Service was again cleared of wrongdoing by a departmental board, a gesture that turned out to mean no more than did Chiang Kai-shek's temporary retirement from the presidency of the Republic of China three days later.

President Truman appointed Dean Acheson secretary of state early in 1949. Truman, bedeviled by accusations from Republicans that his administration had become practically a haven for disreputable characters, had sought to tighten up the loyalty-and-security procedures of the executive branch. It had been the practice of each major department of government to investigate its own employees; Truman now established an umbrella-like entity called the Loyalty Review Board and invested it with authority to supervise the suitability of federal civil servants anywhere, and specifically to function as a sort of court of appeals for those servants who had been unfavorably judged in their own departments.

Acheson took over the State Department just a fortnight before the Chinese Communists took over Peking, they at least doing so undeterred by the shrill protests of such as Senator Pat McCarran, who was demanding that the United States give Chiang Kai-shek a billion and a half dollars to salvage his tottering government. McCarran would devote much of his gamey political career to the subject of China and why and how and by whom it had been lost, but he probably knew less about the situation there in 1949 than did the American Chamber of Commerce in Tientsin. The chamber was fed up because Tientsin had long been under siege by the Communists, and the Nationalists had not done anything to alleviate the city's distress. The United States consul general at Tientsin, Robert Lacy Smyth (whose next consulate, when the Old China Hands were dispersed, would be the one at Vancouver, British Columbia), informed the State Department on March 15:

Americans in Tientsin who had the unhappy experience two months ago of witnessing the capture of Tientsin by Communist armies equipped almost entirely with American arms and other military equipment handed over practically without fighting by Nationalist armies in Manchuria, have expressed astonishment at radio reports from the U.S. during the last two or three days to the effect that a bill may be presented to the Congress to extend further military and economic aid to the Nationalist Government in the sum of a billion and a half dollars.

Americans in Tientsin feel the only result of further U.S. aid to a Government which has proved so ineffective that most of our previous aid has passed to the Communists will be to further strengthen the Communists. They feel that the apparent retirement of the Generalissimo has had little effect on the character of the Nationalist Government, particularly in view of the reported selection as new Premier of General Ho Ying-chin, considered the archetype of the Chinese who have brought the National Government to its present sorry state. They feel that our global policy of opposition to Communism should not oblige us to support a hopelessly inefficient and corrupt government which has lost the support of its people. They believe that at this juncture it would be useless to extend further aid to a government which is so far gone. They feel that the present situation must be solved by the Chinese and that for the time being we should adopt a hands-off policy.

Why did so many respectable Americans—those living closest to him conspicuously excepted—continue to stand up for Chiang Kai-shek as a symbol of probity? To many of his supporters in the United States, he was both the paragon of foreign statesmen (the Americans who were fond of him were often inclined to look askance at Winston Churchill, who smoked cigars and drank brandy) and the touchstone of domestic politics (to be even neutral about him, as were most of the Old China Hands, was *ipso facto* a sign of untrustworthiness). He was personally unknown to all but a handful of Americans of any kind, but he came and tried to cling to power at a time when reactionary foreign dictators—unless they went, like Hitler, to gross excesses—tended to be admired by many Americans for the firmness of hand with which they governed. Like his compères in Italy, Spain, Portugal, South Korea, South Vietnam, and South Africa, Chiang appeared to represent *stability* in an era of uncertainty and upheaval.

More importantly, he was, or seemed, a Christian or at least Christianized gentleman, married, all the better, to a cultured, American-educated helpmate (one could picture Henry Luce's set having the Chiangs to dinner, but the Maos—well, really); a man who appeared from afar to be trying to convert the heathen to sensible, God-fearing, Western ways. Many of his adherents in the United States were the same sort of people who had long supported missionaries in their quixotic efforts to tilt the balance of China. (To have China-born sons of missionaries, like Davies and Service, viewing Chiang with a sometimes jaundiced eye made the bile rise higher than ever among his advocates.) Most importantly, he had, at least by 1947, two other things going for him. He was an underdog, an old-time popular champion seeking to defend his title against an upstart bully who did not always fight according to conventional rules. And, finally, during the cold war, when Americans were feverishly looking around for Communists to get mad at, he had one shining attribute: Here was a man who was indisputably engaged in a hot war with genuine Communists, although he did not always battle against them as strenuously as did his American cohorts against imaginary ones.

When the Chinese Communists, oblivious to the wishes of American public opinion, marched into Peking on January 31, 1949, among the Americans nervously watching their entry was Edmund Clubb. (Peking had earlier been under a sort of quasi-siege, but nobody took that seriously; to all Chinese, the city was a very special treasured antique, and there was little likelihood that the Communists would seek to inflict physical damage on it. Indeed, it was so meekly and gently surrendered by its chief Kuomintang defender, General Fu Tso-yi, that the Communists later made him an Honorary Water Commissioner.) Mao's conquering troops strutted pointedly down Legation Street, past the huge European-style mansions built by the foreign diplomatic missions—a thoroughfare from which, in the days of extraterritoriality, all Chinese soldiers had been barred. Clubb, standing on the sidewalk, noticed what the American businessmen in Tientsin had also perceived: The Communists were not only well-accoutred but familiarly so, being in most cases fitted out with American equipment that had been originally given to the Nationalists. A few weeks later, deciding that the capture of the city had been inadequately documented, the Communists restaged the whole march—with motion-picture crews in position to record the warmed-over event for history, and cheering, banner-waving crowds lining the parade route for extra visual and audible effects.

Ambassador John Leighton Stuart was in Nanking when Peking fell to the Communists. He was soon invited to come north to Peking to discuss Sino-American relations with Mao and Chou En-lai, and they attempted to add a festive air to the proposed meeting by suggesting that it be held on Stuart's birthday. The ambassador wanted to accept; he thought such a get-together could be the "beginning of better understanding" between the United States and the by then obvious government-to-be of China, but the State Department overruled him; it was not yet ready (nor would it be for another generation) to recognize the inevitable.

It was at just about this time that John Foster Dulles, a private citizen not yet turned public servant, would in his wisdom deliver himself of the extraordinary observation (one that, being Dulles, he could ignore without blinking after he became secretary of state) that what was occurring in China—the loss of China, if you liked—was certainly not attributable to what any Americans had or had not done; but rather, "the conditions in China themselves are far more responsible for what has happened than what anybody has done or failed to do in the State Department." Indeed, in his book *War or Peace*, published in 1950, Dulles would go so far as to declare that "if the Communist government of China in fact proves its ability to govern China without serious domestic resistance, then it, too, should be admitted to the United Nations."

With the civil war ended in China and the defeated Chiang Kai-shek on his way to Taiwan, the China Lobby, ignoring Dulles's dissent, at once dusted off the old allegation that American bungling had lost China. In an attempt at rebuttal, Secretary of State Acheson, on August 5, 1949, issued a white paper entitled *United States Relations with China* (hereinafter, the White Paper), which covered, in more than a thousand pages, the events of the previous five frustrating years. John F. Melby was its progenitor. A comparative latecomer to the Foreign Service, Melby had first gone to China at the tail end of the Hurley ambassadorship. He was supposed to keep a special eye on what the Russians were up to in that part of the world; he was equally interested to observe how the Old China Hands still in Chungking were going about *their* business: "The principal occupation seems to be eavesdropping and ducking around corners. Those who hew to the line with Ambassador Hurley swagger. Others are mostly evasive."

Melby returned to the United States early in 1949. In the meantime, George Kennan had written his famous "Mr. X" article for *Foreign Affairs*, in which he sought to spell out a rational policy for United States relations with the Soviet Union. It seemed to Melby that someone ought to follow suit in the case of China. He talked to Kennan, then the head of State's Policy Planning Staff, and to Davies, a member of that in-house think tank; both were enthusiastic about the notion. For several weeks Melby tried to put together a suitable article, but the material he had to draw on seemed overwhelming. Then Davies proposed that a full-length white paper might be more appropriate. Kennan concurred, and so, moving up the line of authority, did Acheson and Truman. The president said in mid-April, in fact, that he wanted it ready for distribution in August. Melby was instructed to be coordinator of the project. The facile pen of Philip Sprouse was called upon to write parts of it. The old government hand Philip C. Jessup, who had not served in China and could review what had gone on there with detachment, was asked by Acheson to look over the first draft, which he did with the assistance of another dispassionate diplomat, Charles Yost. The final polishing was done by Acheson, Melby, and Walton Butterworth. Acheson on his own appended to the manuscript a lengthy letter of transmittal, in which he told the president:

> This is a frank record of an extremely complicated and most unhappy period in the life of a great country to which the United States has long been attached by ties of friendship. . . .
>
> The record shows that the United States has consistently maintained and still maintains those fundamental principles of our foreign policy toward China which include the doctrine of the Open Door, respect for the administrative and territorial integrity of China, and opposition to any foreign domination of China. It is deplorable that respect for the truth in the compilation of this record makes it necessary to publish an account of facts which reveal the distressing situation in that country. I have not felt, however, that publication could be withheld for that reason. . . .
>
> Representatives of our Government, military and civilian, who were sent to assist the Chinese in prosecuting the war soon discovered that . . . the long struggle [between the Nationalists and the Communists] had seriously weakened the Chinese Government not only militarily and economically, but politically and in morale. The reports of United States military and diplomatic officers reveal a growing conviction through 1943 and 1944 that the Government and the Kuomintang had apparently lost the crusading spirit that won them the people's loyalty during the early years of the war. In the opinion of many observers they had sunk into corruption, into a scramble for place and power, and into reliance on the United States to win the war for them and to preserve their own domestic supremacy. . . .
>
> It was evident to us that only a rejuvenated and progressive Chinese Government which could recapture the enthusiastic loyalty of the people could and would wage an effective war against Japan. American officials repeatedly brought their concern with this situation to the attention of the Generalissimo and he repeatedly assured them that it would be corrected. He made, however,

little or no effective effort to correct it and tended to shut himself off from Chinese officials who gave unpalatable advice.[10] In addition to a concern over the effect which this atrophy of the central Chinese administration must have upon the conduct of the war, some American observers, whose reports are also quoted in the attached record, were concerned over the effect which this deterioration of the Kuomintang must have on its eventual struggle, whether political or military, with the Chinese Communists. These observers were already fearful in 1943 and 1944 that the National Government might be so isolating itself from the people that in the postwar competition for power it would prove itself impotent to maintain its authority. Nevertheless, we continued for obvious reasons to direct all our aid to the National Government. . . .

The unfortunate but inescapable fact is that the ominous result of the civil war in China was beyond the control of the government of the United States. Nothing that this country did or could have done within the reasonable limits of its capabilities could have changed that result; nothing that was left undone by this country has contributed to it. It was the product of internal Chinese forces, forces which this country tried to influence but could not. A decision was arrived at within China, if only a decision by default.

And now it is abundantly clear that we must face the situation as it exists in fact. We will not help the Chinese or ourselves by basing our policy on wishful thinking. We continue to believe that, however tragic may be the immediate future of China and however ruthlessly a major portion of this great people may be exploited by a party in the interest of foreign imperialism, ultimately the profound civilization and the democratic individualism of China will reassert themselves and she will throw off the foreign yoke. . . .

Among the formidable contents of the White Paper was Wedemeyer's not previously released report on his 1947 mission. The editors had had to be selective, considering that they had literally thousands of documents to draw on; because they had included some and omitted others, a number of Republicans dismissed the entire White Paper as a whitewash of the Roosevelt and Truman administrations, and announced that when *they*

[10]They also gave him false evidence. An American stationed in Kunming at General Chennault's headquarters was depressed by the emaciated and bedraggled appearance of the Nationalist troops in the vicinity. When it was learned that Mme. Chiang Kai-shek was coming down to inspect them, their officers hastily fattened them up and decked them out in new uniforms. After she left, they soon reverted to their original sorry condition.

came into power they would reveal the whole truth about what had *really* happened in Sino-American relations.[11]

In the light of all the confusion that any discussion of Sino-American relations could then instantly engender, it was not surprising that Acheson should have been assailed by the China Lobby wolfpack for having assayed Chiang Kai-shek as candidly as he did; nor that Acheson, the following year, should have acquiesced in the cashiering of Service, who had been saying all along pretty much what Acheson himself said in his letter of transmittal. That this would happen, however, did not occur to many readers of the White Paper at the time of its publication. In New Zealand a political scientist who had known Service there read it and said to an American at the embassy, "Now Jack will certainly be vindicated, because it has all turned out just as he predicted."

It was just the other way around. The feeling among many Kuomintang sympathizers in the United States was that anybody who had said Chiang was doomed probably *wanted* him doomed, and as like as not had helped engineer his downfall. Reaction was thus instantly converted to action, analysis to antagonism, conclusion to conspiracy. Walter Judd, for instance, declared that the omission from the White Paper of the complete text of Service's 1944 Double-Tenth Day memorandum to Stilwell was a newly revealed element of an anti-Chiang plot.[12] Service himself, as it happened, was not altogether happy with the items chosen for publication; he felt that the State Department had not presented a sufficient number of its own directives to its men in the field adjuring them not to get overinvolved in unilateral support of Chiang.

The State Department decided, after Judd began to howl, that Service was too controversial for any job in Washington, even a back-room one, and it assigned him to Calcutta, as consul general. Service went to California for a brief holiday before his departure, and while there he had some consul-general calling cards engraved. But when members of both

---

[11]Following Eisenhower's election in 1952, the new administration did indeed have the complete record printed up and bound, but then Assistant Secretary Robertson advised Secretary Dulles that the overall impact of the material would do Chiang Kai-shek more harm than good, and the massive volumes were squirreled away undistributed, until later administrations finally began to release them; the volume covering 1948 surfaced in 1973.
[12]Inevitably, in alluding to Service, Judd alluded to *Amerasia:* "Suitcases of documents from his office were found by the FBI in the office of a notoriously pro-Communist magazine. The case was hushed up under circumstances never yet disclosed or explained. Since then he has been promoted several times and is now chairman of the committee within the State Department which makes recommendations for all promotions."

houses of Congress then began laying into him on their respective floors, that gave the department pause. Service already held the rank of consul, but to become a consul *general* would require senatorial confirmation, and it seemed perilous to present his name to the Senate when some of that body's eminences could not utter it without cither seeing red or turning red. So instead of consul general, he was assigned to be mere consul. Service, whose aplomb in the face of one unnerving experience after another never ceased to astonish his friends, shrugged and ordered a new set of calling cards. "People sometimes wonder how you keep going," he said years afterward. "You keep going because you can't know what's in store for you. I always thought that sooner or later everything would come out all right." Next the department was informed that certain members of Congress would not consent to Service's being in charge of anything anywhere—not even a Calcutta consulate—so he was transferred to the embassy in New Delhi as counsellor. Service gamely had a third batch of calling cards made up.

Alfred Kohlberg, for his part, asserted that he had discussed the White Paper with Chiang Kai-shek himself. Kohlberg's reaction to it, presumably reflecting the Generalissimo's, was that "its purpose could not be to discredit the Nationalist Government—it charges incompetence, corruption, bad strategy, and poor propaganda, but not bad faith. Nor could its purpose be to excuse State Department failure; throughout it reveals State Department plotting to betray the National Government and nowhere even excuses nonimplementation of the Wedemeyer Report of 1947, which outlined a method for stopping the Communists at a reasonable cost. The real purpose of the White Paper seems, in spite of the omission of many important documents, to be to reveal to the Chancellories of the world the story of the American betrayal of the Republic of China. What could be of greater aid to the Soviet Union than this?"

An echoing note was sounded by a Nationalist Chinese author, Chia-you Chen:

The self-proclaimed China experts have usurped the power of American public opinion and have become a special class in American politics. Their prime concern is to maintain their position as the leading force in American public opinion. Let us make no mistake about it that that special class of self-proclaimed China experts rely on distortion and falsehood. They are intellectually incapable of comprehending the principle of democracy. Their background and their academic standing makes it clear that they lack interest in mankind. They came to power by hypocritical talk and by disguising themselves as idealists. . . .

The condemnation of Chiang Kai-shek's administration as corrupt, inefficient and reactionary was another master design of the International Communist Movement to discredit in order to destroy. It is a general practice for the self-proclaimed China experts to deal only with superficial phenomena. They must carry their lies to fantastic extremes in order to confuse the general public and thus make the public the victim of their propaganda machine. Their condemnation of Chiang Kai-shek was a phase of China that could not be substantiated by facts. It is no surprise that the *White Paper* was decisively biased against the Chinese people and the Chinese government by the subversive heresies of these self-proclaimed China experts.

It was no less surprising that Mao Tse-tung, who never shied from writing position papers, should have something to say about this American paper himself. Within less than a fortnight of its appearance, he was stating, "The publication of these documents reflects the victory of the Chinese people and the defeat of imperialism, it reflects the decline of the entire world system of imperialism. . . . The White Paper goes into particular detail about how, in the five years from the last part of the War of Resistance against Japan to 1949, the United States pursued a policy of support for Chiang Kai-shek and of anti-communism, opposed the Chinese people by every possible means and finally met with defeat. . . ." While he was at it, Mao gave his Chinese readers a brief look, in an instructive footnote, at prior American history: "George Washington (1732–99), Thomas Jefferson (1743–1826) and Abraham Lincoln (1809–65) were well-known bourgeois statesmen in the early days of the United States."[13]

In China, in the Year of the White Paper, the American presence was becoming increasingly attenuated. China had always been treated peculiarly in the conduct of United States foreign relations. Whereas most big

[13]Professor Fairbank has speculated that some of Chairman Mao's resentment of the White Paper may have been semantically inspired. The American document spoke, favorably, of "individualism" and of "freedom." In the translation Mao received, the first word was *"ko-jen chu-i,"* which means "selfishness" or "every man for himself"; the second word became *"tzu-yu,"* which means "to do as one wishes" and, by extension, "being out of control" or "in a state of licentiousness." All of these concepts were abhorrent to the Chinese Communists.

nations to which America sent diplomatic missions received a scarce few consulates general and a much larger number of subsidiary consulates, China, because it contained so many nearly autonomous polities, had been made the seat of a slew of consulates general—for instance, circumstances permitting, in Peking, Canton, Shanghai, Tientsin, Hankow, Mukden, and Harbin. It had been the practice for the consulates, whatever their status, to carry on during changes of regime, or during civil wars, as long as they were tolerated. But when the Communists took over a city, they insisted that the consulates had no legitimacy because the United States didn't recognize the new regime. One by one, they forced the consulates to shut down, first Canton, then Urumchi, Dairen, Kunming, Mukden, and so on. At Mukden the victors had imprisoned Angus Ward, the consul general, and it was up to Clubb, the by now veteran retriever of lost souls, to spring him loose.

Clubb was functioning in Peking, but not without difficulty. The Communists did not interfere with his using his radio, but there were limitations on travel. Foreigners could no longer go at will to the cool and verdant environs of the Western Hills, where the Summer Palace of the dowager empress Tz'u Hsi—who impishly built her fabulous marble boat there in 1888 on the shore of the lovely K'un Ming Lake, with funds allocated for a Chinese navy—represented an oasis-like relief from the dusty capital city; they could travel only as far as Yenching University, about halfway out. The Communists also suspended the activities of the United States Information Agency. Clubb thereupon discharged the Chinese members of its staff, at which point the local authorities hauled him before a labor court on charges of improper imperialistic behavior. Clubb had to conduct his own defense, inasmuch as lawyers were not allowed to practice at that time; and he managed to talk himself out of a conviction, which under the circumstances was something of a triumph.

On October 1, the day the Communists formally raised their flag in Peking, Clubb and all the other foreign consuls on the scene received a formal communication from the local authorities. The outlanders were notified that the usual diplomatic relations could be maintained provided that their governments would recognize the new Communist government and would sever relations with the Nationalists. On instructions from Washington, Clubb refused. Chiang Kai-shek had not yet left the mainland, and the demand was unacceptable in any event. Clubb's response was returned to him without reply, although it had been manifestly opened and presumably read. For a while Clubb went about his restricted duties without special harassment, but he was not particularly happy about the existing state of affairs. "The American side continues to make statements opposing recognition by the USA of Communist China," he confided to his diary. "I should think they might, for a change, say nothing, and let the Communists do a bit of guessing. But our national pride seems to reside in part in 'laying our cards on the table.' That is all very well sometimes, but not when one is dealing with international pirates."

On January 5, 1950, Secretary Acheson laid a couple of his cards on the table. He made the first of a number of statements to the effect that the United States would not even consider recognition of the Communist regime until—he meant it figuratively—the dust settled in Peking. At about the same time, with no apparent causal relationship, the Communist police authorities tacked placards to the front doors of all the Western consulates: In eight days, their former military barracks were going to be requisitioned. The Communists knew, of course, that the premises in which American military personnel had once been housed were now the seat of the consulate general. A few hours before the deadline, Clubb shifted his offices to an adjoining United States compound, where troops had never been quartered; he had foresightedly moved his radio equipment over there several days earlier so that he could enjoy uninterrupted transmission to and from Washington. By then Acheson had decided to pull all American officials out of China no matter what the Communists did. Clubb closed down the Peking consulate on April 10 and headed sadly homeward. He went, customarily, by way of Tientsin, whose consulate was evacuated later in the month. There, Clubb and his wife had their belongings subjected to a thorough customs search. When a shipping company later undertook to send their household goods after them, twenty-five rare Oriental books and fifty *objets d'art* were removed—for more thorough examination, the seizers later advised Clubb by way of Hong Kong; the Clubbs never laid eyes on them again.

Once again a stickler for the niceties of diplomacy, Clubb had taken pains at the moment of the turnover to leave all the doors open with keys in the locks (so he wouldn't have to make the symbolic gesture of opening them for the trespassers) and to have the American flag lowered in advance (so he wouldn't have to make the symbolic gesture of lowering it before them). He also declined to sign a proffered statement to the effect that the Communists were taking over the premises in the normal course of events. After he left, the Communists' documentary-film people came around and restaged a full-scale flag-lowering, with both sides present. Clubb never learned who portrayed him.

On April 15 Clubb told his diary, "And so, away from Communist China. We are now on the right side of the bamboo curtain, and can breathe deeply again."[14] It was a luxury he would not long enjoy; largely unknown to him, the foes of the Old China Hands were already all but breathing down his neck.

---

[14]Not that Clubb was optimistic about what was taking place on that side. Twelve days earlier he had written in the diary, "The one thing that seems certain is that Chiang Kai-shek, even with the help of Judd and Knowland, is not the man to lead New China out of the wilderness."

9

"Oh, Mac has gone out on a limb."

After letting the Bamboo Curtain be drawn behind him, Clubb, who had several months earlier been promoted to the eminent rank of FSO-1, had a good deal of accumulated home leave due him before embarking on his next assignment—to take charge of the Office of Chinese Affairs at the State Department. He had hardly reached the United States, however, when the Korean War began, and he volunteered to cut short his vacation and report immediately for duty.

Even before that foreign war broke out, the pace of the domestic war against the Old China Hands had begun to mount. The loudest guns had been fired just after the start of 1950, on the floor of the Senate, by Senators Knowland and McCarthy. Knowland was a veteran fighter. McCarthy was a rookie. He had never known or cared much about Far Eastern affairs, but he was looking for a stout peg to hang his political hat on, and he had not been nodding when Richard Nixon and other members of the House of Representatives got reams of publicity from their clamorous investigations in the Un-American Activities Committee. On January 5, 1950, accordingly, McCarthy shared with his senatorial colleagues his grave apprehensions about John Stewart Service, to whom he attributed, falsely, the statement that "the only hope of Asia was Communism."

On January 21 Alger Hiss, a principal target of the Un-American Activities Committee, was convicted of perjury. On February 4 the Klaus Fuchs espionage case emerged. McCarthy sensed that the time was ripe to accelerate even further his own activities and accusations against some of the men he had concluded would make inviting adversaries—men whom he would call "individuals who are loyal to the ideals and designs of Communism rather than those of the free, God-fearing half of the world. . . . I refer to the Far Eastern Division of the State Department and the Voice of America."

On February 9, in what had been billed as a routine speech before the Women's Republican Club of Wheeling, West Virginia, McCarthy began to play his numbers games about Communists in the State Department: ". . . I have here in my hand a list of two hundred and five [names of people] known to the Secretary of State as being members of the Communist Party and who nevertheless are still working and shaping the policy of the State Department." Now, he made a slight geographical amendment to his charge that Service wanted all of Asia to be Communistic; the senator accused Service, again falsely, of "stating in unqu...lified terms—and I quote—that 'Communism was the only hope of China.' "
On February 12, at a Republican celebration of Lincoln's birthday in Reno, Nevada, came a fifty-seven-names speech. This one cited four individuals by name, Service among them, as "specific cases of people with Communist connections." Service was the only one of the four still working for State. Then McCarthy began issuing a list of eighty-one cases, no names at first appended.[1] "Oh, Mac has gone out on a limb and kind of made a fool of himself and we have to back him up now," Senator Wherry confided to Emmanuel Larsen.

McCarthy's sweeping allegations prompted the Senate on February 22 to pass a resolution "to investigate whether there are employees in the State Department disloyal to the United States." The job was turned over to a subcommittee, chaired by Senator Millard Tydings, a Democrat from Maryland, of the Foreign Relations Committee, and it conducted hearings from March 8 through June 28.

McCarthy's lists, such as they were, eventually turned out to be based on material that had been presented to Congress in both 1947 and 1948, that had been investigated by at least four House and Senate committees, and that had in no instance persuaded any of the legislators examining it that there was any need for grave governmental alarm. Owen Lattimore turned out to be number one on McCarthy's list of eighty-one; Lattimore, as it happened, had never been an officer of the Department of State.

[1]Freda Utley deemed it evidence of McCarthy's scrupulosity that he kept changing his figures, and that he wouldn't (she stressed the distinction between "wouldn't" and "couldn't") name many names. What most people didn't understand about him, she argued, was that he was a man motivated by a passion for accuracy.

McCarthy's assault on Lattimore, however, gave the victim a chance to come ringingly, in an appearance before a Senate committee, to the defense of the department:

> I say to you, gentlemen, that the sure way to destroy freedom of speech and the free expression of ideas and views is to attach to that freedom the penalty of abuse and vilification. If the people of this country can differ with the so-called China Lobby or with Senator McCarthy only at the risk of the abuse to which I have been subjected, freedom will not long survive. If officials of our government cannot consult people of diverse views without exposing themselves to the kind of attack that Senator McCarthy has visited upon officers of the State Department, our governmental policy will necessarily be sterile. It is only from a diversity of views fully expressed and strongly advocated that sound policy is distilled. He who contributes to the destruction of this process is either a fool or an enemy of his country. Let Senator McCarthy take note of this.

The number two villain proved to be not John Service, as many of the followers of McCarthy's fulminations would have logically surmised, but John Carter Vincent. That urbane Southern gentleman, whose "Bolshevism" had never aroused much interest except among a few bygone college freshmen and Alfred Kohlberg, was reincarnated in the McCarthy view "as (1) a big Communist tremendously important to Russia, as (2) part of an espionage ring in the State Department, and (3) as one who should not only be discharged but should be immediately prosecuted."

For want of much more other solid evidence against Vincent, McCarthy seized upon a raincoat. On February 20, 1950, he told the Senate about one that somebody had left in an outer office of Far Eastern Affairs about four years earlier. Going to lunch one rainy day, Vincent, who had neglected to bring a coat of his own to work, had grabbed the garment, and on returning had himself inadvertently abandoned it in the men's room. When he remembered that and went to retrieve it, it was gone. He called the building superintendent's office and was informed that the security people had it and were curious about it because in one pocket they found a piece of paper with some Russian words on it. Vincent would forever after have to bear the burden of that suspect shroud; the implication was that it was a transmission device for a Communist conspiracy. (What the piece of paper itself bore was never revealed. Vincent always believed that it represented some foreign-language student's attempts to bone up on word endings.)

In first citing Vincent, who was by then minister to Switzerland, as his number two quarry, McCarthy had merely identified him as an American minister in Europe who had been a contact man for a Soviet espionage ring. The next year McCarthy *almost* had some evidence for that. He sent a weird character named Charles Davis to Switzerland to try to frame Vincent. A twenty-three-year-old black man who had once been in the navy, Davis sent a telegram from Geneva to Vincent in Bern, asking for information about an alleged Communist and suggesting that they meet "concerning a matter of interest to us both." Davis signed the message "Emile Staemfli," the name of a Swiss Communist; the idea apparently was to elicit some sort of compromising response from Vincent, or at any rate to establish that the minister had been in communication with a known Communist.

But when the puzzled Vincent, who skipped the proffered rendezvous, turned over the message to the Swiss authorities and they tracked it back to Davis, they regarded the affair not as some American political prank but as a plot against Swiss sovereignty. Davis was convicted of espionage, but inasmuch as he had already spent eleven months in prison while awaiting trial, was merely deported to the United States upon being found guilty. From prison he wrote a letter of apology to Vincent for the mischief he had perpetrated. He fared less well at McCarthy's hands; the senator denied ever having heard of him, until letters from him to Davis were produced in a Lausanne courtroom; McCarthy then maintained that Davis was a casual acquaintance who had never been on his payroll. "I never dreamed the senator would turn his back on me," Davis said while being sentenced.

When McCarthy began launching his arithmetical bombshells, Service was in Berkeley, packing up for his third assignment to India. Every time the senator made a speech, Service would rush over to the public library and peruse the text in *The New York Times*. On carefully studying the case histories in the list of eighty-one, he concluded that none seemed to fit him. He knew he was on the senator's hard-core list of enemies, however, so he phoned the chief of Foreign Service personnel in Washington and asked what he should do. He was told to proceed according to schedule. He did not know that President Truman's all-encompassing Loyalty Review Board was, after studying his clearance by the State

Department's Loyalty Security Board, at that moment recommending that *that* board hold another detailed hearing on him, and this time ask him questions in person.

Service was aboard a freighter, four days out at sea, with his wife, three children, automobile, and household goods, when, on March 14, McCarthy appeared before the Tydings committee and, pressed for names, came up with those of Service and Lattimore. He had dossiers on both, furnished by Alfred Kohlberg, whom he had just met. The sources of most of McCarthy's old information were Patrick Hurley, Paul Yu-pin, and the already much-tarnished *Plain Talk* article credited to Emmanuel Larsen. As for newer information, the senator relied in large part on his imagination: He had Service, for instance, already *in* Calcutta, "where he is helping determine the all-important policy of our Government toward India."

McCarthy also told the Tydings committee that Service was "a known associate and collaborator with Communists" who had been "consorting with admitted espionage agents." This was more or less true. Service had certainly associated with Mao Tse-tung, and they had once collaborated on repairing an airstrip at Yenan; and by Service's own admission he had consorted with Philip Jaffe before the *Amerasia* editor pleaded guilty to, if not espionage, at least the illegal possession of classified documents. But McCarthy had a way of making his accusations sound fresh and foul. Among those he proceeded to let loose was that J. Edgar Hoover had stated publicly, relative to *Amerasia*, that he had had a 100 per cent airtight case against Service (the Department of Justice denied in writing that Hoover had said it), and that Service was one of a dozen top Far Eastern policy makers at State (he was not, and, indeed, much as he might have liked to do so, had never made any policy). All that, however, was before the whole world knew that McCarthy was a liar.

This was too much to swallow for Joseph Alsop, who, just four months after his *Saturday Evening Post* pieces on the loss of China, wrote to Senator Tydings:

> I should like to suggest to your committee that if the test of loyalty is following the line of the Communist Party, you had much better launch an investigation of Senators McCarthy, Wherry, and Taft than an investigation of Messrs. Lattimore, Service, and Vincent. Let the test be a tabulation of the key votes of the three Senators abovementioned on the great postwar measures of foreign policy, and especially of their votes on key amendments by which bills

can be nullified. Unless I am gravely mistaken, such a tabulation will show that these three Senators, and most of the others who have joined them in the present clamor, have voted the straight Communist Party line on every major issue of foreign policy, as laid down in *The Daily Worker*, ever since the end of the war. If temporary agreement with the party line is to be made the test of loyalty, let these men be called to the bar, to explain their records. . . . I submit further that the members of the Senate who are now persecuting these men who made, as I think, mistakes in China, have far more to explain, excuse, and rationalize in their own records. I still believe that the loss of China was unnecessary, but I think it far more important that we should not destroy the decent traditions of American political life. These now seem to be endangered.

Service never got to use any of his three sets of calling cards. The day after McCarthy had him in Calcutta hamstringing American-Indian relations, he got a wireless at sea instructing him to return to Washington by air as soon as his ship reached Yokohama. McCarthy learned this turn of events while he was having lunch in the Senate dining room. Senator Hubert H. Humphrey and the Washington lawyer Joseph Rauh were at a nearby table. They saw McCarthy go to a phone, listen for a moment, and then exult aloud, "They've recalled Service! Now I have got them and him!"

The State Department tried to contend in a statement issued by its deputy undersecretary, John E. Peurifoy, that Service was not being detoured because of anything McCarthy had said or done, but because the Loyalty Review Board wanted him available for questioning by the Loyalty Security Board. "Here, in the person of Jack Service, we have an able, conscientious, and—I say again, as I've already said many times before—a demonstrably loyal Foreign Service officer, a veteran of seventeen years with the Department, and one of our outstanding experts on Far Eastern Affairs," Peurifoy declared publicly. He added that because of Service's being brought back, "the personnel arrangements of which his new assignment to India was an important part are completely disrupted, a chain of other assignments and replacements is for the time being paralyzed, and vital diplomatic operations in this highly strategic area are being interrupted and impaired. . . . What he'll do with his family and belongings when the ship docks and he is met with the message that he's to turn right around and come back—to face another 'loyalty probe' —I don't know; and I don't suppose he or his wife will either. [The family, not knowing how long the paterfamilias would be detained, proceeded on to New Delhi, which had then become his assigned post, and remained there, until it became clear he would never arrive, for ten months.] I do know, though, that it's a shame and a disgrace that he and his family should have to face, once again, such humiliation, embarrassment, and inconvenience; and I'd like to say that the sympathy and good wishes of the entire Department go out to them."[2]

Service reached Washington on March 27, 1950, and was warmly and sympathetically received, in private, by those few of his fellow Far Eastern experts who were still around. A number of government officials even made bold to greet him at the airport; among them was a Japanese-language specialist in the Foreign Service, Marshall Green, who didn't have to worry about losing his job for his comparative temerity because he had independent means.[3] Most of the senior people at the department were, though guardedly, outraged. They could accept calmly one of their own being assailed by a foreign head of state, but Senator McCarthy was another matter.

Service, strapped for funds because he was sending just about everything he had to his absent family, moved into a cheap Washington hotel. When the Fulton Freemans heard of this, they begged him to come stay with them in their Georgetown house; the best they could offer was an

[2]Two years afterward, when Senator McCarthy had one of his *own* versions of this episode published, he wrote, "His [Service's] task was to advise the State Department on a policy toward India. India was then facing a threat from Communism as serious as was China when Service represented the State Department there. I discussed point by point how John Service had contributed to the disastrous policy which sold four hundred million Chinese to Communism. Had I merely discussed in general terms how disastrous our policy in China had been or how seriously India was threatened by Communism, Service obviously would not have been recalled, nor would he have been slowed down one iota in his planning."

[3]As a very junior Foreign Service officer, Green had been Service's subordinate in New Zealand (in 1973 he was appointed United States ambassador to Australia), and had become such a good friend of his that it was said of the two men that they could never play bridge against each other, because they could practically read each other's mind. Green, who has called the McCarthy period "the darkest and most humiliating days of the Foreign Service," escaped humiliation because he was never in China until in 1971, having progressed by then to being assistant secretary of state for East Asian and Pacific affairs, he accompanied President Nixon there. When Service had been invited by Chou En-lai several months previous, diplomatic punctilio was so strongly ingrained in him that before accepting, even though he had nothing to do with the department by then, he first consulted Green, to make sure State would have no objection. On Service's return, the assistant secretary, who wanted to learn as much about China as possible before setting forth with the president, made a special flight to California to talk with him.

uninsulated chamber on the third floor, once a children's playroom, but it sounded better than the fleabag where their friend was holed up. Service demurred; he felt that he was a pariah, a leper; if he accepted their kind offer, Freeman's career might be blighted. "We'll take our chances," Freeman said. So Service moved in and stayed for six months. (He also spent some time at the homes of Philip Sprouse and John Davies.) "He was the greatest house guest anybody ever had," Freeman said years afterward. "He made his own bed and washed everybody's dishes. Not that there were too many. While he was there, you could count our other friends on one hand; practically everybody in Washington cut us off their list."[4]

Deputy Undersecretary Peurifoy, who had defended Service before the Tydings committee, now urged him to get a good lawyer. It was not easy to find one who was available. John Reid, whom he had consulted during the *Amerasia* affair, was a tax man and far from a civil liberties expert. Joseph Rauh, who was, was tied up with William Remington, as was Abe Fortas with Owen Lattimore, and so on. Finally, Adrian Fisher, the department's legal adviser, proposed the firm of Reilly, Rhetts & Ruckelshaus. They were primarily labor lawyers. Gerard D. Reilly, subsequently a judge in the District Court of Appeals, had been counsel to a Senate committee when the Taft-Hartley Act was being framed. Charles Edward Rhetts, who handled Service's case personally, also knew his way around Washington; he had been an assistant attorney general not long before. Rhetts took Service on as a client, with no assurance of any fee, and labored earnestly on his behalf for twelve years, stepping down only when President Kennedy appointed him ambassador to Liberia.[5] (By then, Rauh was free to carry on.) Whenever Service was visiting Washington,

---

[4]Freeman took friendship seriously. In 1970, not long after completing a long and honorable diplomatic career as United States ambassador to Mexico, he was at a dinner party in California. When the ladies excused themselves and left the men to their brandy and cigars, a retired army general began a tirade against, among other peeves of his, the notorious, traitorous, pro-Communistic John Paton Davies. "You can't speak that way about John Davies in my presence," said Freeman, and he stalked out of the room.

[5]An Indianan by birth, Rhetts moved back to his native state from Washington in the early 1950s, hoping to get elected to Congress. But he had been away too long; he had gone to Dartmouth and Harvard Law School, and he had lost his Hoosier twang. During the 1960 presidential campaign he worked hard for the Democrats, and the Kennedy forces promised him an embassy if they won. Rhetts had the impression that he was slated for either Pakistan or Australia, but Liberia was all he was offered. Whether or not his close identification with Service was a factor in his getting that less prestigious post was moot.

during this long stretch, the Rhettses, like the Freemans before them, told him to make their home his own.

During the McCarthy-inspired investigations, Service stayed on the department payroll (he was still technically assigned to India), but State was perplexed about what to do with him. He was put on a vague and undemanding job in something called the Office of Operating Facilities ("Snake-farm duty," Adrian Fisher called it), where, among other things, he was supposed to keep track of typewriter assignments. He kept himself awake by reading Civil War histories (in the evenings, while the Freemans were waiting for their silent phone to ring, their guest would relate some of the livelier anecdotes), making an intensive study of the statuary of the District of Columbia, and trying to get to see congressmen to solicit their support or, at any rate, allay their doubts. To some whom he knew to be Masons he even sent copies of photographs taken of himself in China, in the full regalia of that order. Among others he called on was Senator Knowland. Hoping to melt his iciness, Service mentioned that in 1932 he had won a gold watch in a marathon sponsored by the Knowland family paper, the Oakland *Tribune*. The senator permitted himself a brief smile, but seemed otherwise unimpressed by this credential. (Years later, when the retired senator was back in Oakland running the paper himself, Service, while appearing before the Senate Foreign Relations Committee in Washington, was the subject of a long and friendly article in the *Tribune*. The reporter who sought him out said in advance that the story would have to be cleared with his boss, but there was no indication that Knowland had laid a finger on it.)

Edward Rhetts had problems. To restore Service's good name would require affidavits and testimony from numerous associates of his, and in those days it was chancy for any government employee to stick his neck out in the general vicinity of McCarthy's flailing axe. Professor Fairbank, for instance, who, enjoying tenure on the Harvard faculty, seemed relatively safe, spoke up for Service and was soon afterward refused a military permit to visit occupied Japan. *The New York Times* stopped asking Fairbank to do reviews on important works about Asia for its Sunday book section. Colonel David Barrett, who wasn't afraid of anybody and put friendship ahead of personal preferences, came through with a handsome testimonial from Asia, which may have been another reason why Chiang Kai-shek refused him permanent residence on Taiwan.

The first order of business for Service and Rhetts was the hearings before a triumviral State Department Loyalty Security Board. Its presiding officer was Conrad E. Snow, a retired brigadier general from New Hampshire; his associates were two career men, both oriented toward European affairs, Theodore C. Achilles and Arthur G. Stevens. Their legal counsel was Allen B. Moreland, who probably welcomed the assignment because his regular job, which could not have been a congenial one at the time, was that of liaison officer between State and the House of Representatives.

The hearings got under way on May 26—not long after a troubled Henry L. Stimson, an elder statesman's elder statesman, had sat down in Long Island and written a letter to the *Times* saying that the McCarthy way "is most emphatically not the proper way in which to insure loyalty of government employees. . . . What is at stake is the effective conduct of our foreign policy." (President Truman called the letter a "fine statement.") A feature of the hearings was the appearance of George Kennan, who everybody agreed was an expert on communism and whom not even McCarthy had accused of being a Communist. At the board's behest, Kennan, then counsellor for the State Department, had gone over all the available reports Service had written between May 1942 and May 1945 —126 of them. Not only had he scrutinized them—as well as he could; he had only four days for the stint—but, seeking evidence, if any, of Communist influences, he had compared them to what the Russians were saying over the same period.

Kennan, who had never met Service at the time, had been impressed by one of his memoranda that treated of the Soviet Union, and he called it to the panel's attention: "Chiang unwittingly may be contributing [Service had written] to Russian dominance in eastern Asia by internal and external policies, which, if pursued in their present form, will render China too weak to serve as a possible counterweight to Russia. By doing so Chiang may be digging his own grave; not only in North China and Manchuria, but also national groups such as Korea and Formosa may be driven into the arms of the Soviets." Those were hardly the words, Kennan reflected, of a man who wanted everybody to end up in a smothering Russian embrace:

> My impression is that the facts were substantially as they are here described by Mr. Service in these reports. To the extent that the critical note rings out more sharply than it might otherwise have done, I must say that I find that myself explainable by the natural tendency of all official observers, a tendency that I know very well from my own reporting experience in Moscow and Nazi

Germany, to try to debunk the official propaganda of a foreign government which you feel is trying to put something over on your own government.

Kennan concluded:

I find no evidence that the reports acquired their character from any ulterior motive or association or from any impulse other than the desire on the part of the reporting officer to acquaint the Department with the facts as he saw and interpreted them. I find no indication that the reports reported anything but his best judgment candidly stated to the Department. On the contrary, the general level of thoughtfulness and intellectual flexibility which pervades the reporting is such that it seems to me out of the question that it could be the work of a man with a closed mind or with ideological preconceptions, and it is my conclusion that it was not.

The Loyalty Security Board's eventual finding was favorable to Service, but only tentatively; it had to defer final judgment to hear "new" evidence that the FBI had been accumulating, some of it almost certainly fed to the bureau by Chinese Nationalist emissaries in Washington: that Service was suspected of being a homosexual (this may have been filtered through Senator Wherry, but in any event Service was not), and that he had fathered an illegitimate child (he hadn't been on the same continent with the woman in question for seventeen months before the baby was born). The board examined these gossamer wisps of gossip and found in his favor, unqualifiedly, on October 9.

The Scripps-Howard papers disagreed with this decision and took the position that Service should not be permitted to go to India. Service, whose family was still in New Delhi, offered to take any other assignment if his presence out there was going to be an embarrassment to the department, but he was informed by his superiors that newspapers did not govern State assignments, and his would stand. It didn't. There was still another embarrassment: Service was by then high on a list of Foreign Service officers who were earmarked for promotion from FSO-2 to FSO-1. As long as his name stayed on the roster, nobody beneath him could get advanced. As there was little hope that the Senate would confirm him, he asked to be stricken from the list. He was. In February 1951, nearly a year after departing for India, his family received instructions from Washington to return to the United States.

In the meantime, Service had also appeared before the Tydings committee, and he had been pleased to find its chairman and Democratic members generally sympathetic to his plight. (For that display of compassionateness, among other reasons, Tydings would lose his Senate seat in November, punished by McCarthyites with the aid of a fake photograph purporting to show his intimacy with the Communist Earl Browder.) Before Rhetts had agreed to represent Service, his firm had laid down certain conditions: Their client was under no circumstances to take the Fifth Amendment, and as much as possible of the transcripts of both his Loyalty Security Board hearing and his appearance before the Tydings committee would have to be made public. Tydings agreed to have nearly everything he was in charge of out in the open—save a few executive sessions where classified matters were discussed—and he took care of the State Department board by simply tacking on its proceedings as an appendix to the published account of *his* proceedings.

McCarthy was not a member of the Tydings committee, but he turned up at its public sessions and hung around outside its executive sessions, waiting to be fed confidences by Robert Morris, the counsel for the Republican minority. (As stouthearted a warrior as right-wing America ever recruited to its ranks, Morris became chief counsel to the Senate Internal Security Subcommittee in February 1951, and he spent many more years trying to prove that the Old China Hands had conspired to hand over China to the Communists. In a 1958 book of memoirs entitled, perhaps inevitably, *No Wonder We Are Losing,* Morris—aping Utley, Wedemeyer, et al.—spelt Emmerson's name throughout "Emerson.")

As Service was emerging from one session, tired and hungry, a photographer tried to intercept him for a picture. Service was for brushing by, but Rhetts told him to be agreeable. He paused, and as he did so McCarthy sprang from a doorway with a calico-cat smile on his face, threw an arm across Service's shoulder, and managed to have a shot taken of the two of them in a victor-and-victim pose—a grinning McCarthy and a glum Service side by side. Another day, rushing up to be briefed by Morris, McCarthy bumped into Service and greeted him with a genial "Hello, John." The use of a name that people who were legitimately on a first-name basis with Service never used was indicative of the sloppiness of McCarthy's research.

Before the subcommittee Service once more recapitulated his entire life, once more confessed an indiscreet acquaintance with Jaffe, and once more had his loyalty affirmed. In its report the subcommittee had this to say of Service:

We, therefore, have a picture of a blanket allegation [in regard to sabotaging General Hurley] being made against a man that his reports are "pro-Communist." Five years after the reports were written, it is proposed to penalize a Foreign Service officer by destroying his career and branding him as disloyal for writing what appears to have been the true facts as he saw them.

And of Hurley:

. . . the shoe of "pro-Communist" would appear to fit the foot of Patrick Hurley more snugly than it does John Service. Yet we reject with all our being any suggestion that Patrick Hurley is anything other than a loyal American doing what he conceived to be his patriotic duty and making statements that he believed to be in furtherance of that duty. It is this illustration that to us best proves the fallacy of the method as well as the danger to the United States of hurling [the near pun was doubtless unintentional] unfounded charges against a man's honest reporting.

The Senate, as a whole, approved the subcommittee's report—along strictly party lines, with every Democrat voting for it (and thus, by extension, for Service) and every Republican voting against it (and thus, similarly, for McCarthy). Service was happy at the outcome, naturally—though he would have preferred a less partisan tally—but his ordeal was far from over.

By that time even he had lost track of how often the State Department had, in one fashion or another, studied his case. (The total then was seven times.) America in the early fifties was a fantasy-ridden nation, and with the Korean War under way the search for scapegoats on whom the national travail could be pinned went on unrelentingly.[6] The State Department would continue to reexamine Service's well-thumbed record.

Clubb had thought, in his low-keyed, straightforward way, that it was imperative—yea, patriotic—to cut short his hard-earned holiday because of the Korean War, and to report for duty to Washington. On July 6, 1950, he did. But he found that the knowledge of the Foreign Service officers like himself who were most familiar with the Far East was not used

[6]As G. Howland Shaw succinctly put it in the *Foreign Service Journal*, "The professional informer has become a hero and character assassination a substitute for patriotism of the traditional kind."

as effectively as it might have been to abbreviate that conflict; indeed, the diplomats were, in a number of instances, held accountable for the conflict, especially after the Chinese, provoked by General MacArthur's unfamiliarity with them, had entered it late that fall.

Some of the experts had already been separated from having anything to do with Asia, and were thankful for that. Philip Sprouse went to Paris in the summer of 1950, for example. "I was glad to get out of the holocaust," he said. John Emmerson was *supposed* to go to Paris, too, as a member of the United States delegation to a hastily convened meeting there, on Korea, of the UN General Assembly. A few hours before Emmerson's plane was scheduled to leave, his orders were canceled; someone had told the State Department that he had been conniving with Japanese Communists, and whatever he might have contributed to the deliberations in France went unsaid. John Davies was in Washington, serving under Kennan on the department's Policy Planning Staff, and it was alleged by, among others, *Time* magazine, that he had been instrumental in undercutting MacArthur on the eve of the Korean War (though surely there was never anyone quite so capable of undercutting MacArthur as MacArthur himself).

Time's absurdity provoked Kennan into writing to the magazine that "It was I, after all, not Davies, who was at that time head of the Policy Planning Staff. . . . Do you not mislead your readers when you encourage them to disregard the clear hierarchy of governmental responsibility and to seek in the alleged 'influence' of junior officials the explanation for whatever is found displeasing in the workings of public policy? Must all reverses be attributable to sinister intrigue? Is it not possible that most of them might be the result of a governmental system?—of faultiness in even the most scrupulous human judgment, of blurred spots in even the clearest human vision, perhaps even in the fact that not all of the problems of national policy are readily soluble?"[7]

[7]What *Time* put forth was tame compared to some of the asseverations of those far to its right, to whom sinister intrigue was the keystone of the arch of politics. As late as 1971, the John Birch Society pamphleteer Gary Allen would be writing that John Service was "John Davies' top Comrade in falsifying information being transmitted from China to Washington. . . . Like Davies, Service was one of a ring of Communists and Communist sympathizers who devoted themselves to delivering China to Mao Tse-tung. Also like Davies, John Service never deviated one iota from the Communist Party line in China. . . . A reasonable man might assume that since Mao turned out to be the bloodiest dictator in all history, and since the Red Chinese inflicted unspeakable tortures on American prisoners in Korea . . . that if Davies or Service were ever to show their faces in public they would be summarily lynched by good Americans."

As head of Chinese affairs at State, Clubb in 1950 was directly subordinate to the assistant secretary for Far Eastern affairs, Dean Rusk. Between July and October Clubb three times sent warning memoranda up through channels to the effect that the Chinese could not be expected to stay out of the war in certain circumstances; he observed once that if the United States troops in Korea crossed the Thirty-eighth Parallel that divided the north and south of that country, the Chinese would almost certainly react in kind. As early as July 14 Clubb declared, "The theoretical alternative of the Chinese Communists' remaining passive may be arbitrarily ruled out." He was not alone. Arthur Ringwalt by then was in London, filling a slot reserved for a Far Eastern specialist at the American embassy. Ringwalt learned in early October what the British Foreign Office had just learned from K. M. Panikkar, the Indian ambassador to Peking. Panikkar had been told personally by Chou En-lai, who knew that he would spread the word, that if any United Nations troops other than South Koreans crossed the Thirty-eighth Parallel, the Chinese would enter the war.[8]

Ringwalt alerted Washington to this intelligence well before the conference at Wake on October 15 between President Truman and General MacArthur, during which MacArthur, whose experience with the Chinese was limited,[9] assured Truman that the Chinese would never do anything that ridiculous. Edmund Clubb, out of his broad experience, could have countered the general's views, but although he was head of Chinese affairs, Clubb was not included in Truman's entourage.

That December, just after Mao's "volunteers" stormed south across the Yalu River and split MacArthur's poorly arrayed forces in two, Clubb's reward for having accurately foreseen Chinese intervention was to be investigated. He had finally taken some time off—the week between Christmas and New Year's, when most government offices ran at low gear anyway—and on January 2, 1951, when he returned to his desk, he was handed a Christmas present from the State Department: a notice, dated December 26, that he was to be subjected to an interrogatory about his

[8]When Raymond Ludden, in Dublin, was notified of his sudden transfer to Brussels and was trying to ascertain the reason, he thought Ringwalt might know something about it and phoned him in London. To foil any prospective eavesdropper, they resorted to what was probably as secure a device as any in that part of the world: They talked in Chinese.
[9]Colonel Barrett recalled a visit that MacArthur had made to Taiwan not long before. Chiang Kai-shek sent his vice-president, Chen Cheng, to greet him at the Taipei airport. MacArthur, who evidently never dreamed that he would be welcomed by a second-stringer, strode briskly down the steps of his plane, hand outstretched, and told the startled Chen, "Generalissimo, I've been waiting years for this moment. . . ."

loyalty. The department wanted to know all about his political attitudes, about his "pinkness," and especially about his 1932 visit to the *New Masses* office. This was the first time Clubb had been faced with that matter. He was informed that he had then been carrying a letter back to a woman named Grace Hutchins (Walt Carmon's name had somehow vanished), who worked for something called the Labor Research Association, which was widely thought to be a Communist front; he was also told that when he got to the *Masses* office he had asked to see Mike Gold, the Communist editor.

Having no independent recollection of the episode and being unable to get his own diaries back until the end of May, Clubb looked up Hutchins and Gold to ascertain whether they remembered meeting *him*. (Miss Hutchins said she didn't, and added that if he had planned to call on her, he'd gone to the wrong place; the Labor Research Association's office wasn't in the same building as the *New Masses*.) While he was waiting for the diaries to arrive, his pursuers were not idle. The House Un-American Activities Committee, before which Chambers had first raised the *New Masses* business in secret session in December 1948, summoned Clubb before it on March 14, 1951. Now then, did he know Grace Hutchins? No, not until he sought her out recently; he had learned from her that she had been in China twice, with an Episcopal mission, but that she had left Asia before he ever got there. Did he know Owen Lattimore (yes), John Stewart Service (of course), Earl Browder (no), Emmanuel Larsen (no), Agnes Smedley? Yes, he thought he had first met Miss Smedley in 1931 at the Hankow home of Bishop Logan H. Roots, an Episcopalian minister who was one of Chiang Kai-shek's religious advisers.[10] By now Clubb had done some homework: He was able to inform the committee that if Miss Smedley was all that dangerous a character to be acquainted with, how was it that on May 4, 1934—two years *after* Clubb was supposed to have carried a surreptitious message from her to the *New Masses*—Secretary of State Hull, at the request of Senator Robert F. Wagner of New York, had sent a message of his own to all diplomatic and consular officers in China, asking them to extend suitable courtesies and assistance to the lady?

In April 1951 Truman relieved MacArthur of his Korean command and

---

[10]A notably worldly clergyman, Roots was sometimes called the "pink bishop"; Agnes Smedley addressed him as "Comrade Bishop."

ordered him home, thus infuriating the general's supporters, who tended by and large also to be supporters of Chiang Kai-shek, and who were accordingly disposed to blame the Old China Hands for, having already lost China, now losing MacArthur and, in all likelihood, Korea.[11] Having made a substantial gesture toward the preservation of constitutional government by cracking down on MacArthur, Truman thereupon threw a bone to the largely pro-MacArthur conservative forces with which he had to cope by announcing on April 28 a revision in the criteria for determining the loyalty of individuals in the executive branch of the government. Until then, eligibility for dismissal had been based on "reasonable grounds . . . for belief that the person is disloyal." Now, *dis*loyalty no longer had to be established; a person's judges merely had to find "reasonable doubt of loyalty."

The new regulations were in effect when on June 27 Clubb received a sheet of specific charges from the State Department's Loyalty Security Board. There were ten of them, and they indicated how people's minds were running in those apprehensive days. The tenth charge, Clubb was by then not surprised to perceive, was that he "in 1932 delivered a sealed envelope to the officer of the editor of the *New Masses* magazine, a Communist periodical in New York City, for transmittal to one Grace Hutchins, an avowed Communist employed by the Labor Research Association, an affiliate of the Communist Party." The others—all characterized as "specific"—were that he:

1. Associated with Communists in Hankow, China, in the period 1931–1934;

2. Viewed some aspects of Communism favorably in the period 1932–1934;

3. Had distinct "pink" tendencies at Peiping, China, during the period 1934–1935;

4. Had a marked preference for some Communist principles in the early 1930's;

5. [Was] friendly toward the USSR and Communism during the period 1935–1937;

[11]In Paris, dropping in at the American embassy one Saturday morning, Philip Sprouse was horrified to find a telegram from Washington. Rusk was ill with a kidney stone; Clubb was tied up with security investigations; the department badly needed Far Eastern people, and could Paris spare Sprouse for a while? "Oh, God," thought Sprouse, "to get mixed back up in this show again!" But back he went.

6. [Was] classified as "Mildly Red" and espoused doctrines of a "Communist" nature prior to 1940;

7. [Was] "100% pro-Red" at Shanghai, China, in 1940;

8. [Was] "favorable" to the Communists during the period 1933–1934;

9. [Had or had had] close and habitual association with the following named persons. . . .

There were eleven names on the list—most of them the names that appeared on just about everybody's "Whom-do-you-know?" lists of that era: Philip Jaffe was there, Anna Louise Strong, Agnes Smedley, and so on. Two of the names stumped Clubb, however. One was Claude Buss, and the other was that of Vladimir Mikheev. Clubb knew Buss, of course; they had been Foreign Service officers in China together before Buss left diplomacy for teaching. But Mikheev? Not only was he not a close and habitual associate, but Clubb could not recall ever having heard of him. In due course Clubb was enlightened: It seemed that Mikheev, a Tass correspondent in Chungking in 1945, had been planning a trip to Vladivostok, where Clubb was then stationed. Buss had thought the Russian might find Clubb worth talking to there and had scribbled Clubb's name on one of his calling cards, along with "Greetings through my friend Vladimir Mikheev." But Mikheev had never presented the card, and to the best of Clubb's recollection they had never laid eyes on one another. (How the Loyalty Security Board came to know about the existence of the calling card was never explained to Clubb. As good a guess as any would be that one of Chiang Kai-shek's intelligence agencies had unearthed it somewhere and passed it along to the FBI.) As for Clubb's "pinkness," it developed that Ambassador Gauss, in one of his routine efficiency reports on his subordinates, had dutifully passed along the allegation that someone else had said Clubb had the reputation of being inclined to be "pink." Gauss appeared before the Loyalty Security Board as a witness *for* Clubb; he said he would never have said such a thing about Clubb himself. The board, however, had not consulted Gauss about this before including it as a specific charge that it expected Clubb to disprove.

Clubb was suspended from performing his regular duties the day he received the list of charges against him. (He would have been suspended without pay had he not had a good deal of accumulated leave time.) The noose was beginning to tighten around one Old China Hand after the other. Concurrently, as other investigations proceeded, Davies and Vincent were placed in the same unhappy, stigmatized jeopardy. Vincent was soon shunted off from Switzerland to Tangier, where presumably no one trying to browbeat the State Department could argue that he was in a consequential policy-making post. Davies was dispatched to Germany as a deputy political adviser to the United States high commissioner. For John Service, on the other hand, that particular summer month was a rare good one: He was cleared by the Loyalty Security Board after its eighth review of *his* case.

Clubb's formal hearing before the board began on July 31, with Conrad Snow presiding. It was charged that "he was a member of, or affiliated with or in sympathetic association with the Communist Party . . . [or was] a person who consistently believed in, or supports, the ideologies and policies of the Communist Party . . . or [was] in a habitual and close association with persons known or believed to be [Communists]." Between receiving the list of ten "specific" allegations and his appearance, Clubb had written the board six explanatory letters. Davies, Service, Vincent, and he, although all being tarred more or less simultaneously with the same brush, were trying to defend themselves independently; Clubb, however, thought it would be useful—and succeeded—in getting inserted in the transcript of his hearing some testimony that George Kennan, who was rapidly emerging as one of the staunchest defenders of the Old China Hands, had given the previous month on behalf of Davies: "If there ever creeps into our system an atmosphere in which men do not feel at liberty to state the facts as they see them, knowing that the greatest crime they could commit would be to state them as they did not see them; then, in my opinion, the successful operation of the democratic foreign policy will be out of the question. I feel very deeply about that, and I think that the first requirement we have of officers who are asked to report to the Government is that they report honestly what they believe."

Clubb submitted to the board several hundred of his reports on China and on Sino-Soviet relations; but some of these were long-winded, and he never found out how many of them, if any, his investigators took the trouble to read. In addition, he had accumulated affidavits from, among other old-time acquaintances in China who did not think him Communistic, the former head of the British American Tobacco Company in Hankow, and from Dr. Knight Biggerstaff, a China expert at Cornell University who had known him back in Peking in the 1920s, and who stated, "He is the most scholarly of any of the American Foreign Service officers I have known in China." Dr. Miner Searle Bates, the veteran missionary and onetime professor of history at the University of Nanking, revealed in his affidavit that in 1949 a good many people in Peking had thought Clubb was too rigid in defending American rights and property *against* the Communists. Colonel Barrett, whom Clubb had invited to comment on whether or not he was a security risk, chimed in, "I always thought you were secure to the point of being boring."

The hearings ground on through the fall, and when Clubb was not racking his brains or riffling through yellowed papers to try to find answers about people and events dating back a quarter of a century or more, he was appearing again before the Un-American Activities Committee. The committee had subpoenaed his diaries, and while Clubb was quite willing to turn over pertinent excerpts, he did not want to yield them up in toto, inasmuch as they contained, logically enough, a good many intimate matters. Perplexed about how to handle that situation, Clubb consulted Deputy Undersecretary of State Carlisle H. Humelsine, who proposed that he turn over the complete diaries to the department; he couldn't very well give them to the House Committee if he no longer had them. Clubb did so, and the department passed the diaries along to its Loyalty Security Board, which found them on the whole—and presumably they reflected Clubb's honest thinking at the time he penned them—to contain nothing discreditable, let alone disloyal.

Still another congressional investigating unit had been created in 1950 —the Senate Subcommittee on Internal Security. It immediately began to conduct probes of its own under the chairmanship of Pat McCarran, so staunch an ally of Chiang Kai-shek that in 1949, along with proposing that the Generalissimo be endowed with $1.5 billion, the Nevadan wanted to have American army officers sent to Asia to command National- ist forces in a last-ditch stand against the Communists. Perhaps McCarran had reason to believe that in 1949—in marked contradistinction to the bygone Stilwell days—Chiang might be desperate enough to accept such an arrangement.

The State Department hadn't much use for McCarran, and it hadn't much sense of irony, either; at one point it assigned John Service, tucked away in the Office of Operating Facilities, to compile a card index of all the department people mentioned in the proceedings of the McCarran subcommittee. This roster included Service himself, who was mentioned adversely by, among others, General Wedemeyer, then retired. Wedemeyer had been persuaded by a member of McCarran's staff to agree that a few comments quoted out of context from one Service report meant in 1951 exactly the opposite of what everybody had assumed they meant in context in 1944, when the State Department had pronounced the report in question "excellent." Service was not invited to testify before the McCarran subcommittee; if he had been, he might have been able to correct the blatantly false statement in its eventual report that he had been indicted in the *Amerasia* case.

The McCarran group's excuse for dredging up China was that it was going to investigate the Institute of Pacific Relations. Under that umbrella McCarran found room for everything—for instance, for still another retelling by Whittaker Chambers of his encounter with Clubb in 1932. The committee didn't seem to know much about Clubb. One of McCarran's chief investigators, Benjamin Mandel, said it had no information on him beyond his being consul general at Changchun, and added —this at a time when Clubb and virtually all other Americans had been out of China for a year and a half—"Presumably that is his present position."

All the Old China Hands were considered fair game by McCarran and his cohorts. The week after Chambers was brought in to denounce Clubb, Louis Budenz was put on the stand to have a go at John Carter Vincent. It seemed that during the war the former managing editor of the *Daily Worker* had told Robert Morris, then in naval intelligence, that Vincent was a Communist, and Morris passed the word along. Now Morris and Budenz were contentedly in cahoots again, and to Morris's delight Budenz was telling the McCarran committee that both Vincent and John Fairbank were Communists, and that Service, moreover, had been "designated [by the Politburo of the American Communist party] as a man to be relied upon in the State Department, particularly in 1945 in the campaign against General Hurley."[12]

When Vincent was called home from Tangier the following January to testify before the McCarran committee, he came with a prepared statement:

Mr. Chairman and members of the Committee:

I have requested an opportunity to meet with you for two reasons. First to repudiate under oath certain irresponsible but very grave allegations made

[12]In his *No Wonder We Are Losing*, published in 1958, Morris said, "McCarran was the very essence of integrity at all times, and he pursued the investigation with scrupulous and careful restraint." Scrupulosity, it will be recalled, was the trait that Freda Utley also attributed to Senator McCarthy.

against me before this Committee; and secondly, to give the Committee whatever other assistance I may in the conduct of its investigation.

On August 23, 1951, before this Subcommittee, Mr. Morris asked a witness, Louis Budenz, the following question:

"Mr. Budenz, was John Carter Vincent a member of the Communist Party?"

Mr. Budenz replied, "From official reports I have received, he was." Insofar as the printed record shows, Mr. Budenz did not produce or describe the "official reports" to which he referred.

Later Mr. Morris again inquired:

"Mr. Budenz, is it your testimony that it was an official Communist Party secret shared by few people that at that time John Carter Vincent was a member of the Communist Party?"

"Yes, Sir," replied Mr. Budenz.

Mr. Budenz also testified that I was described "as being in line with the Communist viewpoint, seeing eye to eye with it." When questioned as to his source, he answered: "That was stated by Communist officials in the Politburo at that time, by Mr. Browder and Mr. Jack Stachel."

I have never met either Browder or Stachel, but it is pertinent to recall that Mr. Browder testified before the Tydings Committee that he knew of no connection that I had with the Communist Party either directly or indirectly.[13]

On October 5, 1951, Mr. Budenz again appeared before the Subcommittee.

Mr. Morris asked: "Mr. Budenz, have you identified John Carter Vincent to be a member of the Communist Party before this Committee?"

Mr. Budenz replied: "Yes, Sir, from official communications. . . ."

Gentlemen, anyone, including Budenz, who before this Subcommittee or anywhere else, testifies that I was at any time a member of the Communist Party is bearing false witness; he is, to put it bluntly, lying I do not pretend to know what motives guide Mr. Budenz. In my own case, his motives seem to be clearly malicious. He has endeavored before this Subcommittee to support his allegations by strained suggestion and devious insinuation.

Now, Mr. Chairman and members of the Committee—I am not a Communist and have never been a member of the Communist Party. I have never sympathized with the aims of Communism. On the contrary, I have worked

[13]Browder, asked about Vincent and Service, had said, "I would say regarding the two names you mentioned, to the best of my knowledge and belief, they never had any direct or indirect connection with the Communist Party."

loyally throughout the twenty-seven years of my foreign service career in the interest of our own Government and people. I am strongly attached to the principle of representative democracy and to our system of free enterprise. These being the facts, the members of the Committee will appreciate, I am sure, how disagreeable it is for me to find it necessary to affirm my devotion to our democratic institutions because of unfounded allegations made by Budenz or anyone else.

We cannot dismiss the Budenz testimony as a "mistake." Any attempt through malicious testimony to cause the American people to lose confidence in their officials, or in each other, is in itself subversive to the interests and security of our country. When, as in my case, the official represents his country abroad, the effect may be doubly harmful.

I am in full accord with the objectives of this Subcommittee. The internal security of the United States, now probably more than ever before in our history, is vitally important to all of us. Our American way of life is threatened from within as well as from without. But we cannot . . . defend democracy with perfidy or defeat Communism with lies. And I wish to state, not as an official of our Government who has been falsely accused, but as a citizen who is deeply concerned for the welfare and security of his country, that irresponsible testimony, such as Mr. Budenz is wont to give, might have its use in a totalitarian state but has no place in our American democracy. . . .

But, Gentlemen, my main purpose in seeking an opportunity to come before you has been accomplished. At the Subcommittee Hearings of October 5, 1951, Senator [Willis] Smith [of North Carolina] is reported as saying: "Mr. Vincent should come here and challenge Mr. Budenz's statement and say 'I am not a Communist.' That draws the issue."

Mr. Chairman and members of the Committee, I now solemnly repeat: I am not and never have been a Communist. I so draw the issue.

Previous to his testifying before the McCarran committee, on November 19, 1951, Vincent, who in October had presented himself before the busy Conrad Snow and his Loyalty Security Board, received from that body a statement of charges against *him*.[14] "You were pro-Communist

[14]Walter S. Surrey, who the year before had left a job as legal adviser for the State Department to go into private practice, was Vincent's attorney. Surrey—who called it a "privilege" to represent "a gentle, civilized being with an unbreakable moral fibre and an unimpeachable dedication to service to his country"—wanted to make certain that Vincent's appearance before the subcommittee would be public; it was one of McCarran's tricks first to hold closed hearings and then open ones, which gave it a chance to be

in your views and sympathies in the period 1940–1947," the first charge went. Another related to his stay in Switzerland, which had recognized the People's Republic of China. Mao's representatives in Bern were looking for suitable quarters, and Vincent was accused of having recommended to Washington that the Chinese Communists be aided in their endeavor to take over the vacant former Japanese legation. What had happened was that he had sent a cable, for the information of the State Department, to the effect that the "USSR" would probably be in favor of such a change in tenancy. In transmission, "USSR" had been garbled into "USFR," and in trying to decipher what that meant, someone on the receiving end had deduced that it meant "US and FR"—that is, the United States and the French Republic. There was another charge involving the abandoned raincoat that Senator McCarthy had found so beguiling.

On arriving in Washington in January 1952 for the McCarran hearings, one of the first people Vincent ran into was Alice Roosevelt Longworth, her not yet ancient ear finely attuned to the nuances of the Capitol. "Well, John Carter, I hear they're getting *you*," she said.

Before the McCarran committee, Vincent, once he proceeded beyond his prepared statement and submitted himself to questioning, was less than a triumphant witness in his own behalf. How could Vincent be certain he had not *unwittingly* done what the Communist party wanted done?, he was asked. What Communist books had he read? It developed, somewhat surprisingly, that Vincent was almost illiterate in that area; he hadn't even read any of the works of Chairman Mao. So they turned on

---

selective about what it revealed on the public record. Surrey hoped to get McCarran to commit himself in advance to full disclosure. One of the lawyer's biggest clients was the Chase National Bank. He phoned Winthrop Aldrich, its chairman, and asked him to set up an appointment with McCarran. When Aldrich called the senator, McCarran wanted to know why the Chase had a Communist attorney working for it; only a Communist, McCarran told Aldrich, would represent another Communist. Aldrich hung up in some consternation and got back to Surrey, who reminded him what had happened to J. P. Morgan at a Senate committee hearing, when a midget had sat on his lap; neither financiers nor Foreign Service officers, Surrey argued, should be subjected to undignified treatment, and who knew—Aldrich himself might be the next witness. Aldrich called McCarran again and reported to Surrey that an appointment had been arranged. It was set for 9:30 a.m. on a morning when Vincent was supposed to be on the witness stand at 10:00. Arriving at the Senate with his client, Surrey sent Vincent on alone to the hearing room and proceeded to McCarran's office. He waited for the senator until 10:15, and then asked a secretary where he was. Oh, didn't Surrey know?, the secretary said pleasantly; why, he was in his committee room, conducting a hearing on John Carter Vincent.

him for *that:* "How can a man be a Foreign Service officer these days and not know about Communism?" demanded Senator Homer Ferguson, a Republican of Michigan. Mrs. Vincent, who was in the audience, afterward happened to share an elevator with Ferguson, who didn't recognize her. "We're going to get Vincent on perjury," she heard him say to a companion. (No perjury charges were ever leveled by the subcommittee, drawn issue or no drawn issue, against Vincent. Nor, when it came to that, against Budenz.) Adrian Fisher, the departmental counsellor, had forewarned Vincent that the committee was fond of perjury (it had already tried, as we shall see presently, to pin a perjury rap on John Davies), and that its way of arriving at perjury charges was to subject a person to a barrage of questions for a couple of weeks and then, having got him thoroughly distracted, to confront him with conflicts in his testimony. Fisher had thus urged Vincent to be as careful as he could in his responses, and Vincent's subsequent circumspection was taken for evasion. On being asked, for example, whether he had once sent his regards to Mme. Sun Yat-sen, he said he couldn't remember. Senator Ferguson had swiftly inquired whether he perhaps had the same difficulty recalling what he'd done in the line of work.

"Senator, this all happened seven or eight years ago," Vincent had said.

Chairman McCarran had pounced. "You better answer that question," he snarled.

It took about half an hour for all present to concur that Vincent probably had sent his regards to Mme. Sun Yat-sen seven or eight years earlier.

Vincent was asked, too, about matters more recent than his bygone greetings to Madame Sun—for instance, whether or not he had contributed to a fund that had been set up to defray some of John Service's legal expenses in connection with *his* ordeal. (Its treasurer was John Reid, who had his du Pont affiliations to keep him out of trouble. Even so, Reid was cautious; afraid that some investigator or other might subpoena his records to ascertain who'd been helping Service, he kept two sets of books, one of which he was prepared to yield up, inasmuch as the names in it were exclusively those of unimpeachably stalwart citizens.) And Vincent was asked again, inevitably, if he knew various suspect individuals—Chou En-lai, Chu Teh, Oliver Edmund Clubb, people of that stripe. The roster was alphabetical; Alger Hiss came just ahead of Ho Chi Minh. No, Vincent said as the names were paraded in front of him, he had never met Mao Tse-tung; but he did avail himself of the opportunity to say at this juncture that General Hurley had called the chairman "Mouse Tongue." When it was all over, Vincent was asked if he had had a fair hearing, and he said yes, he had; but afterward he told his wife, "I knew that if I'd said 'No,' they'd have started in all over again." Mrs. Vincent later said, "John Carter had faced death in Mukden and faced terrible danger in Changsha, and in both experiences had been cool as a cucumber. But this was an experience that almost killed him. And the McCarran committee was the worst experience of my life, too. Childbirth was fun compared to that."

No one knew who could be next. Richard Service, in Brussels late in 1951, came home on a holiday leave. Seeing his colleagues—not to mention his brother—in increasing trouble, he kept waiting for someone to ask him about some of his postwar acquaintances in Hong Kong, where, assigned to the American consulate general, he had been in regular, information-gathering contact with the Chinese Communists and with a group called the Democratic League that was pure anathema to Chiang Kai-shek. Indeed, for a while in Hong Kong, he had been the *only* American diplomat who consistently met with the Communists. But nobody ever questioned him about any of this; conceivably his trespasses against righteousness had been filed in his brother's bulging dossier [15]

John Service's brief period of summer euphoria came to a jolting end late in the fall of 1951, when he got a summons to appear before the Loyalty Review Board, the super-agency for determining the fitness of government employees. He was not at first too worried. Its chairman was Hiram Bingham, a former senator from Connecticut, who came from a Pacific missionary family himself; why, Bingham had once dated Service's mother when she was a college girl. (Her son might have been less sanguine had he known that Bingham kept on his desk a copy of Utley's *The China Story*.) The review board was, like a court of appeals, supposed not to consider new evidence but merely to evaluate the findings of lower bodies like the State Department's Loyalty Security Board. The Bingham group, though, had decided (the Supreme Court would later rule that it had decided wrongly) to judge cases *de novo*. In any event, the review

[15]In 1955, however, Richard Service was asked by a State Department security man if he had any comment to make on a letter he had received in Hong Kong seven or eight years earlier from a Chinese woman who wanted to let him know that her husband was trying to escape from the mainland. What puzzled Service most was how anybody knew about the letter, which up to then he had thought was private correspondence.

board told Service, initially, that the charges it would hear against him were the same as those the Loyalty Security Board had pondered: ". . . that you are a member of, or in sympathetic association with, the Communist party . . . and further that . . . you are a person who has habitual or close associations with persons known or believed to be in the category . . . to an extent which would justify the conclusion that you might, through such association, voluntarily or involuntarily, divulge classified information without authority."

When the board had finished, it gave Service and Rhetts, his lawyer, a transcript of the proceedings. They were surprised to find therein a new charge: "Intentional, unauthorized disclosure to any person under circumstances which may indicate disloyalty to the United States, of documents or information of a confidential or non-public character [this, of course, was a long-winded way of referring to the *Amerasia* case] obtained by the person making the disclosure as a result of his employment by the Government of the United States." When Service and Rhetts pointed out to the board that another dimension had been added, the board was embarrassed and admitted it had erred.

But what to do? One possibility was holding a new hearing. Service, though, had had it with hearings. So he and Rhetts—who mistakenly believed that the review board was going to decide in his client's favor— agreed to stipulate that they would accept the already conducted hearing as though the additional charge had been a part of it all along. They would regret that, because on December 13 the Bingham board concluded that Service had been guilty of this appended accusation, and it decreed: "We are not required to find Service guilty of disloyalty, and we do not do so, but for an experienced and trusted representative of our State Department to so far forget his duty to his trust as his conduct with Jaffe so clearly indicates, forces us with great regret to conclude that there is reasonable doubt as to his loyalty. The favorable finding of the Loyalty Security Board of the Department of State is accordingly reversed."

Within a few hours Acheson had fired Service. Service learned the news quite by accident. Raymond Ludden was having his own troubles—who indeed was not?—and he was going to the department's security office to find out where *his* loyalty stood that day. Service, at loose ends, accompanied him. When they got to the office, a man there, thinking Service had come on his own business, turned pale and blurted, "How did you find out?" Service got hold of Edward Rhetts fast, and the two of them tried to see Acheson that evening, but he was unavailable. Besides, they were told by one of his assistants, the decision of the board was binding on the secretary, and a press release about the dismissal had also been distributed. (In the opinion of Adrian Fisher, Acheson's legal adviser, the decision was probably not binding at all. But Fisher was abroad that day, and the lawyer who was acting in his stead had told the secretary he had no options.)

The following evening Eric Sevareid said on the CBS network:

This reporter would like to step a bit out of character, on two counts. I would like to make a few purely personal assertions, unprovable by their nature, but the truth of which I deeply believe, and to make these statements, not about an issue, but about a man. I wish to talk about Mr. John Stewart Service, whose long career as an American diplomat was broken last night, when the federal Loyalty Review Board concluded that his loyalty to his country was in doubt.

This must be personal because my knowledge of this case is personal; I have known John Service over a period of eight years, in China and in Washington. It is my personal conviction, based on much firsthand knowledge, that the American diplomatic service contained no more brilliant, devoted, self-sacrificing field agent—his unusually rapid rise in the service, the extraordinary prophetic quality of his reports from China attest to that. And it is my unshakable personal conviction, based not only on the same testimony the Review Board considered, not only upon intimate memories of the special wartime atmosphere and procedures at the period of the *Amerasia* case, but also upon the instinctive human knowledge which friendship produces, that John Service was, and is, a completely loyal American citizen. That is not only one man's belief; it is the belief of all his colleagues in the diplomatic service; it was the belief not only of the grand jury which first heard the *Amerasia* story; it was the belief of all those able and honorable men who conducted not one, two or three, but six other investigations of this most thoroughly investigated loyalty case in American history.

Certain things must be understood—no new evidence was produced, by Senator McCarthy or before the Review Board; all of it was in, years ago; Service has never withheld a shred of evidence; he told the whole story freely and openly, immediately he realized the *Amerasia* crowd were not the responsible journalists he had been assured they were. It should be understood that the Review Board has not found him to be disloyal; it has decided only that it has a doubt as to his loyalty; under the new ground rules on these cases, that is all it had to find. Under these rules, the accused, contrary to the ancient

rules prevailing in courts of law, does not enjoy the benefit of the doubt. Mere doubt can destroy a reputation, a career, all that makes life worth living for a citizen who happens to be in the federal service.

In a career without blemish before, without blemish since, John Service made one serious mistake; he gave verbal and documentary information about China, as background, to journalists who were not what he thought they were. In wartime, background briefing by diplomats and soldiers was a necessary and commonplace procedure. He gave me similar information in China, when we first met, but not, may I add, without having me vouched for, despite my uniform and my credentials. He was not a careless, loose-tongued man, by any means. But he did make one mistake.

And he was by no means alone in that. At least once, in the war, General George C. Marshall, as Chief of Staff, briefed a number of us on highly secret information, when there was present a journalist who later turned out to be a strict Communist Party liner. Despite their facilities, Marshall's security officers had made a mistake, an honest mistake. The same kind of mistake, I feel certain, has been made time and time again by high-ranking diplomats and officers in briefing groups of reporters. No one has suggested, or would suggest, that there is any doubt, reasonable or otherwise, about the loyalty of those officials. Service's mistake was an honest one. But his career and his name have been destroyed.

I have said all this because a reporter has a special obligation to report any personal knowledge of a public issue, and because friendship carries with it certain obligations, too.

The whole Service family had by then been reunited in Washington, and they had already invited a number of friends to a New Year's Eve party. They decided to go through with it. It would bring tears to Service's eyes twenty years later to recall how many people (among them John Davies and John Melby) turned up that night to comfort him. One can only imagine how he must have felt when it came time to sing "Auld Lang Syne." And there were a few other heartwarming incidents around then —for instance, publication in the January 1952 edition of the *Foreign Service Journal* of an editorial that said, among other things:

> For it is not only Jack Service and the Foreign Service that are victims in this matter. To the Department, the reversal implies that its Loyalty Security Board, despite carefully selected members and diligence in the examinations which preceded its decisions, is either inept or biased or both. For all journal-

ists greater difficulty in obtaining news is created and the ideal of an informed public as a constructive factor in foreign affairs is made more remote. For the American people a fundamental of law and government has been contravened. . . . The *Journal* believes that there is a great deal at stake here for Service, the individual; for the Foreign Service as a group of dedicated government employees; for the Department in its heavy responsibilities of diplomacy; and for the American people and their heritage of justice. Every effort must be made in our collective self-defense to utilize all available means, including the courts, to make certain that justice prevails in the case of the loyalty of John S. Service to the United States.

At the end of 1951 the crazy United States was on the verge of embarking on one of its truly whackiest ventures: It was getting set to build a splashy secret installation on the Marianas island of Saipan, where the Central Intelligence Agency proposed to train Nationalist Chinese forces for Chiang Kai-shek's conquering invasion of mainland China. (The invasion never took place, and the place on Saipan was taken over by the headquarters of the Trust Territory of the Pacific Islands, much to the relief of the local Saipanese, who had been pretty much denied access to half their island while the CIA was manicuring it.) At that eerie time Edmund Clubb got another Christmas present—a declaration by the Loyalty Security Board that while there was no reasonable doubt of his loyalty he had been judged a security risk and should therefore be separated from the Foreign Service.

Clubb inquired of Secretary Acheson on what grounds the decision had been reached, and the department agreed to hear an appeal from the verdict.[16] Nathaniel Davis was designated by the secretary to hear Clubb's appeal. Davis let Clubb know right off that one of the things he wanted to hear most about was that 1932 visit to the *New Masses*. Up to then Clubb had not bothered to get an attorney—John Melby had been standing by him to give nonlegal aid and comfort during the early Loyalty Security Board proceedings—and this was probably a mistake, for in his innocence he had tolerated fishing expeditions through the depths of his life that any reputable trial lawyer would have objected to strenuously. Also, Clubb was perhaps too candid. Someone would say to him,

[16]One ground conceivably was that in the fateful summer of 1932, while in Washington, Clubb had had lunch with Lawrence Todd, the chief Tass correspondent in the United States. Indeed he had; Todd was a brother of O. J. Todd, the eccentric engineer whom Clubb knew well when he had wrestled with the banks and the bandits of the Yellow River.

"Now, Mr. Clubb, have you told us everything you know about Agnes Smedley?," and he would say, in effect, "No, but I've told you everything about her that's pertinent," and it would be assumed that he was hiding something *really* pertinent.

During the Un-American Activities Committee questioning, Clubb had for a time been counseled by Gerard Reilly, of the firm that was working for Service, but now during the appeal both Reilly and his partner Rhetts were tied up. This was no time not to have a good lawyer, and Clubb was fortunate to be able to recruit one of Washington's best—Paul A. Porter, of Arnold, Porter & Fortas. Not long after the appeal proceedings got under way, Porter delivered himself of some remarks that were both impassioned and cogent:

> I think that this is perhaps the most unusual kind of situation or case that has come to my attention, in a rather unlimited experience in dealing with matters regarding the loyalty and security of federal employees. . . .
>
> I think perhaps the reason that some of us as private lawyers interest ourselves in these private matters [the "question of morale of our Foreign Service, and of the government itself"] is not only to protect the basic civil rights of persons who may be involved, but also to try to make some contribution against what at times seems to me to have been the real secret weapon of our enemy. There is nothing in this record but suspicion. [As to the morale of the Foreign Service]: I frankly do not know what type of information and reporting we are going to get in this critical period. If this process goes on, and I further, as a citizen—and I am not speaking now as Mr. Clubb's counsel necessarily—would not like to see another scalp added to the belt of the demagogues that have so viciously attacked this Department, and it seems to me, unless there is definite probative proof and something that is more than suspicion both from the standpoint of individual rights and for the good of the Service, this finding of the Board below has got to be reversed and Mr. Clubb's vindication upheld.

It was an addled period. The people in the State Department who had any authority were, by and large, sympathetic to the Foreign Service officers who were being pilloried, yet the department itself was under such assault from outside that to propitiate its enemies it had to provide periodic human sacrifices. In Clubb's case a balance was, in theory, beautifully struck. He was cleared by Davis, and he received a letter reinstating him to the department in good standing, but with it came some bleak news: He was a Class 1 officer, a consul general, a man who by now would have been a career minister had not the government felt in 1949 that it didn't want to elevate the status of its diplomatic mission in Peking, and suddenly he was to be put in something called the Division of Historical Research, and not even in charge of it! Said the Washington *Post* in an editorial, "Like some unfortunate suspect of the Middle Ages whose innocence has been established by walking on hot plowshares, Mr. Clubb has been at once 'cleared' and irremediably crippled."

Clubb was fifty-one years old and had had nearly twenty-four years of far-ranging service. Now he was being waved down a narrow, dead-end street. "I could see the handwriting on the wall," he said. So, regretfully, he took the option open to him of early retirement. He left the Foreign Service at the close of business on February 11, 1952. His salary had been $12,000 a year; his retirement pay would be $5800. (At that, he would be better off than Service, who, having been fired, could expect nothing.) "I face the unavoidable conclusion, at last," said Clubb, "that the same loyalty-security process, while resulting in my vindication, has seriously damaged my future career prospects in the Foreign Service. As it was succinctly put by the August 1951 *Foreign Service Journal* editorial, entitled 'The Cost Is Too High,' 'The person so besmirched can never obtain full retribution, nor can the Government regain the full value of his services.' "

10

"Let history be my judge."

So Clubb was out, and Service was out, and the prospects for Davies's and Vincent's survival were ebbing. What had got the McCarran committee so riled up about Davies that it had sought—unsuccessfully—to have him indicted for perjury was a bizarre minor episode involving him, the Central Intelligence Agency, and still another informant, or informer. This was a man named Lyle H. Munson, who had been working for the OSS and the CIA, seriatim, since 1940. Munson was one of those erratic individuals whom, like Budenz, Robert Morris clearly found congenial. When Munson died in November 1973, he was president of a small right-wing publishing operation called Bookmailer, Inc., which among other pseudo-historical works put out Morris's *No Wonder We Are Losing.*

Davies's connection with Munson, a brief one, began in the fall of 1949, when the diplomat was on Kennan's Policy Planning Staff. The Bamboo Curtain was beginning to drop, and the nation's intelligence-gatherers were scouting about for ways to keep abreast, through clandestine channels, of continuing developments inside China. The CIA proposed to Kennan that he, representing State, get together with it and with the Defense Department to work out some scheme. Kennan had what he thought were a lot of other and more important things to do. He knew Davies well, from their service together in Moscow; he had been impressed there by Davies's firm anticommunism, at times even hawkishness. He had been further impressed by Davies's penetrating analysis of one bothersome situation in the Far East: We should keep our hands off Indo-China, Davies had strongly urged; colonialism couldn't last forever; the French were doomed.

Kennan, accordingly, had designated Davies to represent the State Department in the proposed tripartite discussions. Two CIA men, one of them Munson, had come around to see Davies—"these laddies in the dirty-tricks business," he would later call them—and in chatting with them he had concurred (the idea was never implemented, nor indeed carried much beyond that initial exploratory conversation) that one way of keeping abreast of China might be to enlist on the government's behalf individuals who already had close contacts with the new China elite and who might be able to use these for intelligence purposes. Davies threw out a whole raft of names, among them those of the bookish and apolitical Sinologist Benjamin I. Schwartz of the Harvard faculty, and also of such obvious candidates as Agnes Smedley, Edgar Snow, and John Fairbank.[1] Whether or not any of them would have enjoyed being on retainer from the CIA was moot, but it never came up for a decision because it was never seriously broached to them.

Inasmuch as every covert government operation had to have a code name, this one became known as "Tawny Pipit." The reason was, Edgar Snow believed, that that particular bird had a "loud song delivered in flight"; the Americans involved in Tawny Pipit would have attempted to elicit countercalls from across the Communist borders.[2] The China Lobby version of this scheme was that Davies was maneuvering to infiltrate the United States government with Communist sympathizers who would subvert their own nation in support of the new enemy. The charge of perjury arose because Davies, after word of the abortive idea got leaked, declined to discuss it; he believed that anything involving the CIA was supposed to be off-limits. The leaking came from the CIA man, Lyle Munson. He gave some documents pertaining to it to Alfred Kohlberg,

[1] In March 1952 Morris devoted a good part of one day of the committee's presumably valuable time to questioning Fairbank about a Chicago *Tribune* story that had just come out. It was based on a September 3, 1950, story in a Chinese Nationalist paper, the *Central Daily News*, which had said that when a Chinese Communist named Li Peng was executed in April 1950, his last words before getting his desserts had been to the effect that Fairbank was part of an espionage ring conveying diplomatic secrets to Soviet agents. Morris had a copy of the Chinese text with him, and it was one of the ironies of this inquisitorial incident that he asked Fairbank to translate it into English for him and that Fairbank obliged.

[2] Before the McCarran committee, Davies was being questioned one day by J. G. Sourwine, one of Morris's assistant grillers. Davies mentioned "a cute dish" whom Edgar Snow had known in Moscow, and cheerfully agreed with Sourwine that she might well have been a Soviet intelligence operative. "Since you presumed the young lady to be an NKVD agent," Sourwine asked, "why was it that you told Mr. Snow [in a letter a McCarran agent had evidently glimpsed] the NKVD did not have her yet?" Davies replied lightly, "A totalitarian state devours its own, you know."

who passed them on to Robert Morris, and no doubt also to Senator McCarthy.

Davies found himself in trouble because, in the Tawny Pipit matter, he refused to breach security and talk about it. Kennan, who had got Davies into this quandary in the first place, was furious that Munson, who *had* breached security, was being pictured as the hero in the minor drama and Davies as the villain. Secretary Acheson, beleaguered enough by accusations that he was soft on communism, was loath to get personally mixed up in the absurd contretemps. So Kennan went charging over to the CIA himself and insisted that Munson be fired for his indiscretion. Munson quickly got another job, with an army intelligence unit, but he blamed Davies for his dismissal and was eager a few months afterward to give the McCarran committee his version of the story and thus lay the groundwork for its vain attempt to have Davies branded a perjurer.

Davies himself didn't much care by then what happened. When in the 1952 presidential campaign Dwight Eisenhower would not defend his old mentor George Marshall against allegations of treason, Davies felt that, in his words, the jig was up. True, he was cleared in December 1972 by the Loyalty Review Board, the body that had ruled adversely against both Service and Vincent, but nobody had any faith in the durability of any such board's findings. Not long afterward, more or less to remove Davies as far as possible from the field of vision of his and its detractors, the State Department quietly transferred him from Germany to Peru, as deputy chief of mission and counsellor at the embassy. Davies was not averse to be thus out of the direct line of fire. And Lima had certain attractive features of its own: His wife had Spanish blood, and she was fond of bullfights.

President Eisenhower and Secretary Dulles were both inexperienced at running a nation, but well-versed in expediency. If the mood of the times demanded that in order to retain political power, principle would have to be sacrificed for pragmatism, well, then, people like Vincent and Davies were small potatoes compared to George Marshall before them. As Louis J. Halle put it in *The Cold War and History*, "The new administration felt itself compelled to cut out the horses that had been pulling the carriage in order to feed the wolves that bayed on its trail." In presiding over the State Department, *Dulles* felt, according to his biography by Townsend Hoopes, that "the power to do him in . . . lay with the virulent Communist-haters on the right—the archconservatives, the residual

McCarthyites, the China Lobby—and it was a power they would use if he noticeably softened his position on the basic issues of the cold war. Accommodation of the Right was thus equated with personal survival. . . ."

One of Dulles's first pronouncements vis-à-vis the Foreign Service was to set forth new criteria for performance acceptable to him; it was on January 21, 1953, just one day after Eisenhower's first inauguration, that the secretary said that career diplomats would from then on have to demonstrate "positive loyalty" to whatever the president and Congress might prescribe, and that anything less than that, whatever that was, would be "not tolerable at this time." A new rule was invoked: No Foreign Service officer, no matter how often he might have passed loyalty or security tests in the past, could embark on any new assignment without first undergoing yet another clearance. To supervise the procedure, Dulles hired a new security chief, Scott McLeod, an archconservative McCarthyite who proved to be so objectionable even to his Republican confrères that after a year they eased him out. They made him—to the wry amusement of many Foreign Service officers he badgered and who themselves never got that high up the diplomatic ladder—ambassador to Ireland.

McLeod, a onetime newspaperman from Iowa who became an FBI agent in New Hampshire and later served as an administrative assistant to that state's virulently Communist-hating senator, Styles Bridges,[3] had his own standards by which to measure security. The kind of person McLeod considered trustworthy, he declared, was the kind he would like "to be behind a tree with me in a gunfight."[4] While the dendrophilic New England gunfighter was in the saddle, on May 27, 1953, Eisenhower issued an executive order further refining the official standards governing loyalty and security. Now, reliability and trustworthiness were rated equally with loyalty, and in the case of anyone being evaluated a judgment

---

[3]Bridges—who during the Tydings committee hearings of 1950 once felt inspired to exclaim, "Are we men in Europe and mice in Asia?"—was among the guests at a Washington, D.C., dinner party given by Chiang Kai-shek's ambassador to the United States shortly after Eisenhower's election in 1952. Among others in the assemblage, the cream of the China Lobby, were his fellow Senators Knowland, McCarran, and McCarthy, Representative Walter Judd, and Henry Luce. At an appropriate moment, they all rose to their feet in a "Back to the mainland!" toast to the Generalissimo.

[4]Asked once if it was true that his Bureau of Inspection, Security, and Consular Affairs was checking on which Foreign Service officers subscribed to, among other journals, the not very radical *Reporter* magazine, McLeod replied ambiguously that he would be "disappointed in a Foreign Service officer who failed to acquaint himself with both the liberal and conservative sides of every subject bearing upon his mission of protecting and furthering the interest of this country."

was to be made as to "whether continued employment is clearly consistent with the interests of national security." As long as Scott McLeod was around, according to one man in the State Department who could still bring himself to make small jokes about current events, under the new system hardly anyone could anticipate going about his daily chores Scott-free.

Even before McLeod took over security, the Eisenhower administration had stepped up the pace of the Truman administration's sniping at John Carter Vincent. Vincent had outranked Clubb, Service, and Davies; his scalp would make the finest trophy of all. He had been rather uncritical, all things considered, of the potshots taken at him; in March 1952 he had observed in a letter home, however, that as the excesses of the post-Civil War carpetbaggers had led to the Ku Klux Klan, and as the excesses of Napoleon to the Holy Alliance, so had the poison of Russian communism inevitably produced its own vicious antidotes. "I should be more content, in my present frame of mind, if I could cite the Inquisition," he had added. But even while deploring "irresponsible and malicious attacks" upon himself, he had stated that he had no objections to loyalty and security investigations, "especially as the increased danger of Soviet espionage calls for constant vigilance," and he had said after one four-day, grueling, pre-McLeod State Department loyalty probe, that "the security of the United States transcends considerations of personal feelings."

Spoken like a true Foreign Service officer! And the department had rewarded him for his reaffirmation of patriotism and humility. Sending him back to Tangier from Washington after that early 1952 probe, it had issued a public statement saying that he was returning there (though without any explanation of why he had been there in the first place) with the "Department's full confidence and best wishes." Moreover, Deputy Undersecretary Humelsine had conveyed to him privately the "Department's appreciation of your twenty-seven years of conscientious service and best wishes for the future." "The favorable decision in regard to the loyalty aspects of your case will be referred to the Loyalty Review Board of the Civil Service Commission for post-audit review," Humelsine had added. "The Department's security decision, however, is final." Secure, then, yes; loyal, maybe. In any event, in the last few of his twenty-seven conscientious years Vincent had learned one thing for certain: That in the tortured jargon of the State Department in the cold-war years, there was nothing final about the word *final.*

Vincent had truly enjoyed his postwar stay in Switzerland, despite the mischief Senator McCarthy's ill-fated operative, Charles Davis, had tried to stir up for him. Switzerland had not been Vincent's first choice in 1947. He had asked Secretary Acheson to send him to Czechoslovakia, but the department had deemed it impolitic to put him in a Communist nation. Vincent subsequently agreed with the decision. "Had I gone to Czechoslovakia, I'd have lost Czechoslovakia, too," he said.

Vincent had been stationed in Switzerland once before, in prewar days, when it was an exciting place to be, what with all the refugees from Nazism streaming in, seeking a neutral sanctuary. And although Europe was not his primary beat, between 1947 and 1951 he had applied himself to his Swiss job with such conscientiousness that James MacGregor Byrne, his deputy during that period, would later observe that "the morale of the American Mission in Bern remained at a higher level than that of any other mission I have ever seen or heard described." Speaking of those days at a memorial service for Vincent in December 1972, Byrne said, "It was John Carter's distinguished appearance that first would attract attention at official gatherings. And then, as people saw him more frequently, they would notice he was dignified but never pompous, polite and friendly but never patronizing, courtly and urbane but unmistakably American, shrewd, kindly, sensitive, and very amusing. No wonder he was beloved by everyone, from the President of Switzerland to Edmond, his chauffeur. Even his casual raising of chickens in the Embassy's back yard won for him the support of a hitherto unmoved segment of the population."[5]

[5]Byrne continued, "Of course, the Swiss are probably no different inherently from people anywhere else. It was the institutions that evolved there and the feedback from these institutions on succeeding generations that have given the Swiss a special way of looking at things. It was the Swiss social and political climate, their tradition of freedom and of community responsibility which John Carter found so congenial. For example, it was at a small farewell stag luncheon given by the Foreign Minister, Max Petitpierre (later President of Switzerland), in honor of John Carter that John Carter in responding to the Foreign Minister's very warm and flattering toast said something, in French, to the effect that whereas the sense of well-being and the lifting of the spirit that every tourist feels on entering Switzerland may be due to the sight of its soaring mountain peaks and the inhalation of its champagne-like air, for him, who was not just entering Switzerland, but had been living there for several years, this same continuing sense of well-being and of an uplifted spirit was due rather to the political climate and the enduring evidence of the Swiss people's fervent attachment to their own free institutions. From the looks of pleasure which the high Swiss officials present on that occasion exchanged with one another, I could see that he had truly touched them by referring to the one thing about their country they most cared about and were most proud of."

Toward the end of the Truman administration, however, a large contributor to the Democratic party got bored with being ambassador to a small Latin-American nation and requested a switch to Switzerland. The State Department had it in mind to make Vincent ambassador to Costa Rica, but even that less than titanic transfer would have necessitated facing up to the bugaboo of Senate confirmation, so he had been dispatched instead to North Africa, with the high-sounding but not terribly meaningful titles of Minister to Morocco and Diplomatic Agent at Tangier.

Tangier hadn't been much of a post since 1904, when it had been the scene of a mildly sensational incident. A rich man named Perdicaris, who claimed American citizenship, had been kidnapped and held for ransom by an indigene brigand named Raisuli. The United States had ordered a naval squadron to steam toward the spot, and Theodore Roosevelt had sent the American consul general in Tangier a terse message (written for the president by John Hay and Associated Press correspondent Edward Hood): "We want either Perdicaris alive or Raisuli dead." It happened that arrangements for Perdicaris's release had already been made by the time the ultimatum was delivered, but Roosevelt was wildly acclaimed when he delivered the ringing words at the Republican National Convention.

By 1951 there were four more or less separate influences in Tangier—French, Spanish, Moroccan, and international. The place had become celebrated as a haven of global intrigue, and in diplomatic circles was regarded as a potentially rewarding listening post. By an ionospheric quirk, radio messages that were transmitted in various sections of the world had a way of bouncing down into Tangier. So there was always the possibility of eavesdropping on Russian communications, and perhaps learning something of what secret Soviet intentions were with respect to the military situation in Korea. Moreover, there were no Communist diplomats stationed in Tangier; the State Department could thus send Vincent there without subjecting itself to the charge that he was in a place where he could play footsie with a bunch of Communists.

The Americans assigned to Tangier were delighted to welcome Vincent, who was a companionable addition to the poker and baseball games with which they kept themselves occupied while waiting for messages to drop down from the skies; but they were a bit flustered by his high-ranking presence, because there was really not very much for him to do.

On December 12, 1952, with Eisenhower having been elected but Truman still in the White House, Vincent and his wife were preparing to celebrate Christmas in Tangier when still another holiday announcement emerged from the State Department's own communications network. Hiram Bingham's Loyalty Review Board had adjudged that day, by a 3-to-2 vote, that there was some doubt about Vincent's loyalty after all. It had been a strange proceeding. Originally, a three-man panel of the board had considered Vincent's case and had voted in his favor, 2-to-1; then Chairman Bingham had added two more people and taken a new vote, and this time the verdict had swung in the opposite direction. One of the additional members was a woman who apparently took a dim view of Vincent because he had admittedly contributed fifty dollars to John Service's defense fund.[6]

The Loyalty Review Board's recommendation that "Mr. John Carter Vincent be terminated" was based on weird logic: "Without expressly accepting or rejecting the testimony of Louis Budenz that Mr. Vincent was a Communist and 'under Communist discipline' or the findings of the Senate Committee on the Judiciary (a) that 'over a period of years John Carter Vincent was the principal fulcrum of I.P.R. pressures and influence in the State Department' and (b) that 'Owen Lattimore and John Carter Vincent were influential in bringing about a change in the United States policy in 1945 favorable to the Chinese Communists,' the panel has taken these factors into account." And, further, "The panel notes Mr. Vincent's studied praise of Chinese Communists and equally studied criticism of the Chiang Kai-shek Government throughout a period when it was the declared and established policy of the Government of the United States to support Chiang Kai-shek's Government."

But what kind of mealy-mouthed finding was this? How could rational people take into account something they neither accepted nor rejected? And what did the board mean by "studied," when it came to that? The board of directors of the American Foreign Service Association and the editorial board of its *Foreign Service Journal* jointly endorsed an unusually forthright statement entitled "The Meaning of the Ruling in the Vincent Case for the National Interest and the Foreign Service." In it they said:

---

[6]The Washington *Post*, which evidently had had a peek at the books on Chairman Bingham's desk, remarked editorially, some weeks later, "That the three members of the Loyalty Review Board . . . were so taken in is probably due to the fact that they had imbibed an overdose of Utley." In any event, Vincent's modest gift to his friend Service's cause hardly seemed blameworthy. The previous February a former assistant secretary of state had told the *Foreign Service Journal* that "I shall consider it a privilege, as well as an obligation, to contribute to such a fund."

Members of the Service far from Washington and the sense of things at home who read this letter as a guide to their performance may well feel themselves cast adrift without a compass. . . . We are not sure what the Board meant to imply by its studious use of the word "studied." Surely the key to the case in everyone's mind is whether Mr. Vincent was merely calling things as he saw them, or whether he was distorting his recommendations and suppressing truth in the interests of a Communist conspiracy. If the Board found a probability of the latter, its letter should have said as much. The point is far too important to be conveyed by implications; if there is evidence to support so grave a charge it ought to have been cited more specifically.

To us, as it stands, the letter means that any Foreign Service officer reporting confidentially to his superiors may cast a doubt on his own loyalty if his reports contain criticism of a friendly government. It also serves to mean that he will have to be ultra-cautious in admitting the strength of the opposition. . . .

The Board "calls attention to Mr. Vincent's close association with numerous persons who, he had reason to believe, were either Communists or Communist sympathizers." Nothing is said about the *when, where,* or *why* of these associations but it is implied that these contacts were not blameless. It seems to us that they cannot be divorced from the circumstances. It is an historic fact that as a Nation all of us were associated with Communists in fighting World War II with a Communist ally. Our Foreign Service today cannot do its business in many parts of the world, including the U.N., without rubbing elbows with Communists. Its officers would not be good reporters if they did not know what was in the Communist mind and even anticipate it.

The Board's letter does not dispose of a fear it excites; that a man may be suspected merely because his opinions do not stand up when considered free of the mortal compulsions of the war period and with leisured hindsight. We hope no officer will ever be found disloyal because he lacked a foresight which could be found in no man, or because our national effort to work with a particular group did not succeed.

In addition to its disturbing implications for Foreign Service reporting, the letter inevitably provokes speculation as to the Board's judicial standards and proceedings.

We know that the Board is concerned only with the imprecise zone of "reasonable doubt"; that it does not presume to judge guilt or innocence; and that it is not a judicial tribunal; yet we can only read its letter with minds conditioned to the common law concept of evidence. When we are told, therefore, that the Board has "taken into account" certain "factors" including the testimony of a recanted Communist and the adverse findings of the McCarran Committee, but has done this without "expressly accepting or rejecting" these "factors" we are left pondering the difference between "facts," as they are evidenced in a court of law, and "factors" as in this case. Are we to conclude that any Foreign Service officer or employee accused of disloyalty by anyone must expect the Board to accept the accusations as evidence without expressly passing upon their validity? And, since the Board mentions only the "factors" unfavorable to the accused, are we to assume that it did not "take into account" the other "factors" of his clearance by the Department's Board and by an earlier Senate sub-committee?

We believe that Mr. Vincent's long and close association with our China policy makes it all the more necessary that any "reasonable doubt as to his loyalty" be fully documented and any action taken with respect to his dismissal or reinstatement be subject to every possible administrative and legal review. Whatever the ultimate result, no American or foreigner, friend or foe, should be left under an illusion that the United States Government tries to exculpate itself for failures in China by seeking out individual scapegoats. No one should be entitled even to imagine a parallel between legitimate measures for the protection of the American democracy and the mock trials of the wretched men whom the Kremlin accuses of "sabotaging" its policies.[7]

Understandably anguished as was the reaction in Foreign Service circles to the untoward news about Vincent, the reaction in some Tangier circles was even stronger. The American editor of an English-language newspaper there, the *Moroccan Courier,* printed in full a note he'd written to Vincent about this "grievous calumny" and in capital letters enjoined his circulation:

READERS! SERVE YOUR COUNTRY BY WRITING OR WIRING THE PRESIDENT ABOUT THIS TERRIBLE INJUSTICE TO A GREAT MAN.

A Spanish-language paper reflected that Vincent had demonstrated his fondness for Goya's paintings and that no one who felt that way could be a bad man.

Vincent was suspended as soon as the Bingham board's judgment was handed down, and this proved to be another bad break for him; it made

[7]When it came to parallels, Harrison Salisbury observed that the Russians were sore at losing China, too, but they expressed their irritation by murdering most of their Old China Hands.

254 | The China Hands

it impossible for him to officiate at the one comparatively important matter that had arisen since his arrival. Tangier was the last place on earth where the United States had extraterritorial rights of the sort it had waived in China in 1943. Extraterritoriality was a subject dear to Vincent's heart (his only published work in twenty years of retirement was a monograph on extraterritoriality in China), and now, in Tangier, there was to be a trial in a United States consular court of an American accused of hijacking one hundred thousand dollars' worth of cigarettes from a Dutch ship off the Spanish coast. If convicted, the defendant would have the right to appeal to the American minister—Vincent—but inasmuch as Vincent was suspended, he who was being judged afar, by the board in Washington, was deprived of fulfilling his prescribed judicial role.[8]

In Washington Vincent's lawyer, Walter Surrey, was outraged at the peculiar performance of the Loyalty Review Board. He went to see Dean Acheson, the then lame-duck secretary of state, and Acheson's own legal adviser, Adrian Fisher. By this time Acheson had come to agree with Fisher that the secretary was not bound, as he thought he had been in the case of John Service, by the board's ruling. Neither Acheson nor President Truman wanted to fire Vincent, what was more, and they decided to invite still another high-level five-man body to go over the case and determine Vincent's fitness to remain on duty. Fisher went to New York and recruited a chairman for it—Judge Learned Hand, one of the most respected jurists in the nation.

Surrey, for his part, went to see John Foster Dulles, whom Eisenhower had already designated his secretary of state to be. By the time the Hand panel had arrived at its recommendations, of course, it would be Secretary Dulles, not Secretary Acheson, who would have to act upon them; Dulles, therefore, agreed to prepare himself for that responsibility by making a personal study of the whole Vincent loyalty-security file, which by then had assumed enormous proportions. He took it to Europe with him on his first overseas mission as secretary, and he professed later to have read it in its entirety on his two trans-Atlantic flights, which must have been

[8]The trial was to have been held in the grand salon of the palatial building where the minister lived and had his offices. Mrs. Vincent, a long-time music-lover, had installed two grand pianos there, back-to-back, and she had promised the room to a group of children who wanted to sing Christmas carols. She felt that her husband and she still had certain perquisites; she insisted that the recital go on as scheduled and that the trial—the last one, as it turned out, ever to take place under the rules of extraterritoriality—be conducted in a small back room.

quite a feat considering that he also had to prepare for conferences abroad traveling eastward and write a report for the president on the way back.

On December 24, 1952, again during the transitional period between administrations, Dulles had called on Acheson, who had told him about Judge Hand's group, and Dulles had said that its views would certainly be helpful to him after he became secretary and had to make the final decision on Vincent. (Acheson had told Dulles, "It seemed to me that the opinion of the Loyalty Review Board had passed judgment not on Mr. Vincent's loyalty but on the soundness of the policy recommendations he had made. If disagreements on policy were to be equated with disloyalty, the Foreign Service would be destroyed.") But when Hand wrote Dulles on January 20, as the new administration was about to take over, inquiring whether he and his associates should continue their consideration of the Vincent matter, Dulles replied on January 29 that that wouldn't be necessary; he would handle it himself. And so in due course, Dulles, while absolving Vincent of disloyalty or of being a security risk, decided that he would have to go.

Vincent had been recalled to Washington to get the bad news in person. Dulles advised him that he had the choice of being fired outright and forfeiting all his pension rights, or quietly resigning and receiving $6200 a year. Vincent chose the second alternative. The denouement came on a Saturday, just before noon. Vincent was to present himself at Dulles's home with a letter of resignation. He brought Walter Surrey along. To the lawyer's astonishment, when they arrived, Dulles cordially suggested that they have a drink and sit down and talk. Surrey said he didn't think it was an appropriate occasion for either glass-clinking or chitchat. "No, no," said Dulles. "I want to use this opportunity to ask the Minister some questions about China. After all, he knows the situation there better than just about anybody."

Vincent was ever the gentleman[9] and ever respectful of the wishes of his superiors. So, before Surrey's unbelieving eyes, he accepted a drink,

[9]In retirement at Cambridge, Vincent was told one day there was someone at the door to see him. It was a wet-behind-the-ears young FBI agent, who said right off, "I understand you know Owen Lattimore." "Young man, do you realize where you are?" asked Vincent. His visitor didn't. Vincent thereupon invited him in and chatted away for an instructive hour or so about China. Vincent was unaware that, at about the same time, he was the innocent cause of the rupture of a romance. The beau of a young woman rooming at the Vincents' stopped dating her because she lived where she did and he worked for the National Security Council.

sat down, and—this occurring at almost exactly the same moment that over at the State Department a press release was being handed out saying that Vincent was leaving government service because his judgment had been poor—favored the secretary with his best judgment on the current situation in the Far East. Ironically, the press release quoted Dulles's belief that "Mr. Vincent's reporting of the facts, evaluation of the facts, and policy advice during the period under review show a failure to meet the standard which is demanded of a Foreign Service Officer of his experience and responsibility at this critical time" and his conclusion that "I do not believe that he can usefully continue to serve the United States as a Foreign Service Officer."

On hearing this verdict, ex-Secretary Acheson, who perhaps by now regretted his own earlier waffling with respect to the Old China Hands, remarked, "Mr. Dulles's six predecessors, under all of whom Mr. Vincent had served in the China field, did not find his judgment or services defective or substandard. On the contrary, they relied on him and promoted him." (Acheson had promoted him all the way to Tangier.) The Louisville, Kentucky, *Times,* in an editorial headed "Vincent Is Vindicated but Destroyed," had a more general observation to make: "The nation will have lost much if its diplomats, taking the cue from the Vincent story, decide discretion is better than either integrity or valor."

Vincent had thought about being an agriculturist while an undergraduate at Mercer; now, retiring to Cambridge, Massachusetts, at the age of fifty-two, he would have twenty years to spend tending a garden. He did give a few lectures at Radcliffe, and for a while the Speakers Bureau of the Foreign Policy Association was peddling him around—$125 a shot plus traveling expenses—as a man prepared to talk on "Looking Ahead in Asia," "Our China Problem," and "Switzerland: Pattern of European Neutrality." ("Mr. Vincent is recommended both to the large audience and the seminar type of group," one promotional brochure said. "His friendliness makes him excellent in the question period.") But the pickings were slim, and his few sponsors found that they were likely to be castigated for inviting a notorious pro-Communist to occupy their thitherto untainted rostrums.

Vincent's departure from the government was a major victory for Joe McCarthy, and just as the senior diplomat was going into exile, the senator was racking up another triumph of sorts. His pair of brash roving juniors, Roy Cohn and G. David Schine, had set off on a tour of Europe, checking up to see how many United States Information Agency libraries abroad were tainted by the presence of books they thought unbecoming. Edward Rice, the consul general in Stuttgart, narrowly escaped their ferreting. He had been too busy to decontaminate the library there himself, but the senator's henchmen decided at the last minute to omit that one from their scourgelike itinerary.

Dulles's far-flung security people, however, subjected Rice to a searching interrogatory in Bonn the following year. What were his views on the prevailing situation in China during the Hurley ambassadorship? Rice said that would take a book to answer. What about the famous George Atcheson telegram of February 28, 1945? Rice said he hadn't signed it. What about Hurley's having said of him, "I don't think he's one of *them*, but I can't be sure?" That, Rice replied, sounded like a case of damning with very faint praise. What about his relations in China with John Service and Raymond Ludden? Well, as it happened, he had never laid eyes on either of them during the Hurley regime. Well, what did he know about a certain Annalee Jacobus? Perhaps, said Rice, his questioners meant Annalee Jacoby, the coauthor with Theodore H. White of *Thunder Out of China;* if that was whom they had in mind, all he could recall about the lady, and he felt he had to tell the whole truth because he was under oath, was that her teeth had been discolored in China, conceivably from excess smoking.

Meanwhile, Cohn and Schine did not confine themselves to USIA libraries. Richard Service recalled their arrival in Rome, where they were graciously invited to lunch at the residence of the deputy chief of mission, Elbridge Durbrow. While the rest of the guests were having an aperitif, the two investigators were examining their host's private bookshelves. Inasmuch as Durbrow had just previously served a tour of duty in Moscow and had brought to Italy with him quite a number of books from there of indisputably Communistic origin, Cohn's and Schine's peculiar appetites were sated long before anybody sat down to eat.

By the close of 1953, Vincent, Clubb, and Service had all been disposed of. That left Davies. *His* end-of-year holiday gift from the State Department arrived on December 29. In November Senator McCarthy, trying to hit the Eisenhower administration where he thought it would hurt, had declared that the nation's foreign policy was being wrongly conducted and that one of the proofs of that was the government's continuing to harbor Davies, who "was unanimously referred by the McCarran committee to the Justice Department in connection with a proposed indictment be-

cause he lied under oath about his activities in trying to put—listen to this
—in trying to put Communists and espionage agents in key spots in the
Central Intelligence Agency." Dulles, in a statement approved by the
president, had publicly disputed McCarthy's views, but it was characteristic of both the president's and the secretary's kid-gloves treatment of the
senator from Wisconsin that in rebutting him Dulles refrained from
mentioning his name. ("Do you think he could have been referring to
me?" McCarthy asked archly.)

Four days after Christmas the State Department's Bureau of Security,
where by now Scott McLeod rode firmly in the saddle, decided that under
Eisenhower's newly tightened regulations, Davies should be reinvesti-
gated and, pending that, suspended. Dulles withheld suspension, but he
ordered another look taken at the record. It was Davies's ninth time under
official scrutiny.

It would be charged this time that Davies had "actively opposed and
sought to circumvent United States policy toward China"; that he was
a leading proponent in the department of separating the Chinese Communists from Moscow; that he maintained relationships with Chinese
Communists; and that some of his reports from China were based on
insufficient evidence. "I agreed that they were," Davies wrote:

> In so answering, I was applying perfectionist standards to myself. I was harsher
> toward myself than I think I would be toward others. It is true that, ideally,
> a Foreign Service officer should wait until all the evidence is in before making
> a judgment. But it is often the case, as in a battle, that to wait for all the
> intelligence to come in is to be paralyzed while decisive events pass one by.
> I felt that the board was troubled by the estimate I made of the Chinese
> Communists, politically and militarily. While the evidence was inadequate, it
> was all that I had. The urgency and gravity of the crisis which I believed to
> be descending upon us caused me to come to conclusions more quickly than
> I would have, had I not felt that time was so short. For the same reason, I
> stated my position more flatly than I otherwise would have. Had I been more
> deliberate, had I waited for all the evidence to come in, I would not have made
> some of the errors evident in my memoranda. Nor would I have predicted well
> ahead of the event that, for example, the U.S.S.R. would move into Central
> Europe, that it would enter the Pacific war for its own strategic purposes, that
> a Soviet-Chinese bloc would ensue, that our strategic position in the Pacific
> would be critically affected when we again found ourselves at war in the Far
> East—when none of these ideas were finding general acceptance at that time

among most other Americans. Instead, I would have, along with my compatri-ots, watched events overtake evidence. In short, there do occur situations in which, if one is to anticipate events (which is expected of Foreign Service officers) and not function as a historian, one must speak up on the basis of inadequate evidence.

In Dulles's view, Davies's responses to McLeod's inquiries produced "some matters bearing upon reliability which are susceptible of conflicting interpretations and which seem to call for clarification by testimony under oath by Mr. Davies and others." So on March 23, 1954, the secretary set up something called a Security Hearing Board.[10] None of the members of the new board knew much, if anything, about China; its chairman was the inspector general of the army and its other members were the director of plans and readiness of the Office of Defense Mobilization, the legal assistant to the Federal Communications Commission, the assistant to the director of the Foreign Operations Administration, and the director of the Office of Procurement and Technical Assistance of the Small Business Administration. The board convened in May and held hearings in June and July. Davies came back from Peru to testify. Among those

[10]Two days later, in an editorial entitled "Hearings without End," the Washington *Post* observed, "Surely there is something wrong with a system of checking which has already subjected an official's career and reputation to octuple jeopardy and which now compels him to undergo a ninth ordeal. . . . We hope Mr. Davies will submit to this new interrogation with what patience he can muster, instead of resigning, as he must have been tempted to do. This case long ago became much more than a test of Mr. Davies. It became a test to determine whether a nonpolitical career service can function within our American system. If Mr. Davies is to be cleared for the ninth time, we hope that the coming decision will make two things decisively plain. One is that a ninth clearance will be the last, as far as the Executive Branch can make it the last. A foreign service officer should not have to shuttle between a foreign post and a hearing room in Washington, like the unhappy ferry passenger who found himself moving endlessly between Hongkong and Macao because the authorities in both ports were unwilling to have him land. The second point is more fundamental. It should be decided and proclaimed, so that all can hear, that a career officer's honest reports of years ago, sent to his superiors in performance of his duty, shall not be dredged up to his detriment years later when the political climate at home has changed. If Mr. Davies is to be judged unfit because there was faulty judgment in any of his reports of ten years ago—and we do not know that there was—then we can think of other officials, including Mr. Dulles himself, who should be disqualified for the same offense. The essential point is that American officials must be free to report what they believe to be the truth from a foreign post or in a staff meeting here, without having to guess whether their position will be politically popular a decade later. The stakes in this matter have become very high. The effectiveness and integrity of American diplomacy will depend upon the outcome."

who testified against him were Generals Hurley and Wedemeyer.

For Hurley, the appearance was unusual, if not unique. John Service, for instance, had formally requested that Hurley be examined, and cross-examined, at *his* Loyalty Security Board hearing, but the board had no powers of subpoena, and the general no wish to turn up voluntarily. By the time Davies's case was under consideration, the rules governing such probes had been changed: Cross-examination was forbidden, adversary proceedings were considered "inappropriate." So Hurley had come forward.

He was a muddled witness; he didn't seem able to distinguish between Davies and Service in his angry memory; some of his charges against the former related to activities of the latter. In an attempt to straighten all this out, Davies and his attorney asked Service to come down from New York and testify. "I think it was the most profoundly discouraging day I ever spent," Service said later. "In the first place, the Board seemed not in the least interested in hearing me—or having Hurley's accusations sorted out. In the second place, they showed no slightest clue of comprehension of the political situation in China, the duties and responsibilities of a Foreign Service officer, or how it might be permissible to express opinions counter to those of a presidential representative or ambassador. (Of course, they also made it clear that my 'evidence' was discredited because I had already been fired.) When I got home to New York, I told my wife that John Davies was a 'gone goose.' "

On August 30 the board recommended, in the bleak terminology to which bureaucrats are partial, that Davies be terminated for having "demonstrated a lack of judgment, discretion, and reliability." Secretary Dulles, who would demonstrate his own judgment and discretion that same year by ostentatiously refusing to shake hands with Chou En-lai at a conference in neutral territory, said, "The Board emphasized that it defended Mr. Davies' right to report as his conscience dictated, but found that he made known his dissents from established policy outside of privileged boundaries."[11]

Davies was sent a copy of the unclassified sections of this board's report, which he received at the American embassy at Lima on September 16.

[11]When Davies first received the charges against him, he showed them to his brother Donald, who was then still in the Foreign Service himself. "I looked the stuff over and asked where the rest of it was," Donald Davies recalled, "and John said, 'That's all there is.' I felt as though the floor was dropping out. I had been a county courthouse reporter, and charges as flimsy as those wouldn't have stood up there for ten minutes."

In attempted rebuttal he submitted a long letter to the board. He took it to Washington, arriving on November 4, but he might as well have saved his energy; on November 5, before the board had a chance to mull over it, Dulles called him in and told him he was fired. As Davies was leaving the secretary's office, Dulles said sanctimoniously that if in the course of looking for a new job he needed a character reference, he, Dulles, would be happy to furnish one.

Davies did not reply to that. He did issue a brief statement:

> . . . There has been enough recrimination. I am not prepared to add to it and thereby detract from the strength of my country in its mortal struggle with the Communist enemy. So I shall not contest the Secretary's decision nor seek to compare my record with those of others. I must be content to let history be my judge. And to that end I have informed the Secretary that I would, personally, welcome release to the public of the whole record of my case, including my 1950 recommendations that we seek a preventive showdown with the Soviet Union. I can hope that my departure from its ranks will add to the American people's confidence in their Foreign Service, which has been so unjustly undermined. If this is the practical result of my separation, I can have no real regrets over what is for me, personally, a melancholy outcome.

Davies's young children, down in Peru, didn't have much of an inkling what was going on, but they were disturbed because it was getting near year-end time again and their father was up north. "You *have* to be back for Christmas and bring us presents," one of them wrote him.

Davies liked Peru, and he decided to stay on there. Its government of the moment was a fairly right-wing military dictatorship, the sort that would not be expected normally to encourage the continuing residence of an unemployed alien private citizen patently suspected by his own government of left-wing inclinations. But Davies had become extremely popular in Lima, and, stripped though he was of any credentials, when Parliament opened, he was nonetheless invited to sit in the president's box.[12] Davies himself was far less concerned about his seating arrange-

[12]In the October 1971 issue of *American Opinion*, the Birch Society's historian Gary Allen had it that "After his discharge by State, Davies had apparently been on the C.I.A. payroll for some years while living in Chile. What he did there may have something to do with the fact that Chile now has an openly Communist president." Allen's own facts were shaky. The CIA certainly had a payroll in Chile, but the people on it were trying

ments than his livelihood. A friend told him that the furniture business looked promising: Places like Cuba and the Dominican Republic were just about logged out of mahogany, of which Peru had an abundant supply, and a new Sears Roebuck outlet which was due to open up in Lima would doubtless be a steady customer for locally produced goods. So Davies hired a few carpenters, boned up on furniture trade journals, and even took drawing lessons so he could design his own goods. (A chair and a table of his creation were ultimately awarded prizes by a designers' trade association.) He called his shop Estilo, or Style. After a while he had forty or fifty employees. He ran the establishment alone for four years, but then he had a fall and broke a hip, and his wife helped out—an unusual occurrence in that part of the world, for she was pregnant at the time and Peruvian women of her status simply didn't do that sort of thing in such circumstances.[13]

As a civilian, Davies tended to avoid many Americans who passed through Lima, not wishing to cause them any conceivable embarrassment by being spotted in his tarnished presence. Once when Sargent Shriver, then head of the Peace Corps, appeared unannounced at the front door of Estilo, Davies ducked out the back. Visiting Foreign Service officers from the old days were something else again. When Philip Sprouse was a Foreign Service inspector, his duties took him to Lima, where he dined with the British ambassador, who reported that by common consent the person best informed on foreign affairs in the whole city was John Davies. For several years he wrote a weekly column on politics for the Lima newspaper La Prensa.[14] Davies scarcely ever discussed his Foreign Service

to get President Salvador Allende Gossens deposed. Anyway, Davies wasn't working for the CIA. And he wasn't living in Chile, but in Peru.

[13]One of the few particular pieces of advice that Davies's children could recall his ever giving them was "Never take your pants off standing up." Undressing in the dark so as not to disturb his sleeping wife, he had tripped and fallen and suffered the fracture.

[14]In 1964 he put together some of his columns in a book entitled Foreign and Other Affairs. Among his comments in it were: "The truth is that what will happen in China during the next decade is a mystery. It is a sombre mystery, auguring little hopeful, boding many afflictions." At another point he wrote, "It has been fashionable to say the Foreign Service suffered from stagnation. It is more accurate to say that it suffered from shock. Because it deals with suspect matters like foreigners, strange languages, and diplomacy, the Foreign Service is, to an accentuated degree, subjected to the popular distrust of and distaste for bureaucracies. . . . The attacks from the radical right, culminating in the early fifties, destroyed the striving toward distinction and a personality in the Foreign Service. The violence and subtlety of the purge and intimidation left the Foreign Service demoralized and intellectually cowed. With some doughty exceptions, it became a body of conformists."

troubles in front of his children, to whom Sprouse was merely one of a series of pleasant "uncles" who drifted through their Peruvian lives— Uncle Phil, Uncle Jack (Service), Uncle Jim (Penfield), Uncle Tony (Freeman), and so on. The children also heard about "Mao" and "Chou" —never with avuncular prefixes—but knew not much more about them than that they were a couple of old Chinese acquaintances.

So ignorant were Davies's children, for the most part, of their father's connection with American politics that his oldest daughter, as a ten-year-old Brownie, was overjoyed to join her troop in ceremonially greeting Richard Nixon when he arrived at Lima on a state visit. (Born in Moscow while her father was stationed there, the girl had been named Alexandra and nicknamed Sasha, perhaps as a result of which, although she left the Soviet Union before she was a year old, she would later be accused of having Communist leanings herself.) The vice-president of the United States! Sasha got her mother to press her uniform and wash her white gloves, and thus splendidly accoutered went out to the airport and saluted and squealed and even asked for the important man's autograph. Thrilled to death, she returned home and reported on the experience to her father's Aunt Flossie, who was visiting at the time. Aunt Flossie's explosive reaction to the little girl's euphoria almost sent shock waves through the Andes. But as the children grew older, they learned more. When years afterward Sasha's husband, a television producer, came home one evening and told her agitatedly that he'd just been fired, his wife said, not unkindly, "What are you getting so excited about? I've been through this before."

When one dwells on the troubles of individuals, one is apt sometimes to forget that their suffering and anguish must perforce affect members of their families. In the case of the Old China Hands, one of the extraordinary characteristics of the men involved was that—perhaps because, as John Fairbank once put it, "Representation of one's country abroad, especially in a time of war and revolution, calls for qualities of disinterested devotion and disciplined objectivity"—they were singularly unembittered at what happened to them. "If by some miracle the clock could be turned back and I had my life to relive," John Service said in 1973, "I would still wish to be a Foreign Service officer." And that same year John Emmerson said, "I've had some pretty rough periods, and I would get depressed, but it never occurred to me to *quit.* You joined the Foreign Service and there you were, for better or worse. And I was never asked to quit anyway, so I guess I was lucky."

Some of the men's wives were not so uncomplaining or forgiving, possibly because they were more cognizant than their husbands of the effects the husbands' tribulations were having on their children. And there were effects, some fairly traumatic, on the fourteen children of Clubb, Davies, Service, and Vincent. Vincent's daughter Sheila, for instance, who was born in Peking (her nickname was Hsi-hsi), was attending Goucher College while her father was being tormented by the McCarran committee. A number of girls on campus began to heckle her and to call her a Communist. Finally the president of her dormitory called all its residents together and said, "Hey, guys, this has got to *stop*." The president of the college stopped Sheila on her way to class one day and said he could understand what she must be going through, and his wife and he wondered if she would care to stop by for dinner.

Vincent's son, John Carter, Jr., also born in Peking, was at Exeter at the same inquisitorial time. He was sixteen, quite old enough to be miserably aware of what was going on (he cared about his father's work; John Carter, Sr., had been in the habit of taking him over to the old State Department building in Washington on Saturday mornings and proudly exhibiting to him the pigeons' eggs on its broad window ledges); he avoided the prep school's common room, where there was a radio often tuned in to news programs, which so often seemed to be about his father. The son chose General Marshall's mission to China as his topic for a term paper he had to write as an Exeter senior. He picked it not so much because it was of special interest to him as that it was relatively easy to do; he knew a good deal about it because—in addition to having seen Marshall depart at the start of it—he had heard his father talk so much about it. The young man had also used this material for an undemanding essay at Harvard, where he was a member of the class of 1957 and a member of the Reserve Officers Training Corps to boot.

After college, John Junior considered entering the Foreign Service corps, but elected to go to Harvard Law School instead. By then, having successfully completed his ROTC course, he was a lieutenant in the Civil Affairs reserve, which dealt with military government. During summer vacation, two-thirds of the way through law school, he got a job working for Elliot Richardson, then attorney general of Massachusetts. One day Vincent was asked to drop in at the Boston army base, for what he assumed was a routine security clearance interview in connection with his reserve commission. On arriving, he was surprised to find two counterintelligence corps operatives waiting for him with a tape recorder. They put him under oath and then began questioning him.

"I understand you wrote an English theme at Phillips Exeter Academy."

"Yes, I did, on the modern history of China."

"Concerning a defense of your father's China viewpoints?"

"No, it was not in defense of him, it was on General Marshall's mission to China."

"The theme did not have anything to do with your father's viewpoints?"

There were other questions that struck the young law student as of debatable applicability to himself: "Do you favor U.S. arms and aid to Chiang Kai-shek and the Kuomintang regime?" "Do you think the U.S. should recognize Red China?" "Do you think the Chinese nationals in Formosa will ever return victoriously to the China mainland?"

The stunned young man inquired what the relevancy was of such questions; he was told that the military "wished to have my views on record to see whether they coincided with those my father has held in the past." Then he insisted on getting some of his views unmistakably on that record:

My father served a long and devoted career as a Foreign Service officer. He retired honorably in 1953. I am of course aware that, in the heat of partisan political controversy, he became the object of attacks typical of the McCarthy period along with scores of other devoted public servants. But I find it strange and unwarranted that a security inquiry into my qualifications to do my military duty years later should be made an occasion to reviving the crude injustices of that period. Therefore, I wish to express my objections to certain of the questions—to their political and social implications—believing as I do that a security clearance interview, where one is testifying under oath, is not the proper medium for soliciting such views, and that the basis for deciding that my views on such matters should be made a part of my security clearance record has no justification either in fact or in law.

Vincent *fils* ultimately got his clearance and was appointed intelligence officer of his reserve unit; one of his responsibilities was to check up on individuals suspected of being security risks.

Oliver Edmund Clubb, Jr., after serving with the marines in Korea, took the Foreign Service examinations, but he then decided on an academic career. He became a professor of political science, specializing in Southeast Asia. His sister married an American Foreign Service officer from a missionary family that had served in China. The older of John Service's two sons, Robert, actually did become a Foreign Service officer, though he chose Latin America as his special field. Service *père* told him before he embarked on a diplomatic career that he should be absolutely certain he was *not* doing so to justify his father's existence or clear the family name or anything like that. The son ignored him. "I went into the Foreign Service precisely to vindicate my father," he said later. ("Oh, well," said the proud father, "at least he had the good sense to avoid China.") Service's second son, Philip—named after Sprouse—contemplated taking the Foreign Service exams, too, but then switched to penal administration. The other Service child, Virginia, who later married a professor of mathematics, had been a high school student when her father got fired. During her last semester—the vigilant sentinels of the American Legion outposts in Washington, D.C., apparently having been caught nodding—she was the happy recipient of one of the Legion's much touted awards for good citizenship.

11

"Listen, is this guy by any chance a Communist?"

From the moment John Service was fired, he was determined to win reinstatement, and many of his colleagues began raising money to help finance an appeal he soon began making through the federal courts. Service was aware that this could take a long time. Meanwhile, like Davies, he had to earn a living. He was lucky in one respect; his children had their way paid through college—Virginia receiving, on top of her American Legion testimonial, a scholarship at Oberlin. Her father hoped initially that he might land a job with a foundation or with a company that had international operations, and with that in mind he hastily applied for a civilian passport to replace his canceled diplomatic credentials. He was issued one without demurrer. (Things were not always that easy for Service at this time. When he tried to convert a life-insurance policy he had had as a Foreign Service officer to a larger amount of term insurance, the agent said politely that that would be impossible, for how could they be sure he wasn't going to jump out of a window?)

There was no stampede of employers to avail themselves of his skills, though one man who heard Eric Sevareid's broadcast did offer him a job running a small boat-supply business in New England. Then out of the blue came a letter from a man named Clement Wells, in New York, who said he had no idea what Service's plans were, but might he be interested in working for Wells's company, Sarco, which made steam traps?

Service had never heard of a steam trap, and expressed to a number of Washington friends, among them John Reid, his apprehensions about even looking into something about which he was totally ignorant. Reid told him that made no difference; there was no subject a reasonably intelligent man couldn't bone up on with three weeks' diligent research; why, that was the essence of the whole practice of law. So Service went to a library to find out what a steam trap was. (It is an automatic valve that opens to water and closes to steam.)[1] Then he hied himself to New York and met Wells, a septuagenarian Englishman, who offered him a job at a starting salary of $9000. This was $3000 less than Service had been getting from the government, but it was $9000 more than anyone else had proposed, and he accepted it. He began at the bottom, spending three weeks in a Sarco factory, one of these on an assembly line where steam traps were put together.[2] His pay increased as time went on (although Wells would never make any long-term commitments; he had a theory that people worked harder if their future was uncertain), and he became so knowledgeable about steam traps that, with the help of a professor of mechanical engineering, he ultimately devised and patented a new variety. At about this time Wells, who was retiring, gave Service a chance to pick up two hundred shares of Sarco stock for $5000. Service borrowed the money and bought the stock, and soon afterward, owing in large part to his invention, Sarco's business boomed.

The Services spent five and a half years in New York. They became more and more keenly aware of what it meant to be smeared by McCarthy —particularly after their rejection from the apartment house in New York despite Dean Rusk's having expressed willingness to vouch for them. (The turndown had a ripple effect; in Washington John Reid sternly rebuked the venerable law firm of Covington & Burling because one of its major clients was a big insurance company that held the mortgage on the building that barred its doors to Service.) Upon finally finding an apartment where he was acceptable, in Kew Gardens, Service became moderately active on a citizens' committee for Adlai Stevenson in the 1952 campaign. After the election he agreed to help reconstitute the battered group on a permanent basis, but presently a delegation came around and, after a good deal of throat-clearing and foot-shuffling, made him realize that it would be happy if his name were removed from the list of organizers. *Who's Who in America*, which had piped him aboard after

[1]He also took the precaution to ask, through Robert Barnett, who was still at the State Department, whether Wells or Sarco had any political or ideological affiliations that could conceivably get him into further trouble. Barnett was able to reply that there was nothing objectionable about the company or its officers; his source of that reassuring information was, ironically, General Snow of the Loyalty Security Board.
[2]Several years later, when Sarco was threatened with a strike, Wells asked Service to try to settle the company's differences with the union involved, and Service succeeded after spending two days in a hotel room with the union's bargaining agent. The fact that Service, alone of all Sarco's management people, had actually labored in the factory was generally considered to have made the settlement possible.

his 1948 promotion, threw him over the side.

From time to time Service would see some of his old Foreign Service friends socially, but the only time anybody from the State Department consulted him on business was during the preparation of biographies of obscure Chinese figures with whom he was acquainted. Such inquiries were always addressed to him after hours, at home. His only formal contact with the government during this period came in the fall of 1953. For Sarco, Service was bidding on government heating-installation contracts and spending a good deal of time talking to plumbing and heating jobbers.[3] One afternoon the phone rang at his office and a man's voice said, "My name's Cohn." Service knew a plumbing-supply salesman by that name and thought it was he on the wire.

But it was Roy Cohn, back from his bibliographic swing around Europe, and he was demanding that Service present himself instantly at the Federal Courthouse in New York, where Senator McCarthy was holding a one-man session of his Subcommittee on Investigations. Service demurred; he wasn't going to meet McCarthy anywhere without a lawyer, and he didn't think he could find one within minutes. When he said he might be able to make it the following morning, Cohn got angry. "This is a telephone subpoena," he declared. By the next morning Service had recruited Gerard Reilly, who rushed up from Washington and instructed him to say right off at the courthouse that he was not appearing under subpoena but voluntarily. That annoyed Cohn, who was already put out because McCarthy and he had had to cool their heels overnight in New York, awaiting Service's appearance. Cohn and Service were sparring back and forth about who was inconveniencing whom when McCarthy stepped in. He had in his hand a signed affidavit, he said, to the effect that Service was in the employ of the CIA, and what did the witness have to say about *that?* Service replied, truthfully, that he was not, and McCarthy peremptorily excused him. As far as anybody knows, the affidavit, if there was one, was never mentioned again.

What McCarthy and Cohn evidently didn't know was that three years earlier, anguished by all the investigations the State Department was

[3]In the mid-fifties Sarco had some office space in a New York building that also housed the United States delegation to the UN, of which President Eisenhower had made Senator Knowland a member. Inevitably, Knowland and Service found themselves in the same elevator one day. Knowland seemed startled to see his old California adversary, but recovered quickly and in the brief time they spent together asked Service, with what appeared to be genuine interest, how he was making out in civilian life.

putting him through, Service had listened approvingly to the suggestion of the Department's chief of personnel that he remove himself from public sight for a while, join the CIA as a behind-the-scenes operative, and thus acquire for himself, before resurfacing, some gilt-edged patriotic credentials. Service had gone to see a man he knew who had been with the Office of Strategic Services in China and was now in the dirty-tricks section of the CIA, and he had applied for a clandestine job somewhere on the periphery of China, where he could perhaps look and listen to advantage. The CIA man had thought it an absolutely gung-ho notion, but had called back a couple of weeks later and said his superiors had vetoed the proposition.

Meanwhile, Edward Rhetts, Service's chief Washington lawyer, went on trying to clear his client's name. One of Service's arguments for filing a complaint against the State Department was that he had been dismissed in part, at least, for not having satisfactorily explained his monitored conversation at the Statler Hotel with Philip Jaffe; how could he be expected to explain it, he contended, when he had never been made privy to the authentic wording of it? The case moved sluggishly through one federal court after another. In 1955 a judge ordered that the finding of "reasonable doubt of loyalty" be stricken from his record—on the ground that Hiram Bingham's Loyalty Review Board "had no authority to review, on post-audit, determinations *favorable* to employees made by department or agency authorities, or to adjudicate individual cases on its own motion." That court, though, declined to order the government to reinstate Service.

In 1956 the Supreme Court agreed to reconsider *that* matter. On June 17, 1957, it found in Service's favor, 8-to-0. Justice Tom Clark abstained; he had been attorney general twelve years earlier, at the time of the federal grand-jury proceedings in the *Amerasia* case. The court's opinion, written by Justice John Marshall Harlan, was, in sum, that Secretary Acheson's dismissal of Service contravened the existing State Department rules under which such actions could or could not be taken. Acheson, Justice Harlan asserted, had erred in neglecting to be bound by his own regulations.[4]

On July 3, 1957, a federal district judge, in conformity with the Su-

---

[4]In a 1974 federal court decision to the effect that the firing of Archibald Cox as special Watergate prosecutor was illegal, Judge Gerhard A. Gesell followed very closely the reasoning used by Justice Harlan in the earlier Service verdict.

preme Court's ruling, restored Service's status as of December 14, 1951, the day Acheson fired him. Few people around the State Department seriously believed that Service would actually want to come back to work there, but even before the Supreme Court decision, to the surprise of the Foreign Service, he had alerted its director general that if the court upheld him, he had every intention of returning to active duty. Following its favorable verdict, he was informed by Washington that one thing the Supreme Court had not restored to him was a security clearance; before he could embark on any meaningful work, that would have to be resolved. Service replied that that was fine with him; he'd report in after Labor Day; he had some unfinished Sarco business to clear up in any event. This last involved a trip to Europe, to smooth over some snags in a deal Sarco was making with an English company. Before the British Treasury would approve it, Service—highly flattered by the demand—had to agree solemnly that he would stay out of the steam-trap business for a number of years.

That business had taken a delightfully uphill turn, and the stock that Service had bought for $5000 he was now able to sell for $320,000. After capital-gains taxes he had a windfall of more than a quarter of a million dollars. He gave a substantial portion of this to the various lawyers, principally Rhetts, who, with little hope of suitable reimbursement, had put in a dozen years of steady, devoted work for him. (His total outlay for legal costs during his ordeal came to $70,000, of which about one-tenth was raised through the fund John Reid handled.) And the work was not finished. There was still the question of back pay due him from the government, and it would take six more years of struggling through the Court of Claims before the government grudgingly settled its accounts for $24,000, which was about $60,000 less than his accountants and attorneys had calculated he was due.[5]

---

[5]Service had earned $61,000 in salary from Sarco in his six-year involuntary leave of absence; the government argued, successfully, that this should be subtracted from the total amount of restitution. In 1972 a friend suggested a possible way of Service's getting even. Service received a letter that year from the Truman Memorial Library in Missouri. Since he had worked for the Truman administration, the letter went, did he perhaps have any papers he'd care to add to the library's collection? Service replied, somewhat tongue-in-cheek, that he did not, but he did happen to have a lot of files relating to a loyalty-security case that had mostly occurred during that administration. The library responded with a cordial note to the effect that they'd certainly like to have those files. So Service shrugged and decided to send them on some day in the future. His friend pointed out that inasmuch as the cost of accumulating those files—lawyers' fees alone—had come to more than the

Upon returning to work at the department in September, Service was instructed to help form something called the Division of Transportation Management. His superior was an assistant secretary who was many years his junior, and Service's main responsibility was to find ways of saving money on the movement around the world of Foreign Service personnel, their household goods, and their office supplies. (In this job, he earned the resentment of some of his former colleagues, because the economy measures he instituted, though they saved the department a quarter of a million dollars a year, resulted in increased breakage.) His security clearance had not yet come through, and as a result security-obsessed CIA people, many of whom in foreign posts pretend to be State Department employees, would not talk to him. An assistant would sit at Service's desk whenever a CIA man or woman came around to discuss a move abroad and, after the visitor had left, would report to Service on what had been said. During this period the department had a training program in Washington for young men destined to become its future Chinese-affairs experts. The students, understandably, wanted to talk with Service, and two successive groups did, but the meetings were always held at one of their apartments.

As long as Service was merely pushing around unclassified papers, the State Department did not have to confront the issue of trying to get a security clearance for him, and thus conceivably incurring congressional wrath. According to departmental regulations, no Foreign Service officer could be posted abroad, no matter how menial his duties, without a clearance. So some of Service's supporters at State began urging that he be assigned overseas; they felt the issue *had* to be confronted. In 1959, accordingly, the department tentatively assigned him to the embassy at Bonn as an administrative officer. The State Department's security people submitted him to another ten days' worth of the same old questions about *Amerasia* and everything else, and Service got a clearance—though a slightly less sweeping one than he'd had in China. Service prudently refrained this time from having any calling cards printed up in advance, but he did take a sixteen-week cram course in German. Then the Department of Defense objected to his proposed assignment; State canceled it and shipped him to Liverpool.

---

government pay he had not retroactively collected, the amount of the tax deduction he should seek to take for the gift should be no less than the $61,000 he had claimed the government owed him because of the Truman's administrations actions. But changes in the law of the land made this—as Richard Nixon would soon come to realize—impossible.

Service's hopes of moving on to something more stimulating were dashed in 1961, when he returned to Washington on home leave and learned from a branch of the State Department called Career Management that while there was nothing in his dossier that specifically said he could not be promoted again, he was characterized therein as a fellow who had had a hard time of it and could be presumed to be suffering from shellshock, and thus disinclined to come to firm grips with disagreeable situations. Soon afterward, after nearly three years in Liverpool, Service concluded glumly that the Kennedy administration was never going to offer him anything better. In May 1962, at the age of fifty-three, he chose early retirement. Because he had had no promotion since 1948, the pension he got was some $7,000 a year less than the one he would have had if he had received the promotion for which he was recommended back in 1951.

Like some other Foreign Service career men, Service had no permanent home in the United States. But his wife and children had lived in Berkeley during the war, so on his retirement he moved there and put part of his Sarco profits into a house. It was one kind of security he could provide for himself.[6] Another reason for settling in Berkeley was that he had it in mind to go back to school and get an M.A. and a Ph.D. in political science. Still another attraction was a Center for Chinese Studies on the University of California's Berkeley campus. University officials, after examining a transcript of Service's dusty Oberlin record, pointed out that his acquaintance with political science seemed minimal, whereupon he signed up for five undergraduate courses in the field.

One of these was given by Chalmers Johnson, then a thirty-one-year-old assistant professor, who, lecturing confidently one day on Stilwell's China experiences, was so shaken to find out who was among his students that he had trouble continuing. A few months later Johnson announced that he needed a graduate student to read examination papers for him and could pay $1.37 an hour; he was startled again when Service volunteered. Not everyone was as awed as Johnson at Service's presence on campus. When Service telephoned another young professor at his home, he got the man's wife. She asked his name and if he was a student. She had never heard of the name and on his saying yes, he was a student, she said, "Well,

---

[6] In 1973 Service discovered, to his surprise and delight, that he had worked just long enough for Sarco to be eligible for Social Security benefits.

I'm sorry, but the Professor does not receive calls at home from students."
Two years later, Service attended an academic conference at the Chinese-
studies center at the University of Michigan, where he sought out still
another young professor, a Sinologist with whose work he was familiar. He
walked up and said, "I'd like to meet you. My name is Jack Service." "I
was flabbergasted," the younger man said afterward, "because for certain
people in our discipline Service was the real Living Buddha, with all the
connotations of quietness that that implies, and quietness isn't characteristic of all the other dudes in our field."

Service got his M.A. in 1964. He enrolled in a Ph.D. program, but then
Johnson, who was affiliated with the Center for Chinese Studies (he later
served as its director), suggested that Service be asked to fill a modest
part-time opening there, as curator of its library. Service jumped at the
opportunity. "It's hard to imagine how glad I was for employment which,
however distantly, put me back in contact, after a long enforced absence,
with the eternally absorbing and important subject of China," he once
wrote. The center also arranged for Service to be made an assistant
specialist, a category that was originally designed to accommodate agricul-
turists connected with state universities.

It was soon suggested by the Senate Subcommittee on Internal Security
that Service's appointment was somehow linked with a State Department
anti-Chiang Kai-shek cabal.[7] In reality, Service's only contact with the
department, following his move to Berkeley, was to receive from it in 1966
a fancy certificate, suitable for framing, that designated him a member
of something called a Reserve Consultants Roster.

Under President Lyndon Johnson, while William P. Bundy was running East Asian and Pacific affairs, some modest attempts were made to
consult the views of various China experts. Once the administration set
up something called a China Advisory Panel. Philip Sprouse was on it, but
John Davies was not; he was too well known, too hot. John Fairbank did

---

[7]The committee seemed to include in this plot even the conservative Sinologist Robert
A. Scalapino, a full-time member of the Berkeley faculty. One of the witnesses summoned
before the committee was another far from radical Sinologist, Allen S. Whiting, who was
then in charge of the Far East subdivision of the State Department's Bureau of Intelligence and Research. Sourwine, the committee's perennial investigator, began asking
questions about a memorandum Whiting had written mentioning Scalapino, whose name
Sourwine mistakenly gave as "Scalapini." He went on and on asking Whiting if he knew
this "Scalapini," and Whiting, who knew Scalapino very well, could, to his delight, deny
under oath that he did; it was a small but agreeable nit-picking victory over a professional
nit-picker.

make it. From 1950 on he hadn't been invited to Washington by any government agency for some dozen years, and the first time he was asked, he was considered too controversial a figure to be admitted inside the State Department building, so the officials who wanted to pick his brains arranged for a dinner meeting at the house of John D. Rockefeller IV, then on the department's Indonesian desk. All concerned felt that getting together with Fairbank, even under those discreet circumstances, was a brave breakthrough. (Fairbank was less impressed. "As usual at such gatherings," he recalled afterward, "the academic person becomes little more than a symbol. People tell you things, and you don't get a chance to open your mouth. That night, I would occasionally start to say something about the role of the village in Chinese society, and then everybody else would jump in and start talking about villages to demonstrate that they knew all about the subject.")

The sorry state of governmental knowledge about and interest in China at that time was later recounted by James C. Thomson, Jr., a China-born missionary son who, on getting his Ph.D. under Fairbank at Harvard in 1956, hadn't dared use his professor's name as a reference while seeking a job. Thomson, who finally got one anyway, working for a while first at State and then under Bundy's brother McGeorge in the National Security Council, recalled that in the mid-sixties the seventh floor of the State Department building, where the policy makers held sway, contained a couple of Russian experts but not a single Chinese one. "In the policy-making process of the '60s," Thomson wrote, "the 'China generation gap' —the glaring lack of senior China careerists—seems to me a very central factor. In their absence, U.S. policy was inevitably skewed towards Moscow to an unhealthy degree; indeed, vivid Soviet descriptions of Chinese 'irrationality' began to be accepted and repeated among American policy-makers." Averell Harriman concurred. When he became assistant secretary of state for Far Eastern affairs in the fall of 1961 he found his area, he said, a "wasteland."

Nobody at State ever formally consulted Service about anything. It was possible that the Senate subcommittee's revived interest in him and his activities at Berkeley had been stirred by a Chiang Kai-shek spy at the center, or perhaps by a reactionary Catholic group in the community that circulated some tracts denouncing the "pro-Communist" Service's associations with the university. (When a friend brought a copy to the Services' home for their perusal, Jack thought it rather droll, but Caroline wasn't the least bit amused and threw it into a fire.) Every such Chinese-studies center at an American university was, and is, presumed to have its resident Nationalist agent; the suspected one at Berkeley got drunk one night and confessed that he rather liked Service; soon afterward he disappeared from the scene. When the Nationalist Chinese consul in San Francisco learned that the Old China Hand was in the area, however, he invited Service to a Double-Tenth Day party. Service was bemused, but he went, and his presence made the newspapers back in Taipei.

One reason for Service's having been invited may have been that when Nationalist Chinese dropped in at the center and asked to be shown around, he was always available, in pointed contrast to one or two other scholars there who, just because the outsiders *were* partial to Chiang, refused to have anything to do with them. A number of the visitors for whom Service acted as escort were surprised to find him so mild-mannered; evidently they had heard a good deal about him from Nationalist historians and had expected he would be some kind of monster. Once, when a man came to him at Berkeley for some help on a research project, there was something about him that bothered Service, so he went to Chalmers Johnson and said, "Listen, is this guy by any chance a Communist? Because if he is, I don't want to get in that box again."

It is difficult, and sometimes embarrassing, to be a nonacademic in a community where scholarly credentials often count as much as, if not more than, knowledge or experience. In the spring of 1969, therefore, the center resolved to advance Service to the highest nonacademic rank available—full-fledged specialist, which in pay, if not in prestige, was roughly the equivalent of a full professor. With the help of a testimonial from Professor Fairbank, who wrote to Johnson, "I would recommend Assistant Secretary [of State] for East Asia, but I suppose you want him in Berkeley. . . . I privately rate him in the class of national resource and culture hero," Service got the promotion. "In Chinese terms, I gained some face," he told a friend.

When he first moved to Berkeley, Service, as dedicated as ever to physical fitness, used to jog a lot through the hills that overlook San Francisco Bay. In 1971, though, he damaged an Achilles' tendon and was slowed to a walk. On days when he had no lunch date, he would generally stroll from his office at the center to a drugstore a mile or so away, to pick up *The New York Times* (in whose index he is forever enshrined under "U.S.—Espionage"), which he would read at a small Chinese restaurant nearby. He felt an affinity with its proprietor, who was a Chinese diplomat until *he* became disenchanted with Chiang Kai-shek. (On Service's return from his 1971 trip to China, he gave a menu from a dinner in his honor at Hangchow to another Chinese restaurateur, who received it as reverently as though it were a Ming vase.) On getting home from the office, Service would ritually drink tea, but it was English tea, not Chinese.

In Berkeley, too, Service got mildly involved in community affairs. For a while, he was a deputy registrar of voters. Once he put in six weeks as a civil-court juror. "I was rather surprised, in view of everything that had happened, that I was found acceptable for jury duty," he said. The only time he was challenged was in connection with some litigation over an estate whose assets included property abroad. Service was asked to step down because he had been so long and so closely associated with the Foreign Service.

Of all the Old China Hands, Service, Davies, Vincent, and Clubb were the most thoroughly hectored and the most shabbily treated, but few of the others went through the fifties and sixties entirely unscathed. Even Everett Drumright left the diplomatic service—after more than thirty-one years in it—somewhat more abruptly than he'd anticipated. In his case it was a question of politics being a two-way street; he retired soon after the onset of the Kennedy administration, when it became apparent that that government regarded him as a man who had been not too hostile toward Chiang Kai-shek, but too affectionate.

Drumright had by then been ambassador to Taiwan for four years, and he told Secretary of State Rusk that he'd be glad to stay on there or take some other position of comparable stature. (During the ambassador's long stay in Taipei—even though what Davies, Service, Vincent, et al. were supposed to have done was alleged to have been instrumental in Chiang Kai-shek's involuntarily having landed there—Drumright never once heard either the Generalissimo or his wife mention any of these Americans by name.) The Kennedy administration had decided, however, to accord diplomatic recognition to the new satellite nation of Outer Mongolia, which was applying for membership in the United Nations. One of the principal reasons for this was to demonstrate that the United States could be as flexible toward Communist states in Asia as in Europe; another, more down-to-earth one was to establish a convenient listening post during the Sino-Soviet dispute. Such a gesture on the part of the United States would not sit at all well with Chiang Kai-shek, who still claimed that Mongolia was part of China; and Drumright, from Taipei, echoed the Generalissimo's views by arguing strongly against recognition—"perhaps more strongly," he would say afterward, "than a discreet ambassador should have." Because of a determined last stand by the remnants of the China Lobby, the recognition did not materialize (although, with Drumright putting discreet pressure on the Generalissimo not to sabotage it, Outer Mongolia joined the UN); nor, after his emphatic remonstrances against Washington's proposed recognition, did a good new job for Drumright. So he put in for retirement.

James Penfield, when Kennedy took office, had just about despaired of ever becoming an ambassador anywhere. At the age of forty-eight, in 1955, he had been the top man on the list of Class 1 Foreign Service officers earmarked for promotion on merit to career minister. But one could not hold that rank under the age of fifty, and by the time Penfield became chronologically eligible, the mood in Washington was not conducive to sending his name to the Senate. He was too closely identified with the wrong side in China. When, to his surprise and delight, the new administration decided to propose him as ambassador to Iceland, the Senate Subcommittee on Internal Security invited him up to Capitol Hill before the Senate Foreign Relations Committee could exercise its normal confirmation functions. McCarran was dead, and James O. Eastland had succeeded to the chairmanship; Penfield found himself in a room alone with Eastland and the indestructible Sourwine.

The hosts were almost obsequiously polite, but there were, they informed their reluctant guest, a couple of minor matters they felt required clarification. For one, what about a certain letter he had written to John Service from Chengtu in 1944? (It was a letter, evidently, that the FBI had appropriated when it went through Service's desk drawers at the State Department at the time of his *Amerasia* arrest.) Who was this "Tung Pi Wu" mentioned in it? Wasn't he, to come right down to it, a Communist? He was indeed, Penfield conceded, though he was hard put to determine the relevancy of the question, inasmuch as his only reference to Tung Pi Wu in the letter had been a facetious aside.[8] Next, Sourwine wanted to know about something that had happened in Austria in 1956, while Penfield was stationed there. Was it true that at his instigation the

[8]In 1943 Tung Pi Wu was a Chinese Communist spokesman in Chungking, and as such was naturally sought out by the American Foreign Service officers whose job it was to learn as much as they could of Mao's activities and aspirations from—Yenan not yet being accessible to them—whatever authoritative sources they could make contact with. In 1966, when Liu Shao-ch'i was purged as chief of state of the People's Republic, Tung Pi Wu was designated his successor.

United States had ceased publishing a journal it had been putting out, thus leaving the foreign-propaganda field in Vienna wide open to the Russians? Penfield had to confess that he honestly did not know; his vague recollection was that the publication had been dropped either because someone in Washington had cut the budget of the American mission to Austria or because the Viennese hadn't especially seemed to want to read it. After a few more such nonsensical inquiries about bygone days, Eastland and Sourwine finally let his appointment go ahead without interference, but the confrontation—a routine one for them, probably—left him shaken. "It was quite frightening, in a way," he said later.

A Foreign Service inspector when the Kennedy era began, Philip Sprouse was temporarily detached from that duty and sent by Secretary Rusk to Nicosia, Cyprus, where Undersecretary Chester Bowles was holding a conference of ambassadors from all over Europe; the object was to make the Foreign Service more efficient by reducing its numbers and improving its reports. Sprouse spent a day getting there, a day getting back, and thirty minutes with Bowles, in the course of which the only substantive idea the undersecretary put forth was that perhaps it would be helpful if Foreign Service officers got out from behind their desks and spent more time following peasants plowing their furrows. "All I could think," Sprouse said later, "was 'My God, that was what we were doing in China, and look what we got out of it!' "

Fulton Freeman was at Brussels at the end of 1960, serving as deputy chief of mission to Ambassador William A. M. Burden, a noncareer diplomat. Burden, who as an investment banker of considerable financial clout had influence with both Republicans and Democrats, had—like Clare Boothe Luce before him—an unqualifiedly high opinion of Freeman. He told him after Kennedy's election that he was going to use all his influence to get his deputy a mission of his own. What would he like? Freeman would have liked anything, but had doubts by then that anything would ever come his way; but as long as he was being asked, he said he thought Thailand would be nice; he could certainly put his Chinese to better use in Bangkok than in Brussels.

In February 1961 Burden, back in the United States, phoned Freeman, still in Belgium, to report that when he had been in Washington talking to people at State, someone had proposed Freeman as ambassador to Colombia; but Burden, knowing Freeman wanted Thailand, had scotched that. "Bill, you *didn't!*" Freeman exclaimed. He thought his first—and conceivably last—chance of getting his own embassy had gone down the drain out of misdirected friendship. Freeman had a hunch he'd never get any embassy in Asia, and told Burden he'd *love* Bogotá; most Old China Hands at that time would have taken Ouagadougou. Burden said he'd try to undo what he had done, and succeeded, and Freeman got Colombia —with, it will be recalled, Mike Mansfield's formidable backing—after all.

In some respects John Emmerson had as traumatic an experience as anyone, for what he went through resulted—completely inadvertently, on his part—in a diplomat's dismal death. Emmerson had been called before the State Department's Loyalty Security Board in 1952 for a discussion of his associations with, attitudes toward, and alleged assistance to Japanese Communists; he had thought that matter had been thoroughly looked into and disposed of. But among the other Japanese-language experts in the Foreign Service had been a couple of older men who had launched most of the unsavory rumors about him in the first place and were indisposed to see them deflated. One of them, who had also served in Tokyo under MacArthur, had missed out on a promotion he thought he deserved, and he blamed Emmerson and George Atcheson for his not getting it.

By the mid-fifties, though, both these adversaries had retired, and Emmerson, after a couple of years out in Pakistan, had been transferred to Lebanon. He was in Beirut early in 1957, when the State Department once again tried to use his talents as a member of a delegation to the United Nations. It was a time of crisis in UN circles, with both Hungary and the Suez Canal high on the international diplomatic agenda, and Emmerson was supposed to be the delegation's liaison man with the Middle-East nations. Then Senator Jenner, by this time the ranking Republican member of the Internal Security Subcommittee, spoke up. He asserted that two diplomats, Robert C. Strong and John Emmerson, had been among those who had lost China, and now the devious Department of State was trying to make it possible for them to lose the Middle East.[9]

Strong was fortunate. He was in Damascus and was not ordered back to the United States. But Emmerson was available for questioning, and the Senate Internal Security Subcommittee—Eastland now presiding—

---

[9]By the time Strong got to China in 1947, its destiny had been all but settled. He was one of the last Foreign Service officers to see duty on the mainland, serving as chargé d'affaires at Canton and Chungking and then moving with Chiang Kai-shek's government to Taipei. Strong had lost something: He had been president-elect of the Rotary Club of Tsingtao when the revolution made that honor academic.

jumped to have the first whack at him. On Capitol Hill Robert Morris and J. G. Sourwine took turns, for three days, badgering him with alleged misdemeanors. They considered it significant, for instance, that his name had been found in an appointment book of John Service's that the FBI had unearthed twelve years before.

The dramatic moment came on March 14, 1957, when Morris asked Emmerson if he knew a man named Herbert Norman. Of course, said Emmerson; they had served together in Tokyo on MacArthur's occupation staff. Norman, born in Japan of missionary parents, was a forty-eight-year-old Canadian diplomat whose own government had absolved him in 1951 of charges that he'd been a Communist in 1938, while attending college. Now, said Morris to Emmerson, the committee had had reports that Norman was a Communist, and what did he have to say about that? Emmerson said he had never heard anything to indicate Norman was anything of the sort. Well, did Emmerson happen to know where Norman was at the moment? Of course, Emmerson replied; he was Canada's ambassador to Egypt and also its minister to Lebanon; they had had lunch in Beirut not long before, when Norman had flown in from Cairo to present his credentials to the Lebanese government.

Morris seemed thunderstruck. Norman, too, in the Middle East! At this precarious moment! It was apparently a revelation to the committee's inept investigators. The hearing was supposed to be an executive session, but the committee's own internal security arrangements had never been especially foolproof, and all at once there were scary headlines about a Communistic Canadian prowling around the Mediterranean. Prime Minister Lester Pearson's Canadian government was furious and said so; the State Department declared piously that the allegation that Norman was a Communist wasn't the opinion of the American *administration*. Emmerson, the subcommittee's interest in him having waned when it sensed it was on the trail of bigger game, was detached from his UN assignment and sent back to Lebanon. While calling on a government official there on April 14, he received some shocking news: Norman had jumped off the roof of a nine-story building in Cairo, leaving behind a note that said, "I have no option. I must kill myself, for I live without hope."

Inasmuch as Norman was close to Prime Minister Pearson, his suicide had all sorts of repercussions. Canada felt, not unreasonably, that the American witch-hunters had hounded him to death. President Eisenhower had a press conference the day the news arrived from Cairo (it was a pleasant day in Washington; Eisenhower also worked in a round of golf at Burning Tree) and was asked to comment on the incident and on whose responsibility it was. "As usual, I shall not criticize anybody," he said. "Indeed, it is my hope that this thing can now be dropped, if possible. . . ."

Emmerson felt for the rest of his life that he had somehow been responsible for Norman's death. He was not, of course, but he could never forget the incident because he wasn't allowed to. Throughout the remainder of his government service, he was periodically called up for interrogation, and almost every time he was, his relationship with the Canadian, such as it had been, was reexamined; and at the same time that Emmerson's feelings of guilt were being rekindled, his questioners would attempt to find him guilty of improper associations. Dispatched to Nigeria and then to Rhodesia, frustrated in his hope of becoming ambassador to Tanganyika (who would send the name of a friend of Herbert Norman's up to the Hill for confirmation?), he had all but forgotten about Japan, the place upon which his whole career had been focussed.[10] But then President Kennedy named Edwin Reischauer as his ambassador to Tokyo, and Reischauer—supported by Averell Harriman, by then assistant secretary for Far Eastern affairs—specifically requested Emmerson as his deputy chief of mission.[11]

Emmerson had a new hurdle to vault. The Herbert Norman suicide, and his unwitting involvement in it, had been widely publicized in Japan, and the growing right-wing movement there, when it learned of his appointment, ran all over Tokyo denouncing the imminent arrival of an

[10]Emmerson tried to keep up his language proficiency by chatting with Japanese diplomats he encountered at cocktail parties in various world capitals, but that wasn't easy, because most of them knew English and wanted to demonstrate their proficiency in *that*. Their wives proved much more satisfactory: Some of them knew only Japanese and were accustomed to standing around mutely at social levees; they were overjoyed to meet up with a Westerner who could and eagerly would communicate with them.

[11]Reischauer himself did not get appointed without difficulty. Some of the old-timers at State thought he was too liberal, and that he would be handicapped because his wife was Japanese. Dean Rusk thought he was too academic. But Chester Bowles, then Undersecretary of State, was for Reischauer, and so was Chairman Fulbright of the Foreign Relations Committee. The turning point came when one of Bowles's deputies, who was against Reischauer, brought the undersecretary a top-secret FBI report that said Reischauer was alleged to have consorted with a suspicious character, John K. Fairbanks (sic). Both, of course, were professors at Harvard. Bowles got Reischauer's nomination pushed through by observing to his deputy that if the FBI was really concerned about Fairbank's associates, perhaps they should begin with his then brother-in-law, Arthur M. Schlesinger, Jr., over at the White House.

alleged crony of an alleged Communist. Emmerson did finally arrive in July 1962, and a crowd of photographers was awaiting him at the Tokyo airport. It was a bright, hot day, and as he started to get off the airplane, he put on a pair of sunglasses. It was sixteen years since he'd been in Japan, and he'd forgotten something a diplomat should have remembered: that in Japan dark glasses were considered the hallmark of a suspicious character. It was some time before he was totally excused in Japan for his optometric gaffe. Emmerson's reacquaintance with Japan eventually turned out to be so congenial that he bought a house there, at Nikko, where in retirement he would spend a few tranquil months every year.

John Davies moved from Peru to Washington, D.C., in 1964. His seven children were growing up (the oldest was sixteen, the youngest, one), and he felt it was time they got acquainted with their own country. By now Davies had himself become acquainted with Walter Surrey, the lawyer who had defended Vincent; Surrey, indeed, had managed to persuade the General Accounting Office, which operated independently of the recalcitrant State Department, to grant him a pension of $4000 a year. Surrey had never met Davies when he accomplished this; he had been approached by four retired Foreign Service officers who asked him to see what he could do. Later Surrey had gone to Lima on other business, *had* met Davies, and had asked him if he wanted to try to get his name cleared. Davies had said no, it didn't matter, that was over and done with; but when he returned to Washington he changed his mind—for the sake of, in order, his children, his wife, and himself.

The question was: How? Davies, unlike Service, had absolutely no wish to go back to work for the State Department. He just wanted it established as a matter of principle that he was a trustworthy man. Surrey and his legal associates spent hours talking over the situation with various high officials of the government, nearly all of whom were sympathetic but few of whom were minded to do much about it. Then in the summer of 1967, toward the end of the Johnson presidency, Surrey had an idea. What Davies needed was a security clearance, and since it wasn't going to be obtained directly through a connection with State, it would have to come from some other source.

Adrian Fisher had left the State Department and was at the Arms Control and Disarmament Agency, which had given a contract to the Massachusetts Institute of Technology for a study of the employment of small arms in Latin America. Now, if MIT decided to hire Davies as a consultant (after all, he knew Latin America), and if it requested a security clearance for him because some of the material he would have to look at would be classified, and if Arms Control and Disarmament suggested to State that its request for clearance be approved, and if State concurred —why, then, the delicate mission would be accomplished.

There were a lot of intermediate complications, but that was essentially the way things worked out. Still, it took time. Secretary of State Rusk divorced himself from the whole affair, because he was an old friend of Davies.[12] Undersecretary Nicholas deB. Katzenbach took over and pushed the clearance through, ultimately taking it all the way up to President Johnson. A few details had not yet been taken care of by November 1968, at which point Nixon was elected and Fisher learned he was going to be superseded in Arms Control and Disarmament by Gerard K. Smith. Recalling the fiasco that had occurred in the Truman-Eisenhower interregnum when Judge Learned Hand's panel had been assembled and then dismantled with John Carter Vincent's case hanging, Fisher went to see Smith. Fisher said that while he realized his successor naturally couldn't be committed to any arrangement that was being made on Davies's behalf between the agency and MIT, he hoped Smith would view it favorably. "Oh, I had dinner with Davies the other night," Smith said. "Nice chap. We'll go right ahead."

By the time Davies's clearance actually took effect, the MIT project was just about completed. But he went to Cambridge one day, was shown one sheet of paper with a security classification stamp on it, and that was all that mattered; he was vindicated. The grateful Davies presented Surrey with one of the finest products of his recently shut-down furniture factory —a massive mahogany desk that, unfortunately, proved to be too big to be edged through the doors of the attorney's office.

"This belated correction [of a "shocking and inexcusable injustice"] will not restore to the public life of the country the decade and a half of the services of a talented, dedicated, and wholly patriotic Foreign Service officer that were forfeited as a consequence of it," George Kennan wrote *The New York Times.* "But if it will help to engender in American public opinion a more incisive revulsion at the spectacle of political figures

[12]Early in the Kennedy administration, Rusk had sent an emissary to a few of the departed China hands, to inquire whether they were interested in having their cases reexamined, with the end of clearing their names. But before anything happened, the Secretary backed away from the notion.

playing fast and loose with the reputation of others for political gain, and if the memory of it will inspire the Department of State to a somewhat greater sense of loyalty to its own personnel, then perhaps the anguish caused not just to an innocent man but to his family and friends as well by this breaking of an honorable career will have served some useful purpose."

12

"A very strange turn of fate."

Less than a quarter of a century after the end of the Second World War, most past sins, real or fancied, had just about been universally forgotten or forgiven. West Germany and Japan were among the closest allies of the United States. But as the People's Republic of China remained outside the American pale at the start of the 1970s, so were the men who were supposed to have lost China not yet redeemed. In the case of the People's Republic, the prolonged life, liberty, and pursuit of happiness of Chiang Kai-shek were, of course, paramount factors. They affected the fate of the Old China Hands, too, but what was an even greater factor in their case was the unrelenting vengefulness of the men and women who had practically made a career out of baiting the alleged China-losers. Patrick J. Hurley died in 1963; eight years later, his daughter, Patricia J. Hurley, was still to be found buzzing around the right-wing lecture circuit, crying "Sabotage!" to one enthralled, hot-eyed audience after another.

In Berkeley John Service, who had always been a gifted writer (that was partly what had got him into trouble in the first place), had quickly gained a reputation as a deft editor of other people's manuscripts—someone who had not only a solid grasp of Chinese affairs but a marvelous knack of coping with the hyphens and apostrophes that challenge scholars trying to romanize the Chinese language. ("When it comes to determining whether 'ssu' is preferable to 'szu,' or 'szu' to 'ssu,'" one of his peers declared, "I'd take Jack's opinion over just about anybody else's.") Service's colleagues at the Center for Chinese Studies kept urging him to do some writing of his own, particularly about the wartime episodes he had had to recount so often before boards of inquiry, but he would merely mumble something about doing that someday for his grandchildren (he had six) and change the subject. He rarely even talked about his nightmare. Some of Service's close friends thought that one reason for his reticence was that while he believed that his wartime analyses and recommendations about China had been valid, he feared 'that if he began to relive that period and delve into all its ramifications afresh, he might somehow conclude that in some way he had been wrong; and that, psychically, would have been the straw, as it were, that broke his already burdened back.

But then one day early in 1970, Service got mad. His anger was aroused by Anthony Kubek, then a professor at a small Catholic institution, the University of Dallas, whose founding president was Robert Morris. Kubek, who held a Ph.D. from Georgetown University in American diplomatic history, had in 1963 published his magnum opus, *How the Far East Was Lost: American Policy and the Creation of Communist China, 1941–1949.* He had been assisted in preparing it by Morris, who had also helped promote it, as had General Hurley. The tone of *How the Far East Was Lost* was typified by such passages as ". . . some American officials and Foreign Service officers sedulously and deliberately usurped the authority to establish U.S. policy towards Nationalist China" (a statement that led straight into a discussion of Lenin) and as "A gullible victim of any left-wing scheme, Henry Wallace was used by the Davies-Service clique while in Chungking."

Kubek was also a longtime aficionado of the China Lobby; he had been engaged by the Internal Security Subcommittee, Robert Morris's fiefdom, to prepare, presumably with public funds, an introduction to the publication of the subcommittee's own resurrection of the *Amerasia* case. This Kubek opus, entitled *The* Amerasia *Papers: A Clue to the Catastrophe of China,* in two volumes totaling nearly two thousand pages, was rushed into print by the subcommittee at the end of 1969. There seemed to be no plausible explanation for the haste (the manuscript had been lying around for some time), other than that the Nixon administration was resuming conversations in Warsaw with the Chinese Communists and that Senator Eastland and his staff hoped that by rehashing the story they could arouse some new support for Chiang Kai-shek in his moment of need. Senator Eastland's own explanation, in a foreword, was that "in telling and retelling of the *Amerasia* story there is a lesson for all of us, and especially for all the officials in our government, whether or not in the diplomatic service, who would learn and benefit from the mistakes of the past."

The Government Printing Office, which does not ordinarily make a promotional fuss over its plodding output, used not Kubek's mostly unknown name in advertising this sample but Service's very well-known one, and it touted the book with come-ons like "These documents read like a spy thriller, but is [sic] all the more interesting because it is true. . . . Part III presents an analysis of some of the documents, herein published in full text, which were written in 1943–45 as official despatches by one of the arrested six, John Stewart Service, then a young career diplomat on station in China." There was no mention in the ads that the grand jury had declined, 20-to-0, to indict the young career diplomat after his arrest.

Kubek's introduction, 113 pages long, turned out to be largely an assault on Service, who in turn called it "a systematic attempt at fraudulent deception of the reader."[1] So questionable in its facts, let alone its interpretations, was Kubek's blast at Service that Professor Fairbank thought of asking the Ethics Committee of the American Historical Association to scrutinize it. Fairbank held back. "It would have created the assumption that the man is a historian," he said. (At the Stanford Center for East Asian Studies, Professor Van Slyke asserted, "Mr. Kubek is of course entitled to his opinions, but in my view, the bias, tendentiousness, and general absence of integrity which characterize this essay are an insult to scholarship. . . .") The Kubek attack, however, was gleefully received on Taiwan, and his introduction was translated into Chinese and brought out separately in hardcover for local consumption; Kubek himself was invited to Taipei, where he had a private audience with the Generalissimo and, all around, got more publicity than the Apollo XII astronauts, who were there on a good-will tour that overlapped his visit. A government press attaché who was assigned to Kubek during his stay declared, "Dr. Kubek is saying what we've believed for a long time but were afraid to say because it would be called propaganda. That's why we're so grateful to Dr. Kubek."

---

[1]Kubek referred to Service, Davies, et al., during their subservience to General Stilwell, as "liaison personnel" from the State Department. That phrase made Service wonder whom Kubek was using for sources. "Anyone knowing Chinese (which Kubek apparently does not) will also be struck by some of the language in these quotations," Service wrote in rebuttal. "This description ('liaison personnel') of our duties and status is not only incorrect; it is also one that was never used by ourselves, by the Army, by the State Department, or—so far as I know—in the writings of American historians dealing with this period. It is, however, a literal translation of a very common Chinese term (lien-lo jen-yuan), and has been carried over in this verbatim form in English-language Kuomintang accounts. It is of course appropriate for Kubek, as a historian, to consult all sources. But when he is in effect quoting from Chinese sources, why not acknowledge the fact?"

The gist of the Kubek diatribe was that the most important of hundreds of documents found in several raids on the *Amerasia* premises had been written by Service and had also been stolen by him from State Department files. Some of the documents of Service's composition mentioned by Kubek had demonstrably been passed to *Amerasia* by other people. In any event, of 923 *"Amerasia"* documents that Kubek claimed to have examined, he had selected 315 for analysis and had published 142. Of these, 101 had been written by Service. (The next most generously represented contributor of dispatches, out of a roster of twelve authors, was Edward Rice, with 8.) Sixty-nine of the Service papers had nothing at all to do with *Amerasia;* they had, rather, been lifted from Service's own files by the FBI. In one way, Service was not sorry to see them in print. Kubek was at least making available to him some of his writings that he hadn't had access to for more than twenty-five years.

At first Service wanted to sue Kubek, but instead, at the urging of his associates at the center, he decided to write a monograph that was in part a reply to the Kubek charges and in part an account—his first ever—of some of the aspects of wartime China that seemed to him most worth recalling. He came to that conclusion just before the annual Christmas banquet of the center, on which gala occasion Chalmers Johnson—who had heard more clarion cries than he could recall about "unleashing" Chiang Kai-shek so he could retake mainland China—was thus privileged to announce, "At last we have unleashed Jack." Writing at night mostly, after office hours, Service completed his rejoinder in two months; it was characteristic of his meticulousness that he used two typewriters—one for the main body of the text and the other for footnotes. Entitled *The Amerasia Papers: Some Problems in the History of U.S.-China Relations,* Service's work was published by the center in May 1971. In a foreword Johnson observed that in Service's case "America reenacted the ancient tragedy of the Persian generals who killed the messengers who brought bad news," and he noted that "future generations of historians will benefit from both his foresight and his hindsight."

The monograph was reviewed in the *Foreign Service Journal*—twenty years after it had run its editorial trying to rally the State Department to Service's cause—by Armistead Lee, a Foreign Service officer who had been with Service in New Zealand. "Few indeed of Senator McCarthy's victims have been so thoroughly vindicated," Lee wrote. "It was a triumph shared vicariously by his many admirers in the service. . . . Some day, there may be a plaque in the Department, honoring those officers who resisted these [McCarthy's] efforts at great personal sacrifice, men such as Jack Service, the finest and most capable officer I have known in 25 years." The Moscow journal *Problemy Dal'nego Vostoka* also reviewed the monograph, saying that Service's book "indicates the aspiration of U.S. ideologists to place a theoretical basis under Washington's new China policy directed at the nationalistic and great-power oriented forces in the Chinese Communist Party. Adherents of the new U.S. approach to the China policy would like to conceal true goals of imperialist diplomacy and its aggressive essence from the world community and the Chinese people."

Inasmuch as Kubek had been published by Congress, Service hoped to get his rejoinder at least inserted in the *Congressional Record*. Senators Birch Bayh and Sam J. Ervin, Jr., were members of the subcommittee under whose aegis Kubek's revisionisms had been issued, and Service and some of his friends in Washington thought they might be persuaded to put his monograph in the *Record* to make Congress's record more balanced. But that effort got nowhere.

In due course, though, the monograph came to the attention of Senator J. William Fulbright, who thereupon invited Service—along with Davies and Fairbank—to testify on China before his Foreign Relations Committee that July. "I am sure you can appreciate what it means for me to be here," Service said. "It is the first Senate meeting where I have appeared without need for counsel." (Davies thought the occasion was one "of considerable irony.") Senator Fulbright, for his part, said, "It is a very strange turn of fate that you gentlemen who reported honestly about the conditions [in China] were so persecuted because you were honest about it. This is a strange thing to occur in what is called a civilized country." No one thought to comment on the strange willingness of a presumably civilized country's principal legislative body to condone one of its Democrat-headed committees' trying to hang a citizen at the same time that another Democrat-headed committee was patting him on the back.

Soon after that, some other strange things occurred—strange, at least, in Service's long and trying relationship with his critics. When, following his appearance before the Fulbright committee, a commentator on the CBS radio network disparaged Service's loyalty, CBS actually got in touch with Service and offered him equal time to reply—which he did. Concurrently, James B. Reston was talking in Peking with Chou En-lai, who told him that four Old China Hands—Fairbank, Vincent, Lattimore, and Service—were welcome to visit China.

When this indirect invitation was conveyed to Service through *The New York Times*, he was eager to accept it—and to accept it at once, since the Berkeley center, anxious to get its man to China before the East Asian Center at Harvard got Fairbank there, offered to furnish him with a round-trip ticket to Hong Kong. Caroline Service had also been invited; her husband paid for her ticket. (The invitation had made it clear that while the Services were in the People's Republic they would be guests, like many other contemporary visitors, of the Chinese People's Association for Friendship and Cultural Relations with Foreign Countries.) After hearing from Marshall Green that the State Department would have no objection to his going, Service wrote to Chou En-lai and also to another old friend from Yenan, Huang Hua, then ambassador to Canada.[2] Within a couple of weeks, Service was informed that he could pick up his visas at Ottawa, and when he arrived there Huang invited him to dinner. Service told his host that he expected to report to his government on the journey, and Huang assured him that that would be all right with the People's Republic.

The Services arrived in Peking on September 26, 1971, and spent six and a half weeks in China. For much of that time they went through the usual tourist routine—visits to factories (in one of which he was pleased to espy a Chinese-manufactured steam trap of excellent quality), to a hydroelectric project, to a zoo, and to several hospitals, where there were the usual demonstrations of acupuncture in lieu of conventional anaesthesia.[3] They dropped in on Nanking, Shanghai, Hangchow, and Canton, the regular tourist stops; but they also, at Service's request, revisited some of the areas of the north and northwest that had such poignant associations for him: Chungking, Yenan, and especially Chengtu, where few Westerners had been seen since 1949, and where, accordingly, the Ser-

[2]Mao Tse-tung spoke Chinese in a Hunan dialect, with which Service was not fully conversant; during their wartime talks, accordingly, Huang Hua had several times sat in to bridge the conversational gaps between them.
[3]The Services were offered a chance to witness three operations: one abdominal, one gynecological, and one for the removal of some knee cartilage. The gynecological one he passed up as improper for him to witness—once a missionary's son, perhaps, always a missionary's son; the abdominal one he also passed up, because he thought watching it might make him pass out; the knee operation he gazed at intently, and, as have so many Americans lately in China, with amazement and awe.

vices' presence attracted large crowds.[4] "My Chinese, though rusty, gave me ears and at least half a mouth," Service recounted afterward, with characteristic—and not un-Chinese—diffidence. His father's YMCA had been taken over by an epidemic-control bureau, and the mission residence was occupied by fourteen families, none of whom had ever heard of him.

In the more sophisticated cities of the People's Republic, however, Service met up with quite a few Chinese who—perhaps because his arrival had been preceded by newspaper stories identifying him as an old friend of Chairman Mao's—remembered him; there were even a handful of them who spoke with knowledge, if not nostalgia, about Patrick J. Hurley. Being a man with *kuan-hsi*, who would never affront anybody or act in a pushy fashion, Service was quick to observe at the first of several dinners given in his honor by revolutionary committees along his route that his toasts to Mao Tse-tung seemed to embarrass his hosts. Guessing that this might be because they did not want to have to toast Nixon in response, he substituted a general invocation to international friendship, and that seemed more acceptable.

When, on Service's return to America, nearly everyone he met asked him what had happened to the minister of defense, Lin Piao, he could say truthfully that he had no idea, because he hadn't pressed the point. Nor had he requested a meeting with Mao; he had felt that any such overture should come from the chairman. Service did have amiable reunions with Dr. Ma Hai-teh, his onetime fellow cave-dweller at Yenan, and with Chiao Kuan-hua, soon the deputy foreign minister, to whom he had unavailingly tried to give his blood; and he did further convey to the Chinese People's Association his hope of getting together again with Chou En-lai. He had seen Chou briefly at a large reception just after his arrival, but they hadn't had a chance to speak. As Service and his wife traveled around the country, there had been no further word from Chou, and Service had begun to wonder if there would be. The premier, he knew, was busy: Emperor Haile Selassie was in China on a state visit.

---

[4]Twenty miles outside Chungking, during the war, the senior officials of the Kuomintang had built themselves fancy homes, beyond the usual target areas of Japanese bombers. In 1971 Service found these converted into workers' sanitaria. There was a swimming pool on the scene, and Service, never a man to forgo a chance to enhance physical fitness, persuaded his guides and drivers to join him in a muscle-toning plunge. At Yenan Service found that Mao Tse-tung's wartime residence had been converted into a sort of George-Washington-slept-here shrine, and the eight loess caves the Dixie Mission had occupied into a middle school.

Service did run into Chou again at a reception—this one for all the Americans then in Peking (Huey Newton was among them)—and although on this occasion Chou made a point of being flatteringly attentive to him, he said nothing about a private meeting.

Next, Henry Kissinger turned up in Peking on one of his trips to pave the way for Nixon. Apparently on the premise that it was perfectly appropriate for United States government officials to solicit views *in camera* abroad that they could not openly solicit at home, Kissinger requested a secret meeting with Service. Adhering once again to protocol, Service assented, but only after being assured by his Chinese hosts that they had no objection. The rendezvous was arranged with typical Kissinger furtiveness, but nothing much came of it; Kissinger, unlike most senior members of the United States Senate, didn't seem to be aware that Service had ever met Mao. Also, Kissinger was apparently under the impression that the room Service and he were talking in was bugged, so after a few guarded exchanges he suggested that they get together again back in California, perhaps in the secure environs of San Clemente. Service never heard from him after that.

Service was unprepared, accordingly, when, on the next-to-last day of his visit to China, he was suddenly summoned to see the premier. Chou began with a polite passing reference to the hard times that Service had experienced, and he inquired about some of their mutual friends—Dave Barrett, John Davies, John Emmerson, and John Carter Vincent, for instance—and said that they, too, would naturally be welcome if they chose to come to China. (The premier was evidently contrite that Colonel Barrett had once been accused of a plot against Chairman Mao's life, and in any event Barrett had no wish to return to a Communist China;[5]

---

[5]"The government in Peking is just a bunch of namby-pamby do-gooders," Barrett said in 1973. "The Chinese aren't Chinese any more. I don't expect China to put up indefinitely with all this Communist hogwash. I think they'll eventually get tired of it. They used to like to dress up and have a good time; why, today, they can't even gamble any more." In retirement Barrett had become generally pessimistic about China. "In all sincerity, at the risk of oversimplification," he wrote Lyman Van Slyke in 1968, "it is doubtful if anything could have prevented us from 'losing' China as we did, as long as we remain essentially an anti-Communist country, for China was doomed to go Communist as the sparks fly upward, as long as it was governed by the Kuomintang. The blind stupidity and arrogant stubbornness of Chiang Kai-shek did much to accelerate the loss of China to the Reds, and our well-meant, but fumbling and poorly directed, efforts to help were of little avail, and with the economy of the country in complete chaos, collapse of the government, which of course meant a take-over by the well-organized opposition, was inevitable. Whatever our faults in dealing with China, we have paid for them through our

neither Davies nor Emmerson had much of a yen to go back, either; Vincent, who probably more than the others would have enjoyed a return trip, was in failing health.) Then Chou En-lai launched into a three-hour discourse on world affairs, ranging from de Gaulle's handling of the Algerian situation to the status of Taiwan. At one point he said that if Chiang Kai-shek would give up his government there Peking would be happy to find the Generalissimo an honorable position in *its* government. Service did not pass this intelligence along to the Senate Internal Security Subcommittee.

In February 1972, however, one week before President Nixon went to China, Service—along with Raymond Ludden and Warren I. Cohen, a Sinologist from Michigan State University—was asked to reappear before the Foreign Relations Committee that had welcomed him the year before —to reminisce about, as he put it, "Americans who, shall we say, had had a bad time because of some of their views and recommendations concerning China in the 1940's." He added, "My own recent visit to China has demonstrated, to me at least, that many of the roots of the Chinese present may be found in what we saw and reported from the Communist base on Yenan in 1944 and 1945. . . . I think that our involvement in Vietnam, our insistence on the need to contain China and to prevent what we thought was the spread of Communist influence in Southeast Asia, was based very largely on our misunderstanding and our lack of knowledge of the Chinese, the nature of the Chinese Communist movement, and the intention of their leaders. We assumed that they were an aggressive country, and I don't believe that they really have been, and, therefore, I think we got into Vietnam largely, as I say, through the misinterpretation and misfounded fear of China."

Professor Cohen, in his turn, said that General Hurley had left behind him, when he resigned his ambassadorship at the end of 1945, "a dung heap of irresponsible charges in which ambitious politicians would soon revel." Cohen thought that the abuse of Service, Vincent, Clubb, and

---

teeth, and I can see nothing but much worse times ahead. Mao can't last much longer, but when he goes, we may find ourselves looking back on his time as the good old days. With Red China apparently falling more and more into the hands of totally irresponsible people, I think war between us and that country is inevitable just as soon as the leaders of our enemy feel they stand even a slight chance of success. One of the things which is going to work to our great disadvantage . . . in future attempts to cope with China will be the almost complete lack of people who have first-hand knowledge of the country. . . . Let me assure you, Kuomintang-run Taiwan is a hell of a long way from being China, and as for Hongkong, it of course doesn't even faintly resemble it."

Davies constituted "one of the most shameful and destructive episodes in the history of the United States" and that the four of them "are guaranteed a higher place in the annals of man than that accorded to their accusers, but the damage done to them personally can never be repaired."

Ludden, when his time came, said he found the rediscovery of China by the Nixon administration rather "amusing," and added that he was using the adjective "wryly."

"You are entitled to be wry in view of your experience," Senator Fulbright told him.

Among the other remarks Fulbright made on that pivotal eve of a new era in Sino-American relations were, "For too many years Americans have found it difficult, if not impossible, to engage in rational, dispassionate discussion of China. . . . We considered ourselves uniquely qualified to play the role of China's savior. . . . These Foreign Service officers in China served their country well, but their country did not always serve them well. . . . They were transferred from China and were denied deserved promotions. Their loyalty was questioned; some were hounded from the Foreign Service. As a result, it was recognized as unwise and unsafe to write about the 'real' China whether one was in or out of the Government. . . . Much that has been written about China since the late 1940's was thus an exercise in demonology."

Senator Fulbright's efforts to redress past wrongs, while not widely popularized, were deeply appreciated by the people affected. At a memorial service for John Carter Vincent less than a year later, Abbot Low Moffat, who had served under Vincent when he was director of the Bureau of Far Eastern Affairs, said, "I am . . . glad that there has at long last been public recognition of the penetrating reporting and analyses by certain of the Foreign Service officers then in China; what as yet has had less public understanding is that the far harder task devolved on John Carter to consider all reports from China, to evaluate them, and, drawing on these and his knowledge of their authors and their abilities and perceptiveness and on his own years of experience in China, to determine the basic facts and trends as best he could, and then to recommend to the Secretary the policies that he thought should obtain. Only now is it being realized how much wiser John Carter was than his later detractors."

And Walter Surrey added, "One might reflect, as a John Carter Vincent never would, what enlightened hindsight concerning past events and sins has taught us. Such reflection permits us to speculate that if we had today a Foreign Service composed totally of John Carter Vincents, we would not today be engaged in a war that nobody wants; we would not be running the risk of becoming engaged in future wars that nobody will want; and, we would have today a Foreign Service which could not only stand up to any new McCarthy attack, but also could enjoy the novelty of being the target of public support and gratitude."

13

"It's very pleasant to be here."

Can there be anyone among that group who reported from China during World War II who, watching an American president journey in person to Communist China in 1972, was not conscious of an irony so acute as to make him shiver? Could anyone remembering past attitudes look at that picture of President Nixon and Chairman Mao in twin armchairs, with slightly queasy smiles bravely worn to conceal their mutual discomfort, and not feel a stunned sense that truth is indeed weirder than fiction?

The speaker was Barbara W. Tuchman, and the occasion was another stunning one—a lunch given at the State Department on January 30, 1973, by the American Foreign Service Association. The gathering could scarcely have been contemplated, let alone held, had not Nixon gone to China the year before. The president, to put it mildly, was no particular friend of the Foreign Service officers to whom Mrs. Tuchman alluded. In fact, he had precious little use for—nor much comprehension of—career diplomats, "too many [of whom], according to my experience," he wrote in *Six Crises*, "prefer to compromise, to avoid conflict, to play it safe." In the same book he recalled having told President-elect Kennedy after their 1960 race, "The foreign service needs a leavening of top-notch, hard-driving, non-career people who will not be completely controlled by the more rigid, even stodgy, career officers. It needs an element of no vested interests."

This had been written before Nixon, as president, peddled embassies to the highest bidders, but after President Eisenhower sent Scott McLeod to Ireland. When one of Nixon's own appointments of a career ambassador to be an assistant secretary of state ran afoul of a Senate committee, he had his press secretary declare with a straight face that the president believed "it is not in the interest of the Foreign Service or the United

States that career officers become subject to retribution for diligent execution of their instructions." Secretary of State William B. Rogers chimed in by asserting that "loyalty, energy, imagination, and courage" were "the best qualities that a diplomat can place at the service of his country," adding that "Foreign Service officers must be able to serve a President without being cited as a symbol by some senators opposed to Presidential policies."[1]

Attorney General John Mitchell had long since said, of course, that the Nixon administration should be judged not by its words but by its deeds. When Nixon went to call on Mao, he took along practically no China-language Foreign Service officers (by then a new crop had, not without some difficulty, been grown), except for a very few junior ones who acted mainly as messengers. Those who were left behind in Washington, watching Nixon and Kissinger on television as they hobnobbed with their hosts in Peking and Shanghai, kept exclaiming to each other, "My God, they don't know who's sitting next to them!" And when the Nixon party returned, there was never any organized debriefing by the State Department of its members, to ascertain to whom they'd talked, and to whom they hadn't, and who had initiated what conversations on what topics, and how this was done—procedures that are normally followed in the conduct of sensible foreign relations.

But at least Nixon had gone to the People's Republic of China and returned alive, and so now on January 30, 1973, 250 individuals could safely gather in the stately Benjamin Franklin Room, on the eighth and topmost floor of the State Department building, in response to invitations from the Foreign Service Association. The chairman of its board of

---

[1]To cite anomalies, ambiguities, ambivalences, and sheer hypocrisies during Mr. Nixon's incumbency is a pointless exercise, but it is perhaps worth noting that on February 5, 1972, when he knew he was going to China, he wrote to Edgar Snow, dying of cancer in Switzerland (the Chinese government had sent Dr. Ma Hai-teh there to tend him in his last days), ". . . your distinguished career is deeply appreciated." The letter was probably drafted for Nixon by some Foreign Service officer, who may or may not have reminded the president, never revealed before as an admirer of Snow's, that in *Journey to the Beginning* Snow had written, "There has seldom been such successful demagoguery, conspired in by a responsible American political party, as the 'twenty-years-of-treason' hoax which helped carry the Republican Party to power in 1952. Nor was there in our history any campaign more costly to the American people, to our prestige abroad and to our internal unity and self-respect, than the triumph of lies and slander, spearheaded by McCarthy and Nixon, which charged Roosevelt, Marshall, Stilwell, Truman, Acheson and loyal men of the U.S. Foreign Service with betrayal of our country and 'selling China to the Russians.' "

directors, William C. Harrop, had told his prospective guests in a rather unusually worded invitation to the meal:

> The President's trip to Peking, and the new era he has opened in American/Chinese relations, have drawn attention to the prophetic quality of much that was written about China by Foreign Service professionals serving there during the years 1942–1945.
>
> Historians have praised the perception and candor of the analysis that was produced by Foreign Service officers in Embassy Chungking and elsewhere in China during that turbulent period. The facts they reported were unwelcome at home. Many of these officers suffered harsh domestic criticism and were unable to continue their careers.
>
> At a luncheon on the Department of State's 8th floor at noon on Tuesday, January 30, 1973, the American Foreign Service Association will honor those Foreign Service Officers in China during the early 1940's who demonstrated their professionalism and integrity by reporting events as they saw them. . . .

Far more people than the Benjamin Franklin Room could hold wanted to attend the signal gathering (John Davies's brother couldn't manage a ticket), so the proceedings were carried to another audience of six hundred, elsewhere in the building, by closed-circuit television. The lunch was not an official State Department affair. Secretary Rogers was invited, but begged off; he was too busy, he explained (his office was on the floor below the dining room), to attend. Henry Kissinger couldn't make it, either. The highest-ranking State Department official who turned up was U. Alexis Johnson, the undersecretary for political affairs. He did not speak, nor did Assistant Secretary Marshall Green, who sat at a place of honor at the head table. Green did remark, afterward, "This has done more to tie together the Foreign Service than anything in recent history."

Some of the men scattered around the room—Averell Harriman and Nicholas Katzenbach, for instance—were nationally prominent figures, but the guests who counted most that day were those who had been intimately concerned with the events Harrop had cited in his invitation. Edmund Clubb was there, at seventy-one, a now widely respected historian, whose *Twentieth Century China* and *China and Russia* grace the shelves of any library where serious scholars converge. ("It's very pleasant to be here," Clubb said at lunch. "I hadn't thought about the possibility, I must say.") John Emmerson was there, now a scholar in residence at

Stanford; and Arthur Ringwalt, up from his retirement home at Chapel Hill, North Carolina; and Walton Butterworth, Robert Barnett, and Fulton Freeman. That morning Freeman had been talking on the phone to Mike Mansfield, and on learning that the senator had never met John Service, whom Harrop had announced would speak at the lunch, Freeman had taken Service over to see the majority leader of the legislative body so many of whose members had caused him so much grief. Mansfield and Service had had a pleasant get-together.[2]

John Davies, writing a book across the Atlantic in Malaga, was missing from the scene. "Washington would have been a long way to go for lunch," he said later. John Carter Vincent had died the month before, but his wife was present and able to hear Service say of him, "We all knew him as a staunch friend, and as a capable, courageous, and loyal chief. He was the man who should be standing here today." Jim Penfield, Ed Rice, Phil Sprouse, Ray Ludden, and John Melby were all absent. (Most of them could not make it. Ludden could have, but did not want to. His reaction to the invitation conveyed to him, indeed, was rather sulphurous. A mild paraphrase of it might go, "God damn it, what the hell did the Foreign Service Association ever do for us? Where in hell were they when we needed them?") "I never thought I'd live to see the day," wrote Melby in the course of conveying his regrets. And among the men and women who turned up were some whose legal counsel and friendship had been stout crutches for the Old China Hands to lean on in their beleaguered years—Adrian Fisher, Joseph Rauh, John Reid, and Walter Surrey. Supreme Court Justice William Douglas sent Service a note regretting that the pressing business of the court precluded his attendance.

When John Service was introduced, he received a long standing ovation. Service! Acclaimed in the State Department at last! In point of fact, the standing ovation was not unanimous. There were a couple of senior Foreign Service officers in the room who had never been especially sympathetic to the victimized China Hands, and who now kept their seats, just as in years before they—and, when it came to that, the Foreign Service institutionally—had been notably lukewarm in siding with their colleagues against their attackers. Service did not want to allude directly to any of this on a preponderantly happy occasion, but he did remark in his

---

[2]No member of the Senate came to the lunch, but shortly after it was over Senator James L. Buckley, the Conservative from New York, wrote to Secretary Rogers complaining about the State Department's having made its premises available for it.

address, "I wish I could say . . . that the Foreign Service itself has always supported the value of reporting and area expertise. I imagine we can all think of negative examples: they have not been few."

Service's prepared text began, "Let me, first of all, say simply that my family and I appreciate your invitation to be here." And then he added, extempore, "and that is probably the understatement of the year." His speech was about Foreign Service reporting, but it was not so much what he was saying that enthralled his audience as that he was saying it where he was saying it.

There's more to reporting, of course [Service said], than merely being on the ground. In October, 1946, I arrived in Wellington, New Zealand, as Deputy Chief of Mission. It was just before a national election. Ambassador Avra Warren, an old professional, had assigned a young, new-minted third secretary the task of making an analysis and electoral prediction. Pouch day was upon us—our last chance to get a prediction to Washington. The Ambassador thought the third secretary a capable young man—"likely to do well in the Service"—but had grave reservations about his prognosis. The third secretary conceded that the election would be close, but firmly concluded that Labour (the incumbents) would win by certainly three, and probably four seats. "Hell," said the Ambassador, "almost all the press supports the Tories; everyone I know outside the government is going to vote Tory; and everyone tells me the Tories are going to win." Furthermore, the Ambassador had a theory (call it history or political science) that democracies change parties after a long war.

My *immediate* task was to read the report and advise whether it should go forward. I knew nothing about New Zealand politics. Having transferred direct from Tokyo, there had not even been the chance for a briefing by the country desk. So I talked to the understandably uptight third secretary about his sources, and how he had gone about collecting the information for what appeared to be a superbly documented, realistic analysis. On this basis, I told the Ambassador that I thought we should send it. In contrast to one other Ambassador I have known, he took my advice.

The wait seemed long but election day finally came. Labour did win by four seats, but one seat was so close that for a while it seemed that the margin might be only three.

A few comments. Most important, the report was right—right on the button. That's what the game is all about. But more. The officer had a talent for developing contacts among the right people—though in this case the right people were clearly to the left of the Ambassador's circle. Furthermore, those contacts led to the development of useful information; we've all seen high-powered social types who "know everybody" but somehow lack a nose for news. And finally, he knew what to do with the information. Some officers accumulate a terrific amount of data in their heads or personal files; but it doesn't mean a thing in the Department if they can't organize it to produce a cogent, timely report.

Also, the reporting officer had done his work so well that he had the courage of his conclusions—despite the intimidating effect (even if not intended) of the Ambassador's doubts. The Ambassador deserves credit, too, for a broad concept of reporting, and for willingness to trust the judgment of the officer.

Incidentally, the young third secretary was Marshall Green. . . .[3]

Service concluded his remarks in a curious fashion—an almost Chinese fashion, some of his auditors thought: He told a story about another Foreign Service officer whose blighted career (he had left China for good long before General Hurley came on the scene) had terminated in an obscure consulate in England:

When the Sino-Japanese War commenced and the Japanese occupied Shantung in 1937 and 1938, our consul in Tsingtao was Samuel Sokobin. He was a capable, conscientious officer—a China specialist of long experience. As is often the case, he had come to have a genuine liking and respect for the Chinese. Eventually, Chinese guerrillas began to be active in Shantung. Soon the Chinese press was carrying dramatic accounts of heroic exploits in crippling the Japanese-held railways and denying the Japanese the important agricultural and mineral resources of the province. In his post at the main port,

---

[3]Service's account of what had happened in the New Zealand elections had latter-day implications that few in the audience probably grasped. A couple of months before the lunch, there had been another general election in New Zealand, and this time the American ambassador, a conservative Texan who was emphatically a noncareer diplomat, had refused to pass along his junior officers' conclusion that Labour would very likely win, and had flatly predicted a Tory victory. The outcome of the election was not without interest to Washington, for the incumbent government of New Zealand had sent a small detachment of troops to Vietnam, a gesture that the Labour party disapproved of. When Labour did win, accordingly (it soon afterward recalled the troops), Washington was surprised.

After the lunch Marvin Kalb, the CBS reporter, to whom the implications had been clear, came up to Green and asked, "By the way, how did your boys do on that recent election in New Zealand?" Green blandly ignored the question, and Kalb did not pursue it.

and making intelligent use of excellent contacts in shipping and business circles, Sokobin came to realize the gross exaggeration in these claims. The Japanese were maintaining and increasing the flow of these strategic materials to Japan.

Sokobin did not consider that a responsible officer needed to be told when (or what) to report. He commenced a series of reports thoroughly documenting the success of the Japanese in countering the guerrillas and in exploiting the resources of their occupied territory. He should, of course, have been commended; but the reaction his reports received was very different. He was upsetting the picture, then the accepted line, of a Chinese resistance not only brave but also effective. Sokobin's reports were harshly depreciated. He was cruelly and ridiculously accused of being "pro-Japanese." And, with a perverted idea of justice, his transfer was arranged to Kobe, Japan. He was never returned to service in China.

Sokobin's career might never have reached the heights—one can never know. But in 1947 he finished thirty-three and one-half years of loyal service as Class 3 and consul in Birmingham.

Substitute "Service" for "Sokobin," "Liverpool" for "Birmingham," change a few numbers, and the last paragraph could have been autobiographical. It was close enough to home, at least, to make Service's eyes brim with tears as he uttered it.

Even more curiously, Service did not intend his story about Sokobin to be in any way autobiographical. He had hoped by citing it to remind his audience again, in a gentle fashion, that the State Department had been as guilty in the past as any outsider groups of destroying its own men. Months after the lunch he tried to put it all into reflective context:

Toward the end of 1951, the whole China group was clearly becoming involved in Loyalty-Security troubles, and in Congressional committee attacks. The people included Clubb, Davies, Emmerson, Ludden, Melby, Fisher, Sprouse, Freeman, Vincent, and myself. In some cases, there had been formal charges and hearings. Others were still in the "interrogatory" stage—which appeared increasingly clear as a first stage toward more serious charges. I had been, of course, a vulnerable and obvious target because of the *Amerasia* connection. But as the process moved on to engulf the rest of us, it was obvious that the issue was not loyalty-security but our political reporting and policy recommendations. We felt (with Clubb, as I recall, taking the lead) that this was an issue that involved the integrity of the Foreign Service and State

Department; and that it should be the concern of our representative body, the Foreign Service Association.

One aspect, for instance, was the fact that our views (and, to some extent, our recommendations) had been accepted and even commended by our superiors. Was there not such a thing as executive responsibility, from several Secretaries of State downward? This sort of thing might be exemplified by the China White Paper's timidity that obscured the fact that the February 28, 1945, recommendations of the Chungking Embassy had been approved by State all the way to the top. We held several meetings of our group and produced several drafts of a letter to the Foreign Service Association. None of us opposed the loyalty-security program as such. But we argued that what was happening was a distortion and perversion of any proper concept of loyalty-security. Alas, it was all wasted effort. We never, as I remember it, presented a formal communication to the Association. But from discussions with its directors, we had it made clear to us that they regarded it as too delicate a political issue for the Association to get involved in. As a body, the Association remained silent.

Ludden felt that this was incredible, as well as shameful. He had just been serving in Brussels, and the Ambassador he had served under was a "real man" who had guts and courage, could understand the issue, and would "stand up and fight." This man was Robert Murphy, Eisenhower's wartime political adviser, unassailable politically, one of the "big" men in the Foreign Service. Murphy was then in Washington. So Lud and I went around to talk to him. He was very friendly, very sympathetic. But so far as being willing to stand up, the result was zero. So the hard fact was that we were on our own. The Foreign Service Association averted its eyes and walked by on the other side of the road. Not all the members of the Service. Many were distressed at what was happening. And I think every member could believe he was sincere in upholding a statement in favor of the integrity of Foreign Service reporting (vide the editorials in the Foreign Service Journal, though on the whole the people editing it tended to have more guts than the governing body of the Association). But beyond that, no action.

It was the firing of Davies, I think, that finally sent a shock wave through the Foreign Service. Up to that point we had been a group—relatively small, specialized, and outside the mainstream of the Service—whose views seemed wildly eccentric and to many people, in those Cold-War days, hopelessly in error, if not actually dangerous. But the Davies case, by the time he was fired in 1954, was something very different. John had served in Moscow, had enjoyed Kennan's confidence and played a prominent role on the Policy

Planning Staff (during the heyday of that Staff, and probably the *only* period when it enjoyed prestige and really amounted to much), had served in Germany, and in South America. However "radical" his views had been in China, he had now become a doughty, valued, and staunch contributor to the current policy of containment. If John could be fired, who might not be affected? "For whom the bell tolls," and all that. It was because of the Davies case that the five old worthies—the retired diplomats—wrote their letter to the *Times*.[4] And so far as I know, after John there were no more firings. One could say, of course, that there was no one left to fire.

If there ever *is* another firing of an officer of the experience and stature of Davies, on such flimsy and transparent grounds, I think it very unlikely that the Foreign Service Association, or the Foreign Service as a group, will sit by passively and wring their hands in private. The Association has changed in character. It used to be a do-nothing club of the most senior officers. Now it has been taken over by "young Turks" who have made it into something like a trade union. Active pursuit of the interests of its members is a part of its platform. I used these arguments—unsuccessfully—to try to persuade Ludden to come to the lunch. It was unfair, I suggested, to charge the Association of today with the sins—of omission, at least—of the old Association. The new people were trying to make some amends. When I said at the lunch that "negative examples . . . have not been few" I was thinking of all these things. My introduction of the China Service's cruelty to Sokobin, to one of its own men, because of a disagreement with *his* reporting, was not intended as a device for asking sympathy for myself.

There were many newspaper editorials about the lunch at the State Department. In a *New York Times* one about this "poignant occasion," it was said that "Here, in effect, was the last step in the vindication of the 'old China Hands,' whose careers had been ruined or tarnished because they correctly predicted the victory of the Chinese Communists over the ineffective Kuomintang Government of Chiang Kai-shek." But in his final sentence, the editorial writer must have had second thoughts about that "last step." For now he was hedging: "It would be naive to think that what happened to the 'old China hands' in the postwar era could never happen again."

The cautionary note was well sounded. For even at the very lunch itself

---

[4]This was the letter from Messrs. Armour, Bliss, Grew, Phillips, and Shaw mentioned on page 34.

an ugly dissonance had intruded. A man identified as John David Hemenway—a right-wing ex-Foreign Service officer who had been let go by the
State Department four years earlier—had come to the party and, while
the other guests were in an anteroom drinking cocktails and congratulat-
ing one another on being present at the historic moment, had wandered
into the dining room and scattered mimeographed tracts on the tables.
"Some Questions for John Service," they were headed. There were eight
questions, all "suggested by" an organization called "Concerned Voters,"[5] and it was easy to see whoever drew them up had had recourse to
Anthony Kubek's introduction to the Senate Internal Security Subcommittee's report. One question dealt, inevitably, with *Amerasia.* Another
went: "John Leighton Stuart, our last ambassador to China on the mainland, wrote in his memoirs: 'We Americans mainly saw the good things
about the Chinese Communists, while not noticing carefully the intoler-
ance, bigotry, deception, disregard for human life and other evils which
seem to be inherent in any totalitarian system.' A study of your reports
from China reveals much praise of the Communists, but we were not able
to find any criticism of them. Were you blind to their faults, as suggested
by Ambassador Stuart?" And so on and so on.[6]

Hemenway and his Concerned Voters were not alone. On April 1,
shortly after the lunch at the State Department, a District of Columbia
group called the Council Against Communist Aggression held a dinner
at a Holiday Inn in Alexandria, Virginia. The invitations to *that* social
affair went:

> Our dinner this year will honor those who have steadfastly fought for the
> freedom of the people of China for over a quarter of a century. This theme
> was suggested by the luncheon given by the American Foreign Service Associ-
> ation on January 30, 1973, to honor Foreign Service Officers whose reporting
> and conduct in China in 1944–45 helped bring about the Communist take-
> over. We are now told that these men were right because they foretold the
> victory of communism. Actually, they were *wrong,* because they recom-

---

[5]A Washington, D.C., postoffice box was given as the address for Concerned Voters, who
seemed more interested in asking than answering questions. An inquiry to that address
as to who their officers were and as to what connection, if any, they had with John
Hemenway received no reply.

[6]Stuart suffered a stroke while writing the memoirs, and they were finished for him by
Stanley Hornbeck, who had, and expressed, views on China that were quite different from
those of the nominal author of the published book.

mended policies that helped bring about that victory. They said the communists were really democrats.

The American Foreign Service Association refused to hold a luncheon to honor the China experts who correctly described the Chinese Communists as totalitarians and who accurately predicted what their victory would mean for China and America.

The Council Against Communist Aggression is therefore proud to honor at its Annual Award Dinner representatives of the China experts who stood for freedom in China and who were right even though freedom itself was snuffed out.

Among the experts listed were Professor Anthony Kubek, Robert Morris, Freda Utley, Lyle H. Munson, Dr. Walter H. Judd, and General Albert C. Wedemeyer.

So the long battle, thirty years after General Stilwell had gone to China, might seemingly still be far from over. McCarthy was dead and McCarran was dead, but it was beginning to appear that as long as any of the pursuers of the Old China Hands retained the breath of life, the controversy would continue. Yes, Nixon had gone to China, and the China Hands had gone before the Senate without lawyers, and the Foreign Service Association had put on a bang-up lunch, but who could say for sure that some headline-hunting congressional committee chairman or Dallas kindergarten student or ambitious grandnephew of a Wellesley classmate of Mme. Chiang Kai-shek might not take it into his or her head one week or month or year to demand, or initiate, a full-scale inquiry into the allegedly secrecy-shrouded *Amerasia* case or to come to grips with the main issue of who lost China? A partial vindication the Old China Hands had certainly achieved, but as John Fairbank was saying, more than two thirds of the way through the twentieth century, to some young China-language Foreign Service officers with whom, by then, he could at least openly communicate, "Remember, the pendulum could swing the other way. It always does."

Postscript

"Quemoy and Matsu are not likely to be remembered in history among the outposts of the free world, but there was a time when it was a matter of grave policy whether the United States would defend the islands. . . . Indeed, Quemoy and Matsu were a major issue of the 1960 Presidential campaign. . . .

"Asked what the present United States policy on Quemoy and Matsu was, a State Department spokesman said he didn't know but suspected there wasn't any."

—*The New York Times*, August 25, 1974

A Glossary of
Old China Hands

David D. Barrett. Born Central City, Colorado, 1892. Graduated University of Colorado, 1915. U.S. Army, 1917–1952. Chinese-language training, Peking, 1921–1925. Most of military career spent in China: with Fifteenth Infantry, 1931–1934; assistant military attaché, 1936–1942; commander of first military observer group to Yenan (the Dixie Mission), 1944. Recommended for promotion to brigadier general, 1944. Highest rank achieved: colonel. Military attaché, Taiwan, 1950. Retired to San Francisco, 1952.

Oliver Edmund Clubb. Born South Park, Minnesota, 1901. A.B., University of Minnesota, 1927; M.A., California College in China, 1940. U.S. Army, 1918–1919. Joined Foreign Service, 1928. Language officer, Peking, 1929. Served between 1931 and 1950 at Hankow, Tientsin, Nanking, Shanghai, Hanoi, Chungking, Urumchi, Vladivostok, Mukden, Changchun, Peking. Interned by Japanese after Pearl Harbor, volunteered upon release to return directly to China. Last U.S. consul general in Peking, 1950. Director, Office of Chinese Affairs, Department of State, 1950–1952. Highest rank: Class 1 Foreign Service officer. Forced into retirement, February 1952.

John Paton Davies, Jr. Born Kiating, China, of missionary parents, 1908. Student, Yenching University, Peking, 1929–1930. B.S., Columbia University, New York, 1931. Appointed foreign service officer, 1931. Served in Asia at Kunming, Peking, Mukden, Hankow, Chungking. First secretary at American embassy, Moscow, 1947. Member, State Department Policy Planning Staff, 1950. Highest rank: Class 1 Foreign Service officer. Last post: Lima, Peru. Fired by Secretary of State Dulles, 1954.

Everett F. Drumright. Born Drumright, Oklahoma, 1906. B.S., University of Oklahoma, 1929. Appointed Foreign Service officer, 1930. Served in China at Hankow, Peking, Swatow, Nanking, Sian, Shanghai (where interned by Japanese after Pearl Harbor), Chungking. Chief of Office of Chinese Affairs, Department of State, 1945. Postwar service in London, Tokyo, Seoul, New Delhi, Bombay. Consul general, Hong Kong and Macao, 1954. Ambassador to Republic of China (Taiwan), 1958–1962. Retired to Poway, California, 1962.

John K. Emmerson. Born Canyon City, Colorado, 1908. A.B., Colorado College, 1929. M.A., New York University, 1930. Appointed Foreign Service officer,

1935. Japanese-language specialist. Served in Tokyo, Lima, Chungking, Yenan, Moscow, Karachi, Beirut, Paris, Lagos, and Salisbury, Rhodesia. Highest rank: Class 1 Foreign Service officer. Last job, counsellor and deputy chief of mission, American embassy, Tokyo, 1962. Diplomat in residence, Stanford University, 1967. Retired to Los Altos Hills, California, 1968.

Fulton Freeman. Born Pasadena, California, 1915. Student, Lingnan University, China, 1934–1935. A.B., Pomona College, 1937. Appointed Foreign Service officer, 1939. Language officer, Peking, 1941. Interned by Japanese after Pearl Harbor. Served in Chungking, 1943–1945. Acting deputy director, Office of Chinese Affairs, State Department, 1949. Further diplomatic stations: Rome, Norfolk, Virginia, Brussels. Ambassador to Colombia, 1961. Ambassador to Mexico, 1964. Highest rank: career minister. Retired to California, to become president of Monterey Institute of Foreign Studies, 1969. Died December, 1974.

Raymond P. Ludden. Born Fall River, Massachusetts, 1909. B.S., Georgetown University, 1930. Appointed Foreign Service officer, 1931. To Tsinan, China, 1932. Served in Mukden, Peking, Canton, until interned by Japanese after Pearl Harbor. Upon release volunteered to return directly to China. Served in Chungking, Kunming, Yenan. Four months on reconnaissance behind enemy lines. Left China for last time, 1949. Further service in Dublin, Brussels, Paris, Stockholm. Last job, consul general, Düsseldorf. Highest rank: Class 1 Foreign Service officer. Retired to South Yarmouth, Massachusetts, 1961.

James K. Penfield. Born New York City, 1908. A.B., Stanford University, 1929. Appointed Foreign Service officer, 1930. To Asia, 1931. Served in Canton, Mukden, Peking, Kunming, Chungking. Deputy director, Bureau of Far Eastern Affairs, State Department, 1945. Postwar service in Prague, London, Vienna, Athens, and Washington, as deputy director for African Affairs. Ambassador to Iceland, 1961. Highest rank: Class 1 Foreign Service officer. Retired to Longbranch, Washington, 1970.

Edward E. Rice. Born Saginaw, Michigan, 1909. B.S., University of Illinois, 1930. Appointed Foreign Service officer and sent to China, 1935. Served in Peking, Canton, Foochow, Kunming, Chungking. Assistant chief, Office of Chinese Affairs, State Department, 1946. Postwar service abroad at Manila, Stuttgart. To Policy Planning Staff, Washington, 1959. Deputy assistant secretary of state for Far Eastern Affairs, 1962. Consul general, Hong Kong and Macao, 1964–1967. Diplomat in residence, University of California, Berkeley, 1968. Retired to Tiburon, California, 1969.

Arthur R. Ringwalt. Born Omaha, Nebraska, 1899. Studied at Sorbonne, Paris. Appointed Foreign Service officer and first assigned to China, 1928. Stationed at Shanghai, Kunming, Peking, Kweilin, Chungking. Chief, Office of Chinese Affairs, State Department, 1946. Postwar service abroad at London and Kingston, Jamaica, where served as consul general from 1957 until retirement to Chapel Hill, North Carolina, 1959.

John S. Service. Born Chengtu, China, 1909, of missionary parents. A.B., Oberlin College, 1931. Appointed Foreign Service officer, 1935. Served in Kunming, Peking, Shanghai, Chungking, Yenan. Arrested in *Amerasia* case, 1945. Dismissed from State Department, 1951. Reinstated by Supreme Court, 1957. Assigned to Liverpool as consul, 1959. Highest rank: Class 2 Foreign Service officer. Retired to Berkeley, California, 1962.

Philip D. Sprouse. Born Greenbriar, Tennessee, 1906. A.B., Washington and Lee, 1928. Further study at Institut de Tourain, Paris, and Princeton. Appointed Foreign Service officer, 1938. Service in China at Peking, Hankow, Chungking, Kunming, Shanghai. In China with General George C. Marshall, 1946. Director, Office of Chinese Affairs, State Department, 1949. Subsequent service in Paris, Brussels. Highest rank: career minister. Foreign Service inspector, 1959–1962. Ambassador to Cambodia, 1962. Retired to Orinda, California, 1962.

John Carter Vincent. Born Seneca, Kansas, 1900. U.S. Army 1918. A.B., Mercer University, 1923. Appointed Foreign Service officer, 1925. Served in Asia at Changsha, Hankow, Swatow, Peking, Mukden, Nanking, Dairen. Counsellor, American embassy, Chungking, 1942. Director, Bureau of Far Eastern Affairs, State Department, 1945. Career minister, 1946. Envoy extraordinary and minister plenipotentiary to Switzerland, 1947–1951. Diplomatic agent, Tangier, 1951–1952. Forced to resign from Foreign Service, 1952. Retired to Cambridge, Massachusetts, where died December 1972.

Notes on Sources

Many, though far from all, reports home from the China Hands have been published in the volumes relating to China in that massive documentary series issued from time to time by the Government Printing Office in Washington, D.C., and called "Foreign Relations of the United States." References herein to this series identify it as "FRUS," with the appropriate year appended. "LSB" stands for Loyalty Security Board. For publishing data on the books referred to herein, consult the *Bibliography*, which follows.

1. "How do you say that in Chinese?"

p. 2: Taft's comment—in Dean Acheson's *Present at the Creation*, p. 364; Vandenberg's —in *The Private Papers of Senator Vandenberg*, ed. by Arthur H. Vandenberg, Jr., p. 535; Senator Dodd's comment was made in the course of a radio address over Station WGMS, Washington, D.C., January 6, 1961.

p. 3: Vincent was quoted in *The New York Times* on his arrival in New York from Tangier on April 29, 1953.

p. 3: Service's "we may save China"—March 20, 1944, FRUS 1944.

p. 4: The "John" mentioned by Geraldine Fitch in her *Formosa Beachhead* was John Allison, later United States ambassador to Japan.

p. 4: Service's comment on the four Johns was made to the Senate Foreign Relations Committee on July 21, 1971.

p. 6: Service's remarks on Mao's China and ping-pong matches—in his *The Amerasia Papers*.

pp. 7–8: Fairbank's statement—quoted by Anthony Lewis in *The New York Times*.

p. 8: Information on Vietnam—provided by a Foreign Service officer stationed there who prefers to remain anonymous.

p. 10: Ludden on Düsseldorf and on the Old China Hands—Ludden to author.

p. 11: Emmerson and Wedemeyer—Emmerson to author.

p. 12: Clubb's resignation statement was issued February 11, 1952.

p. 12: The dinner in Brussels—Richard Service to author.

p. 13: Sprouse-Rusk resignation conversation—Sprouse to author.

p. 13: Hurley and his gun—Ringwalt to author.

p. 18: Henry Luce's reply to Mrs. Vincent shown to author by her and by Gary May, Vincent's biographer.

p. 22: Service's remark on Shanghai—Service to author.

p. 22: Senator Aiken's comment was made during Foreign Relations Committee hearings, February 8, 1972.

p. 23: Penfield-Rusk exchange—Penfield to author. Secretary Rusk's remarks on the government of China were made during a speech in New York City, May 18, 1951.

p. 23: Snow mentions his meeting with Rusk in *The Other Side of the River: Red China Today*, p. 773.

p. 23: Kennedy's speech endorsing Hurley—delivered at Salem, Mass., on January 30, 1949.

pp. 24–25: Information on Kennedy's hopes for rapprochement and rehabilitation—Arthur Schlesinger, Jr., to author.

p. 26: Salisbury in Liverpool—Salisbury to author.

2. "We have no one like them today."

p. 29: Edith Rogers's complaint about Service was made in a letter to Secretary of State Acheson, who she hoped would not send Service to India.

pp. 29–31: Davies and Sevareid—Sevareid's *Not So Wild a Dream* and his CBS radio broadcast of November 8, 1954; also, Davies to author.

p. 33: Davies commented on learning a new trade on NBC television, December 12, 1953.

p. 33: Kennan quotation—*Foreign Affairs*, July 1955; reprinted in *Foreign Service Journal*, September 1955.

p. 34: The letter from the five diplomats appeared in the *Times* on January 17, 1954; the editorial on January 19.

p. 34: Shaw's article—in *Foreign Service Journal*, June 1942.

p. 35: Acheson to Dulles—in Acheson's *Present at the Creation*, p. 712; Dulles's views on loyalty—in a State Department press release, January 22, 1953.

p. 35: Fairbank's comments on *United States Relations with China* (hereafter cited as "White Paper") were written to the Stanford University Press and subsequently used by it in promoting its edition of the document.

pp. 36–39: Information about Barnett, Ludden, Drumright—personal interviews with author.

p. 39: Statistics on Foreign Service applications from William Barnes (with John Heath Morgan), *The Foreign Service of the United States*.

p. 40: Rice's October 2, 1944, report—FRUS 1944.

p. 41: Rice quotation and MacArthur story—Rice to author.

p. 44: Clubb's 1934 statement and 1951 quotation are in the transcript of his hearings before the State Department's LSB during the summer and fall of 1951—made available by Clubb to author.

p. 45: Davies on ambiance of Peking—Davies to author.

p. 47: Peking reaction to Clubb's report Ringwalt to author; Washington reaction to Clubb's passing along Mao's statement—Dorothy Borg's *The United States and the Far Eastern Crisis of 1933–1938.*

3. "It is not only a duty to serve others, but an honor."

p. 48: Clubb's appraisal of Vincent—*The New York Times*, December 5, 1972.

p. 50: Kohlberg's cabal listed in his "China via Stilwell Road," in *China Monthly*, October 1948, pp. 283–87.

pp. 51–53: Ringwalt-Johnson experiences—Ringwalt to author.

p. 52: Johnson's views on Service from the transcript of Service's hearing before the LSB, published by the Government Printing Office as an appendix to the Hearings of a

Subcommittee of the Committee on Foreign Relations [the "Tydings Committee"], U.S. Senate, 81st Congress, 2d Session, Part I. Johnson, incidentally, was the first witness on Service's behalf.

p. 54: Information on the Rev. Davies's later years—Sasha Davies Schnurman, his grand-daughter, to author.

p. 56: Donald Davies on serving the nation—Donald Davies to author.

pp. 58–59: Davies's parody report and his pre-Pearl-Harbor wrestling match—Ringwalt to author; Davies quotation on missionaries—*Dragon by the Tail*, p. 429.

p. 61: Service's accounts of his 1971 trip to the People's Republic of China appeared the following year on the Op. Ed. page of *The New York Times*, January 24 through 27.

pp. 62–63: Service's linguistic skill—Col. David Barrett to author.

pp. 64–65: Gauss's receiving a young diplomat—Harold Roser to author; Gauss's testimony about Clubb—transcript of Clubb's LSB hearings; Gauss's comment to Vincent, made November 23, 1943—reported by Vincent in letter to his wife.

pp. 65–66, 68–69: Gauss's comments about Service—transcript of Service's LSB hearing, May 27, 1950.

p. 67: Mme. Chiang Kai-shek's pun—Service to author; "frozen entities"—Theodore H. White to author.

p. 69: Davies's letter, to Lt. Gen. Daniel Noce, was written in Lima, Peru, on November 2, 1954, and published in the *Foreign Service Journal*, December 1954.

p. 70: Barnett's visit to Taiwan—Barnett to author.

p. 70: The Hornbeck memorandum was written December 14, 1943; copy in possession of Laurence Salisbury.

pp. 70–71: Hornbeck's "In the opinion of the undersigned"—FRUS 1941, p. 673.

p. 71: Salisbury to author.

p. 71: Clubb has a copy of his memorandum on Japanese activities just before Pearl Harbor.

p. 72: Vincent's memorandum for Gauss to send to Hull was written December 14, 1951; his letter was to Lauchlin Currie. Mrs. Vincent has copies of both.

p. 73: Clubb on his internment—Clubb to author.

4. "Where I am, the consulate is."

p. 75: Fairbank on Barrett—Fairbank's Foreword to Barrett's *The Dixie Mission*.

pp. 75–76: Col. Barrett and Gen. Chang—Richard Service to author.

p. 76: ". . . let's get the hell out of here"—Barrett to author.

p. 77: "small-fry colonel"—from *The Stilwell Papers*, ed. by Theodore H. White.

p. 77: Boatner quote from a critique of Barbara Tuchman's *Stilwell and the American Experience in China*, written for John K. Fairbank; copy in library of Center for Chinese Studies, University of California, Berkeley.

p. 80: "My men have worked miracles"—Chennault to Roosevelt, September 21, 1944, in FRUS 1944.

p. 81: Alsop statement on Stilwell, Davies, and Service—Part V, Hearings, Subcommittee on Internal Security [the "McCarran Committee"], Senate Judiciary Committee, 82d Congress, 1951.

p. 82: "an ignorant, illiterate peasant son of a bitch"—Theodore H. White to author.

p. 82: On assassinating Chiang—Chin-tung Liang's *General Stilwell in China, 1942–1944: The Full Story*, pp. 166–167.

p. 83: Penfield at Chengtu—Sept 9, 1944, FRUS 1944.

p. 83: "I am literally encompassed by Soong sisters"—from Vincent letter home quoted by Ross Terrill in his "When America 'Lost' China," *Atlantic*, November 1969, p. 80.

p. 84: Soong to Davies—Davies, *Dragon By the Tail*, p. 266.

p. 84: Vincent commented on assistance to Chiang in a letter to Hull, June 28, 1942; copy in possession of Mrs. Vincent.

p. 84: "thin binding tie"—Davies, *Dragon by the Tail*, p. 246.

p. 84: Gauss's efficiency report on Service was written in August 1942 and published in transcript of Service's 1950 LSB hearings.

p. 86: Mrs. Vaughan has shown the author her late husband's commission as a major general from Generalissimo Chiang Kai-shek.

pp. 87–88: Service's remarks from a report written January 23, 1943, and published in his *Lost Chance in China*, pp. 169ff.

p. 89: "It is almost laughable . . ."—Service, *The Amerasia Papers*, p. 99.

p. 90: Vincent's July 22, 1942, comments to Gauss—FRUS 1942, pp. 212ff; Vincent's comments on Willkie and Mme. Chiang—Mrs. Vincent to author.

p. 91: Stilwell and Chennault confer with Marshall—in Wedemeyer's *Wedemeyer Reports!*, p. 269.

pp. 91–92: Barnett's orientation booklet and what happened to it—Barnett to author.

p. 92: ". . . I shake in my shoes"—the remark, which Kohlberg attributed to Hornbeck, appears in Anthony Kubek's *How the Far East Was Lost*.

p. 95: Service's views on Sinkiang—included in an article by Service in *Foreign Service Journal*, October 1951.

p. 95: Conversation between Clubb and Sheng—Clubb to author.

p. 96: Ringwalt's dispatch—in FRUS 1943, pp. 373–74.

p. 96: Service from Chungking, May 25, 1943—Service, *Lost Chance*, pp. 101ff.

pp. 96–97: Drumright from Sian—December 26, 1943, and January 24, 1944, in FRUS 1944.

pp. 97–98: Davies's report from Chungking—written June 24, 1943, in "White Paper," p. 571.

p. 98: Gauss on Atcheson—comment made in 1950 during Service's LSB hearing, in Tydings committee hearings, p. 2070.

p. 99: Atcheson's report of May 28, 1943—in FRUS 1943.

p. 100: "I was lucky to find old friends . . ."—*The Stilwell Papers*, undated entry from late 1943, p. 257.

p. 100: Liang's quotation—from his *General Stilwell in China*, p. 11; Buss's quotation from his *The People's Republic of China*.

p. 101: Service on being for or against Chiang—answer to question about F. McCracken Fisher during his 1950 LSB hearing.

p. 101: "we should look for some other man . . ."—Tuchman, *Stilwell and the American Experience in China*, p. 410; Frank Merrill's remark—Emmerson to author.

p. 102: Davies wrote Hopkins on December 31, 1943—"Stilwell's Command Problems," in *The China-Burma-India Theatre* by Romanus and Sunderland (U.S. Army in World War II Series, published by the U.S. Government Printing Office: see under United States Government in *Bibliography*).

5. "I was prepared to contradict the ambassador, but . . ."

pp. 104, 105: Davies's reports to Stilwell and to the secretary of state—both from New Delhi, in FRUS 1944.

p. 104: Service's memorandum—in "White Paper," pp. 564 ff.

p. 105: Baker and Graves—memorandum from Davies to the secretary of state, March 10, 1944, FRUS 1944.

p. 105: Drumright's report—March 1944, in FRUS 1944, p. 384.

p. 105: Medical-corps major—Dr. Julius Pearson to author.

p. 106: "there is one detective . . ."—from Mansfield speech, January 3, 1945, reported in Shewmaker's Americans and Chinese Communists, 1927–1947: A Persuading Encounter.

p. 106: Service on Chiang's household—Service, Lost Chance, pp. 93–96.

p. 107: John Service told author about Chiao's laughing, and Harold Roser about his crying.

p. 108: Service's June 20, 1944 memorandum—Lost Chance, pp. 149, 151, 152.

pp. 109–11: The June 21–24, 1944, meetings between Chiang and Wallace—from notes taken by Vincent and published in "White Paper," pp. 549–59.

p. 110: "The Gimo had a good poker face . . ."—Service to author.

p. 111: Vincent asked about riding in the second car—Walter Surrey to author.

p. 111: Wallace report to Roosevelt—New York Times, January 19, 1950 (when the report was first made public).

p. 112: "misguided American opinion with the myth . . ."—statement originally issued by Senators Eastland and Dodd, of Internal Security Subcommittee, 1960; cited by O. Edmund Clubb in unpublished manuscript written that year.

p. 112: Fitch on "agrarian reform"—from her Formosa Beachhead.

pp. 112–13: Ashbrook's remark—from speech before Congress, June 28, 1966, adapted and published 1967 in The Case for Free China, compiled by Anthony T. Bouscaren, p. 19.

p. 112: Mrs. Vincent has a copy of Vincent's memorandum.

p. 113: "They are not Communists in the sense that Russians are . . ."—Congressional Record, January 16, 1945, pp. 279–80; "We are always social revolutionaries . . ."—Snow's Journey to the Beginning, p. 229.

p. 113: Fitch on Marshall—Formosa Beachhead, p. 109.

p. 113: "I was prepared to contradict the ambassador . . ."—Rice to author.

p. 113: ". . . a comparatively small measure of agrarian reform . . ."—Freda Utley's China at War, p. 260.

p. 114: "Well, the order to represent . . ."—Budenz quoted on p. 805 of Tydings committee hearings.

p. 114: Lattimore quotations—from his Ordeal by Slander; Utley on Lattimore—Tydings committee, May 1, 1950, p. 755 of report on hearings; Service on "agrarian reform"—Tydings committee hearings, p. 1372.

p. 114: Budenz on Wallace—McCarran committee hearings on Institute of Pacific Relations, quoted in Herbert Packer's Ex-Communist Witnesses.

p. 115: Gauss to Hull—July 12, 1944, in FRUS 1944.

p. 115: ". . . I survived the purge"—Rice to author.

p. 116: "the high point of official contact . . ."—Fairbank's Foreword to Barrett's *Dixie Mission.*

p. 116: Service's July 28, 1944, report—FRUS 1944, pp. 517–20; Communist directive quoted in article by K. Kukushkin, "CPC Central Committee Directive in Diplomatic Work, Moscow," *Problemy Dal'nego Vostoka,* 1972.

p. 117: "looked like a Welsh coalminers' choir . . ."—Barrett in his *Dixie Mission.*

p. 118: Hopkins's message to Roosevelt about Service—cited in Herbert Feis's *The China Tangle.*

pp. 118–19: Service's August 3, 1944, memo and Gauss's comment on it—FRUS 1944.

pp. 119–21: Service and Mao—in Service's *Lost Chance,* pp. 299, 300, 301, 302, 303, 306, 307.

p. 121: "the only man I ever saw who can strut sitting down"—George Hill to author.

pp. 121–22: "I have never killed a mule"—Don Lohbeck's *Patrick J. Hurley,* p. 5.

pp. 122–23: Hurley's talkativeness—Chiang in FRUS 1944, Mansfield in FRUS 1945, Barrett in *Dixie Mission,* and Rice and Sprouse to author.

p. 123: Gauss called Hurley a liar during Service's LSB hearing, in Tydings committee hearings, p. 2066.

p. 124: Roosevelt on Hurley—quoted in Russell Buhite's *Patrick J. Hurley and American Foreign Policy.*

p. 125: Roosevelt's instructions to Hurley in Lohbeck's *Patrick J. Hurley.*

pp. 125–26: Service on Communists, September 4, 1944—*Lost Chance,* pp. 194, 197, 218, 219, 224.

pp. 126–27: Messages to and from Hull, Gauss, Roosevelt, Chiang—FRUS 1944.

pp. 127–28: Ludden's report, written on February 2, 1945, and Drumright's April 5 comments thereon in FRUS 1945, pp. 200 et. seq.

p. 129: Hurley to Roosevelt—Buhite's *Patrick J. Hurley.*

pp. 129–31: Service's October 10, 1944, memorandum—in *Lost Chance,* pp. 161–66.

p. 132: Judd's statement—made October 19, 1949, in *Congressional Record,* and Tydings committee hearings, p. 1985.

p. 132: Judd talking to Vincent—FRUS 1944.

p. 132: Vincent and Judd in postwar Washington—Sheila Vincent Cox to author.

pp. 133–34: Service's conversations with Hurley and Hopkins—Service to author.

p. 133: Gauss to Wedemeyer—Wedemeyer's *Wedemeyer Reports!,* p. 295.

p. 134: Vincent to Grew—FRUS 1944.

6. "Hit him on the other side, Charlie!"

p. 135: Hurley to Roosevelt, November 7, 1944—FRUS 1944.

p. 135: Barrett and Chou dialogue—Barrett to author.

pp. 136–37: Davies and Mansfield quotes—FRUS 1944.

pp. 137–38: Barrett on Hurley in Yenan—Barrett to author.

p. 138: Hurley's five points—"White Paper," p. 74.

pp. 138–39: Davies's November 15, 1944, comments on Chiang—"White Paper," p. 574.

p. 139: Hurley to Roosevelt—"White Paper," p. 73.

p. 139: Barrett, Mao, and Chou—Barrett report from Yenan, December 10, 1944, in FRUS 1944, pp. 727ff.

p. 140: Barrett's comments on Hurley and Wedemeyer—Barrett to author.

p. 141: The comic strip, headed "American Spy Activities," was published in a Peking newspaper in the fall of 1951; in 1966 Barrett had it reproduced and appended his own comments.

p. 141: Stimson's letter to Stettinius—FRUS 1944.

p. 141: Wedemeyer quotations—from his *Wedemeyer Reports!*, pp. 312–13, 319–20.

pp. 142–44: Wedemeyer's testimonial to Service—produced during Service's LSB hearing, 1950, in Tydings committee hearings, p. 2477.

pp. 143–44: Nosaka's journey—Emmerson to author.

p. 144: Hurley in Chungking—Fulton Freeman to author.

p. 144: Buhite told of the Chungking raids; Lohbeck of the raid at Yenan. Both had access to, and were probably taken in by, Hurley's papers.

p. 145: Hurley and gun—Ringwalt to author.

p. 146: Davies's quotation—from his letter to Gen. Noce; State Dept. policy paper—in Tuchman's *Stilwell;* Wedemeyer instructions—in Service's *The* Amerasia *Papers;* Vincent to secretary of state, January 29, 1945—FRUS 1945.

p. 146: Ringwalt, Hurley, and Soong—Ringwalt to author.

p. 147: Hurley and Grew—FRUS 1945, p. 406.

p. 148: Wedemeyer on Yeaton—Wedemeyer's *Wedemeyer Reports!*, p. 285.

p. 149: Hurley and Davies—*Wedemeyer Reports!*, p. 319; Davies report—written December 12, 1944, quoted in Buhite's *Patrick J. Hurley.*

p. 149: Ludden-Hurley dialogue—Ludden to author.

p. 149: Davies report—November 15, 1944; in "White Paper," p. 574.

pp. 150–51: Ludden-Service report, February 14, 1945—FRUS 1945.

p. 152: Message of February 28, 1945, and Vincent memorandum about it—FRUS 1945; Atcheson's comment on it—Freeman to author.

p. 153: Hurley comments on Service—Service's *Lost Chance,* p. 358; Atcheson comment on Hurley—made on December 8, 1945, FRUS 1945, p. 734; Ballantine comment—FRUS 1945.

pp. 153–54: Drumright, March 2, 1945—FRUS 1945.

p. 154: Byrnes to Foreign Relations Committee, December 7, 1945—FRUS 1945, p. 739.

p. 155: Service's report on Communist congress, from Yenan, March 11, 1945—Kubek's *The* Amerasia *Papers,* pp. 1390–93.

pp. 155–56: Service-Mao conversation, April 1, 1945—Service's *Lost Chance,* p. 383.

p. 157: Roosevelt-Snow conversation—Snow's *Journey to the Beginning,* pp. 347–48.

p. 157: Leahy's quotation—from his *I Was There,* p. 337.

p. 157: Hurley and Donovan—On May 25, 1950, Donovan told an assistant counselor of the Tydings committee about their getting together in London and his having asked if Mrs. Vincent wasn't a Communist, quoted in Tydings committee hearings, p. 1919.

p. 158: Kennan on Hurley—from Service's LSB hearing, in Tydings committee hearings, p. 2124.

p. 159: Stanton's memorandum, April 28, 1945—FRUS 1945.

p. 160: Robertson to Ringwalt—Ringwalt to author.

p. 160: Robertson on the Chinese Communists—in Townsend Hoopes's *The Devil and John Foster Dulles*.

7. **"The Foreign Service is not an exhilarating business."**

p. 162: Mao's remark to Jaffe—in T. A. Bisson's *Yenan in June 1937: Talks with the Communist Leaders*.

p. 162: Granich in Shanghai—John Carter Vincent's *The Extraterritorial System in China*, and Granich to author.

pp. 164–65: Fisher's career—Fisher to author.

p. 165: Service on Ellsberg—Service to author.

p. 166: The Services and Larsens in Chengtu—from Grace Service's unpublished memoir.

p. 166: Larsen's charge against Fairbank and Fairbank's rebuttal occurred during Service's LSB hearing in 1950.

pp. 167–68: The transcript of the alleged conversation between Service and Jaffe can be found on pp. 87–90 of the majority report of the Tydings committee.

pp. 168–69: Ludden, Wedemeyer, and the FBI—Ludden to author.

p. 169: Larsen's account of his conversation with Drumright—Tydings committee hearings, p. 2218; his conversation with Service—Service to author.

p. 169: Service's feelings when arrested—Service to author.

pp. 170–71: Reactions in Yenan to Service's arrest—Service's *Lost Chance*, p. 390.

p. 171: Reid's exchange with Rogers—Reid to author.

p. 172: Grew made his chicken-coop statement at a press conference after the *Amerasia* arrests; on McCarthy's "forced to resign," see Earl Latham's *The Communist Controversy in Washington*.

pp. 173–74: Chiang's letter was dated September 19, 1945—see *The Reporter*, April 15 and 22, 1952.

p. 174: Hurley's statement on the Foreign Service men—Foreign Relations Committee hearings, December 5, 1945.

p. 174: DeLacy's speech—*The New York Times*, November 27, 1945.

pp. 174–75: Hurley's letter of resignation to Truman, November 26, 1945—FRUS 1945, pp. 722–26.

p. 176: Atcheson to Salisbury—Salisbury to author; Atcheson to Secretary of State Byrnes, November 30, 1945—FRUS 1945, pp. 726–27.

p. 176: Wedemeyer in Tokyo—Sprouse and Service to author.

pp. 177–78: Hurley's statements in transcript of December 1945 Foreign Relations Committee hearings, published in 1971.

p. 178: Byrnes's memorandum to Hackworth, December 7, 1945—FRUS 1945, pp. 729–730.

p. 178: Freeman and Ringwalt as spectators—Ringwalt to author.

p. 179: According to Larsen's testimony during Service's LSB hearing (in Tydings committee hearings, p. 2229), his meeting with Wherry was "about May 1, 1950."

pp. 180–83: Service and Atcheson, from Tokyo—FRUS 1945, pp. 728–38.

p. 183: Davies quotation from letter to his family, December 14, 1945—cited in his *Dragon by the Tail*, p. 421.

p. 183: Byrnes, Davies, and Molotov—ibid.

8. "Sticking to verified and documented facts."

p. 184: Departure of Marshall for China—J. C. Vincent, Jr., to author.

p. 184: Sprouse on Chinese affairs—Sprouse to author.

pp. 185–86: Ludden's conversation with Marshall—Ludden to author.

p. 186: Truman to Chiang, August 10, 1946—FRUS 1946.

p. 186: "The salvation of the situation . . ."—"White Paper," p. 218.

pp. 186–87: "MacArthur flatly refused . . ."—in Kubek's *How the Far East Was Lost;*
Sir Patrick Duff wrote a letter on Service's behalf that was introduced during his 1950
LSB hearing.

p. 187: Service on promotions—Service to author.

p. 188: "They went to lunch . . ."—Larsen gave one account of this to the Hobbs
subcommittee on May 13, 1946, and another on June 2, 1950, under cross-examination
by C. Edward Rhetts during Service's LSB hearings.

pp. 189–90: ". . . verified and documented facts"—from Isaac Don Levine's *Eyewitness
to History;* Larsen on being rewritten—Tydings committee hearings, p. 2200; conclusion
of Tydings committee on pp. 147–48 of its report.

p. 190: Kohlberg on MacArthur and treason—*China Monthly,* June 1948.

p. 190: Wedemeyer mentions the War College appearance in his *Wedemeyer Reports!,*
pp. 370ff.; Freeman's experience—Freeman to author.

p. 191: Vincent on Vietnam—*Pentagon Papers,* Gravel Edition, Vol. I, p. 29.

p. 192: Bridges's accusations against Vincent can be found in Part 13 of the published
transcript of the McCarran committee hearings on the Institute of Pacific Relations, pp.
4540–47.

p. 192: Penfield on personnel management—letter from Penfield to author.

pp. 193–94: Wedemeyer's instructions—"White Paper," p. 255.

p. 194: Wedemeyer's statements—ibid., pp. 257–58.

pp. 194–95: Wedemeyer's report on his trip was finally made public in 1949—*The New
York Times,* August 6, 1949.

p. 195: "In China today I find apathy . . ."—"White Paper," p. 257.

p. 197: Chambers quotes from pp. 270–71 of his *Witness.*

p. 198: Barr report—cited in Seymour Topping's *Journey between Two Chinas.*

p. 199: Even in 1974 the former State Department official who spoke to the author about
security and loyalty programs preferred to speak off the record.

pp. 200–201: Smyth's comments, inspired by the American Chamber of Commerce in
Tientsin—"White Paper," p. 300.

p. 202: "beginning of better understanding"—quoted in Topping's *Journey between Two
Chinas.* Stuart made the remark on May 13, 1949.

p. 203: Dulles's remark was made on June 29, 1949, in a talk with, among others, Edward
R. Murrow and Eric Sevareid—cf. Guhin's *John Foster Dulles.*

p. 203: ". . . eavesdropping and ducking around corners . . ."—Melby's *The Mandate of
Heaven.*

p. 206: The New Zealand man's statement was cited by Armistead Lee in *Foreign Service
Journal,* November 1971, p. 29.

p. 206: "Suitcases of documents . . ."—Rep. Judd in Congress, October 19, 1949.

p. 207: "You keep going . . ."—Service to author.

p. 207: ". . . What could be of greater aid to the Soviet Union than this?"—Kohlberg's "Who Is Responsible for China's Tragedy?," *China Monthly*, December 1949.

pp. 207–208: Chia-you Chen—article in *China Monthly*, February 1950.

p. 208: Mao's reaction to the "White Paper"—English-language edition of *Collected Works of the Chairman*, published in Peking.

9. "Oh, Mac has gone out on a limb."

p. 213: "Oh, Mac has gone out on a limb . . ."—Tydings committee report, p. 149.

p. 213: McCarthy's scrupulosity—Utley's *The China Story.*

p. 214: Lattimore's statement appears on p. 441 of the Tydings committee report; McCarthy's charge against Vincent—ibid., p. 95.

p. 217: "They've recalled Service!"—Rauh to author.

p. 217: Peurifoy's statement—reported in *The New York Times*, March 17, 1950, p. 10.

p. 218: McCarthy's reflections on Service and India presented in McCarthy's *McCarthyism, the Fight for America.*

p. 218: "the darkest and most humiliating days . . ."—Marshall Green to author.

p. 219: ". . . the greatest house guest anybody ever had"—Freeman to author.

p. 225: *Time's* story was published in its issue of November 3, 1952, and Kennan's letter in the December 29, 1952, issue.

p. 225: The Gary Allen statement appeared in his article "Betraying China—Why Mr. Nixon Must Not Go to Peking," *American Opinion*, October 1971.

p. 226: MacArthur's gaffe at Taipei—Barrett to author.

pp. 228–29: Clubb has shown author a copy of the charges against him.

p. 233: Browder's statement about Vincent and Service was made to the Tydings committee.

pp. 234–35: Information on McCarran hearings—Walter Surrey to author.

pp. 234–35: Charges against Vincent shown to author by Mrs. Vincent and Gary May; Mrs. Vincent is source also for quote from Alice Longworth.

p. 237: Mrs. Vincent's remarks made to author.

p. 241: The author is personally acquainted with Saipan and its peculiar history.

p. 243: The Washington *Post* editorial ran on Feb. 13, 1952.

p. 243: Clubb's vision of the handwriting on the wall—Clubb to author.

10. "Let history be my judge."

p. 245: Snow tells the story of Sourwine and Davies and the NKVD in *Journey to the Beginning.*

p. 246: Munson, Acheson, and the CIA—Kennan to author.

p. 247: Dulles on "positive loyalty"—State Department press release, January 22, 1953.

p. 247: Bridges's men-or-mice attitude—cited in Foster Rhea Dulles's *American Policy toward Communist China;* The China Lobby dinner—described by W. A. Swanberg in his *Luce and His Empire.*

p. 247: McLeod's remark on trustworthiness and trees—cited by C. L. Sulzberger in his column in *The New York Times*, November 8, 1954; McLeod's views on magazine-reading —*Foreign Service Journal*, June 1954.

p. 248: Vincent's remarks on Inquisition—letter from Tangier, March 17, 1952.

p. 248: Humelsine's statement on Vincent—incorporated in State Department press release issued February 19, 1952.

p. 249: Text of Byrne's remarks at Vincent memorial service—courtesy of Mrs. John Carter Vincent.

p. 250: Information on Tangier—Stuart Gates, who served with Vincent there, to author.

pp. 250–54: Material on Vincent's departure from the ranks—*Foreign Service Journal,* January and April 1953.

p. 251: The Washington *Post* editorial ran on March 5, 1953.

p. 253: The outcry over Vincent appeared in the *Moroccan Courier* on December 22, 1952.

p. 253: Salisbury's comment appeared in a review he wrote of Service's *Amerasia* book in *The New York Times* in 1971.

p. 255: Acheson's statement to Dulles in regard to Vincent and the Loyalty Review Board —in Guhin's *John Foster Dulles.*

p. 255: Dulles offering Vincent a drink—Surrey to author.

p. 256: "Mr. Dulles's six predecessors . . ."—Acheson's *Present at the Creation.*

pp. 257–58: McCarthy and Dulles views reported in *The New York Times,* December 2, 1953.

pp. 258–60: Material on Davies hearing—*Foreign Service Journal,* May and December 1954, and January 1955, and from Service to author.

p. 260: Flimsiness of charges against Davies—Donald Davies to author.

p. 263: The Davies children's "uncles"—Sasha Davies Schnurman to author.

p. 263: Fairbank's remarks were made at a memorial service in Cambridge, Mass., for Vincent; Service's at a lunch for Foreign Service officers in Washington, D.C.; Emmerson's to author.

pp. 264–66: Information and documentation relating to John C. Vincent, Jr., and counterintelligence corps interrogatory—John C. Vincent, Jr., to author.

11. "Listen, is this guy by any chance a Communist?"

p. 274: "Scalapini"—Whiting to author.

p. 275: ". . . the academic person becomes little more than a symbol"—Fairbank to author; Thomson quotation—from his "On the Making of US-China Policy, 1961–69," in the April-June 1972 issue of *China Quarterly.*

p. 277: Service's comment on jury duty—Service to author.

p. 277: Drumright's remark and his reflections on the scene in Taipei—Drumright to author.

p. 278: Account of Penfield interrogatory—Penfield to author.

p. 279: ". . . My God, that was what we were doing in China . . ."—Sprouse to author.

p. 279: "Bill, you *didn't?*"—Freeman to author.

pp. 281–82: Text of Norman suicide note—Cedric Belfrage's *The American Inquisition, 1945–1960;* Eisenhower comment in *The New York Times,* April 5, 1957.

pp. 282, 284: Reischauer and Rusk incidents—James C. Thomson, Jr., to author.

p. 284: Smith's remark about Davies—Adrian Fisher to author.

12. "A very strange turn of fate."

p. 288: Service's comments on "liaison personnel"—from an unpublished manuscript of his.

p. 288: Fairbank's comment on Kubek—letter to author (who happened to be in Taipei, incidentally and coincidentally, with Kubek and the Astronauts); Van Slyke's assessment —letter he wrote to a third party.

pp. 291–92: Service's account of his trip to China, as noted earlier, appeared in *The New York Times*, January 24–27, 1972.

p. 293: Kissinger-Service meeting—Service to author.

p. 293: "The Chinese aren't Chinese any more"—Barrett to author.

13. "It's very pleasant to be here."

p. 297: The Foreign Service officer was G. McMurtrie Godley, who had been ambassador to Laos and had been slated to take over East Asian [née Far Eastern] affairs. The American Foreign Service Association couldn't decide whether Godley's turndown was good or bad, but it did announce that the Senate committee action "had the effect of generating concern within the Foreign Service about career people being able to carry out their professional responsibilities honestly and loyally without worrying about possible future retribution."

p. 298: Nixon's letter to Snow—cited by Service in his "Edgar Snow: Some Personal Reminiscences," *China Quarterly*, April-June 1972.

p. 300: ". . . a long way to go for lunch"—Davies to author.

pp. 301–303: Service's remarks—published in *Foreign Service Journal*, March 1973.

pp. 303–305: Service's retrospective view—Service to author.

p. 307: "Remember, the pendulum could swing the other way"—reported to author by a Foreign Service officer who, because he is still on active duty, prefers—not unreasonably —to remain anonymous.

Bibliography

Along with many magazine and newspaper articles (notably in the *Foreign Service Journal* and *The New York Times*), the following sources have been consulted:

Acheson, Dean. *Present at the Creation: My Years in the State Department.* New York: W. W. Norton & Co., 1969.

Allen, Gary. "Betraying China: Why Mr. Nixon Must Not Go to Peking." *American Opinion,* October 1971.

Barnes, William (with John Heath Morgan). *The Foreign Service of the United States.* Washington, D.C.: Department of State, 1961.

Barrett, David D. *Dixie Mission: The United States Army Observer Group in Yenan, 1944.* Berkeley: China Research Monographs, University of California, 1970.

Belfrage, Cedric. *The American Inquisition, 1945–1960.* Indianapolis and New York: Bobbs-Merrill Co., 1973.

Bisson, T.A. *Yenan in June 1937: Talks with the Communist Leaders.* Berkeley: China Research Monographs, University of California, 1973.

Borg, Dorothy. *The United States and the Far Eastern Crisis of 1933–1938.* Cambridge, Mass.: Harvard University Press, 1964.

Bouscaren, Anthony T., compiler. *The Case for Free China.* New York: Twin Circle Publishing Co., 1967.

Buhite, Russel D. *Patrick J. Hurley and American Foreign Policy.* Ithaca: Cornell University Press, 1973.

Buss, Claude A. *The People's Republic of China.* Princeton: D. Van Nostrand Co., 1962.

Chambers, Whittaker. *Witness.* New York: Random House, 1952.

Clubb, O. Edmund. *Communism in China as Reported from Hankow in 1932.* New York: Columbia University Press, 1968.

———. *Twentieth Century China.* New York: Columbia University Press, 1964.

———. *The Witness and I.* New York: Columbia University Press, 1974.

Davies, John Paton, Jr. *Dragon by the Tail: American, British, Japanese and Russian Encounters with China and One Another.* New York: W. W. Norton & Co., 1972.

———. *Foreign and Other Affairs.* New York: W. W. Norton & Co., 1964.

Decter, Moshe (with James Rorty). *McCarthy and the Communists.* Boston: Beacon Press, 1954.

Dulles, Foster Rhea. *American Policy toward China: The Historical Record.* New York: T. Y. Crowell, 1972.

Emmerson, John K. *Arms, Yen and Power: The Japanese Dilemma.* New York: Dunellen Publishing Co., 1971.

Fairbank, John K. *The United States and China.* Cambridge, Mass.: Harvard University Press, 1948. Third Edition, 1971.

Feis, Herbert. *The China Tangle: The American Effort in China from Pearl Harbor to the Marshall Mission.* Princeton: Princeton University Press, 1953.

Fitch, Geraldine. *Formosa Beachhead.* Chicago: Henry Regnery Co., 1953.

Flynn, John T. *While You Slept.* New York: Devin-Adair Co., 1951.

Guhin, Michael A. *John Foster Dulles: A Statesman and His Times.* New York: Columbia University Press, 1972.

Halberstam, David. *The Best and the Brightest.* New York: Random House, 1972.

Halle, Louis J. *The Cold War and History.* London: Chatto & Windus, 1967.

Handbook on China. U.S. Army Forces, CBI Theater, 1942.

Hoopes, Townsend. *The Devil and John Foster Dulles: The Diplomacy of the Eisenhower Era.* Boston: Atlantic Monthly Press-Little Brown, 1973.

Keeley, Joseph C. *The China Lobby Man: The Story of Alfred Kohlberg.* New Rochelle, N.Y.: Arlington House, 1969.

Kennan, George F. *Memoirs: 1925–1950.* Boston: Atlantic Monthly Press-Little Brown, 1967.

Koen, Ross Y. *The China Lobby in American Politics.* New York: Harper & Row, 1975.

Kubek, Anthony. *The Amerasia Papers: A Clue to the Catastrophe of China.* Washington, D.C.: U.S. Government Printing Office, 1970.

_____. *How the Far East Was Lost: American Policy and the Creation of Communist China, 1941–1949.* Chicago: Henry Regnery Co., 1963.

Latham, Earl. *The Communist Controversy in Washington: From the New Deal to McCarthy.* Cambridge, Mass.: Harvard University Press, 1966.

Lattimore, Owen. *Ordeal by Slander.* Boston: Atlantic Monthly Press-Little Brown, 1950.

Leahy, William D. *I Was There.* New York: McGraw-Hill, 1950.

Levine, Isaac Don. *Eyewitness to History.* New York: Hawthorn Books, 1973.

Liang, Chin-tung. *General Stilwell in China, 1942–1944: The Full Story.* Jamaica, N.Y.: St. John's University Press, 1972.

Lohbeck, Don. *Patrick J. Hurley.* Chicago: Henry Regnery Co., 1956.

Mao Tse tung. *Selected Works.* Peking: Foreign Language Press, 1967.

McCarthy, Joseph R. *McCarthyism, the Fight for America: Documented Answers to Questions Asked by Friend and Foe.* New York: Devon-Adair Co., 1952.

Melby, John F. *The Mandate of Heaven.* Toronto: University of Toronto Press, 1968.

Morris, Robert J. *No Wonder We Are Losing.* New York: The Bookmailer, 1958.

Neustadt, Richard E. *Presidential Power.* New York: John Wiley & Sons, 1960.

Packer, Herbert L. *Ex-Communist Witnesses: Four Studies in Fact Findings.* Stanford: Stanford University Press, 1962.

Pentagon Papers. Boston: Beacon Press, 1971.

Red China and Its American Friends. Washington, D.C.: American Council on World Freedom, 1971.

The Reporter. Articles on the China Lobby, issues of April 15 and April 22, 1952.

Rice, Edward E. *Mao's Way.* Berkeley: University of California Press, 1972.

Rigg, Robert B. *Red China's Fighting Hordes: A Realistic Account of the Chinese Communist Army by a U.S. Army Officer.* Harrisburg, Pa.: Military Service Publishing Co., 1951.

Rovere, Richard H. *Senator Joe McCarthy.* New York: Harcourt, Brace & Co., 1959.

Service, Grace B. "Golden Inches." Unpublished manuscript.

Service, John S. *The Amerasia Papers: Some Problems in the History of US-China Relations.* Berkeley: China Research Monographs, University of California, 1971.

_____. *Lost Chance in China.* Edited by Joseph W. Esherick. New York: Random House, 1974.

_____. "Edgar Snow: Some Personal Reminiscences." *China Quarterly,* April-June 1972.

Sevareid, Eric. *Not So Wild A Dream.* New York: Alfred A. Knopf, 1946.

Shewmaker, Kenneth E. *Americans and Chinese Communists, 1927–1947: A Persuading Encounter.* Ithaca: Cornell University Press, 1971.

_____. "The 'Agrarian Reformer' Myth." *China Quarterly,* April-June 1968.

Snow, Edgar. *Journey to the Beginning.* New York: Random House, 1958.

_____. *The Other Side of the River: Red China Today.* New York: Random House, 1962.

_____. *Red Star over China.* New York: Random House, 1938.

Stanton, Edwin F. *Brief Authority: Excursions of a Common Man in an Uncommon World.* New York: Harper & Bros., 1956.

Stuart, John Leighton. *Fifty Years in China: The Memoirs of John Leighton Stuart, Ambassador and Missionary.* New York: Random House, 1954.

Swanberg, W.A. *Luce and His Empire.* New York: Charles Scribner's Sons, 1972.

Terrill, Ross. "When America 'Lost' China." *The Atlantic,* November 1969.

Thomas, John N. *The Institute of Pacific Relations: Asian Scholars and American Politics.* Seattle: University of Washington Press, 1974.

Thomson, James C., Jr. "On the Making of U.S. China Policy, 1961–69: A Study in Bureaucratic Politics," *The China Quarterly,* April-June 1972.

Topping, Seymour. *Journey between Two Chinas.* New York: Harper & Row, 1972.

Tsou, Tang. *America's Failure in China: 1941–1950.* Chicago: University of Chicago Press, 1963.

Tuchman, Barbara W. *Stilwell and the American Experience in China, 1911–45.* New York: Macmillan, 1971.

_____. *Notes from China.* New York: Collier Books, 1972.

United States Government. Hearings, 92d Congress, 1st Session, *The Evolution of US Policy toward Mainland China* (includes Hearings, Committee on Foreign Relations, 79th Congress, 1st Session, *The Situation in the Far East, Particularly China.*) Washington, D.C.: U.S. Government Printing Office. 1971.

_____. Hearings, House of Representatives, Committee on Un-American Activities, 82d Congress, 1st Session. Washington, D.C.: U.S. Government Printing Office, 1951.

_____. Hearings, Senate Committee on the Judiciary, Internal Security Subcommittee, 82d Congress, 2d Session. Washington, D.C.: U.S. Government Printing Office, 1952.

_____. Hearings, U.S. Senate, 81st Congress, 2d Session, before Subcommittee of the Committee on Foreign Relations, Employee Loyalty Investigation. Washington, D.C.: U.S. Government Printing Office, 1950.

_____. *The China-Burma-India Theatre* by Charles Romanus and Riley Sunderland. Washington, D.C.: United States Army in World War II Series, U.S. Government Printing Office, 1953, 1956, 1959.

_____. *United States Relations with China, 1944–1949* (The White Paper). Washington, D.C.: U.S. Government Printing Office, 1949.

_____. *Foreign Relations of the United States.* Washington, D.C.: U.S. Government Printing Office, annual series published by Department of State, 1941–1945.

Utley, Freda. *China at War.* London: Faber & Faber, 1939.

_____. *The China Story.* Chicago: Henry Regnery Co., 1951.

Vandenberg, Arthur H. *The Private Papers of Senator Vandenberg, 1884–1951.* Edited by Arthur H. Vandenberg, Jr. Boston: Houghton Mifflin Co., 1952.

Van Slyke, Lyman P. (ed.). *The Chinese Communist Movement: A Report of the United States War Department, July, 1945.* Stanford: Stanford University Press, 1968.

Vincent, John Carter. *The Extraterritorial System in China, Final Phase.* Cambridge, Mass.: Harvard East Asian Monographs, 1970.

Wedemeyer, Albert C. *Wedemeyer Reports!* New York: Henry Holt & Co., 1958.

Westerfield, Holt Bradford. *Foreign Policy and Party Politics: Pearl Harbor to Korea.* New Haven: Yale University Press, 1955.

White, Theodore H. (ed.). *The Stilwell Papers.* New York: William Sloane Associates, 1948.

——— (with Annalee Jacoby). *Thunder Out of China.* New York: William Sloane Associates, 1946.

Index

Acheson, Dean, 22, 172, 204; Edmund Clubb and, 241; John Davies and, 246; as Secretary of State, 200; John Service and, 9, 26, 35, 206, 238, 270–71; John Vincent and, 192, 254–55, 256
Aiken, Senator George D., 22
Alexander Meiklejohn College, 56
Alsop, Joseph W., 81, 81n, 109, 216–17
Amerasia case, *see* Service, John Stewart, *Amerasia* case
Amerasia Papers: A Clue to the Catastrophe of China (Kubek), 287–88
Amerasia Papers: Some Problems in the History of U.S.–China Relations (Service), 289
American China Policy Association, 18, 49, 191
American Communist Party, 168
American Foreign Service Association, 28, 251–52, 297–305, 307
Andrews, Roy Chapman, 45
Armour, Norman, 34
Ashbrook, Rep. John M., 112
Asian Affairs, National Council of, 15
Asia Society, 36
Atcheson, George, 31, 73, 98, 98n, 99, 144n, 150; attitude toward Chinese Communists, 101; Chiang Kai-shek and, 174; defends against attacks, 180–83; Patrick Hurley and, 157, 174, 176, 178, 180–83; replaced by Walter Robertson, 159–60; reporting of, 152–53, 154; in Tokyo, 172
Atkinson, Brooks, 106, 164

Ballantine, Joseph, 58, 153, 166
Barnett, Robert W., 14, 36, 70, 91–92, 92n, 286n, 300
Barr, Major General David, 198
Barrett, David, 90, 156n, 226n; accused of assassination attempt, 141, 293; and Chiang Kai-shek, 140, 220; Chinese Communists and, 147–48, 293n–294n; defends Edmund Clubb, 231; defends

John Service, 220; on Dixie Mission, 104–105, 117, 148, 149; Foreign Service career, 309; and Patrick Hurley, 122–23, 135, 139n, 148; and Mao Tse-tung, 139, 139n, 293; sent to Kunming, 148
Bates, Dr. Miner Searle, 230–31
Benedict, Ruth Fulton, 15
Bielaski, Frank, 163, 163n
Biggerstaff, Dr. Knight, 230
Bingham, Hiram, 237, 238, 251, 270
Birch, John, 48n, 160n
Bird, Willis H., 147–48
Bisson, T. A., 162
Bliss, Robert Wood, 34
Boatner, Haydon L., 77
Bohlen, Charles, 37n, 42n
Borg, Dorothy, 47
Bowles, Chester, 279, 282n
Boxer Rebellion of 1900, 74
Bridges, Sen. Styles, 177, 179n, 192, 247, 247n
Browder, Earl, 168, 223, 233, 233n
Bruce, David, 10
Budenz, Louis F., 100, 114, 114n, 232, 233, 234, 251
Buhite, Russel D., 122
Bunker, Ellsworth, 17
Burden, William A. M., 279–80
Buss, Claude A., 100–101, 229
Butterworth, W. Walton, 193, 204, 300
Byrne, James MacGregor, 249, 249n
Byrnes, James F., 154, 174, 176, 178, 183n

Cairo Conference, 101
California, University of, at Berkeley, 60, 63; Center for Chinese Studies, 273–74, 286, 291
Carlson, Evans, 58
Carmon, Walt, 197
Carnegie Corporation, 161
Casablanca Conference, 88
Chamberlain, Culver B., 31
Chambers, Whittaker, 196–97, 197–98
Changchun, 185, 195–96